THE NEW
COMPLETE BOOK OF
Herbs, Spices,
and Condiments

THE NEW COMPLETE BOOK OF
Herbs, Spices, and Condiments

CAROL ANN RINZLER

Foreword By
WENDELL L. COMBEST, PH.D.

Checkmark Books®
An imprint of Facts On File, Inc.

THE NEW COMPLETE BOOK OF HERBS, SPICES, AND CONDIMENTS

Checkmark Books
An imprint of Facts On File, Inc.
11 Penn Plaza
New York, NY 10001

Library of Congress Cataloging-in-Publication Data

Rinzler, Carol Ann
The New Complete Book of Herbs, Spices, and Condiments / Carol Ann Rinzler
p. cm.
Includes bibliographical references and index.
ISBN 0-8160-4153-9 (hardcover : alk. paper)—ISBN 0-8160-4152-0 (pbk : alk. [paper])
1. Herbs. 2. Spices. 3. Condiments. I. Title
TX406 .R55 2001
641.3′57—dc21
00-032164

Checkmark Books are available at special discounts when purchased in bulk quantities for businesses, associations, institutions or sales promotions. Please call our Special Sales Department in New York at (212) 967-8800 or (800) 322-8755.
You can find Facts On File on the World Wide Web at http://www.factsonfile.com

Text design by Erika K. Arroyo
Cover design by Semadar Megged

Printed in the United States of America

MP Hermitage   10 9 8 7 6 5 4 3 2 1
        (pbk)   10 9 8 7 6 5 4 3 2 1

This book is printed on acid-free paper.

Contents

❧ Foreword ❧

This comprehensive book on herbs, spices, and condiments will be a useful resource for anyone interested in the nutritional and/or medicinal value of plants. It will be especially useful to nutritionists and other health care professionals as a guide for making recommendations on dietary supplements. This book complements nicely Ms. Rinzler's earlier book *The New Complete Book of Food*.

Our knowledge base in the field of herbs and spices has dramatically increased in the past few years. Correspondingly, many publications have surfaced on this topic. Ms. Rinzler's book helps to clarify this overwhelming literature. Essential information on each herb, spice, or condiment, presented in alphabetical order, is clearly written in an easy-to-read monograph style. Each monograph is divided into sections concerned with information about the plant and its constituents, followed by a discussion of its benefits as well as adverse effects and possible drug interactions. When relevant, information is given concerning potential effects in women who are pregnant or nursing. A unique feature of these monographs is the sections offering culinary and gardening information about the plant. Potentially unsafe or toxic plants are featured in the appendix.

A major strength of this book is its comprehensiveness and user-friendly organization. Rarely do you see information on medicinal and/or culinary herbs and spices and condiments like salt substitutes and vinegar presented in a single volume. This book will be useful to the pharmacist as well as physician who may be interested in alternative nonpharmacological therapies or are concerned about interactions of dietary supplements with conventional drugs. Finally, this book will be a welcome addition to everyone's home library, providing needed information to guide us in selecting useful nutritional supplements to our diet.

Wendell L. Combest, Ph.D.
Associate Professor of Pharmacology
Shenandoah University School of Pharmacy
Winchester, Virginia

~ *Introduction* ~

The information in this book regarding the medical benefits or adverse effects of herbs, spices, and condiments, as well as their possible interactions with medical drugs or medical tests, is drawn from sources current as the book was written. It is for your information only and should never be used in place of your own doctor's advice or without his or her consent. Because your doctor is familiar with your personal medical history, he or she is best qualified to advise you on medical matters.

Please note that the effects attributed to some of the plants and condiments listed here may not happen to everyone who uses the seasonings or occur every time the seasoning is served.

CAUTION: All plants contain oils whose constituents give the plant its flavor and aroma. Although many of the naturally occurring chemical compounds found in these oils are potentially hazardous, kitchen herbs and spices are generally considered safe in the amounts used in food. HOWEVER, SOME PLANT OILS ARE AVAILABLE IN CONCENTRATED FORM FOR USE IN MAKING YOUR OWN PERFUMES AT HOME. UNLIKE THE FLA-VORING LIQUIDS SOLD AS FOOD IN GROCERY STORES, THESE OILS ARE NOT SAFE FOR USE IN COOKING. THEY ARE POTENTIALLY POISONOUS AND MAY PROVE FATAL IF INGESTED. THEY MAY ALSO BE HAZARDOUS IF APPLIED DIRECTLY TO YOUR SKIN IN CONCENTRATED FORM. ANY MENTION OF OIL IN THIS BOOK REFERS TO THE OIL FOUND NATURALLY IN PLANTS, NOT THE OILS USED IN PERFUMES.

Before using any herbs from the garden, always wash them thoroughly to remove dirt and debris. Many products used in the garden are poisonous. NEVER USE ANY PLANT AS FOOD UNLESS YOU ARE ABSOLUTELY CERTAIN IT HAS NOT BEEN TREATED WITH GARDEN CHEMICALS INCLUDING, BUT NOT LIMITED TO, INSECTI-CIDES. THIS INCLUDES PLANTS GROWING WILD.

ᴥ How to Use This Book ᴥ

Authors who write about specific subjects such as nutrition always like to keep up with what's happening — new studies, new reports, new books. As a result, we generally like to check out one another's work to see if there's anything we've missed. Naturally, we pay our debt to other authors by crediting them in the text or listing their books in our bibliographies.

While doing research for this new edition of *The Complete Book of Herbs, Spices, and Condiments*, I came across one such bibliography that described this book as an "orthodox medical viewpoint on herbs."

That's precisely right. The information you find here comes from authoritative medical sources based on research with animals or human beings. No speculation. No what-if. No, "My best friend's uncle tried this and it worked, so . . ." In other words, the emphasis is placed squarely on science, not magic.

The New Complete Book of Herbs, Spices, and Condiments presents these foods and flavorings as individual health products, each one dressed in the same sort of nutritional and medical regalia you would expect to find in any volume on prescription drugs, over-the-counter medications, or nutritional supplements.

Throughout the book, I use the word *plant* to describe, well, plants. This is simply more direct than either *herb* (customarily used for flowering plants such as marjoram and thyme) or *spice* (customarily used to describe seasonings such as cinnamon and pepper from woody plants). You can rightly call any seasoning a condiment, but here the word *condiment* describes a prepared product, such as ketchup, mayonnaise, or Worcestershire sauce.

The plants and condiments included here are grouped into three broad categories. First, plants and condiments used in food and beverages. Second, plants used only in medicine. Third, hazardous plants. In each group, the information is presented in alphabetically arranged entries; for example, from ACESULFAME-K to ZEDOARY. Sometimes the name in the heading may not be familiar to you or it just may not be the one you ordinarily use, i.e. PEPPER, BLACK instead of "pepper." For consistency's sake, all the names agree with those used in *The Complete German Commission E Monographs, Therapeutic Guide to Herbal Medicine*, currently the most widely recognized authority on the medical properties of herbs. If you can't find the entry you're looking for by thumbing through the book, check the index.

Each entry has four basic sections: ABOUT THIS PLANT (or CONDIMENT), ABOUT THIS PLANT (CONDIMENT) AS FOOD OR DRINK, HOW THIS PLANT (CONDIMENT) AFFECTS YOUR BODY, and HOW TO USE THIS PLANT (CONDIMENT).

ABOUT THIS PLANT (CONDIMENT). This chart is a quick summary. Because so many common names for plants look or sound alike, it's important to be sure you're talking about the right one. So the chart begins with the BOTANICAL (or CHEMICAL) NAME. Next come

COMMON NAME(S), such as "green onions" for "scallions." Move down a line, and you'll see NATIVE TO, a useful bit of information for identifying flavor and aromas of specific ethnic dishes. You'll also want to identify the PARTS USED AS FOOD/DRINK (which includes herbal teas, a category that enables me to include well-known herbs such as SENNA, which are never used in food).

Does this plant or condiment appear on the U.S. Food and Drug Administration's GRAS ("Generally Recognized As Safe") List? The answer here is either "yes," indicating the herb or spice has been approved for use in food, or "no" which may mean "not yet," or "not applicable." "No" does not necessarily mean the herb, spice, or condiment is regarded as unsafe. It may signify that the plant is not approved or simply recognize the obvious: that the plant is not on the list because it is itself a food, not an ingredient. For example, coffee is not on the GRAS list.

Finally, the chart lists the plant or condiment's MEDICINAL PROPERTIES and OTHER USES, such nonfood uses as perfume or maybe even a natural insecticide.

ABOUT THIS PLANT (CONDIMENT) AS FOOD OR DRINK. This section provides a general description of how the plant or condiment is grown or manufactured. It also includes a NUTRITIONAL PROFILE listing the amounts of vitamins, minerals and other nutrients you can expect to find in a common serving of each seasoning. The nutritional profiles are based primarily on figures from the U.S. Department of Agriculture (USDA) Nutrient Database, which is available at http://www.usda.gov. For those herbs, spices, and condiments for which the USDA has not yet created nutritional listings, the nutritional profile section has been marked with three asterisks. This does not mean that the seasoning has no nutrients, only that no authoritative nutritional analysis is currently available.

HOW THIS PLANT (CONDIMENT) AFFECTS YOUR BODY. We commonly use such small amounts of plants and condiments as kitchen seasonings that you may reasonably wonder whether we can really expect seasonings to contribute significant amounts of nutrients to our diet. In many cases, the answer is yes because of the IMPORTANT PHYTOCHEMICALS (*phyto* means "plant") or CHEMICALS including vitamins and minerals. For example, just 1 teaspoon of paprika has 1,200 IU (international units) vitamin A, 24 percent to 30 percent of the recommended daily dietary allowance (RDA). One teaspoon of dill seed has 32 mg calcium, which is 4 percent of the RDA for a man and 3 percent of the RDA for a woman, twice as much as half a medium grapefruit and 50 percent more than one cup of canned peas. One-half cup of chopped fresh parsley has 27 mg vitamin C, 50 percent of the RDA.

This section also spells out specific BENEFITS associated with this plant/condiment and tells you whether the plant is an "approved medical herb" — a term signifying that the German Commission E has named this plant a safe, effective drug.

Some plants and condiments have POSSIBLE ADVERSE EFFECTS even in the amounts commonly used as food or medicine. For example, an ordinary dusting of black or red pepper may irritate anybody's stomach lining. Pepper can also irritate the skin (which is why it is sometimes used as a "warming" poultice) and the urinary tract (which is why it is sometimes mistakenly regarded as an aphrodisiac). Even one cup of chamomile tea may trigger an allergic reaction in people sensitive to ragweed. "Normal" servings of salt, MSG (monosodium glutamate), and soy sauce may be hazardous for people on low sodium diets. They are listed here, along with INFORMATION FOR WOMEN WHO ARE PREGNANT OR NURSING. Finally, if you are taking medication, pay special attention to the section on PLANT/DRUG INTERACTIONS.

Note: Plants not listed as "approved" may be either ineffective or harmful. However, it may simply be that there are as yet no reliable scientific studies of the plant's effects. Similarly, the symbol ∗ ∗ ∗ doesn't necessarily mean that there are no benefits or adverse effects, only that as of this printing there may be no precise information available.

HOW TO USE THIS PLANT (CONDIMENT). The last section in each entry offers a brief but practical guide to using plants and condiments IN COOKING, AROUND THE HOUSE, IN THE GARDEN, AS A HOME REMEDY, and for INDUSTRIAL USES.

In compiling all this information, I am grateful to many experts who were willing to take the time to discuss and explain their subjects. In particular, I wish to thank Alan Schwartz of *U.S. Pharmacist*, as well as James A. Duke, Walter H. Lewis and Varro E. Tyler, each of whom was kind enough to share with me information about the medical effects of plants. I am also thoroughly appreciative of the time and effort of my editor James Chambers, copy editor Laura Magzis, and all the people at Facts On File, Inc. Without their gracious comments and assistance, I could not have hoped to complete this project.

—Carol Ann Rinzler

ABBREVIATIONS AND MEASUREMENTS USED IN THIS BOOK

g = gram
mg = milligram
mcg = microgram
One gram = 1,000 milligrams
= 1,000,000 micrograms
l = liter
ml = milliliter
One liter = 1,000 milliliters
oz = ounce
One ounce (solid) = 28 grams
One ounce (liquid) = 30 milliliters
IU = international units
tsp = teaspoon
tbsp = tablespoon

Acesulfame-K

ABOUT THIS CONDIMENT

Chemical name(s): 6-Methyl-1,2,3-oxathiazin-4(3H)-one 2,2-dioxide; acesulfame potassium

Common name(s): Sunett

Native to: ∗ ∗ ∗

Parts used as food/drink: ∗ ∗ ∗

GRAS list: No

Medicinal properties: Nonnutritive sweetener

Other uses: Pharmaceutical sweetener

ABOUT THIS CONDIMENT AS FOOD OR DRINK

Acesulfame-K, a crystalline compound 150 to 200 percent sweeter than SUGAR (sucrose), was approved by the U.S. Food and Drug Administration in 1988 but has not yet been approved for use in Canada. It dissolves in water and retains its sweetness when heated, so it is used as a tabletop sweetener, as a sweetening agent in beverage mixes such as flavored instant coffees and instant teas, as well as in gelatins, pudding mixes, and chewing gum.

NUTRITIONAL PROFILE

Acesulfame-K has no nutritive value. One packet contains approximately 0.4 g acesulfame-K.

HOW THIS CONDIMENT AFFECTS YOUR BODY

Important Chemicals   The "K" in acesulfame-K is the chemical symbol for potassium.

Benefits   Your body does not digest acesulfame-K, which simply passes unchanged through your intestinal tract. Therefore, its chief benefit is its ability to sweeten without calories. It is useful in diets designed to control weight and for people with diabetes who must control their sugar intake.

Possible Adverse Effects   Because the chemical structure of acesulfame-K is similar to the chemical structure of SACCHARIN, some consumer advocates believe it may be a carcinogen, at least in large doses for laboratory animals. However, there is no evidence to show that it has any effect at all on the human body.

Information for Women Who Are Pregnant or Nursing   * * *

Condiment/Drug Interactions   * * *

HOW TO USE THIS CONDIMENT   * * *

Agar

ABOUT THIS PLANT

Botanical name(s): Rhodophyceae (algae)
Common name(s): Agar-agar, Bengal or Ceylon or Chinese isinglass
Native to: Pacific and Indian Oceans
Parts used as food/drink: Extracted gum
GRAS list: Yes
Medicinal properties: Laxative, demulcent
Other uses: Cosmetic and pharmaceutical gel

ABOUT THIS PLANT AS FOOD OR DRINK

Agar, also known as Chinese or Japanese isinglass, is a complex sugar compound extracted from algae and dried to make an odorless, tasteless, colorless powder used as a thickener in ice creams, salad dressings, icings, and glazes.

Nutritional Profile 3.5 ounces (100 g) dried agar has 306 calories. It provides 6.2 g protein, 0.3 g fat, 80.9 g carbohydrates, 7.7 g dietary fiber, no vitamin A or vitamin C, 625 mg calcium, 21.4 mg iron, and 102 mg sodium.

HOW THIS PLANT AFFECTS YOUR BODY

Important Phytochemicals The active ingredients in agar are alginates, thickeners that form a strong gel at about 96 degrees F (36 degrees C), and remains firm even at temperatures as high as 202 degrees F (95 degrees C).

Alginates are effective, bulk-forming laxatives. They are also demulcents, substances that soothe irritated mucous membranes.

Known Benefits * * *

Possible Adverse Effects * * *

Information for Women Who Are Pregnant or Nursing * * *

Plant/Drug Interactions * * *

HOW TO USE THIS PLANT

Industrial Uses Agar is used commercially to make medical gelatin capsules and dentures, as fabric and paper sizing, in adhesives, and as a medium in which to culture bacteria.

Alfalfa

ABOUT THIS PLANT

Botanical name(s): *Medicago sativa*
Common name(s): Buffalo grass, lucerne
Native to: Europe
Parts used as food/drink: Sprouted seeds
GRAS list: Yes
Medicinal properties: Hormonal (estrogen) effects
Other uses: Animal feed, paper manufacturing

ABOUT THIS PLANT AS FOOD OR DRINK

Alfalfa is perennial plant and a member of the pea family. It is most commonly used as cattle feed, but its fresh sprouted seeds can be added to salads. In addition, pulverized dried alfalfa is packaged and sold in health food stores as a tea or in tablets and capsules.

Nutritional Profile   One-half cup (33 g) raw, sprouted alfalfa seeds has 5 calories. It provides 0.5 g protein, a trace of fat, 0.5 g carbohydrates, 0.5 g dietary fiber, 25 IU vitamin A, 1.5 mg vitamin C, 5.5 mg calcium, 0.2 mg iron, and 1 mg sodium.

HOW THIS PLANT AFFECTS YOUR BODY

Phytochemicals in This Plant   Alfalfa contains the phytoestrogen coumestrol, a steroid-like compound with effects similar to those of the mammalian female hormone estrogen. In animals, a diet high in coumestrol may cause infertility, and laboratory animals fed zearalenone, a similar compound produced by moldy grain, often experience changes in ovarian, cervical, and breast tissue. There are no studies showing similar effects in human beings.

Benefits   * * *

Possible Adverse Effects   In 1998, following an outbreak of *Salmonella* and *Escherichia coli* 0157:H7 food poisoning associated with eating raw alfalfa sprouts, the U.S. Food and Drug Administration issued a warning cautioning those at high risk of food-borne illness not to eat raw sprouts. The high risk group includes children, older adults, and people with weakened immune systems (for example, those who are HIV-positive). In June

1999, USDA tests suggested that irradiating the sprouts and treating them with a chlorine solution could eliminate the organisms and prolong the sprouts' shelf life.

Alfalfa is a potential allergen. Animals foraging on the plant may develop photosensitivity (an allergic sensitivity to sunlight) and people with hay fever or asthma may be allergic to the plant or to alfalfa teas, tablets, and capsules.

A 1981 article in the British medical journal *Lancet* reported that people who eat large quantities of alfalfa seeds every day may develop a blood disorder called *pancytopenia*, a reduction in the number of red cells, white cells, and platelets in the blood that makes it difficult for blood to clot. This was confirmed in a 1984 report in the *American Journal of Clinical Nutrition*. The condition is potentially serious but reversible when alfalfa seeds are eliminated from the diet.

When laboratory monkeys are fed alfalfa seeds and sprouts, they develop symptoms similar to those in people with systemic lupus erythematosus (SLE), an inflammatory immune disorder of the connective tissue in which the body seems to attack itself. People in whom SLE is in remission may suffer a relapse after taking alfalfa tablets or capsules. The culprit appears to be L-canavarine, a compound in alfalfa seed and sprouts that is similar to arginine, a nonessential amino acid.

Information for Women Who Are Pregnant or Nursing   There are no studies documenting the effects of coumestrol on women who are pregnant of nursing.

Plant/Drug Interactions   * * *

HOW TO USE THIS PLANT

Industrial Uses   Alfalfa is used as a source of carotenoids (the deep orange and yellow pigments in plants) and chlorophyll; alfalfa fiber is used in manufacturing paper.

Allspice

ABOUT THIS PLANT

Botanical name(s): Pimenta dioica, Pimenta officinalis
Common name(s): Eugenia pimenta, clove pepper, Jamaica pepper, pimenta
Native to: West Indies, Central America, Mexico
Parts used as food/drink: Fruit
GRAS list: Yes
Medicinal properties: Antiseptic, fungicide
Other uses: Fragrance

ABOUT THIS PLANT AS FOOD OR DRINK

Allspice is the dried, nearly ripe fruit of an evergreen tree that grows in Jamaica, Mexico, Guatemala, and Honduras. It gets it name from the fact that it tastes like a natural combination of CINNAMON, NUTMEG, and CLOVES. Outside the United States, allspice is commonly known as pimento (which is not the same as pimiento, another name for some sweet red peppers).

Allspice is used in liqueurs (notably benedictine and Chartreuse) and as a flavoring for ice cream, candy, baked goods, and chewing gum. Allspice oleoresin (a combination of its resins and oils) is used in sausages.

Nutritional Profile   One teaspoon (2 g) ground allspice has 5 calories. It provides 0.1 g protein, 0.2 g fats, 1.4 g carbohydrates, 0.4 g dietary fiber, 10 IU vitamin A, 0.7 mg vitamin C, 13 mg calcium, 0.1 mg iron, and 1 g sodium.

One tablespoon (6 g) ground allspice has 16 calories. It provides 0.4 g protein, 0.5 g fat, 4.3 g carbohydrates, 1.3 g dietary fiber, 32 IU vitamin A, 2.4 mg vitamin C, 40 mg calcium, 0.4 mg iron, and 5 mg sodium.

HOW THIS PLANT AFFECTS YOUR BODY

Important Phytochemicals   The primary flavor and aroma ingredient in allspice is eugenol, an oily substance that accounts for up to 80 percent of the oil extracted from allspice berries and up to 96 percent of the oil in the leaves.

Eugenol, which is also found CINNAMON, CLOVES, and NUTMEG, is an antiseptic, a fungicide (an agent that kills fungi and mold), and a counterirritant, an agent that irritates the skin, causing small blood vessels underneath to expand so that more blood flows in and the skin feels warmer.

Allspice also contains astringent tannins; they are mild local anesthetics.

Benefits   Eugenol is used in dentistry to relieve the pain of a toothache.

Caution: This is not a home remedy. Concentrated eugenol is a potentially toxic essential oil that may cause nausea, vomiting, central nervous system slowdown, and convulsions.

Counterirritants such as eugenol are used in over-the-counter products designed to relieve the pain of arthritis. Natural counterirritants such as allspice are sometimes used in folk medicine as wet dressing to provide the same temporary relief, but the commercially produced creams and gels are more effective.

Possible Adverse Effects   Eugenol is an allergen and an irritant. Handling the spice may cause itching, burning, stinging, and reddened or blistered skin.

Information for Women Who Are Pregnant or Nursing   * * *

Plant/Drug Interactions   * * *

HOW TO USE THIS PLANT

In Cooking   Allspice is available as whole, small reddish brown berries or as a powder.

Provided you use the same form of the spice (that is, whole allspice for whole cinnamon sticks, ground allspice for ground nutmeg) you can use allspice measure for measure as a substitute for these other warm, spicy flavorings.

As a substitute for allspice, combine 1 part nutmeg with 2 parts each cinnamon and cloves.

Around the House   Allspice is an effective air freshener. To mask kitchen odors, boil 1 teaspoon whole or ground allspice in 2 cups water on top of the stove, and let the aroma drift pleasantly. To perfume a room, a closet, or a cabinet, use 4 whole allspice berries in a potpourri.

Aloe

ABOUT THIS PLANT

Botanical name(s): Aloe vera, Aloe barbadensis, Aloe capensis
Common name(s): Barbados aloe, Cape aloe, Curaçao aloe
Native to: Africa, Mediterranean region
Parts used as food/drink: Leaf (extract)
GRAS list: No
Medicinal properties: Laxative, emollient
Other uses: Cosmetic

ABOUT THIS PLANT AS FOOD OR DRINK

The aloe plant is a succulent with narrow, prickly-edged leaves. It is a member of the lily family native to Africa and the Mediterranean region, but now grown in the Southwest United States.

Aloe extract, a bitter liquid from the leaf, is used to flavor commercially produced candies, baked goods, gelatins, and alcoholic beverages such as aromatic BITTERS, cordials (liqueurs), and vermouth.

Nutritional Profile * * *

HOW THIS PLANT AFFECTS YOUR BODY

Important Phytochemicals The aloe plant produces two fluids. The first is aloe juice, a bitter yellow liquid (latex) from the cells just under the surface of the leaf. The second is aloe gel, a thick, clear, slippery liquid from the center of the leaf. Aloe juice contains the cathartics (strong laxatives) aloin, isobarbaloin, and aloe-emodin. Aloe gel is relatively free of cathartics; when aloe leaves are processed to make aloe gel for skin lotions and other cosmetics such as shampoo, the cathartic compounds are removed entirely.

Several laboratory studies testify to the ability of fresh aloe gel to soothe small cuts and burns, but exactly how and why remains a mystery. Aloe gel is often added to cosmetics for hair and skin, but there is no proof that the processed, purified gel used in commercial lotions and shampoos has the same healing effect as fresh gel.

In 1997, aloe was the sixth best-selling herbal supplement in health food stores in the United States, behind ECHINACEA, GARLIC, GINKGO BILOBA, goldenseal, and SAW PALMETTO. (Despite its popularity, goldenseal is not used in food, has no proven medical benefits, and is toxic in large doses.)

Benefits   In 1985 and 1993, the German Commission E approved the use of preparations of dried latex from aloe leaves to relieve constipation. In its approval, the commission cautioned against the use of aloe for children younger than 12 or for people with intestinal obstruction; inflammatory intestinal diseases such as Crohn's disease or ulcerative colitis; appendicitis; or abdominal pain from an unknown cause.

Possible Adverse Effects   The cathartics in aloe juice, found in commercial laxative products, may irritate the lining of the intestinal tract, causing strong intestinal contractions. They have been reported to cause severe intestinal cramps.

Long-term use of cathartics or even one very large dose may lead to potassium deficiency resulting in disturbances in heart function, a slowdown of the natural action of the intestinal tract, and kidney damage. Commercial laxatives containing aloe-emodin may cause a harmless red discoloration of urine.

Information for Women Who Are Pregnant or Nursing   Owing to a lack of information on its long-term effects, Commission E advises that aloe latex should not be used during pregnancy or when a woman is nursing.

Plant/Drug Interactions   Using aloe-emodin laxatives while taking a diuretic (a drug that increases urination), cortisone products, or a product containing LICORICE root may increase potassium loss.

HOW TO USE THIS PLANT   ✳ ✳ ✳

Angelica

ABOUT THIS PLANT

Botanical name(s): Angelica archangelica; Angelica fructus, angelica herbs
Common name(s): Archangel, European angelica, garden angelica, dong quai
Native to: Northern Europe
Parts used as food/drink: Stems, seeds, leaf stalks
GRAS list: Yes
Medicinal properties: Antispasmodic; antiflatulent
Other uses: Perfume

ABOUT THIS PLANT AS FOOD OR DRINK

Angelica, a large plant with fragrant leaves, is a member of the carrot family, native to Northern Europe and related to the American angelica (*Angelica atropurpurea*). The plant is a biennial, meaning that it lives for two years.

Angelica seeds and stalks contain an essential oil with a faint licorice flavor that is used in liqueurs such as benedictine and Chartreuse. The seeds are also used in baking, to lend a licorice flavor to cookies and cakes, while angelica stalks, which look like CELERY stalks, are sometimes used as a vegetable; the stems may be candied and used as a garnish.

Caution: Never gather wild angelica. Water hemlock (*Cicuta maculata*), a deadly poisonous plant, has leaves that look like and may be mistaken for angelica.

Nutritional Profile   One-eighth ounce (3.5 g) dried Chinese dong quai has 4 calories. It provides 0.5 g protein, less than 1 g fat, 6 g dietary fiber, 71 IU vitamin A, 1.8 mg vitamin C, 11 mg calcium, and 3 mg iron.

HOW THIS PLANT AFFECTS YOUR BODY

Important Phytochemicals   The primary flavor and aroma compound in angelica oil is angelica lactone. The oil also contains angelicin, bergapten, and xanthotoxin.

Angelica lactone is an irritant. Angelicin, begapten, and xanthotoxin are photosensitizers, substances that make your skin more sensitive to sunlight ("photosensitivity"), mutagens (substances that cause genetic changes in cells), carcinogens (chemicals that cause cancer).

Benefits   In 1990, the German Commission E approved the use of angelica root products as an appetite stimulant, an intestinal antispasmodic, and an antiflatulent (a drug used to relieve intestinal gas).

Possible Adverse Effects   Angelica lactone may be absorbed through your skin. Handling the angelica plant may cause contact dermatitis (itching, burning, stinging, reddened, or blistered skin), a reaction most commonly seen in food workers who handle the angelica plant. To avoid this, always wear protective gloves when handling angelica plants in the garden and wash your hands thoroughly after handling the herb in the kitchen.

Information for Women Who Are Pregnant or Nursing   Angelica is best avoided while nursing because very little is known about its effects on a nursing infant.

Plant/Drug Interactions   * * *

HOW TO USE THIS PLANT

In Cooking   To candy angelica stems, cut the stems into 2-inch lengths, enough for 1 cup. Put the stems in a bowl and add $1/4$ cup salt dissolved in 1 cup boiling water. Cover the bowl and refrigerate it overnight. In the morning, drain the stems, peel them, and wash once more in cold water to rinse off all the salt. Cook 1 cup sugar in 1 cup water until it makes a thick syrup. Then add the angelica stems and simmer slowly for 15 minutes. Drain the stems in a colander or sieve, saving the syrup. Store the syrup in the refrigerator. Lay the stems on a wire rack in a cool place to drain and dry for three days. On the third day put the stems and the syrup into a saucepan, bring to a boil and simmer for 15 minutes. Drain the stems once more, discard the syrup and store the candied stems in a tightly covered container in a cool place. Use the stems as needed for garnish. If you keep them longer than a day or two, always check for mold before using them. If you find any mold, discard all stems.

As a Home Remedy   The suggested daily dose is 4.5 g dried angelica root.

Commercial Uses   The essential oil of angelica is used in perfumes and as a flavoring in cigarettes.

Anise

ABOUT THIS PLANT

Botanical name(s): *Pimpinella anisum*
Common name(s): Aniseed, anise seed, sweet cumin
Native to: Egypt, western Asia
Parts used as food/drink: Fresh leaves, dried fruit (a.k.a. seeds)
GRAS list: Yes
Medicinal properties: Antiflatulent; expectorant; antispasmodic
Other uses: Pharmaceutical flavoring agent, perfume, rodent bait

ABOUT THIS PLANT AS FOOD OR DRINK

A member of the carrot family, anise is an annual plant native to Egypt and western Asia and widely cultivated in southern Europe, India, and the United States. Anise "seeds"—actually the ripe fruit of the plant—and anise leaves have a faint LICORICE flavor and aroma.

Anise seed and anise seed extract are used in commercial baked goods, as well as the licorice-flavored liqueurs ouzo and anisette, a safe substitute for absinthe, a licorice-flavored liqueur whose flavor came from the poisonous oil of WORMWOOD (*Artemisia absinthium*). It is also used to flavor cough syrups, cough drops, toothpastes and tooth powders, and as a scent in cosmetics, especially soaps.

Nutritional Profile One tablespoon (7 g) anise seed has 23 calories. It provides 1.2 g protein, 1 g fat, 3.4 g carbohydrates (including 1 g dietary fiber), 311 IU vitamin A, 10 mcg folate, 1.4 mg vitamin C, 43 mg calcium, and 2.5 mg iron.

HOW THIS PLANT AFFECTS YOUR BODY

Important Phytochemicals Anise's licorice flavor and aroma come from anethole (also known as anise camphor). The other important flavor compounds in anise are methylchavicol, a relative of chavicol, one of the flavoring agents that gives BLACK PEPPER its bite, and anisaldehyde, which has a faint vanilla flavor.

Anethole, which is also found in BASIL and FENNEL, is an irritant and a potential allergen.

Benefits   Anethole contains a compound called transanethole which appears to be an effective antiflatulent (a substance that helps expel gas from the intestinal tract), a mild antispasmodic, and an expectorant (a substance that helps break up and expel mucus from the respiratory tract). In 1988, the German Commission E approved the use of anise seed preparations to relieve upset stomach and respiratory congestion.

Anise seed is an excellent source of iron: One tablespoon provides 16 percent of the RDA for a man and 24 percent of the RDA for a woman. A 1990 study from Germany suggested that it increases iron absorption in laboratory rats.

Possible Adverse Effects   Anise seeds and toothpastes flavored with anethole have both been reported to cause cheilitis—peeling, cracking, or bleeding of the lips sometimes mistaken for the simple chapping caused by cold weather.

Anethole is an irritant that may cause redness, scaling, and blistering when applied directly to the skin. In laboratory animals, it is poisonous when absorbed through the skin. Sensitive individuals may develop contact dermatitis when handling the anise plant or products containing anethole; others may experience symptoms of respiratory or intestinal allergy when exposed to anise.

Information for Women Who Are Pregnant or Nursing   Some anethole compounds behave like weak estrogens. Since neither anise nor anethole have been tested in pregnant women, there is no information, one way or the other, as to how these compounds may affect a developing fetus.

Plant/Drug Interactions   * * *

HOW TO USE THIS PLANT

In Cooking   Anise is available as anise seed and as an extract (typically, 70 percent alcohol plus water and a very small amount of oil of anise). Licorice-flavored anise leaves, almost certainly available only from your own garden, can be used fresh in salads and as a garnish.

To make an anise-flavored vodka or brandy, add $1/4$ cup fresh anise leaves or 2 tablespoons crushed anise seeds to 1 quart plain, unflavored vodka or 1 quart brandy. Close the bottle tightly and let it steep for 24 to 48 hours, then strain and taste a sample of the vodka or brandy. When you find the flavor pleasing, strain to remove the herb.

Around the House   The scent of anise is attractive to mice and rats; adding anise seeds or fresh leaves to your rodent traps may make them more effective.

As a Home Remedy   The suggested daily dose is a tea brewed from 3 g anise seed.

Anise Hyssop

ABOUT THIS PLANT

Botanical name(s): Agastache foeniculum
Common name(s): Blue giant hyssop, fragrant giant hyssop
Native to: North America
Parts used as food/drink: Leaves, flowers
GRAS list: No
Medicinal properties: * * *
Other uses: Perfume in cosmetics

ABOUT THIS PLANT AS FOOD OR DRINK

Anise hyssop is a member of the mint family, a relative of BASIL, LAVENDER, ROSEMARY, SAGE, and THYME, with LICORICE-scented leaves rarely used in cooking.

Nutritional Profile * * *

HOW THIS PLANT AFFECTS YOUR BODY

Important Phytochemicals   Anise hyssop contains two important aroma compounds, vanilla-scented anisaldehyde and sharp, spicy pulegone, whose odor is reminiscent of peppermint or camphor.

Anisaldehyde is used in perfumes and toilet soaps, but anise hyssop itself is simply a garden plant with no reported history of use in folk medicine. There appears to be no scientific evidence of any effects (good or bad) on the human body.

Benefits   * * *

Possible Adverse Effects   * * *

Information for Women Who Are Pregnant or Nursing   * * *

Plant/Drug Interactions   * * *

HOW TO USE THIS PLANT

In Cooking   To brew a licorice-flavored tea, steep anise hyssop leaves in boiling water. Anise hyssop's violet blue flowers, which bloom from late summer through fall, may be used fresh or dried to garnish fruit dishes or desserts.

In the Garden   Like some other pungent herbs, anise hyssop is a natural insect repellent and insecticide. The plant, which grows to a height of 4 feet, is a useful addition to the garden.

Annatto

ABOUT THIS PLANT

Botanical name(s): Bixa orellana
Common name(s): Achiote, arnotta, annotta
Native to: Caribbean region
Parts used as food/drink: Seed
GRAS list: No
Medicinal properties: * * *
Other uses: Fabric dye, coloring agent (paints and varnishes)

ABOUT THIS PLANT AS FOOD OR DRINK

Annatto is the spice obtained from the seeds and seed coats of *Bixa orellana*, a tree native to the Caribbean region and cultivated in Brazil, Mexico, and India. You are most likely to find annatto powder in Latin American grocery stores, particularly in Puerto Rican neighborhoods, where it is sold under the name *achiote*.

Annatto is an excellent source of the carotenoid pigments bixin and norbixin, which are extracted from the seed and used as natural food coloring agents. Concentrated annatto pigments are red. Diluted for use in food processing, they make a peach- to buttery-yellow dye once used to standardize the color of commercial butters. Today annatto pigments are used commercially in a variety of dairy products, including cheese, ice cream, imitation creams and whipped toppings; as a coloring in some mixed seasonings; and to color frankfurters and other sausages.

Nutritional Profile   The nutritional values for annatto may vary. One-eighth ounce (3.5 g) annatto has 2–12 calories. It provides less than 1 g fat and dietary fiber, up to 0.5 mg vitamin C, up to 2 mg calcium, and less than 1 mg iron.

HOW THIS PLANT AFFECTS YOUR BODY

Important Phytochemicals   Coloring agents (see above).

Benefits   Many carotenoid pigments such as as beta-carotene and alpha-carotene (found in yellow fruits and vegetables) are converted to vitamin A in your body. Others, such as the bixin and norbixin in annatto and the red lycopene in tomatoes, have little or no vitamin A activity.

Possible Adverse Effects   * * *

Information for Women Who Are Pregnant or Nursing   * * *

Plant/Drug Interactions   * * *

HOW TO USE THIS PLANT

In Cooking   Despite its versatility and the fact that it turns up in recipes in many well-known cookbooks, annatto is not widely available. That's a pity, because it is an inexpensive cheap substitute for SAFFRON, the world's most expensive seasoning. But use annatto sparingly: its bitter flavor can overwhelm a dish. As a rule, to maintain the proper flavor, commercial food processors use no more than 1 part annatto to every 400 parts of food.

Industrial Uses   Pigments derived from annatto are also used to dye silk fabrics and in the manufacture of wood stains and varnishes.

Arrowroot

ABOUT THIS PLANT

Botanical name(s): *Maranta arundinacea*
Common name(s): Bermuda arrowroot
Native to: West Indies
Parts used as food/drink: Root
GRAS list: No
Medicinal properties: Demulcent
Other uses: Cosmetic, glue base

ABOUT THIS PLANT AS FOOD OR DRINK

Arrowroot is a starch from the rhizomes (underground stems) of *Maranta arundinacea*, a plant that grows on St. Vincent's Island in the West Indies. Although arrowroot is most commonly used as a thickener for sauces, it can also be boiled and served as a vegetable.

Nutritional Profile One ounce (28 grams) arrowroot has 45 calories. It provides 0.7 g protein, a trace of fat, 11 g carbohydrates, 0.5 g dietary, 3 mg vitamin C, 6 mg calcium, and 1 mg iron.

HOW THIS PLANT AFFECTS YOUR BODY

Important Phytochemicals Complex carbohydrates (starches). See below.

Benefits Like other starches, arrowroot soothes the skin. It can be used as a dressing powder to reduce friction and prevent irritation, and it keeps skin dry by absorbing water.

   If you are not sensitive to arrowroot (see below), you may add a cup of powdered starch to a warm bath to soothe irritated skin. In a pinch you can use the powdered starch as a substitute for dusting powder. More, though, isn't better: Too much powdered starch will make a sticky paste on the skin.

Possible Adverse Effects Arrowroot is a potential allergen that may cause skin rashes, stuffy nose, and reddened eyes in sensitive people. Be cautious in using arrowroot for infants and children who may have as-yet-unidentified allergies.

Information for Women Who Are Pregnant or Nursing * * *

Plant/Drug Interactions * * *

HOW TO USE THIS PLANT

In Cooking All starches, including arrowroot, consist of molecules of complex carbohydrates packed into bundles called starch granules. The carbohydrates inside the starch granule are amylose (a long, straight molecule) and amylopectin (a short, branched molecule). When you heat a starch in liquid, its starch granules absorb the heated water. The amylose and amylopectin molecules inside relax, breaking some of their internal bonds (bonds between atoms on the same molecules) and forming new bonds between atoms on different molecules. The result is a network of carbohydrate molecules that traps and holds water molecules, immobilizing them and thus thickening the liquid.

It takes less energy (heat) to break and re-form bonds between the long, straight amylose molecules than it takes to do the same thing with the short, branched amylopectin molecules. Therefore, starches such as arrowroot, which have a higher proportion of amylose molecules, "cook" at a lower temperature than starches such as cornstarch and wheat starch, which are higher in amylopectin. As a result, you are much less likely to burn a sauce made with arrowroot. Arrowroot also has less protein than cornstarch and wheat starch, which is why it makes a clear sauce rather than a protein-clouded one. Finally, because it has virtually no flavor of its own, arrowroot is particularly useful for delicate fruit sauces.

Note: As a thickener, $1^1/_2$ teaspoon arrowroot is equivalent to $1^1/_2$ teaspoon cornstarch or 1 tablespoon wheat flour. The arrowroot thickens at a lower temperature.

Industrial Uses Arrowroot is used as a base for some commercially produced glues.

Artichoke Leaf

ABOUT THIS PLANT

Botanical name(s): Cynara scolymus (plant), Cynara folium (leaf)
Common name(s): Artichoke
Native to: Southern Europe
Parts used as food/drink: Leaf
GRAS list: No
Medicinal properties: Choleretic
Other uses: * * *

ABOUT THIS PLANT AS FOOD OR DRINK

The globe artichoke is the prickly plant from which we get artichoke hearts and artichoke leaves. Note: The Jerusalem artichoke, also known as the sunchoke, is the edible root of a plant related to the American sunflower.

Nutritional Profile   The leaves and heart of one 10-ounce cooked globe artichoke have 60 calories. They provide 4 g protein, 13 g carbohydrates, 10 g dietary fiber, less than 1 g fat, 54 mg calcium, 61 mcg folate, 12 mg vitamin C (20 percent of the RDA), and 1.5 mg iron (15 percent of the RDA).

HOW THIS PLANT AFFECTS YOUR BODY

Important Phytochemicals   The most interesting natural ingredient in artichokes is cynarin, a sweet-tasting derivative of caffeoylquinic acid. Cynarin dissolves in water, including the saliva in your mouth, so it sweetens the flavor of anything you eat after you've eaten an artichoke.

Benefits   Cynarin is a choleretic, a substance that stimulates bile production and may relieve symptoms of nausea, vomiting, and bloating due to certain kinds of digestive disorder. In one 1994 randomized study among 21 German men suffering from digestive disorders due to an inability to digest fat, artichoke extract (the juice from fresh plants) increased bile production and relieved gastric distress. Artichoke juice may also be a milk diuretic, and there is speculation (but currently no proof) that it may also be useful in lowering cholesterol levels.

In 1990, the German Commission E approved the use of artichoke leaf preparations to relieve upset stomach.

Possible Adverse Effects   Because artichoke may effect bile production, people with gall-stones or bile duct obstruction should consult with a physician before using any product containing artichoke leaf.

Cynarin is a potential allergen. People sensitive to the compounds may develop contact dermatitis (itching, burning, reddened skin) when handling artichokes.

Information for Women Who Are Pregnant or Nursing   * * *

Plant/Drug Interactions   The guaiac slide test for hidden blood in feces is done with alpha-guaiaconic acid, a compound that turns blue in the presence of blood. Artichokes contain peroxidase, a naturally occurring compound that also turns alphaguaiaconic acid blue. If you eat artichokes a few hours before taking the guaiac test, the peroxidase may produce a false positive, indicating that you have blood in the stool when you do not.

HOW TO USE THIS PLANT

In Cooking   Raw globe artichokes contain an enzyme that interferes with protein digestion; cooking inactivates the enzyme.

To prepare an artichoke, slice off the stem and trim back the tough outer leaves. Then set the artichoke upside down in a bowl of cold water to flush out any insects and debris. When the artichoke is thoroughly rinsed, put it upside down on a cutting board and slice off the bottom. Cutting into the base of the artichoke tears cell walls and releases polyphenoloxidase, an enzyme that converts phenols in the vegetable to brown compounds that darken the artichoke heart. To slow the reaction, rub the cut surface with a solution of lemon juice or vinegar and water.

The bronze color of fresh artichokes is due to aging that allows the yellow pigments under the green chlorophyll to show through. Cooked artichokes turn bronze when heat causes chlorophyll, the green plant pigment in the leaves, to react with acids in the artichoke or in the cooking water, forming brown pheophytin that combines with natural yellow pigments in the leaves. To prevent this reaction, cook the artichoke very quickly so there is no time for the chlorophyll to react with the acid, or cook it in lots of water to dilute the acids, or cook it with the lid off the pot so that the volatile acids can float off into the air.

Canned globe artichoke hearts packed in brine are a high-salt food; artichoke hearts packed in oil are high-fat; frozen artichoke hearts are nutritionally equivalent to fresh ones.

As a Home Remedy   The suggested daily dose is 6 g dried cut leaves or pressed juice.

Asafetida

ABOUT THIS PLANT

Botanical name(s): Ferula assafoetida
Common name(s): Assafoetida, asant, Devil's dung, food of the gods
Native to: Asia
Parts used as food/drink: Root, rhizome
GRAS list: No
Medicinal properties: Antiflatulent, expectorant
Other uses: Animal repellent

ABOUT THIS PLANT AS FOOD OR DRINK

Asafetida, a member of the carrot family, is a foul-smelling plant native to Afghanistan, Iran, and Turkistan (a region of Asia now divided among China, Russia, and Afghanistan).

The plant tastes and smells like onions and garlic, only stronger. Gum from the asafetida root and rhizome (underground stem) is used as an ingredient in Worcestershire sauce, and small quantities of asafetida are used as a condiment and flavoring in Indian and Iranian cooking.

Nutritional Profile   * * *

HOW THIS PLANT AFFECTS YOUR BODY

Important Phytochemicals   Asafetida's flavor and odor come from acrid sulfur compounds called mercaptans, the same compounds that give ONIONS and GARLIC their characteristic taste and smell. Asafetida also contains irritating oils and sticky, gumlike substances called oleoresins.

Benefits   Asafetida acts as an antiflatulent (a substance that helps break up and expel intestinal gas). Like other plant resins, it has been used as an expectorant (an agent that causes the lining of the respiratory tract to weep watery secretions that make it easier for you to cough up mucus). Some researchers have suggested that asafetida, like oil of garlic, may help lower blood pressure and increase the amount of time it takes for blood to clot. Like garlic, asafetida has been hung around the neck as a talisman or folk remedy to ward off colds and other infectious diseases. But again like garlic, its only true value seems to be its ability to keep other people—and their germs—at arm's length.

Possible Adverse Effects   Like urushiol, the irritant in poison ivy, the oils and resins in asafetida gum may cause contact dermatitis in people who have been sensitized to it. However, the reaction does not occur as frequently nor is it likely to be as severe as the reaction to poison ivy.

Information for Women Who Are Pregnant or Nursing   * * *

Plant/Drug Interactions   * * *

HOW TO USE THIS PLANT

In Cooking   In the United States, asafetida is occasionally found in Indian grocery stores, where it is sold either as a solid lump or as a grainy powder. The lump form is thought to have a purer flavor. To use the asafetida, break off a small chip with a hammer or meat-tenderizing mallet and pound it to a powder between two sheets of waxed paper. Then use as your recipe directs.

In the Garden   Two of the sulfur compounds isolated from asafetida are natural pesticides similar to those in MARIGOLD (marigold) and NASTURTIUM. To make a 2 percent asafetida solution for use in your garden, crush a chip of the resinous lump, then mix 1 ounce of the powdered asafetida with $1^1/_2$ quarts water and shake hard. Use the solution around your garden plants to ward off deer and rabbits.

Asparagus

ABOUT THIS PLANT

Botanical name(s): *Asparagus officinalis* (plant) *Asparagi rhizoma* (underground stem)
Common name(s): Asparagus
Native to: Europe
Parts used as food/drink: Spear
GRAS list: No
Medicinal properties: Diuretic
Other uses: * * *

ABOUT THIS PLANT AS FOOD OR DRINK

The asparagus spear is a green leafy vegetable, high in dietary fiber, the B vitamin folate, and vitamin C. Keeping asparagus cool preserves its vitamins. At 32 degrees F, 8 degrees below the recommended temperature for a home refrigerator, asparagus will retain nearly 80 percent of its vitamin C for up to five days and all its folic acid for at least two weeks. Kept at room temperature, the asparagus would lose 50 percent of its vitamin C in 24 hours and up to 75 percent of its folic acid in 3 days.

Nutritional Profile   A serving of six cooked fresh asparagus spears has 1 g dietary fiber, 490 IU vitamin A (12 percent of the RDA for a woman; 10 percent of the RDA for a man), 10 mg vitamin C (17 percent of RDA), and 131 mcg folate (66 percent of the RDA for a man, 73 percent of the RDA for a woman).

HOW THIS PLANT AFFECTS YOUR BODY

Important Phytochemicals   Asparagus roots contain naturally foaming substance called saponins, plus mildly diuretic sulfur compounds such as methyl mercaptan.

Benefits   Like other green leafy vegetables, the asparagus stalk is high in folate, an important weapon in the war against heart disease and birth defects (see below). In the spring of 1998, an analysis of data from the records for more than 80,000 women enrolled in the long-running Nurses Health Study at Harvard School of Public Health/Brigham and Woman's Hospital in Boston demonstrated that a diet providing more than 400 mcg folate and 3 mg vitamin B_6 per day from either food or supplements—more

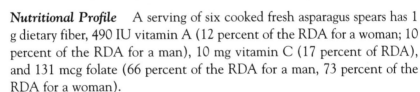

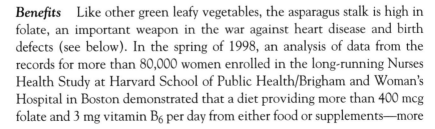

than twice the current RDA for each—may reduce a woman's risk of heart attack by almost 50 percent. Although men were not included in the analysis, the results are assumed to apply to them as well.

In 1991, the German Commission E approved the use of asparagus root/rhizome teas for the relief of inflammation of the urinary tract and prevention of kidney stones. In its approval, the commission cautioned against the use of asparagus root/rhizome products for people with heart disease or kidney disease.

Possible Adverse Effects   After eating asparagus, you excrete a smelly sulfur waste product, methyl mercaptan, in your urine. Whether or not you find this objectionable is an individual matter, since some people are more sensitive than others to the odor.

The asparagus plant is a mild potential allergen that may cause contact dermatitis (itchy, burning, reddened skin) in sensitive people who handle the vegetable's stalk or root.

Information for Women Who Are Pregnant or Nursing   As many as two of every 1,000 babies born in the United States each year may have cleft palate or a neural tube (spinal cord) defect due to their mother's not having gotten adequate amounts of folate during pregnancy. The current RDA for folate is 180 mcg for a healthy woman and 200 mcg for a healthy man, but FDA now recommends 400 mcg for a woman who is or may become pregnant. High-folate foods such as asparagus are an important part of the diet for women of reproductive age. In addition, taking folate supplements before becoming pregnant and through the first two months of pregnancy reduces the risk of cleft palate; taking folate through the entire pregnancy reduces the risk of neural tube defects.

Plant/Drug Interactions   Asparagus is high in vitamin K, the vitamin manufactured naturally by bacteria in our intestines. An adequate supply of vitamin K makes it possible for blood to clot normally. Eating foods high in vitamin K may interfere with the effectiveness of anticoagulants ("blood thinners") such as heparin and warfarin.

HOW TO USE THIS PLANT

In Cooking   The white part of the fresh asparagus stalk is woody and tasteless, so bend the stalk and snap it right at the line where the green begins to turn white. If the skin is very thick, peel it, but save the parings for soup stock.

Chlorophyll, the green coloring in asparagus, is sensitive to acids. When you heat asparagus, its chlorophyll reacts with natural acids in the leaves or in the cooking water, forming a brown compound called pheophytin. The pheophytin in turn reacts with the yellow carotene pigments in the leaves, turning the cooked asparagus bronze. To prevent this color change, prevent the chlorophyll from reacting with the acids by cooking asparagus for as short a time as possible.

Canned green asparagus is less nutritious than fresh. The intense heat of the canning process softens the asparagus, turns their bright green color drab, and reduces the vitamin A, folate, and vitamin C content by at least half. White asparagus is a green vegetable bleached to remove its green color. Both canned white asparagus and canned green asparagus have more than 200 times the sodium in fresh asparagus (236 mg in the canned varieties versus 1 mg in fresh, boiled asparagus).

As a Home Remedy   The suggested daily dose is a tea prepared from 45–60 g cut rhizomes.

Aspartame

ABOUT THIS CONDIMENT

Chemical name(s): N-L-alpha-Aspartyl-L-phenylalanine 1-methyl ester
Common name(s): Equal, Nutrasweet
Native to: * * *
Parts used as food/drink: * * *
GRAS list: No
Medicinal properties: Very low calorie sweetener
Other uses: * * *

ABOUT THIS CONDIMENT AS FOOD OR DRINK

Aspartame, which was approved by the U.S. Food and Drug Administration (FDA) in 1981, is approximately 160 to 200 percent sweeter than sucrose (table sugar). It tastes like sugar and, unlike saccharin, it has no bitter aftertaste. In commercial products such as diet sodas, sugar-free beverages, and sugar-free desserts, aspartame is called Nutrasweet. For home use, it is sold under the brand name Equal, a low-calorie sweetening powder or liquid.

NUTRITIONAL PROFILE

A one-serving packet of powdered aspartame sweetener (Equal) contains 37 mg aspartame. It has 4 calories. It provides less than 1 g fat and less than 1 g carbohydrates. Each Equal packet contains aspartame plus the sweeteners dextrose and dried corn syrup, cellulose and cellulose derivatives for bulk, and two anticaking ingredients, silicon dioxide and tribasic calcium phosphate.

HOW THIS CONDIMENT AFFECTS YOUR BODY

Important Chemicals Aspartame is a white, odorless, crystalline powder made from two commercially produced amino acids, L-phenylalanine and L-aspartic acid.

Aspartic acid is a nonessential amino acid, one your body can manufacture so that you do not have to get it from food. It occurs naturally in food from animals, and in some plant foods, specifically young sugarcane and sugar beet molasses. Phenylalanine is an essential amino acid (one that you must get from food because it cannot be made in your body), a component of tyrosine, another amino acid.

Benefits   Aspartame's chief benefit is its ability to sweeten with fewer calories than sugar, making it useful in a diet designed to control weight. Aspartame is useful for people with diabetes who must control their sugar intake.

Possible Adverse Effects   In the small intestine aspartame breaks down into methanol, phenylalanine and aspartic acid in the small intestine. All these substances are absorbed into your bloodstream. Phenylalanine and tyrosine (which your body makes from phenylalanine) both appear to interfere with the transmission of nerve impulses from one cell to another. Some scientists have suggested that this may cause changes in mood and behavior leading to depression or seizures. However, the FDA concluded in 1987 that although consuming aspartame does increase the amount of phenylalanine in your blood and brain, there is no conclusive evidence to show that it actually affects neurotransmission or changes behavior. In fact, there is less phenylalanine in 500 mg (0.5 g) aspartame than in 3 ounces of beef or 6 ounces of milk. The FDA has set the Acceptable Daily Intake of aspartame at 50 milligrams for each kilogram (2.2 pounds) of body weight. For a 150-pound adult man, this translates to 3.4 grams, the amount of aspartame in 20 cans of diet soda.

Because the chemical structure of aspartic acid is similar to that of MONOSODIUM GLUTA-MATE (MSG), people who are sensitive to MSG may also be sensitive to aspartame, which may cause hives and swelling of tissue in the throat. According to a 1986 study at Washington University in St. Louis, Missouri, these symptoms may show up immediately after a person who is sensitive to aspartame drinks a diet soda, or they may not appear for several hours.

Although some people have complained of headaches after consuming foods that contain aspartame, a 1987 Duke University study of 40 patients with this complaint showed that when the patients were given either a placebo or an amount of aspartame equal to what they would get from 10 diet sodas, the patients who got aspartame were no more likely to develop a headache than the patients who got the placebo.

Information for Women Who Are Pregnant or Nursing   Because your body breaks aspartame down into phenylalanine, the sweetener may be hazardous for children born with phenylketonuria (PKU) and for pregnant women who were PKU infants. People with PKU are unable to metabolize phenylalanine. In newborns and infants the unmetabolized phenylalanine circulating in the blood may damage brain cells, thus causing mental retardation. As a protective measure, all newborns in the United States are given a simple blood or urine test to detect PKU, and PKU babies are put on a special diet low in phenylalanine. In 1981 researchers at the Children's Medical Center in Boston suggested that women who were PKU babies should return to a protective diet (which would exclude foods sweetened with aspartame) when they become pregnant to avoid developing high blood levels of phenylalanine, which might damage fetal brain cells. To protect people with PKU, the 1981 FDA approval for aspartame included a requirement that the label on any product containing aspartame carry the warning "Contains phenylalanine."

Condiment/Drug Interactions   * * *

HOW TO USE THIS CONDIMENT

In Cooking   One packet aspartame sweetener (Equal) has the sweetening power of 2 teaspoons sugar.

Aspartame dissolves better in warm water than in cold. It degrades and loses its sweetness when exposed to high temperatures, so it cannot be used in cooking or baking. It may be added to foods after they have been cooked, used as a sweetener for coffee and tea, or sprinkled over cold cereals.

Always store diet sodas made with aspartame in a cool, dark place to prevent the aspartame from breaking down.

Bacon Bits (Imitation)

ABOUT THIS CONDIMENT

Chemical name(s): * * *
Common name(s): * * *
Native to: * * *
Parts used as food/drink: * * *
GRAS list: No
Medicinal properties: * * *
Other uses: * * *

ABOUT THIS CONDIMENT AS FOOD OR DRINK

Imitation bacon bits are small pieces of meatless "bacon" made from soy products. A typical list of ingredients in imitation bacon bits includes soy flour, soybean oil, salt, natural and artificial flavors, hydrolyzed vegetable protein, caramel, and artificial colors.

Nutritional Profile   Soy flour is very high (37–47 percent) in protein, and products made from soy flour are also high in protein. But the quantity of imitation bacon bits used as a seasoning is generally too small to add any appreciable amounts of protein to your diet. Soy flour is very low (0.9–20 percent) in fat, and soybean oil is composed chiefly (62 percent) of polyunsaturated fats. Neither the flour nor the oil has any cholesterol, so imitation bacon bits are low in saturated fats, contain no cholesterol and may be permitted on a low-cholesterol, controlled-fat diet that prohibits real bacon. They are also useful for vegetarian cooks.

HOW THIS CONDIMENT AFFECTS YOUR BODY

Important Chemicals   * * *

Benefits   Unlike bacon, imitation bacon bits are cholesterol-free.

Possible Adverse Effects   Soy products, artificial colors and artificial flavors may cause allergic reactions in sensitive people. In addition, imitation bacon bits, like real bacon, are high in salt and may be restricted on a diet for people who has heart disease or high blood pressure.

Information for Women Who Are Pregnant or Nursing   * * *

Condiment/Drug Interactions   * * *

HOW TO USE THIS CONDIMENT

In cooking: As a flavoring agent, one tablespoon imitation bacon bits equals one slice of bacon, cooked and crumbled.

Imitation bacon bits dissolve in liquid. Add them to fresh salads or use as a garnish on cooked dishes, preferably a few minutes after they come off the stove or out of the oven.

Baking Powder

ABOUT THIS CONDIMENT
Chemical name(s): Sodium bicarbonate (plus assorted acids)
Common name(s): Baking powder
Native to: * * *
Parts used as food/drink: * * *

Medicinal properties: * * *
GRAS list: Yes
Other uses: * * *

ABOUT THIS CONDIMENT AS FOOD OR DRINK

Baking powder is a leavening agent used to make baked goods rise. It is labeled "double-acting" when it contains both the "slow-acting" leavening agent sodium bicarbonate (BAKING SODA) plus a "fast-acting" leavening agent such as calcium acid phosphate (also known as monocalcium phosphate monohydrate), calcium sulfate, or cream of tartar.

Nutritional Profile One teaspoon double-acting baking powder made with sodium bicarbonate plus sodium aluminum sulfate and calcium acid phosphate (monocalcium phosphate monohydrate) has 5 calories. It provides a trace of protein, no fat, 1 g carbohydrates, 58 mg calcium (7 percent of the RDA for an adult), and 329 mg sodium.

One teaspoon double-acting baking powder made with sodium bicarbonate plus sodium aluminum sulfate, calcium acid phosphate (monocalcium phosphate monohydrate), and calcium sulfate has 5 calories, a trace of protein, no fat, 1 g carbohydrates, 183 mg calcium (22 percent of the RDA for an adult), and 290 mg sodium.

One teaspoon tartrate baking powder (sodium bicarbonate plus cream of tartar) has approximately 2.34 calories and provides a trace of protein, no fat, 0.5 mg carbohydrates, no calcium, 219 mg sodium, and 114 mg potassium.

HOW THIS CONDIMENT AFFECTS YOUR BODY
Important Chemicals See "About this condiment as food or drink."

Benefits * * *

Possible Adverse Effects Because it is high in sodium, baking powder and baked goods made with baking powder may be restricted for people on a low-sodium diet.

Some baking powders contain cornstarch as a filler (a substance that adds bulk to the powder). People sensitive to corn may be sensitive to the baking powders made with corn-starch filler, which can trigger such allergic side effects as hay fever, reddened eyes and stuffy nose.

Information for Women Who Are Pregnant or Nursing   * * *

Condiment/Drug Interactions   * * *

HOW TO USE THIS CONDIMENT

In Cooking   When you mix flour with water and beat the batter, the long protein molecules in the flour relax and unfold. Internal bonds (bonds between atoms on the same molecule) are broken and new bonds form between atoms on different molecules, creating a network of elastic protein known as gluten. When you add baking powder to the batter, its fast-acting ingredient releases carbon dioxide immediately (you can see the carbon dioxide as bubbles in the batter). The slow-acting sodium bicarbonate releases carbon dioxide later, when the batter is heated in the oven, stabilizing the batter's protein network into its final ("risen") form.

The combination of a slow-acting and a fast-acting leavening agent, first used around 1835 in England and available commercially since about 1850, works best in thin batters such as pancakes and quick breads or muffins. These cook too quickly to be made with yeast, which releases carbon dioxide very slowly.

Tartrate baking powders have the quickest reaction time. They release their carbon dioxide as soon as they are added to the batter and should be used only in batters that will go straight into a heated oven. Never use a tartrate baking powder in a dough you plan to refrigerate.

To protect the potency of your baking powder, store it tightly closed in a cool place. Even under the best conditions baking powders become less potent with time. To test the powder, add 1 teaspoonful to a cup of water. If it bubbles, the powder is still working.

Baking Soda

ABOUT THIS CONDIMENT

Chemical name(s): Sodium bicarbonate, sodium hydrogen carbonate
Common name(s): Baking soda, bicarbonate of soda
Native to: * * *
Parts used as food/drink: * * *
GRAS list: Yes
Medicinal properties: Antacid, antipruritic (relieves itching)
Other uses: Cosmetics, household cleansers, fire extinguishers

ABOUT THIS CONDIMENT AS FOOD OR DRINK

Sodium bicarbonate is a white powder prepared from sodium carbonate (a naturally occurring crystal), water, and carbon dioxide (gas). Baking soda is used as an ingredient in baking powder (see BAKING POWDER) and carbonated beverages.

Nutritional Profile   One teaspoon baking soda contains 821 mg sodium.

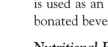

HOW THIS CONDIMENT AFFECTS YOUR BODY

Important Chemicals   See above, "About this condiment as food or drink."

Benefits   When sodium bicarbonate is moistened, it decomposes into sodium carbonate and carbon dioxide. Sodium carbonate, a base (alkali), neutralizes acids. As a result, sodium bicarbonate is commonly used as an antacid to relieve the pain of indigestion. The U.S. Food and Drug Administration's Advisory Review Panel on OTC (over-the-counter) Miscellaneous Internal Drug Products rates it safe for occasional use, but adds that there is no scientific research that actually proves its effectiveness.

Sodium bicarbonate moistened to a paste or diluted in bath water may be used to soothe the itch of a mosquito bite, relieve the pain of minor sunburn, or ease the discomfort of "weepy" poison ivy. Caution: sodium bicarbonate solutions are drying to the skin.

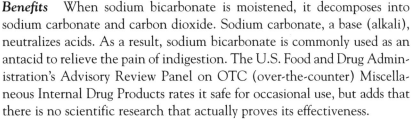

As an oral rinse, sodium bicarbonate ($\frac{1}{2}$ teaspoon in 1 cup warm water) may relieve the pain of canker sores. The FDA Advisory Review Panel on OTC Oral Cavity Drug Products rated a solution of one teaspoon baking soda and $\frac{1}{2}$ teaspoon salt in an 8-oz glass of warm water a safe and effective treatment for minor sore throat, softening mucus so that you can

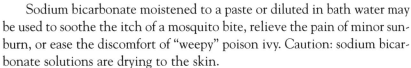

spit it out. Caution: White spots in your mouth may be an early sign of oral cancer. Any sore that does not disappear within 10 days should be examined by your dentist.

Sodium bicarbonate is sometimes added to vaginal douches on the theory that it will make the vagina more basic (alkaline) and thus less hospitable to various microorganisms. The FDA Advisory Review Panel on OTC Contraceptives and Other Vaginal Drug Products concluded that while sodium bicarbonate is a safe ingredient there is no scientific research to show that it has any effect on organisms in the vagina.

Possible Adverse Effects   Over-the-counter medications such as antacids, pain relievers, or laxatives that contain sodium bicarbonate may be high-sodium products.

Frequent use of a sodium bicarbonate antacid or very large doses may cause belching and bloating or fluid retention or distend the walls of the stomach. In one case reported during the 1980s, this distention was severe enough to rupture the stomach wall.

Information for Women Who Are Pregnant or Nursing   * * *

Condiment/Drug Interactions   Sodium bicarbonate increases the effects of pseudoephedrine, a decongestant found in many allergy and cold products.

In large doses, sodium bicarbonate decreases the effectiveness of aspirin, the diabetes drug chlorpropamide (Diabinese), as well as the mood-stabilizing drug lithium (Cibalith-D, Eskalith, Lithobid, Lithonate, Lithotabs); and tetracycline antibiotics.

Frequent use of sodium bicarbonate may reduce your body's absorption of iron supplements.

HOW TO USE THIS CONDIMENT

In Cooking   When you mix flour with water and beat the batter, the long protein molecules in the flour relax and unfold. Internal bonds (bonds between atoms on the same molecule) are broken and new bonds form between atoms on different molecules, creating a network of elastic protein known as gluten. Leavening agents release carbon dioxide to stabilize the batter's protein network into its final ("risen") form.

Sodium bicarbonate, a "slow-acting" leavening agent, stabilizes the protein network as the batter bakes. As a result, it is used in combination with a "fast-acting" leavening agent to make baking powder. The following combinations have the same leavening power as one teaspoon baking powder:

$1/4$ teaspoon baking soda + $1/2$ cup buttermilk; $1/2$ cup yogurt; or $1/4$ cup to $1/2$ cup molasses.

Around the House   Sodium bicarbonate is an effective dry scouring powder for the kitchen sink, pots, and utensils. To make an all-purpose liquid household cleanser, dissolve 2 tablespoons baking soda in 1 quart warm water and use on bathroom tile, sink, and tub.

In your refrigerator, an open box of sodium bicarbonate traps odoriferous particles. Eventually, oxygen and moisture in the refrigerator break sodium bicarbonate crystals into sodium carbonate and carbon dioxide. Some of the trapped odor particles stay stuck in the carbonate crystals; the rest float away in the carbon dioxide gas. If you change the box of used baking soda after three months, you eliminate, most of the smelly particles. For best results replace the box every three months.

As a Cosmetic   Sodium bicarbonate is an inexpensive substitute for effervescent bath salts and underarm deodorant. *Caution #1*: Baking soda is drying to the skin. If this is not a problem for you, one cup baking soda in a tub full of warm water can be substituted for bath salts. *Caution #2*: Baking soda is not an antiperspirant.

Basil

ABOUT THIS PLANT

Botanical name(s): Ocimum basilicum
Common name(s): Common basil, sweet basil
Native to: India, Africa, southern Asia
Parts used as food/drink: Leaves
GRAS list: Yes
Medicinal properties: Antibacterial
Other uses: Perfumery, insect repellent

ABOUT THIS PLANT AS FOOD OR DRINK

Basil is a member of the mint family, a bushy annual with broad, light green, oval leaves that release a spicy scent when bruised.

The herb is widely available fresh or dried and ground. The fresh leaves are much more flavorful, and they are easy to grow in a garden or in a window box. In addition to plain basil, you may want to try dark opal basil, whose peppery, purple leaves have overtones of mint and CLOVES; or anise basil with its licorice-flavor leaves; or lemon basil, which tastes lemony; or cinnamon basil, which has a flavor reminiscent of CINNAMON. These unusual varieties are not widely available; you may have to grow them yourself.

Nutritional Profile   One ounce (28 g) fresh basil leaves has 12 calories. It provides 0.9 g protein, 0.3 g fat, 2 g carbohydrates, 91 mg calcium, 0.3 mg iron, approximately 12,380 IU vitamin A, and 8 mg vitamin C.

Five fresh basil leaves (3 g) have 1 calorie, 0.1 g protein, a trace of fat, 0.2 g carbohydrates, 0.2 g dietary fiber, 205 IU vitamin A, and 1 mg vitamin C.

One teaspoon (1 g) ground basil has 4 calories. It provides 0.2 g protein, a trace of fat, 0.9 g carbohydrates, 0.6 g dietary fiber, 30 mg calcium, 0.6 mg iron, 131 IU vitamin A, and 0.9 mg vitamin C.

HOW THIS PLANT AFFECTS YOUR BODY

Important Phytochemicals   Basil's aroma and flavor come from anethole, the major constituent of oil of basil as well as oil of ANISE, the flavoring in anise, STAR ANISE, and FENNEL. Basil also contains estragole, which tastes like TARRAGON; spicy eucalyptol, which is also found in BAY LEAVES, CARDAMOM, cloves, and EUCALYPTUS; clove-scented eugenol, the major constituent of oil of cloves; and LAVENDER-scented linalool, also found in bay leaves and CORIANDER.

Anethole, estragole, and eugenol are all irritants and potential allergens.

Benefits   Like other dark green leafy vegetables, basil is a good source of deep yellow carotenoid pigments such as beta-carotene that are converted to vitamin A in your body. A diet rich in carotenoids appears to reduce the risk of some forms of cancer. It also protects your eyes as your body converts beta-carotene to 11-cis retinol, the most important constituent of rhodopsin, a protein in the rods in your retina (the cells that enable you to see in dim light).

In theory, this should make basil a highly nutritious addition to our diet. However, we use basil in such small amounts that its nutritional contribution is very slight. Five basil leaves, a common serving, weigh only about one-tenth of an ounce. For example, one ounce fresh basil leaves has about as much vitamin A as 1.75 ounces of boiled carrots, 309 percent of the vitamin A a healthy woman needs each day and 247 percent of the daily requirement for a healthy man.

Possible Adverse Effects   Very large servings of basil might be hazardous rather than healthful because the essential oil in basil contains estragole, a potential carcinogen which has caused tumors when fed or injected into laboratory rats and mice, and safrole, a known carcinogen.

Prolonged handling of the basil plant may cause itching, burning, stinging, and reddened or blistered skin, and sensitize you to other plants and chemicals.

Information for Women Who Are Pregnant or Nursing   The FDA classifies basil as a safe food, but the German Commission E report on basil warns against the use of basil in medicinal concentrations, against long-term use of the herb, and against consumption of the herb by toddlers, infants, and women who are pregnant or nursing.

Plant/Drug Interactions   * * *

HOW TO USE THIS PLANT

In Cooking   Basil, which is particularly tasty with tomatoes, is characteristically identified with Italian tomato sauces, pizza, or pesto, the oil-and-herb Italian condiment, but it also tastes good with fruit. As an experiment, sprinkle some on a baked apple.

Chlorophyll, the green coloring in basil leaves, is sensitive to acids. When basil is heated, its chlorophyll reacts with natural acids in the leaves or in the cooking water, forming a brown compound called pheophytin. The pheophytin in turn reacts with the yellow carotene pigments in the leaves, turning the cooked basil bronze. To prevent this color change, prevent the chlorophyll from reacting with the acids by adding basil at the very last minute. (Commercial herb packagers preserve the color of basil and other green herbs by drying the leaves at a very low heat.)

To protect the flavor and aroma of fresh basil leaves, pack them in a tightly sealed glass jar and store in the refrigerator. To maintain basil's flavor and aroma during longer storage, blanch the leaves, then wrap them whole or minced in tightly sealed plastic bags and store in the freezer.

In the Garden   Like MARIGOLD, ROSEMARY, SAGE, TANSY, and a number of other plants with a strong aroma, basil is a safe, natural insect repellent for your garden. Oil of basil repels houseflies and mosquitoes; one of its components, eucalyptol, also repels cockroaches.

Bay Leaf

ABOUT THIS PLANT

Botanical name(s): *Laurus nobilis*
Common name(s): Sweet bay, bay laurel, Grecian laurel, sweet laurel
Native to: Mediterranean region
Parts used as food/drink: Leaf
GRAS list: Yes
Medicinal properties: Antibacterial
Other uses: Insect repellent

ABOUT THIS PLANT AS FOOD OR DRINK

The bay leaves used in food come from an evergreen tree that may grow to a height of 40 feet in its native Mediterranean area. The leaves have a spicy fragrance; when crushed, they emit an aroma similar to that of bay rum.

Leaves from the California laurel (*Umbellularia californica*), also known as bay laurel, Pacific myrtle, or pepperwood, are often sold as "bay leaves," but they taste and smell bitter. Leaves from the West Indian bay tree (*Pomenta acris*) are not used in cooking, but they are distilled to produce oil of bay (oil of Myrcia), used in making bay rum and as a fragrance in medicines. The primary constituent of oil of bay is eugenol, also found in CLOVES.

Bay leaves are used in pickling spice, to flavor vinegars, and to flavor or scent various cosmetics and over-the-counter drugs including tooth pastes and tooth powders.

Caution: Leaves from the mountain laurel (*Kalmia latifolia*) or the cherry laurel (*Prunus laurocerasus*) are poisonous. The leaves of the cherry laurel contain prulaurasin, a compound that releases cyanide in your stomach. All parts of the mountain laurel contain andromedotoxin, a poison that may slow your pulse, lower your blood pressure, impair your coordination and cause convulsions, paralysis, and death. Andromedotoxin is potent enough to poison honey made by bees that alight on the mountain laurel.

Nutritional Profile One teaspoon crumbled bay leaf has 2 calories. It provides a trace of protein and fat, 0.5 g carbohydrates, 0.4 g dietary fiber, 37 IU vitamin A, 0.3 mg vitamin C, 5 mg calcium, and 0.3 mg iron.

HOW THIS PLANT AFFECTS YOUR BODY

Important Phytochemicals   The aroma and the flavor of bay leaves used in food comes from laurel leaf oil, whose major constituent is camphor-scented eucalyptol. The oil in bay leaves also contains rose-scented geraniol, lavender-scented linalool, turpentine-scented pinene, and phellandrene, a constituent of eucalyptus oil.

All these aromatic compounds are irritants and potential allergens.

Benefits   * * *

Possible Adverse Effects   Foods made with bay leaves and toothpastes made with bay oil have been reported to cause cheilitis (peeling and bleeding of the lips).

Information for Women Who Are Pregnant or Nursing   * * *

Plant/Drug Interactions   * * *

HOW TO USE THIS PLANT

In Cooking   Bay leaves are one of the few herbs that should be added early in cooking because they require a lot of simmering or marinating before their flavor permeates food.

Bay leaves are most often used in tomato sauces or in stews. For an unusual flavor, try adding a bay leaf to the water in which you boil potatoes, rice, or pasta.

Caution: Whole bay leaves MUST be removed before a dish is served. They are large enough to stick in the throat making them particularly dangerous for young children because they can obstruct a child's throat, cutting off the air supply and causing suffocation. Even a swallowed bay leaf can be hazardous. Bay leaves are very hard to digest. They may actually remain intact long enough to obstruct the intestines, in which case they may have to be surgically removed.

Around the House   Eucalyptol is a natural insect repellent which chases away roaches, moths, and fleas. Put a whole leaf in a canister of flour to keep the insects out, or put whole leaves on the floor of your closet, in drawers where woolen clothes are stored or around the drain under the sink in your kitchen. *Caution:* Keep the leaves out of reach of children and pets.

Bilberry Fruit

ABOUT THIS PLANT

Botanical name(s): Vaccinium myrtillus
Common name(s): European blueberry, huckleberry
Native to: Europe, North America
Parts used as food/drink: Dried ripe fruit
GRAS list: No
Medicinal properties: Anti-inflammatory, antidiarrheal
Other uses: * * *

ABOUT THIS PLANT AS FOOD OR DRINK

Bilberries, better known as huckleberries, are related to blueberries, but they have more seeds and the seeds are much larger.

Nutritional Profile * * *

HOW THIS PLANT AFFECTS YOUR BODY

Important Phytochemicals   Bilberries are colored with anthocyanin pigments, the same pigments that are found in blueberries. Bilberries also contain antioxidant flavonoids, natural compounds in plants that prevent molecular fragments from joining to form potentially carcinogenic compounds. Flavonoids are also anti-inflammatory.

Finally, bilberries get their tangy flavor from astringent tannins which coagulate proteins on the surface of skin or mucous membranes. Tannins are antidiarrheal; drying the berries increases the amount of tannins per gram, increasing the antidiarrheal effect.

Benefits   In 1990, German Commission E validated the long-standing use of dried bilberry teas as a folk remedy, approving these products to relieve occasional diarrhea. Oral rinses may be used to relieve mild inflammation of the mucus membranes of the mouth and throat.

Possible Adverse Effects   According to *The Merck Manual*, 16th edition, berries are one of the 12 foods most likely to trigger the classic food allergy symptoms: hives, swelling of the lips and eyes, and upset stomach. The others are chocolate, corn, eggs, fish, legumes (green peas, lima beans, peanuts, soybeans), milk, nuts, peaches, pork, shellfish, and wheat.

Information for Women Who Are Pregnant or Nursing * * *

Plant/Drug Interactions   * * *

HOW TO USE THIS PLANT

In Cooking   Bilberries are used only in recipes that allow you to cook the berries and strain out the seeds—jellies, jams, and sauces, but not pies.

Cooking destroys some of the vitamin C in fresh berries and allows water-soluble B vitamins to leach out. It also dissolves dietary fiber (pectin) in the berry walls, so that cooked berries are softer than fresh ones. They may also be a different color. Like blueberries, bilberries get their color from natural blue pigments called anthocyanins. Ordinarily, anthocyanin-pigmented fruits and vegetables turn reddish in acids (lemon juice, vinegar) and deeper blue in bases (baking soda). But some blue berries also contain yellow pigments called anthoxanthins. In a basic (alkaline) environment, such as a muffin batter with too much baking soda, the yellow and blue pigments will combine, turning the formerly blue berries greenish blue. This simple chemical reaction can be used for some kitchen magic. Want to find out whether canned fruits or juices have picked up metal ions (basic) from the cans? Just add a teaspoon of canned juice or fruit to some huckleberry juice. If the mixture turns greenish, the canned fruit contains some basic metal ions.

As a Home Remedy   The suggested daily dose is 20–60 g dried bilberries steeped in hot water (an infusion).

Birch Leaf

ABOUT THIS PLANT

Botanical name(s): Betula pendula (a.k.a Betula verrucosa), Betula pubescens
Common name(s): Birch
Native to: Europe, northern Asia, northern North America
Parts used as food/drink: Extracts
GRAS list: No
Medicinal properties: Diuretic, counterirritant
Other uses: * * *

ABOUT THIS PLANT AS FOOD OR DRINK

There are about 40 species of birch, including the black birch, a tree native to Europe, northern Asia, and northern North America that also grew in the Appalachians. Birch is not used as food, but it is a common herbal tea.

Nutritional Profile * * *

HOW THIS PLANT AFFECTS YOUR BODY

Important Phytochemicals The only birch species approved as a medical herb are the European white birch or silver birch. Fresh or dried leaves from these trees are rich in antioxidant flavonoids and astringent tannins.

The minty aroma of birch leaves comes from an essential oil known as sweet birch oil or birch tar oil, a dark brown liquid with high concentrations (up to 98 percent) methyl salicylate, a compound related to acetylsalicylic acid, the active ingredient in aspirin.

Methyl salicylate is a mild counterirritant, a substance that irritates the skin causing small blood vessels underneath to expand so that the flow of blood to the skin increases and the skin feels warmer. Birch leaf dressings have been used as a folk remedy for muscle or joint pain; methyl salicylate is sometimes included in liniments, ointment and other products used to relieve joint pain and inflammation associated with arthritis.

Caution: Methyl salicylate is toxic, used only for external dressings. Products containing oil of birch or methyl salicylate should be used only as directed on the package. They should never be applied when you have been perspiring heavily or in very hot weather, as these conditions increase your absorption of potentially poisonous methyl salicylate.

Benefits Teas brewed from birch leaves (which are available in tea bags) have traditionally been used as diuretics.

In 1986, the German Commission E approved the used of birch leaf tea to relieve bacterial and inflammatory diseases of the urinary tract and for the relief of arthritis, cautioning that the tea should be accompanied by "copious" amounts of fluids. In its approval, the commission cautioned against the use of birch leaf products for people with swelling due to fluid retention resulting from heart disease or kidney disease.

Possible Adverse Effects   Diuretics increase urination, leading to the loss of fluid and electrolytes, minerals that regulate fluid balance. As a result, they should be used only with the advice of your physician.

Information for Women Who Are Pregnant or Nursing   * * *

Plant/Drug Interactions   * * *

HOW TO USE THIS PLANT

As a Home Remedy   The suggested daily dose is a tea brewed from 2–3 g of fresh or dried birch leaves.

Bitter Orange Peel

ABOUT THIS PLANT

Botanical name(s): Citrus aurantium
Common name(s): Bitter orange
Native to: India, China
Parts used as food/drink: None
GRAS list: Yes
Medicinal properties: Appetite stimulant
Other uses: * * *

ABOUT THIS PLANT AS FOOD OR DRINK

Bitter orange peel is the dried rind of ripe bitter orange varieties such as the Seville, Bouquet de Fleurs, or Chinotto, each a highly acidic fruit with a distinctive aftertaste. The peel should be free of the white material underneath.

Nutritional Profile * * *

HOW THIS PLANT AFFECTS YOUR BODY

Important Phytochemicals   The flavor of bitter oranges comes from two flavonoids, naringin (the primary bitter component in grapefruit juice and grapefruit peel) and hesperidin (also found in other citrus fruits). Flavonoids are anti-inflammatory compounds, natural antioxidants that prevent molecular fragments in your body from joining to form potentially carcinogenic compounds.

Bitter oranges also contain acrid resins, gums, and astringent tannin.

The scent of bitter orange peel comes from bitter orange oil (neroli oil), which accounts for up to 2 percent of the weight of the peel. Neroli oil, which is also used as a perfume and as a fragrance in cosmetics, contains lemon-scented limonene and citral, lavender-scented linalool, and terpineol, an antiseptic also found in pine oil.

Limonene, linalool, terpineol, and some of the other pungent compounds in bitter orange oil are irritants, potential allergens, and photosensitizers, chemicals that make your skin more sensitive to light, increasing the risk of sunburn, particularly for fair-skinned people.

Caution: Although the small amounts of bitter orange peel used in food are considered nontoxic, pure bitter orange oil is poisonous; in 1995, the East African Medical Journal carried reports of convulsions and deaths among young children who ate large quantities of bitter orange peel.

Benefits   Like other astringent herbs, dried bitter orange peel appears to be an effective appetite stimulant. In 1990, the German Commission E approved the use of preparations of the peel for this purpose.

Possible Adverse Effects   Bitter orange oil is irritating to the skin and intestinal tract. People with ulcers should avoid this fruit and its peel.

Information for Women Who Are Pregnant or Nursing   * * *

Plant/Drug Interactions   * * *

HOW TO USE THIS PLANT

In Cooking   Bitter orange juice can be used in place of lemon juice, adding warm orange tones along with its bite.

Dried bitter orange rind gives orange marmalade its characteristic flavor. The rind is also used to lend dash to marinades, sauces, and baked goods.

As a Home Remedy   The suggested daily dose is 4–6 g of dried peel steeped in hot water to make a tea.

Bitters

ABOUT THIS CONDIMENT

Botanical name(s): * * *
Common name(s): Angostura, et al.
Native to: * * *
Parts used as food/drink: * * *
GRAS list: No
Medicinal properties: Appetite stimulant
Other uses: * * *

ABOUT THIS CONDIMENT AS FOOD OR DRINK

Bitters is an alcohol-based liquid flavoring agent made of distilled spirits plus the roots and rhizomes (underground stems) of GENTIAN. The finished product is 22–45 percent alcohol by volume (ABV), a relatively high amount, but we use bitters in such small amounts that the alcohol content is virtually irrelevant. (ABV describes the percentage of the liquid composed of alcohol. It is a new term that will replace the older term *proof* on labels for beverage alcohol products. To translate ABV to proof, multiply by 2. To translate proof to ABV, divide by 2. For example, A product that is 22 percent to 45 percent ABV is 44 to 90 proof.)

Nutritional Profile * * *

HOW THIS CONDIMENT AFFECTS YOUR BODY

Important Phytochemicals A gentian-based aromatic bitters contains amarogentian and gentiopicrin, the flavoring agents in the herb; as well as gentisic acid, an analgesic and antirheumatic compound related to salicylic acid; and gentianine, another possible anti-inflammatory.

Like other bitter herbs, gentian is reputed to stimulate appetite by irritating the lining of the stomach and triggering the secretion of gastric acid which sets off the gastric contractions we call hunger pangs. Some other herbs regarded as appetite stimulants are CARAWAY and MUSTARD.

Benefits * * *

Possible Adverse Effects Gentian is a choleretic, an agent that stimulates the liver to increase its production of bile, the yellow brown or green fluid that helps emulsify fats in your duodenum and increases peristalsis, the rhythmic contractions that move food through your gastrointestinal

tract. Choleretics are ordinarily beneficial for healthy people but may pose some problems for people with gallbladder or liver diseases. There is no evidence of harm linked to bitters. Some other choleretic herbs are ONION, OREGANO, and PEPPERMINT.

Information for Women Who Are Pregnant or Nursing * * *

Condiment/Drug Interactions * * *

HOW TO USE THIS CONDIMENT
In Cooking To retain the full flavor of bitters, add the liquid just before serving. Bitters is also a common ingredient in many cocktails.

Black Cohosh

ABOUT THIS PLANT

Botanical name(s): Cimicifuga racemosa
Common name(s): Black snakeroot, bugbane, squaw root
Native to: North America
Parts used as food/drink: * * *
GRAS list: No
Medicinal properties: Hormonal (estrogen) effects
Other uses: Insect repellent

ABOUT THIS PLANT AS FOOD OR DRINK

Black cohosh, an herb native to the eastern United States, is a tall plant with irregular leaves and fragrant white flowers. Its botanical name, *Cimicifuga*, comes from the Latin word for "bug repellent." Its common name comes from the Algonquin word for "rough," an accurate description of its roots, and the dark color of its racemes (underground stems). The herb is not used as food or flavoring, but may be available as an herbal tea.

Caution: Black cohosh should not be confused with BLUE COHOSH (*Caulophyllium thalictroides*), an unrelated poisonous herb that is also be known as squaw root.

Nutritional Profile * * *

HOW THIS PLANT AFFECTS YOUR BODY

Important Phytochemicals Black cohosh root contains triterpene glycosides, steroid-like compounds that seem to behave like estrogen, latching onto estrogen receptor sites in sensitive tissue; suppressing the secretion of lutropin (also known as luteinizing hormone or LH), the hormone that stimulates the final reopening of an ovarian follicle; and stimulating contractions of the smooth muscle lining of the uterus.

Native Americans used the fresh or dried rhizome (underground stem) and roots of the black cohosh plant to relieve menstrual cramps and to ease the pain of childbirth, which is how it got the name squaw root. Black cohosh was one of the principal ingredients in Lydia Pinkham's Vegetable Compound, the legendary 19th-century "female tonic." For years, it was also included in the *United States Pharmacopoeia—The National Formulary*, an authoritative listing of all recognized drugs. By 1986, however, it was no longer used in medicine in this country.

Actein, a steroidal derivative in black cohosh, has been found to lower blood pressure in laboratory cats and rabbits; there is no evidence of such an effect in human beings.

Benefits   In 1989, the German Commission E approved the use of black cohosh root preparations to relieve signs of premenstrual discomfort (PMS) or irregular menstrual periods, conditions for which doctors commonly prescribe oral contraceptives. However, the U.S. Food and Drug Administration, which considers black cohosh ineffective and potentially unsafe, lists it as an herb of "undefined safety."

Possible Adverse Effects   In large doses, black cohosh may cause upset stomach (nausea and vomiting) and dizziness.

Information for Women Who Are Pregnant or Nursing   Black cohosh may trigger contractions of smooth muscle, including the muscle of the uterus. It should not be used by pregnant women.

Plant/Drug Interactions   * * *

HOW TO USE THIS PLANT

Around the House   Black cohosh's botanical name, *Cimicifuga*, is derived from the Latin words *cimex* (bug) and *fugare* (drive away). Like ASAFETIDA, BASIL, and BAY LEAVES, black cohosh has been used as a natural insect repellent. *Caution:* This herb may be hazardous to children and pets.

Blackberry

ABOUT THIS PLANT

Botanical name(s): *Rubi fruticosi*
Common name(s): Brambleberry
Native to: Europe
Parts used as food/drink: Fruit
GRAS list: No
Medicinal properties: Anti-inflammatory, antidiarrheal
Other uses: Inks, dyes for paper and fabrics, photographic developer

ABOUT THIS PLANT AS FOOD OR DRINK

Blackberries (also known as brambleberries) are an English import, brought here by the early colonists who used them in pies and other desserts. Blackberries belong to the rose family, which also includes the STRAWBERRY and the RASPBERRY. (Like the raspberry, a blackberry is a group of several small fruits, each with its own tiny seed.)

Nutritional Profile   One cup fresh blackberries has 75 calories. It provides 1 g protein, 0.6 g fat, 18 g carbohydrates, 7.6 g dietary fiber, 238 IU vitamin A, 48.9 mcg folate, 30 mg vitamin C, 47 mg calcium, and 0.8 mg iron.

HOW THIS PLANT AFFECTS YOUR BODY

Important Phytochemicals   The leaf and the dried bark of the blackberry's rhizome (underground stem) and roots contain astringent tannins and gallic acid, plus saponins such as villosin, a naturally occurring plant compound that foams in water. Many saponins have antibiotic activity.

Benefits   Blackberry leaf, rhizomes and root have been used as antidiarrheals in folk medicine. In 1990, German Commission E approved the use of blackberry leaf tea as an antidiarrheal and to relieve mild inflammation of the mouth and throat.

Possible Adverse Effects   According to *The Merck Manual,* 17th edition, berries are one of the 12 foods most likely to trigger the classic food allergy symptoms: hives, swelling of the lips and eyes, and upset stomach. The others are chocolate, corn, eggs, fish, legumes (green peas, lima beans, peanuts, soybeans), milk, nuts, peaches, pork, shellfish and wheat.

Information for Women Who Are Pregnant or Nursing   * * *

Plant/Drug Interactions   ✳ ✳ ✳

HOW TO USE THIS PLANT

In Cooking   Store berries, unwashed, in the refrigerator. When you are ready to use them, rinse thoroughly to remove all dirt and debris, and pick over to eliminate crushed berries.

Cooking destroys some of the vitamin C in fresh berries and allows water-soluble B vitamins to leach out. It dissolves dietary fiber (pectin) in the berry walls, making cooked berries softer than fresh ones. And it may also change the color of the fruit. Like BILBERRIES (huckleberries), blackberries contain natural blue pigments called anthocyanins. Ordinarily, anthocyanin-pigmented fruits and vegetables turn reddish in acids (lemon juice, vinegar) and deeper blue in bases (baking soda). But some blue or black berries also contain yellow pigments called anthoxanthins. In a basic (alkaline) environment, such as a muffin batter with too much baking soda, the yellow and blue pigments will combine, turning the formerly blue berries greenish blue. This simple chemical reaction can be used for some kitchen magic. Want to find out whether canned fruits or juices have picked up metal ions (which are basic) from the cans? Just add a teaspoon of canned juice or fruit to some blackberry juice. If the mixture turns greenish, the canned fruit contains some basic metal ions.

As a Home Remedy   The suggested daily dose is 4.5 g dried leaves, steeped to make a tea.

Industrial Uses   The blackberry yields a dark blue liquid used commercially in inks and paper and fabric dyes, and as a photographic developer.

Borage

ABOUT THIS PLANT

Botanical name(s): *Borago officinalis*
Common name(s): Beebread, bee plant, burage
Native to: Europe, Mediterranean region
Parts used as food/drink: Leaves, flowers
GRAS list: No
Medicinal properties: * * *
Other uses: Honey plant

ABOUT THIS PLANT AS FOOD OR DRINK

Borage is a decorative garden plant with coarse, hairy stems and leaves.
The leaves, which can be eaten raw or cooked, taste and smell like cucumber. They are sometimes added to salads or used as a garnish for cold drinks.

Borage is rarely available in grocery stores. If you like its flavor, you'll
have to grow your own.

Nutritional Profile   One-half cup (44 g) raw borage contains 9 calories,
0.8 g protein, 0.3 g fat, 1.4 g carbohydrates, 00 g dietary fiber, 1,848 IU vitamin A, 15.4 mg vitamin C, 41 mg calcium, and 1.5 mg iron.

One-half cup cooked borage has 25 calories, 2 g protein, 0.8 g fat, 3.6
g carbohydrates, 00 g dietary fiber, 4,385 IU vitamin A, 32.5 mg vitamin
C, 102 mg calcium, and 3.64 mg iron.

HOW THIS PLANT AFFECTS YOUR BODY

Important Phytochemicals   Borage's crisp flavor comes from astringent
tannins, which coagulate the proteins on the surface of the mucous membrane lining of your mouth, making the tissues pucker. A second flavoring
agent in borage is malic acid, the naturally occurring sour compound in
immature apples. Finally, borage contains potassium nitrate, which has a
cool, pungent flavor. (Potassium nitrate is used in matches, firecrackers,
and gunpowder, and is added to tobacco to make cigarettes burn more
evenly. It is what makes burning borage pop and crackle.)

Benefits   Like other dark green leafy vegetables, borage is a good source
of deep yellow carotenoid pigments such as beta-carotene that are converted to vitamin A in your body. A diet rich in carotenoids appears to
reduce the risk of some forms of cancer. It also protects your eyes as your

body converts beta-carotene to 11-cis retinol, the most important constituent of rhodopsin, a protein in the rods in your retina (the cells that enable you to see in dim light).

One cup raw borage leaves gives a woman 46 percent of the vitamin A she needs each day and a man 37 percent of what he requires. Three and a half ounces of cooked borage provides 109 percent of the RDA for a woman, 88 percent for a man. Borage is also rich in vitamin C. One-half cup of fresh borage has 26 percent of the RDA for healthy adults; 3.5 ounces (100 g) cooked borage, 54 percent.

Like many greens—collard, DANDELION, mustard, and turnip—borage is rich in calcium. Three and a half ounces cooked borage provides 13 percent of the calcium an adult needs each day. Borage rivals spinach as a source of nonheme iron, the kind of iron found in plants. (The form of iron found in meat, fish, poultry, milk, and eggs is called *heme iron*.) One-half cup fresh borage leaves provides 15 percent of the RDA for iron. To increase the amount of iron you absorb from borage, serve the vegetable with meat. The meat increases the secretion of stomach acids, and iron is absorbed more easily in an acid environment. The vitamin C in borage also makes its iron more easily available by changing nonheme iron from ferric iron to ferrous iron, a form of iron your body absorbs more easily.

In late 1999, researchers at the Mayo Clinic reported to the American Society of Anesthesiologists that feeding borage seed oil through stomach tubes to 150 hospitalized patients reduced by 35 percent the death rate from acute respiratory distress syndrome, respiratory failure caused by trauma (such as an automobile accident) or infection. The scientists suspect that the benefits are due to gammalinolenic acid, an anti-inflammatory substance in borage seed oil.

Possible Adverse Effects   The borage plant is an irritant and a potential allergen: Its bristles may scratch your skin, and handling the plant may cause contact dermatitis (itching, burning, stinging, reddened, or blistered skin) in sensitive people.

Because borage is high in calcium, it may be prohibited to people who form calcium oxalate kidney stones. Large doses of potassium nitrate may cause violent gastric upset; repeated exposure to small amounts over a long period of time may cause anemia and kidney damage (neither effect has been reported in people who eat borage).

In 1984, food chemists discovered that borage contains small amounts of lycopsamine and supinidine viridiflorate, members of a class of chemicals called pyrrolizadine alkaloids which are known to be toxic to the liver; in animal studies, they also appear to be carcinogenic. As a result, some experts advise limiting your consumption of the vegetable despite its vitamin content (see above).

Information for Women Who Are Pregnant or Nursing   * * *

Plant/Drug Interactions   * * *

HOW TO USE THIS PLANT

In Cooking   Borage is generally served as a vegetable, but it has also been used to flavor wine and in sweet products such as jellies and candies.

Do not tear or cut borage leaves until you are actually ready to use them. When you cut into a food rich in vitamin C, its cells release an enzyme called ascorbic acid oxidase which destroys vitamin C and reduces the nutritional value of the food.

Do not cook borage in an aluminum or iron pot; its tannins react with ions from the metal to form dark pigments that discolor the pot and darken the borage. To prevent this chemical reaction, cook your borage in a glass or enameled pot.

Chlorophyll, the green coloring in borage, is sensitive to acids. When borage is heated, its chlorophyll reacts with natural acids in the leaves or in the cooking water, forming a brown compound called pheophytin. The pheophytin in turn reacts with the yellow carotene pigments in the leaves, turning the cooked borage bronze. To prevent this color change cook borage quickly.

Bouillon Cubes (packets)

ABOUT THIS CONDIMENT

Botanical name(s): * * *
Common name(s): Herb-ox, et al.
Native to: * * *
Parts used as food/drink: * * *
GRAS list: No
Medicinal properties: * * *
Other uses: * * *

ABOUT THIS CONDIMENT AS FOOD OR DRINK

Bouillon cubes and powders are dried soup bases that can be used as a seasoning or reconstituted with water to make a hot beverage.

A representative bouillon cube (packet) contains salt, soy protein, sweeteners (sugar), fat (vegetable oil), yeast extract, natural and artificial flavors, spices (onion powder), and preservatives. Beef, chicken, and fish bouillon cubes may contain dehydrated beef, chicken, or fish.

Nutritional Profile   One representative dry beef bouillon cube (3.5 g) has 5 calories. It provides less than 1 g carbohydrates and 900 mg sodium.

One representative dry packet beef bouillon (6 g) has 14 calories. It provides 1 g protein, 2 g carbohydrates, 1 g fat (0.3 g saturated fat), 10 mg calcium, and 1,361 mg sodium.

HOW THIS CONDIMENT AFFECTS YOUR BODY

Important Chemicals   The only meaningful nutrient in bouillon cubes/powders is the sodium in salt. Sodium is a mineral essential to life. It is an electrolyte, a substance that helps regulate fluid balance—the amount of liquid flowing into and out of every body cell—and it maintains the body's pH (acid/base balance).

Benefits   A warm salty solution such as a bouillon cube (packet) reconstituted with hot water is soothing to swollen mucous membranes. A cup of bouillon may soothe a sore throat associated with a cold or upper respiratory infection. The warm liquid also loosens mucus so that it is easier to clear your throat or blow your nose.

Possible Adverse Effects   Bouillon cubes may be on the restricted list for people with high blood pressure who are sensitive to sodium.

Salt holds water in body cells. Even healthy people who consume excessive amounts of sodium may retain large amounts of water, a condition that produces edema (swelling), usually of ankles and wrists.

Information for Women Who Are Pregnant or Nursing   See above.

Condiment/Drug Interactions   * * *

HOW TO USE THIS CONDIMENT

Storage   Keep bouillon cubes and packets in tightly closed containers to prevent their absorbing moisture and caking.

Buchu

ABOUT THIS PLANT

Botanical name(s): *Barosma betulina*
Common name(s): Short buchu, bucco, bucku, buku
Native to: Southern Africa
Parts used as food/drink: * * *
GRAS list: No
Medicinal properties: Urinary antiseptic
Other uses: Veterinary drug, artificial flavoring

ABOUT THIS PLANT AS FOOD OR DRINK

Buchu, a low flowering shrub native to Southern Africa (the Cape of Good Hope), is sometimes used to scent mixed teas or as artificial black currant flavoring. There are three varieties of buchu plants, each identified by the shape of its leaves: *Barosmae betulina* (short buchu), *Barosmae crenulata* (ovate buchu), and *Barosmae serratafolia* (long buchu).

Nutritional Profile   * * *

HOW THIS PLANT AFFECTS YOUR BODY

Important Phytochemicals   The active ingredients in buchu are the antioxidant flavonoids hesperidin and diosmin (buchu resin), plus bitter diosphenol (buchu leaf camphor) and pulegone, an oil with an aroma reminiscent of peppermint.

Hesperidin, diosmin, and diosphenol are mild diuretics, which accounts for buchu's having been used in African folk medicine for centuries and for buchu leaves having once been part of the National Formulary of the United States. Today, while the herb is considered safe, it has never been proven effective. A U.S. Food and Drug Administration advisory review panel ruled against allowing its use in over-the-counter products for the relief of premenstrual discomfort such as bloating.

Benefits   * * *

Possible Adverse Effects   Diosmin and pulegone may be irritating. The British Herbal Medicine Association's Herbal Compendium recommends that people using buchu products take them with food to prevent gastric upset.

Information for Women Who Are Pregnant or Nursing   Buchu may trigger contractions of the smooth muscle lining the uterus; the British Herbal Medicine Association warns against its use by pregnant women.

Plant/Drug Interactions   * * *

HOW TO USE THIS PLANT

In Veterinary Medicine   Buchu is sometimes used as a diuretic or urinary antiseptic in veterinary medicine.

Buckthorn

ABOUT THIS PLANT

Botanical name(s): *Rhamus frangula* (buckthorn bark) *Rhamus catharticus*
  (buckthorn berry)

Common name(s): Alder buckthorn, black dogwood, berry alder, arrow
  wood

Native to: Eurasia

Parts used as food/drink: * * *

GRAS list: No

Medicinal properties: Cathartic (strong laxative)

Other uses: * * *

ABOUT THIS PLANT AS FOOD OR DRINK

Buckthorn trees, which are native to Europe, Russian Asia, and the
Mediterranean coast of Africa, are not used as food.

Nutritional Profile * * *

HOW THIS PLANT AFFECTS YOUR BODY

Important Phytochemicals Buckthorn bark and buckthorn berry, the tree's
dried fruit, contain frangulin, emodin, and chrysophanic acid, a trio of
strong laxatives.

Benefits Laxative products containing buckthorn bark or berries stimulate contractions that move food quickly through the intestinal tract.
These substances also stimulate the secretion of the mineral chloride,
which increases the amount of water in the intestines and in stool. This,
too, moves waste faster through the intestinal tract.

In 1993, the German Commission E approved the use of buckthorn
bark and buckthorn berry liquids (teas, decoctions, elixirs) as laxatives, but
cautioned against their use for children younger than 12 and for people of
any age with intestinal obstruction, gastric inflammatory disorders such as
Crohn's disease or ulcerative colitis, appendicitis, and abdominal pain of
unknown origin.

Possible Adverse Effects Fresh buckthorn bark causes severe vomiting
and intestinal spasms. The buckthorn bark used in commercial laxative
preparation is aged naturally for at least one year or artificially aged by

heating it and exposing it to air. Nonetheless, buckthorn products may cause intestinal cramps.

As with any laxative, long-term use of buckthorn products may lead to a potassium deficiency or a loss of other electrolytes (the minerals that regulate the body's fluid balance). A continuing potassium deficiency can lead to muscle weakness, including weakness of the heart muscle. No laxative, including buckthorn products, should be used for longer than one to two weeks without your doctor's advice.

Information for Women Who Are Pregnant or Nursing   Because the exact nature of buckthorn's laxative activity has not been documented, German Commission E warns against its use by pregnant women or women who are nursing.

Plant/Drug Interactions   Because buckthorn is a diuretic, it increases the loss of potassium and other important minerals caused by diuretics ("water pills"), laxatives, steroid drugs, or herbal products containing LICORICE.

HOW TO USE THIS PLANT
See above.

Burdock Root

ABOUT THIS PLANT

Botanical name(s): Arctium lappa
Common name(s): Great burdock, lappa
Native to: Europe
Parts used as food/drink: Leaves, roots, stems
Gras list: No
Medicinal properties: Skin protectant/antiseptic
Other uses: * * *

ABOUT THIS PLANT AS FOOD OR DRINK

Burdock is a tall weed whose leaves, stems, and roots may be used a vegetable. Dried burdock root, used to brew an herbal tea, is sometimes sold in health food stores under the name *lappa*.

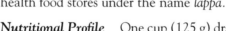

Nutritional Profile One cup (125 g) drained boiled burdock root has 110 calories, 2.6 g protein, 0.2 g fat, 26.4 g carbohydrates, 62 mg calcium, and 0.9 mg iron.

HOW THIS PLANT AFFECTS YOUR BODY

Important Phytochemicals The starchy burdock root is composed largely (45 percent) of the complex carbohydrate inulin, the starch that gives the Jerusalem ARTICHOKE its characteristic sweet flavor. The root also contains sucrose, bitter resin, and some fats, plus organic chemicals called lactones which are potential allergens.

Benefits Inulin is sometimes used as a substitute for sucrose (table sugar) in baked goods for people with diabetes who do not produce insulin to metabolize (digest) sucrose.

Like other starches, inulin appears to form a protective, soothing film when spread on the skin. Some studies suggest that there are antiseptic or antibacterial compounds in fresh burdock root (they disappear when the root is dried), but there is currently no scientific proof that burdock root is effective either as a soothing dressing or as an external antiseptic.

Possible Adverse Effects Handling burdock may cause contact dermatitis (itching, burning and stinging, reddened or blistered skin) in sensitive people.

Information for Women Who Are Pregnant or Nursing * * *

Plant/Drug Interactions   * * *

HOW TO USE THIS PLANT

In Cooking   Fresh burdock leaves may be used in salads. Burdock stems can be peeled, boiled, and eaten like ASPARAGUS or candied like ANGELICA. Burdock's long roots, which are grayish-brown on the outside and white on the inside, can be sliced into soups, stews, or stir-fries, or boiled, buttered, and served like turnips or potatoes. The roots contain creamy anthoxanthin pigments that turn dark when they react with ions from an iron or aluminum pot. To keep cooked burdock roots white, prepare them in a glass or enameled pot.

Burnet

ABOUT THIS PLANT

Botanical name(s): *Sanguisorba minor* (garden burnet), *Sanguisorba officinalis* (greater burnet)

Common name(s): Salad burnet, garden burnet

Native to: Europe (salad burnet), Eurasia (garden burnet)

Parts used as food/drink: Leaves

GRAS list: No

Medicinal properties: Astringent

Other uses: * * *

ABOUT THIS PLANT AS FOOD OR DRINK

The burnets are members of the rose family native to Europe (greater burnet) and Eurasia (garden burnet). The main difference between them is the color of their flowers, light green to yellow green for garden burnet, red for greater burnet.

Burnet leaves, which taste like cucumber, are used fresh in salads or as a garnish for cool summer drinks.

Nutritional Profile   One ounce (28 g) burnet has 3.2 g protein, 3.8 g fat, and 2.2–7 g dietary fiber.

HOW THIS PLANT AFFECTS YOUR BODY

Important Phytochemicals   The crisp, refreshing flavor of burnet leaves comes from tannins, astringents that coagulate proteins on the surface of your skin or the mucous membrane lining of your mouth and make the tissues pucker, creating a sensation of coolness.

In folk medicine, high-tannin plants such as the burnets were commonly used as a remedy for diarrhea, to soothe minor burns, or to stop bleeding from open wounds (*Sanguisorba*, the burnets' botanical genus name, means "blood absorber"). There are no scientific studies to demonstrate these effects.

Benefits   * * *

Possible Adverse Effects   * * *

Information for Women Who Are Pregnant or Nursing   * * *

Plant/Drug Interactions   * * *

HOW TO USE THIS PLANT

In Cooking   Burnet is almost never available in groceries. To try it, you are likely to have to grow your own. Use fresh-picked burnet leaves as quickly as possible; their flavor lessens significantly as the leaves dry.

Butcher's Broom

ABOUT THIS PLANT

Botanical name(s): *Rusci aculeati*
Common name(s): Box holly, pettigree
Native to: Mediterranean region
Parts used as food/drink: * * *
GRAS list: No
Medicinal properties: Anti-inflammatory
Other uses: * * *

ABOUT THIS PLANT AS FOOD OR DRINK

Butcher's broom, a relative of the ASPARAGUS plant, is an evergreen shrub native to the Mediterranean region that now grows in the southern United States. It was once used as a vegetable.

Nutritional Profile * * *

HOW THIS PLANT AFFECTS YOUR BODY

Important Phytochemicals The dried rhizomes (underground stems) and roots of the butcher broom plant contain several steroid-like compounds: ruscin, ruscoside, ruscogenin, and neuroruscogenin.

Benefits In laboratory studies with hamsters and dogs, extract of butcher's broom appeared to strengthen blood vessel walls. In a few small studies with human beings, extract of butcher broom given together with aspirin and the antioxidant flavonoid hesperidin appears to relieve leg cramps, numbness, and swelling associated with varicose veins.

In 1991, the German Commission E approved the use of butcher's broom extract for this purpose as well as to relieve itching and pain due to hemorrhoids. The U.S. Food and Drug Administration has not approved the plant for this use. Note: Butcher's broom should not be used as a home remedy; if you have varicose veins and hemorrhoids severe enough to require treatment, the safest course is to seek a doctor's advice rather than to self-medicate.

Possible Adverse Effects Butcher's broom may (rarely) cause upset stomach or nausea.

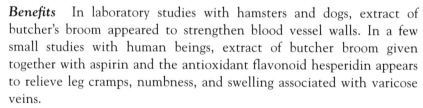

Information for Women Who Are Pregnant or Nursing   * * *

Plant/Drug Interactions   * * *

HOW TO USE THIS PLANT   * * *

Capers

ABOUT THIS PLANT

Botanical name(s): Capparis spinosa
Common name(s): * * *
Native to: Southern Europe, Mediterranean region
Parts used as food/drink: Flower buds
GRAS list: Yes
Medicinal properties: * * *
Other uses: * * *

ABOUT THIS PLANT AS FOOD OR DRINK

Capers are the unripe flower buds of a spiny shrub native to southern Europe and the Mediterranean region. The buds are picked before they have a chance to open and then pickled in vinegar or salted.

Caution: The caper spurge (*Euphorbia lathyris*) is an unrelated poisonous plant whose buds are sometimes mistaken for capers. Consuming caper spurge buds may cause a burning sensation in the mouth, nausea and gastric upset, paleness, irregular pulse, dizziness, delirium, and collapse.

Nutritional Profile One tablespoon drained canned capers has 2 calories. It provides 0.2 g protein, a trace of fat, 0.4 g carbohydrates, 0.3 g dietary fiber, 12 IU vitamin A, 2 mcg folate, 0.2 mg vitamin C, 0.1 mg iron, and up to 255 mg sodium.

HOW THIS PLANT AFFECTS YOUR BODY

Important Phytochemicals * * *

Benefits * * *

Possible Adverse Effects Capers made with salt are a high-sodium food (defined as more than 125 mg sodium per serving). They may increase your body's retention of fluids and raise your blood pressure.

Information for Women Who Are Pregnant or Nursing * * *

Plant/Drug Interactions * * *

HOW TO USE THIS PLANT

In Cooking   Capers add a salty, sour piquancy to salad dressings or meat and chicken stews. They are particularly good in a sour cream sauce.

Capers can also be used as a substitute for *toushi,* an Asian condiment consisting of fermented black beans.

In the Garden   The caper plant is a perennial that thrives in mild winter climates. It can be started indoors from seed and then, once the threat of frost has passed, it can be moved outside where it will tolerate dryness but requires full sun. To harvest the capers, pick off the flower buds before they show any color and steep them in vinegar to taste.

Caraway

ABOUT THIS PLANT

Botanical name(s): Carum carvi, Carvi aettheroleum (caraway oil), Carvi
   fructus (caraway seed)
Common name(s): Roman cumin
Native to: Asia
Parts used as food/drink: Leaves, fruit ("seeds")
GRAS list: Yes
Medicinal properties: Antiflatulent, antispasmodic
Other uses: Pharmaceutical flavoring, cosmetic scent

ABOUT THIS PLANT AS FOOD OR DRINK

The caraway plant is a member of the carrot and PARSLEY family, native to
Europe and Asia, now cultivated in Great Britain, Russia, and the United
States. Caraway's crunchy brown dried ripe fruit, called seeds, give rye bread
and the rye-flavored liqueur kummel their characteristic flavor and aroma.
Young and tender caraway seeds can be used to garnish and flavor salads.

Nutritional Profile   One tablespoon (7 g) caraway seeds has 22 calories.
It provides 1.32 g protein, 1 g fat, 3.3 g carbohydrates, 2.5 g dietary fiber,
24 IU vitamin A, 1.4 mg vitamin C, 46 mg calcium, and 1.09 mg iron.

   One teaspoon (2 g) caraway seeds has 7 calories. It provides 0.4 g protein, 0.3 g fat, 1.1 g carbohydrates, 0.8 g dietary fiber, 8 IU vitamin A, 0.4
mg vitamin C, 14 mg calcium, and 0.3 mg iron.

HOW THIS PLANT AFFECTS YOUR BODY

Important Phytochemicals   Caraway's flavor and aroma come from an oil
whose main constituent is carvone (50–60 percent), the flavoring agent
used in kummel, a liqueur. Caraway oil also contains lemon-scented
limonene, also found in oil of DILL, LEMON, and BITTER ORANGE PEEL.

   Carvone is an antispasmodic, an agent that relaxes muscle spasms, and
an antiflatulent, an agent that helps expel gas from the intestinal tract. It
is also an irritant. Limone is an irritant, a potential allergen, and a photosensitizer, a substance that makes your skin more sensitive to sunlight (a
condition known as photosensitivity).

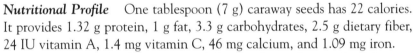

Benefits   In 1990, the German Commission E validated caraway's long-standing reputation as a folk remedy for intestinal gas and intestinal spasms, approving the use of preparations of crushed caraway seeds (which contain caraway oil) for these purposes.

Possible Adverse Effects   Handling the caraway plant or caraway seeds may cause contact dermatitis (itching, burning, stinging, reddened or blistered skin) in sensitive individuals, including people sensitive to daisies.

Information for Women Who Are Pregnant or Nursing   Theoretically, carvone, an anti-spasmodic, might relax the smooth muscle lining of the uterus, but Commission E's report does not list this effect.

Plant/Drug Interactions   * * *

HOW TO USE THIS PLANT

In Cooking   To protect the flavor of whole caraway seeds, store them in airtight containers in a cool, dark cabinet.

Add caraway seeds to a sauce after the dish is cooked; long cooking can turn their flavor bitter.

Caraway is sometimes called Roman cumin because ground caraway has a flavor similar to—though slightly "lighter" than—ground CUMIN. You can grind or mash caraway seeds and use them as a substitute for cumin in homemade CURRY POWDER or CHILI POWDER.

Cardamom

ABOUT THIS PLANT

Botanical name(s): Elettaria cardamom
Common name(s): Cardamom seed
Native to: India
Parts used as food/drink: Dried fruit
GRAS list: Yes
Medicinal properties: Antiflatulent
Other uses: Pharmaceutical flavoring

ABOUT THIS PLANT AS FOOD OR DRINK

Cardamom is the world's third most expensive spice, right behind SAFFRON and VANILLA. Dried cardamom (that is, cardamom seeds) is sold whole or ground. Some Indian grocery stores also stock cardamom seed pods, either black (sun-dried, deeply flavored) or green (milder flavored, dried indoors in large kilns).

Cardamom is used in curry powders, baked goods, and candies; its oil is used to flavor liquors and pharmaceutical drug products.

Nutritional Profile One tablespoon (6 g) ground cardamom has 18 calories. It provides 0.6 g protein, 0.4 g fat, 4.0 g carbohydrates, 1.6 g dietary fiber, 1.2 mg vitamin C, 22 mg calcium, and 0.8 mg iron.

One teaspoon (2 g) ground cardamom has 6 calories. It provides 0.2 g protein, 0.1 g fat, 1.4 g carbohydrates, 0.6 g dietary fiber, 0.4 mg vitamin C, 8 mg calcium, and 0.3 mg iron.

HOW THIS PLANT AFFECTS YOUR BODY

Important Phytochemicals Cardamom's flavor and aroma come from oil of cardamom, a pale yellow liquid that contains spicy, camphor-scented eucalyptol (also found in CLOVES), lemon-scented limonene and terpinene, and peppery borneol (also found in CILANTRO, CINNAMON, and GINGER).

Borneol, eucalyptol, and limonene are irritants. Limonene is also a potential allergen and a photosensitizer, a chemical that makes your skin more sensitive to sunlight (a condition known as photosensitivity).

Benefits Cardamom is reputed to be an antiflatulent, a substance that breaks up intestinal gas. In 1990, the German Commission E approved the use of preparations of ground cardamom seeds to relieve upset stomach, but cautioned that people who have gallstones should not use cardamom or cardamom preparations without consulting a physician.

Possible Adverse Effects   Prolonged handling of cardamom seeds may cause contact dermatitis (itching, burning, stinging, reddened, or blistered skin) or result in sunburn in sensitive individuals.

Information for Women Who Are Pregnant or Nursing   * * *

Plant/Drug Interactions   * * *

HOW TO USE THIS PLANT

In Cooking   A pinch of cardamom adds piquancy to after-dinner coffee. Cardamom is most commonly used in spicy curries and chili dishes or to add dash to ground beef.

Around the House   Eucalyptol, found in BAY LEAVES as well as cardamom, is an insect repellent. Several laboratory studies have shown that scattering bay leaves under the sink or in kitchen cabinets will repel cockroaches. There are no similar studies with cardamom pods, perhaps because cardamom is so much more expensive than bay leaves. But if you have cockroaches in the kitchen and you can find cardamom pods, you may wish to try your own experiment by placing a pod or two under the sink and seeing if they reduce the insect population.

Carob

ABOUT THIS PLANT

Botanical name(s): Ceratonia siliqua
Common name(s): Carob, locust bean gum
Native to: Mediterranean region
Parts used as food/drink: Pods
GRAS list: Yes
Medicinal properties: Absorbent, demulcent
Other uses: * * *

ABOUT THIS PLANT AS FOOD OR DRINK

Carob is an evergreen tree native to the Mediteranean region. Carob flour, milled from dried carob beans and pods, looks like cocoa, but it tastes like beans until it is mixed with sweeteners to make a substitute for cocoa powder or combined with fats and sweeteners to produce candy that looks and tastes like honey-sweetened milk chocolate.

Like other legumes (beans and peas), carob is a high-carbohydrate food. It contains sugars (including raffinose and stachyose, two complex indigestible sugars commonly found in beans), starches, and dietary fiber (soluble gums and pectins). Carob has more protein and calcium but fewer calories per ounce than chocolate.

Nutritional Profile One cup (103 g) carob flour has 394 calories. It provides 5 g protein, 92 g carbohydrates, 13 g dietary fiber, 1 g fat, 30 mcg folate, 358 mg calcium, and 3 mg iron.

HOW THIS PLANT AFFECTS YOUR BODY

Benefits Carob is a useful substitute for people who are sensitive to chocolate. Like ARROWROOT and BAKING SODA, carob can be used as a soothing skin powder.

Possible Adverse Effects * * *

Information for Women Who Are Pregnant or Nursing * * *

Plant/Drug Interactions * * *

HOW TO USE THIS PLANT

In Cooking Three tablespoons carob flour plus 2 tablespoons of water is equivalent to one ounce unsweetened chocolate.

To use carob flour in baked goods, substitute $1/4$ cup carob flour plus $3/4$ cup regular flour for each cup ordinary flour.

Unlike cocoa powder, carob flour contains virtually no fat. It will burn, not melt, if you heat it in a saucepan.

All starches, including carob, consist of molecules of complex carbohydrates packed into bundles called starch granules. The carbohydrates inside the starch granule are amylose (a long, straight molecule) and amylopectin (a short, branched molecule). When a starch is heated in liquid, its starch granules absorb the heated water. The amylose and amylopectin molecules inside relax, breaking some of their internal bonds (bonds between atoms on the same molecules) and forming new bonds between atoms on different molecules. The result is a network of carbohydrate molecules that traps and holds water molecules, immobilizing them and thus thickening the liquid.

Cascara

ABOUT THIS PLANT

Botanical name(s): *Cascara sagrada*

Common name(s): Sacred bark, chittem bark, Persian bark, bearberry bark

Native to: United States

Parts used as food/drink: Bark

GRAS list: No

Medicinal properties: Laxative

Other uses: * * *

ABOUT THIS PLANT AS FOOD OR DRINK

Cascara, the dried bark of a tree native to the Pacific Northwest from Idaho west to California, is a laxative. It is not used as food but may (rarely) be brewed into an herbal tea.

Nutritional Profile * * *

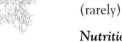

HOW THIS PLANT AFFECTS YOUR BODY

Important Phytochemicals Native Americans were the first to use cascara. They made a laxative tonic by stripping the bark from the tree, aging it for at least a year, then steeping it in boiling water. This remedy was effective and was adopted by the Spanish explorers who colonized California. They gave cascara recipes to U.S. physicians, and in 1894 cascara was included in the U.S. Pharmacopoeia. Today, the plant is still used in many commercial laxatives.

The laxative compounds in cascara bark are aloe-emodins. The emodins are similar to laxative compounds in ALOE, BROOM, BUCKTHORN, and SENNA. Emodins irritate the intestinal walls, stimulating contractions that move food through the intestinal tract.

Benefits Cascara bark is a milder laxative than broom, buckthorn, and senna. In 1993, the German Commission E approved the use of cascara preparations for the relief of constipation. However, the commission cautions against prescribing cascara for children younger than 12 or for people of any age with intestinal obstruction or gastric inflammatory disorders such as Crohn's disease or ulcerative colitis or appendicitis or abdominal pain of unknown origin.

Possible Adverse Effects   Only dried (aged) bark is used as a laxative. Using fresh cascara bark may cause nausea. Long-term use may cause chronic diarrhea.

As with any laxative, repeated use of cascara may cause excessive fluid loss leading to a potassium deficiency or an imbalance in other electrolytes (the minerals that regulate the body's fluid balance). A continuing potassium deficiency may cause muscle weakness, including weakness of the heart muscle. No laxative, including cascara products, should be used for longer than one to two weeks without your doctor's advice.

Information for Women Who Are Pregnant or Nursing   Exactly how cascara works remains unknown. Because it causes intestinal contractions, it should not be used by women who are pregnant or nursing.

Plant/Drug Interactions   By increasing defecation, cascara increases the loss of liquids, potassium and other electrolytes. It should not be taken by people who are also taking diuretic drugs ("water pills"), steroid drugs, or herbal products containing LICORICE, another diuretic.

HOW TO USE THIS PLANT
See above.

Cassia

ABOUT THIS PLANT

Botanical name(s): *Cinnamomum aromaticum, Cinnamomum cassia*
Common name(s): Chinese cassia
Native to: Asia
Parts used as food/drink: Bark, buds
GRAS list: Yes
Medicinal properties: Carminative
Other uses: Perfumery

ABOUT THIS PLANT AS FOOD OR DRINK

The cassia tree, a relative of *Cinnamomum verum* (true cinnamon), is an evergreen belonging to the laurel family. Cassia bark, also known as "the poor man's cinnamon," and cassia buds, the clovelike dried fruit of the tree, are highly aromatic spices.

In their native China, cassia buds are used to add a cinnamon flavor to candy and sweet pickles, but it's unlikely you will ever find them sold under their own name. Instead, cassia is ground, mixed with true cinnamon, and marketed as "ground cinnamon." Or the bark may be rolled into sticks and sold as "stick cinnamon." True cinnamon sticks look like quills (a single tube); "stick cinnamon" made from cassia is rolled from both sides toward the center so that it ends up looking like a scroll.

The marriage of cassia and cinnamon works well. Cassia adds a stronger aroma, a bitter note to cinnamon's warm, sweet flavor, and a dark, reddish brown tinge to cinnamon's natural tan.

Caution: The cassia used in food is not related to other similarly named herbs such as *Cassia fistula* (also known as cassia pods, Indian laburnam), *Cassia marilandica* (also known as wild senna) or *Cassia senna* (also known as senna). These plants contain strong cathartics that may cause violent purging; they are never used as food.

Nutritional Profile   One teaspoon (2.3 g) dried cassia has 6 calories. It provides 0.1 g protein, 0.1 g fat, 1.8 g carbohydrates, 28 mg calcium, 6 IU vitamin A, and 0.7 mg vitamin C.

HOW THIS PLANT AFFECTS YOUR BODY

Important Phytochemicals   Both oil of cassia (also known as oil of cinnamon) and oil of true cinnamon (also known as oil of cinnamon, Ceylon) derive their flavor and aroma from cinnamaldehyde, a yellow, oily liquid with a strong cinnamon scent. The value of oil of cassia is determined by its cinnamaldehyde content, which can run higher than 80 percent; oil of cinnamon, Ceylon, is only 50 percent to 65 percent cinnamaldehyde.

Cinnamaldehyde is an antiflatulent, an agent that helps to break up intestinal gas. It is also an irritant and potential allergen.

Benefits   * * *

Possible Adverse Effects   Some people find cassia and cinnamon irritating to the stomach.

Handling cassia or cinnamon may cause contact dermatitis (itching, burning, even blistered skin). Eating a cassia or cinnamon-flavored dish may cause cheilitis (irritated, peeling lips).

Information for Women Who Are Pregnant or Nursing   * * *

Plant/Drug Interactions   * * *

HOW TO USE THIS PLANT

Around the House   To freshen the air in your kitchen, put one-half teaspoon cassia in 2 cups water and boil on top of your stove. To scent your drawers, put scrolls of cassia in the back.

Catnip

ABOUT THIS PLANT

Botanical name(s): Nepeta cataria
Common name(s): Catnip, catmint, field balm
Native to: Europe, Asia
Parts used as food/drink: Leaves
GRAS list: No
Medicinal properties: * * *
Other uses: Pharmaceutical fragrance, attractant for cats; insect repellent

ABOUT THIS PLANT AS FOOD OR DRINK

Catnip is a member of the mint family. A native of Europe and Asia, it is now grown in the United States. As you might expect, its name comes from its best known characteristic, its ability to attract cats, who become ecstatic when they smell it. (Feeding catnip to a cat produces no such effect.)

One intriguing bit of misinformation about catnip comes from a 1969 article in the *Journal of the American Medical Association* that2

mistakenly concluded that smoking catnip cigarettes produces euphoria in human beings. The error arose from the authors' confusing a drawing of the catnip plant with a drawing of the marijuana plant.

Fresh catnip leaves, with their pleasant scent of mint, may be used in salads or steeped in boiling water for a mint-flavored tea. Dried catnip tea bags are often available at health food stores.

Nutritional Profile   One-eighth ounce (4 g) dried catnip has 0.4 g protein, a trace of fat, 22 mg calcium, and 4.9 mg iron.

HOW THIS PLANT AFFECTS YOUR BODY

Important Phytochemicals   Catnip's flavor and aroma come from nepetalactone, a compound whose chemical structure is similar to that of the valpotriates, natural sedatives found in VALERIAN, an herb often used as a sedative in Europe. Some studies with laboratory animals suggest that nepetalactone has sedative effects and that it acts as an antiflatulent (an agent that breaks up intestinal gas), but there is no scientific evidence that it is effective for human beings.

Benefits   * * *

Possible Adverse Effects   Drinking excessive amounts of tea brewed from catnip leaves may cause gastric upset, including vomiting.

Information for Women Who Are Pregnant or Nursing   * * *

Plant/Drug Interactions   * * *

HOW TO USE THIS PLANT

In Cooking   To coax the most flavor from catnip leaves, chop them or rub them against the side of a colander or sieve to release their nepetalactone-flavored oil.

Around the House   Give your cat a special treat by rubbing fresh catnip leaves against his or her scratching post.

In the Garden   Catnip has a long-standing reputation as a cockroach, spider, fly, cricket, and rodent repellent, but it was not until August 1999 that this was confirmed when two Iowa State University researchers released data from a study showing that German cockroaches—cricket-size insects common throughout the United States—really are repelled by two forms of nepetalactone. The researchers say the naturally occurring compound is about 100 times more effective than chemical roach poisons; they suggest its discovery may lead to the creation of a new form of anti-insect product, repellents rather than poisons.

Conduct your own experiment by planting catnip in a border around your garden. But keep a sharp eye on the catnip: You must clip off the flowers early, before the seeds are ready to fall. If you don't, the catnip, which grows aggressively from seed, will begin to take over your garden.

Celandine

ABOUT THIS PLANT

Botanical name(s): *Chelidonium majus*
Common name(s): Celandine herb
Native to: North America
Parts used as food/drink: * * *
GRAS list: No
Medicinal properties: Mild antispasmodic
Other uses: Dye (yellow) for wool

ABOUT THIS PLANT AS FOOD OR DRINK

Celandine is a perennial herb that grows among rocks and bushes on the edges of forests in northeastern Canada and the United States. Its name comes from *chelidon,* the Greek word for swallow (the bird, not the action). Fresh celandine is not edible; dried, treated celandine leaves (see below) may be used as an herbal tea.

Nutritional Profile * * *

HOW THIS PLANT AFFECTS YOUR BODY

Important Phytochemicals The active ingredient in celandine is chelidonine, an antispasmodic that is also a strong irritant and a central nervous system depressant.

Benefits In 1985, the German Commission E approved the use of preparations of dried, "aboveground" parts of the plant, presumably chelidonine-free celandine leaves, to relieve intestinal spasms.

Possible Adverse Effects Handling the fresh celandine plant may cause severe irritation of the skin.

    If swallowed, the chelidonine in fresh celandine may depress respiration and heartbeat. In studies with laboratory mice, the LD50 [the amount that kills 50 percent of the animals] was 35 mg [approximately $^1/_{1000}$ oz] chelidonine per kg of body weight.

Information for Women Who Are Pregnant or Nursing * * *

Plant/Drug Interactions * * *

HOW TO USE THIS PLANT
Steep dried, treated leaves as tea.

In Cooking * * *

Celery

ABOUT THIS PLANT

Botanical name(s): *Apium graveolens*
Common name(s): * * *
Native to: Europe, Asia, Africa
Parts used as food/drink: Leaves, stalks, fruit ("seeds")
GRAS list: Yes (celery seed)
Medicinal properties: * * *
Other uses: Cosmetic scent, birdseed

ABOUT THIS PLANT AS FOOD OR DRINK

Celery seeds do not come from ordinary celery; they are the dried fruit of smallage, a wild celery that is the ancestor of the modern celery first cultivated in Europe during the 17th century.

Celery (smallage) seeds are the tiniest of all the seeds used as flavorings; it takes as many as 700,000 seeds to make one pound. The seeds contain proportionately much more oil of celery than do celery stalks and leaves, so they are more intensely aromatic.

Celery stalks and leaves are used as vegetables; celery seeds, as seasoning in soups and stews. Or they may be ground and mixed with salt to make celery salt. Oil of celery pressed from the seeds is used to flavor celery tonic and liqueurs, and to scent cosmetic products such as soap.

Nutritional Profile One cup diced celery stalk has 19 calories. It provides 1 g protein, less than 1 g fat, 4 g carbohydrates, 2 g dietary fiber, 160 IU vitamin A, 8 mg vitamin C, 48 mg calcium, and 0.5 mg iron.

One tablespoon (7 g) celery seed has 25 calories. It provides 1.2 g protein, 1.6 g fat, 2.7 g carbohydrates, 0.8 g dietary fiber, 1.1 mg vitamin C, 115 mg calcium, and 3 mg iron.

One teaspoon (2 g) celery seed has 8 calories. It provides 0.4 g protein, 0.5 g fat, 0.8 g carbohydrates, 0.2 g dietary fiber, 0.3 mg vitamin C, 35 mg calcium, and 0.9 g iron.

HOW THIS PLANT AFFECTS YOUR BODY

Important Phytochemicals Oil of celery is a pale yellow liquid scented and flavored with apiin, a sugar/alcohol compound also found in PARSLEY;

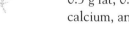

plus lemon-scented limonene, also found in CARAWAY, DILL, and LEMON or LIME peel; and bitter bergapten and hydroxymethoxypsoralen.

Limonene, bergapten, and hydroxymethoxypsoralen are allergens and photosensitizers, substances that can make your skin more sensitive to sunlight, increasing the risk of sunburn, especially for fair-skinned people.

Although celery has long been used in folk medicine as a diuretic (a drug that increases urination), there is no scientific evidence to back up this claim.

Benefits   Celery stalks and leaves are a moderately good source of dietary fiber including insoluble dietary fiber (cellulose, hemicellulose, and lignin). They are also rich in vitamin C and a source of carotenoid pigments your body converts to vitamin A.

According to the American Heart Association and the American Cancer Society, eating foods high in dietary fiber, vitamin A, and vitamin C may reduce the risk of heart disease and some forms of cancer. Vitamin A also protects vision; the carotenoids from fruits and vegetables are converted to 11-cis retinol, the most important constituent of rhodopsin, a protein in the rods in your retina (the cells that enable you to see in dim light).

Possible Adverse Effects   People sensitive to celery may develop contact dermatitis (itching, burning skin) when they handle celery, or mild to severe allergic reactions (hives, difficulty in breathing, or potentially fatal anaphylactic shock (system-wide collapse) if they eat it. Note: Bruised or rotting celery may contain up to 100 times as much photosensitizing psoralens as fresh, healthy celery.

Like beets, eggplant, lettuce, radishes, spinach, and collard and turnip greens, celery stalks and leaves contain nitrates, naturally occurring compounds that are converted to nitrites in your stomach. Some of the nitrites combine with amines to form nitrosamines, which are known carcinogens. This natural chemical reaction presents no known problems for a healthy adult. However, when nitrate-laden vegetables are cooked and left standing for a while at room temperature, microorganisms that convert nitrates to nitrites begin to multiply, and the amount of nitrites in the food rises. The resulting higher-nitrite foods may be dangerous for infants; there have been several reported cases of "spinach poisoning" among infants fed unrefrigerated cooked spinach.

Celery stalks and leaves contain about 50 mg sodium in an average serving; the sodium content of celery seeds is much lower, only 3 mg per teaspoon. Celery (the vegetable) is often limited on a sodium-restricted diet. Celery seeds give you the flavor without the sodium.

Information for Women Who Are Pregnant or Nursing   * * *

Plant/Drug Interactions   * * *

HOW TO USE THIS PLANT

In Cooking   Rinse celery under cold running water to remove all sand and dirt. Cut off the leaves, blanch them, dry them thoroughly and rub them through a sieve or food mill. The dry powder can be used to season salt or frozen for later use in soups or stews.

Chlorophyll, the green coloring in celery, is sensitive to acids. When celery is heated, its chlorophyll reacts with natural acids in the leaves or in the cooking water, forming a brown compound called pheophytin. The pheophytin in turn reacts with the yellow carotene pigments in the leaves, turning the cooked celery bronze. To prevent this color change, prevent the chlorophyll from reacting with the acids by cooking celery quickly. (Commercial herb packagers preserve the color of celery leaves and other green herbs by drying the leaves at a very low heat.)

A commercial celery salt is approximately 10 to 25 percent ground celery seed. A simple way to make your own celery-flavored salt at home is to stir 2 teaspoons celery seeds into 6 teaspoons table salt, mixing thoroughly. Store the celery/salt mixture in a salt shaker, adding a few grains of rice to keep the salt from caking. Let the salt sit for a few days, and then use as needed. For a more intensely flavored celery salt, chop the seeds into small pieces before stirring them into the salt. When you cut the seeds, you tear the walls of cells inside the seed, releasing the oil of celery stored there.

Chamomile

ABOUT THIS PLANT

Botanical name(s): Matricaria recutita

Common name(s): German chamomile, Hungarian chamomile, wild chamomile

Native to: Europe

Parts used as food/drink: Flowers

GRAS list: Yes

Medicinal properties: Anti-inflammatory, antiflatulent, antispasmodic

Other uses: Hair color rinse

ABOUT THIS PLANT AS FOOD OR DRINK

German chamomile is a member of the daisy family with pale-green, feathery leaves and white, daisy-like, edible flowers native to northern Europe. The flowers, with their faintly bitter yellow centers, can be used in salads or as edible decoration. A related plant, Roman chamomile (also known as *Chamaemelum nobile* or *Anthemis nobilis*), has similar edible flowers but many more branches on its stems. Both varieties of chamomile smell faintly like apples.

Nutritional Profile   One-eighth ounce (4 g) dried German chamomile has 11 calories. It provides 0.4 g protein, 0.2 g fat, 0.3 g fiber, 13 IU vitamin A, 1 mg vitamin C, 24 mg calcium, 0.6 mg iron, and 8 mg sodium. One eight-ounce cup of chamomile tea has nine calories. It provides 47 IU vitamin A, 4.7 mg iron, and 2.4 mg sodium.

HOW THIS PLANT AFFECTS YOUR BODY

Important Phytochemicals   Chamomile flowers are flavored with coumarin, a vanilla flavored compound, and the bitter flavonoid pigments apigenin, luteolin, and quercitrin. (Quercitrin, a pale yellow pigment, is also found in white wines. As the wine ages, the quercitrin turns browner; the darker the wine, the older it is.)

Flavonoids are antioxidants (compounds that prevent molecular fragments in your body from joining to form potential carcinogens) and antispasmodics (compounds that relax muscle spasms and are often used to soothe an upset stomach). The oil in chamomile flower heads also contains chamazulene, a potent antioxidant that is also an antiinflammatory and a mild antibacterial.

Benefits   In 1988 and 1990, the German Commission E approved the use of preparations of German chamomile to relieve spasms and inflammatory disease of the gastrointestinal tract. The commission has also approved the use of chamomile infusions as a soothing wash or bath to relieve skin irritations. The effectiveness of the related plant Roman chamomile has not been documented; Commission E lists it as a safe but "unapproved" herb.

Possible Adverse Effects   Chamomile plants are related to ragweed, asters, and chrysanthemums. People sensitive to these plants may also be sensitive to chamomile, which means they may develop hives, hay fever, or asthma from eating chamomile flowers or drinking chamomile tea.

Handling chamomile plants may cause contact dermatitis (itching, burning, stinging, reddened, or blistered skin). One 1990 study of seven patients reported in the Annals of Allergy showed that chamomile tea used as an eye wash for conjunctivitis caused an inflammatory reaction in a majority of patients.

Information for Women Who Are Pregnant or Nursing   * * *

Plant/Drug Interactions   * * *

HOW TO USE THIS PLANT

In Cooking   Rinse fresh chamomile flowers thoroughly to get rid of insects that may be hiding in the flower heads. Or spread the flowers on a cookie sheet and dry them in an oven at 120 degrees F for half an hour. Then sift them in a strainer or colander and discard the debris. Store the dried flowers in an airtight container. Use as desired for teas. Dried chamomile is also available in tea bags at health food stores. German chamomile is generally preferred because, while not as strongly scented as Roman chamomile, it is sweeter.

As a Cosmetic   For a golden rinse to highlight blond or light brown hair, steep chamomile flowers in hot water, let the water cool, and use as a rinse after shampooing. For an apple-scented bath, add $1/2$ pound chamomile flowers (an enormous amount!) to $2^1/2$ quarts water. Bring the water to a boil to force the flowers to release their scented oil. Then let the water cool, and strain out the flowers. Add the water to your bath.

In the Garden   Both German chamomile and Roman chamomile are easy to grow from seed. Both prefer full sun. Roman chamomile, an erect plant, is neater in the garden. German chamomile, which crawls along the ground, turns weedy if left untended.

As a Home Remedy   The suggested dose is 1 heaping tablespoon (3 g) German chamomile steeped in 5 ounces (150 ml) boiling water for 5–10 minutes, then strained and drunk as tea or used as a gargle.

Chervil

ABOUT THIS PLANT

Botanical name(s): *Anthriscus cerefolium*
Common name(s): French parsley, skirret
Native to: Northern Europe, Russia
Parts used as food/drink: Leaves
GRAS list: Yes
Medicinal properties: * * *
Other uses: * * *

ABOUT THIS PLANT AS FOOD OR DRINK

Chervil is a member of the carrot family, a fernlike plant with light green lacy leaves that look like PARSLEY. "True chervil" has curly leaves. However, both curly-leaved chervil and flat-leaved chervil have the same sweet pleasant flavor with a hint of LICORICE and a highly aromatic scent some consider similar to that of TARRAGON.

Chervil is one of the green herbs included in the classic French culinary bouquet known as *fines herbes:* BASIL, CHIVES, parsley, SAGE, SAVORY, and TARRAGON.

Nutritional Profile   One tablespoon (2 g) dried chervil has 4 calories. It provides 0.4 g protein, a trace of fat, 0.9 g carbohydrates, 0.2 g dietary fiber, 111 IU vitamin A, 1 mg vitamin C, 26 mg calcium, and 0.6 mg iron.

One teaspoon (1 g) dried chervil has 1 calorie. It provides 0.1 g protein, a trace of fat, 0.3 g carbohydrates, 0.1 g dietary fiber, 35 IU vitamin A, 0.3 mg vitamin C, 8 mg calcium, and 0.2 mg iron.

HOW THIS PLANT AFFECTS YOUR BODY

Important Phytochemicals   Chervil is almost never mentioned in herbal medicine, and to date there is no scientific evidence to support folk claims that it is useful as a diuretic or a digestive.

Benefits   * * *

Possible Adverse Effects   * * *

Information for Women Who Are Pregnant or Nursing   * * *

Plant/Drug Interactions   * * *

HOW TO USE THIS PLANT

In Cooking   Curly-leaved chervil is prettier and more decorative than flat-leaved chervil.

Use chervil fresh whenever possible, and add it just before serving a hot dish. Chervil's delicate flavor disappears quickly when the leaves are heated or dried.

Chlorophyll, the green coloring in chervil, is sensitive to acids. When chervil is heated, its chlorophyll reacts with natural acids in the leaves or in the cooking water, forming a brown compound called pheophytin. The pheophytin in turn reacts with the yellow carotene pigments in the leaves, turning the cooked chervil bronze. To prevent this color change, prevent the chlorophyll from reacting with the acids by adding chervil at the last minute. (Commercial herb packagers preserve the color of chervil and other green herbs by drying the leaves at a very low heat.)

If your grocery store doesn't stock fresh chervil, try a substitute made of 1 part fresh chopped tarragon with 2 parts fresh chopped parsley.

Chickweed

ABOUT THIS PLANT

Botanical name(s): *Stellaria media*
Common name(s): Mouse ear, satinflower, starweed
Native to: Europe
Parts used as food/drink: Leaves
GRAS list: No
Medicinal properties: * * *
Other uses: Bird food

ABOUT THIS PLANT AS FOOD OR DRINK

Chickweed was named *Stellaria* by the great Swedish botanist Linnaeus in honor of its star-shaped white flowers. The blossoms open on sunny days and close when it rains. The herb is not a common food, but it has been used as a seasoning or pot herb.

Nutritional Profile   One ounce (28 g) chickweed has 61 calories, 6.2 g protein, 1.4 g fat, 3.1 g dietary fiber, 2,065 IU vitamin A, 2 mg vitamin C, 345 mg calcium, 72 mg iron, 714 mg zinc.

HOW THIS PLANT AFFECTS YOUR BODY

Important Phytochemicals   Chickweed leaves contain antioxidant flavonoids such as rutin, fatty acids, and moderate amounts of vitamin C. The leaves, once used to treat scurvy, a disease of vitamin C deficiency, are no longer used in medicine. In addition, there are no scientific studies of chickweed's claimed ability to soothe injuries, burns, and psoriasis or to relieve arthritic joint pain.

Benefits   * * *

Possible Adverse Effects   Like beets, CELERY, eggplant, lettuce, radishes, spinach, and collard and turnip greens, chickweed leaves contain nitrates, naturally occurring compounds that are converted to nitrites in your stomach. Some of the nitrites combine with amines to form nitrosamines, which are known carcinogens. This natural chemical reaction presents no known problems for a healthy adult. However, when nitrate-laden vegetables are cooked and left standing for a while at room temperature, microorganisms that convert nitrates to nitrites begin to multiply, and the amount of nitrites in the food rises. The resulting higher-nitrite foods may be dangerous for infants; there have been several reported cases of "spinach poisoning" among infants fed unrefrigerated cooked spinach. In addition, there have been reports of animals suffering nitrate poisoning after grazing on chickweed.

Information for Women Who Are Pregnant or Nursing   * * *

Plant/Drug Interactions   * * *

HOW TO USE THIS PLANT

In Cooking   Chlorophyll, the green coloring in chickweed leaves, is sensitive to acids. When the leaves are heated, their chlorophyll reacts with natural acids in the leaves or in the cooking water, forming a brown compound called pheophytin. The pheophytin in turn reacts with the yellow carotene pigments in the leaves, turning them bronze. To prevent this color change, prevent the chlorophyll from reacting with the acids by adding the leaves at the last minute. (Commercial herb packagers preserve the color of green herbs by drying the leaves at a very low heat.)

Chicory

ABOUT THIS PLANT

Botanical name(s): Cichorium intybus
Common name(s): Coffeeweed
Native to: Europe, India
Parts used as food/drink: Leaves, roots
GRAS list: No
Medicinal properties: Appetite stimulant, choleretic
Other uses: Coffee substitute or flavoring, substitute sweetener

ABOUT THIS PLANT AS FOOD OR DRINK

Chicory is a green-leafed plant with bright blue flowers that open and close at the same time every day. The plant is used as a vegetable and as a coffee flavoring or substitute. Young chicory leaves, with their slightly bitter tang, are used in salads. The older leaves can be cooked and served like spinach and the root may be roasted and used as a substitute for or flavoring in coffee.

Nutritional Profile   One cup (180 g) chopped raw chicory leaves has 42 calories. It provides 3 g protein, 0.6 g fat, 8.4 g carbohydrates, 7,200 IU vitamin A, 44 mg vitamin C, 180 mg calcium, and 1.6 mg iron.

One-half cup (45 g) raw chicory root has 33 calories. It provides 0.6 g protein, a trace of fat, 7.9 g carbohydrates, 3 IU vitamin A, 2.3 mg vitamin C, 18 mg calcium, and 0.4 mg iron.

HOW THIS PLANT AFFECTS YOUR BODY

Important Phytochemicals   Chicory leaves contain bitter substances that appear to trigger the secretion of gastric juices which cause the contractions we call hunger pangs.

Chicory root is composed primarily of inulin, the indigestible carbohydrate that gives the Jerusalem artichoke its characteristic flavor. It also contains fructose; pyrone (a natural flavor enhancer that can make sucrose taste 10 to 300 times sweeter and which has been approved by the U.S. Food and Drug Administration for use in baked goods); oils; bitter flavor chemicals; and astringent tannins. When chicory root is roasted, its inulin is converted to oxymethylfurfurol, which smells like coffee but has no caffeine.

Benefits   Both the leaves and roots of the chicory plant have long been used in folk medicine as a "bitter tonic" for treating digestive problems and as a diuretic or laxative. In 1987 and 1990, German Commission E approved the use of chicory as an appetite stimulant and to relieve upset stomach.

Fresh chicory leaves are a good source of vitamin C. One-half cup of fresh leaves in a salad provides 37 percent of the vitamin C an adult needs each day. Like other dark green, leafy vegetables, chicory is a good source of deep yellow carotenoid pigments such as beta-carotene that are converted to vitamin A in your body. A diet rich in carotenoids appears to reduce the risk of some forms of cancer. It also protects your eyes as your body converts beta-carotene to 11-cis retinol, the most important constituent of rhodopsin, a protein in the rods in your retina (the cells that enable you to see in dim light). One-half cup fresh chicory leaves provides 90 percent of the vitamin A an adult woman needs each day and 72 percent of the RDA for an adult man.

People who are sensitive to caffeine's stimulant effects but don't like decaffeinated coffees may find coffee mixed with chicory a satisfactory alternative. It has less caffeine than plain coffee but is still pleasantly bitter.

Inulin is sometimes used as an ingredient in baked goods for people with diabetes, an illness characterized by an inability to metabolize sucrose (table sugar).

Possible Adverse Effects   People sensitive to chicory may develop contact dermatitis (itching, burning, irritated skin) when they handle the plant.

Chicory is a mild choleretic, a substance that stimulates the liver to increase its production of bile, the yellow, brown or green fluid that helps emulsify fats in your duodenum and increases peristalsis, the rhythmic contractions that move food through your gastrointestinal tract. Choleretics are ordinarily beneficial for healthy people but may pose some problems for people with gallbladder or liver diseases. People with gallstones or gallbladder disease should check with their physician before using this herb.

Information for Women Who Are Pregnant or Nursing   * * *

Plant/Drug Interactions   * * *

HOW TO USE THIS PLANT

In Cooking   Do not tear or cut chicory leaves until you are ready to use them. When you cut into a food rich in vitamin C, its cells release an enzyme called ascorbic acid oxidase which destroys vitamin C and reduces the nutritional value of the food.

Chlorophyll, the green coloring in chicory, is sensitive to acids. When you heat chicory, its chlorophyll reacts with natural acids in the leaves or in the cooking water, forming a brown compound called pheophytin. The pheophytin in turn reacts with the yellow carotene pigments in the leaves, turning the cooked chicory bronze. To prevent this color change, prevent the chlorophyll from reacting with the acids by cooking chicory very quickly.

As a Home Remedy   The average recommended daily dose is 3 g ($^1/_{10}$ oz) chicory, steeped in hot water as a tea.

Chili Powder

ABOUT THIS CONDIMENT

Botanical name(s): * * *
Common name(s): * * *
Native to: * * *
Parts used as food/drink: * * *
GRAS list: No
Medicinal properties: Diaphoretic, irritant
Other uses: * * *

ABOUT THIS CONDIMENT AS FOOD AND FLAVORING

Chili powder is a blend of spices created in the American Southwest during the 19th century. A representative chili powder is mostly red (cayenne) PEPPER, plus CUMIN, OREGANO, SALT and GARLIC powder.

Nutritional Profile   One tablespoon (8 g) chili powder containing red pepper (83 percent), cumin (9 percent), oregano (4 percent), salt (2.5 percent), and garlic powder (1.5 percent) has 24 calories. It provides 0.9 g protein, 1.3 g fat, 4.1 g carbohydrates, 2.6 g dietary fiber, 2,620 IU vitamin A, 4.8 mg vitamin C, 21 mg calcium, and 1.07 mg iron.

One teaspoon (3 g) chili powder with the same ingredients has 8 calories. It provides 0.3 g protein, 0.4 g fat, 1.4 g carbohydrates, 0.9 g dietary fiber, 908 IU vitamin A, 1.7 mg vitamin C, 7 mg calcium, and 0.4 mg iron.

HOW THIS CONDIMENT AFFECTS YOUR BODY

Important Phytochemicals   Chili powder's flavor and bite come primarily from capsaicin (pronounced cap-SAY-i-sun), the most pungent compound in cayenne peppers. Virtually all of chili powder's effects on your body are due to the irritants and diaphoretic compounds capsaicin, nordihydrocapsaicin, and dihycrocapsaicin. (A diaphoretic is a substance that increase perspiration.)

Capsaicins cause pain by hooking onto special sites called receptors on the surface of nerve cells. This causes small channels in the cells to open, permitting calcium particles to flood in. The calcium particles trigger pain at the site of the injury, a reaction similar to what happens when skin is burned.

Note: Peppers are members of the nightshade family, Solanacea. Other members of this family are eggplant, potatoes, tomatoes, and some mushrooms. Nightshade plants produce natural toxins called glycoalkaloids. The toxin in pepper is solanine. It is estimated that an adult would have to eat 4.5 pounds of fresh peppers at one sitting to get a toxic amount of solanine.

Benefits   Very spicy foods, including dishes made with chili powder, irritate the mucous membranes lining your nose and throat and the bronchi in your lungs, making tissues "weep" watery secretions that make it easier for you to cough up mucus or blow your nose, thus temporarily relieving your congestion.

Foods spiced with chili powder may also stimulate your appetite because they irritate the lining of your stomach and trigger the flow of gastric juices, setting off the contractions we call hunger pangs.

Chili powder is high in carotenoid pigments, including beta-carotene, a deep yellow coloring agent your body converts to a form of vitamin A. According to the American Cancer Society, a diet rich in these foods may lower the risk of some forms of cancer. Vitamin A also protects your vision. In your body, the vitamin A from chili powder is converted to 11-cis retinol, the most important constituent of rhodopsin, a protein in the rods in your retina (the cells that enable you to see in dim light). One tablespoon chili powder provides 66 percent of the vitamin A a woman needs each day and 52 percent of the RDA for a man.

VITAMIN A AND VITAMIN C CONTENT OF PEPPERS			
Pepper	Serving	Vitamin A (IU)	Vitamin C (mg)
Chili powder	1 tablespoon	2,620	4.8
Chili powder	1 teaspoon	910	1.7
Bell pepper (green)	1 whole	470	66
Bell pepper (red,chopped)	1 cup	5,700	190
Hot green chili peppers (canned)	1/2 cup	410	46
Hot red chili pepper (raw, diced)	1 tablespoon	1.010	23
Jalapeno peppers (canned)	1/2 cup	1,160	9

Source: USDA Nutrient Database: http://www.nal.usda.gov/fnic/cgi-bin/nut_search.pl
Nutritive Value of Foods, USDA Home and Gardens Bulletin Number 72 (Washington, D.C., USDA, revised 1989)

Capsaicin extracted from hot peppers is included in over-the-counter pain relievers for the skin. In a 1991 study at the University of Florence (Italy), 39 men and women suffering from cluster headaches (a form of migraine) obtained relief by squirting a capsaicin-containing solution into the nostril on the headache side of the face. WARNING: CAPSAICIN IS ONLY EFFECTIVE WHEN USED AS A MEDICATION. HOT PEPPERS DO NOT RELIEVE PAIN. THEY ARE HAZARDOUS AND SHOULD NEVER BE ALLOWED TO TOUCH SKIN OR MUCOUS MEMBRANES.

Possible Adverse Effects   Capsaicins irritate the lining of the mouth and esophagus and may cause heartburn. Note: Capsaicin dissolves in milk fat or alcohol, not water. If eating a dish flavored heavily with chili powder makes your mouth burn, water won't help. You need either a glass of cold milk or a glass of chilled beer to relieve the sting.

The oils of strong spices, including chili powder, may irritate the lining of urinary tract, triggering frequent urination.

Information for Women Who Are Pregnant or Nursing   * * *

Condiment/Drug Interactions   * * *

HOW TO USE THIS CONDIMENT

In Cooking   Store chili powder tightly closed in a cool place to protect its flavor and color. You can enrich the flavor of any chili powder and make it more interesting by adding a pinch of one of the "sweet" spices: ALLSPICE, CINNAMON, CLOVES, or ONION.

Chives

ABOUT THIS PLANT

Botanical name(s): *Allium schoenoprasum*
Common name(s): * * *
Native to: Northern Europe, Asia
Parts used as food/drink: Leaves
GRAS list: Yes
Medicinal properties: * * *
Other uses: Insect repellent

ABOUT THIS PLANT AS FOOD OR DRINK

Chives are members of the ONION family. They have mildly flavored bulbs and hollow, flat, green leaves with a pleasant, onionlike flavor and aroma. The young pink, lavender, purple, or white flower clusters of the chive plant are edible if used before seeds form. Once flowers appear, the leaves become much less flavorful.

Garlic chives (*Allium tuberosum*), also known as Chinese chives or Oriental chives, have a mild garlicky flavor.

Nutritional Profile One tablespoon (3 g) chopped raw chives has 1 calorie. It provides 0.08 g protein, 0.02 g fat, 0.11 g carbohydrates, 2 mg calcium, 0.05 mg iron, 192 IU vitamin A, and 2.4 mg vitamin C.

One tablespoon (0.2 g) freeze-dried chives has about 1 calorie. It provides 0.04 g protein, 0.01 g fat, 0.13 g carbohydrates, 2 mg calcium, 0.04 mg iron, 137 IU vitamin A, and 1.3 mg vitamin C.

HOW THIS PLANT AFFECTS YOUR BODY

Important Phytochemicals Like onions, chives get their flavor and aroma from mustard oils, sulfur compounds with antibiotic properties similar to those of alliin and allicin, the antibacterials in GARLIC.

Benefits A diet rich in onions and garlic is reported to lower blood levels of low-density lipoproteins (LDLs), the "bad" cholesterol that clings to artery walls. But because we use such small amounts of chives to season foods, we are unlikely to experience any benefit.

Possible Adverse Effects * * *

Information for Women Who Are Pregnant or Nursing   * * *

Plant/Drug Interactions   * * *

HOW TO USE THIS PLANT

In Cooking   The chopped tops of green onions (scallions) can be used as a substitute for chives, but they are much more strongly flavored.

Freezing chives is the best way to preserve their flavor for long storage. Blanch the leaves and chop them, then store in airtight, freezer-proof containers. Use as needed right from the container; there's no need to defrost them first.

Chlorophyll, the green coloring in chives, is sensitive to acids. When chives are heated, their chlorophyll reacts with natural acids in the leaves or in the cooking water, forming a brown compound called pheophytin. The pheophytin in turn reacts with the yellow carotene pigments in the leaves, turning the cooked chives bronze. To prevent this color change, prevent the chlorophyll from reacting with the acids by adding chives at the last minute or after the dish is removed from the stove. (Commercial herb packagers preserve the color of chives and other green herbs by drying the leaves at a very low heat.)

In the Garden   Many insects are repelled by the odors of garlic and onion plants, including chives, which appear to act as safe natural pest repellents that keep the bugs away without poisoning people or pets.

Chutney

ABOUT THIS CONDIMENT

Botanical name(s): * * *

Common name(s): * * *

Native to: India

Parts used as food/drink: * * *

GRAS list: No

Medicinal properties: * * *

Other uses: * * *

ABOUT THIS CONDIMENT AS FOOD OR DRINK

Chutneys are spicy relishes first created to be served with or spooned over Indian dishes ranging from plain rice to elaborate curries. Indian chutney is a fresh, uncooked relish. Cooked chutney, a British invention originally based on mangoes, is actually pickled fruit sauce. The fruit—plums or tamarinds or apples or rhubarb or tomatoes or the ubiquitous mango—is cooked until soft then covered with a mixture of vinegar, sugar, salt, and spices. The distinguishing flavor is sweet-and-sour.

Nutritional Profile   One tablespoon (21 g) of a representative mango chutney has 45 calories. It provides 12 g carbohydrates (sugar), a little more than 1 mg iron, and 210 mg sodium.

HOW THIS CONDIMENT AFFECTS YOUR BODY

Important Phytochemicals   Chutneys are fat free, high sodium, high sugar foods.

Benefits   Like KETCHUP, MUSTARD, and other fat-free flavorings, chutneys are useful for people on low-fat or reducing diets because they make food taste good without adding many calories.

Possible Adverse Effects   Given their high sodium content, chutneys may be on the restricted list for people with sodium-sensitive high blood pressure.

Information for Women Who Are Pregnant or Nursing   * * *

Condiment/Drug Interactions   * * *

HOW TO USE THIS CONDIMENT

In Cooking   To protect your chutneys from airborne mold and yeast, you must keep them tightly covered, even in the refrigerator.

Cilantro

ABOUT THIS PLANT

Botanical name(s): Coriandrum sativum
Common name(s): Chinese parsley
Native to: Mediterranean region, eastern Europe
Parts used as food/drink: Leaf
GRAS list: Yes
Medicinal properties: * * *
Other uses: * * *

ABOUT THIS PLANT AS FOOD OR DRINK

Cilantro is the Spanish name for the young, flat leaves of the plant whose fruits ("seeds") are sold as coriander. The leaves, which are also known as Chinese parsley, taste like a blend of lemon and parsley, with a pungent odor some people find unpleasant.

Cilantro is used in Mexican and Asian cuisine. It is widely available fresh, dried or freeze-dried.

Nutritional Profile One ounce (28 g) fresh cilantro leaves has 6 calories, 0.3 g protein, 0.1 g fat, 0.2 g dietary fiber, 790 IU vitamin A, 3 mg vitamin C, 28 mg calcium, and 0.6 mg iron.

One tablespoon (1.86 g) dried cilantro has 5 calories. It provides 0.4 g protein, 0.1 g fat, 0.9 g carbohydrates, 0.2 g dietary fiber, 105 IU vitamin A, 10.2 mg vitamin C, 22 mg calcium, and 0.8 mg iron.

One teaspoon (1 g) dried cilantro has 2 calories. It provides 0.1 g protein, a trace of fat, 0.3 g carbohydrates, 0.1 g dietary fiber, 35 IU vitamin A, 3.4 mg vitamin C, 7 mg calcium, and 0.3 mg iron.

HOW THIS PLANT AFFECTS YOUR BODY

Important Phytochemicals Cilantro's flavor and aroma come from peppery borneol (also found in CARDAMOM and CINNAMON), lemon-scented limonene, lavender-scented linalool, sour malic acid (which gives immature apples their bite), astringent oxalic acid, and tannic acid. Linalool, also found in BITTER ORANGE PEEL, CARDAMOM and many other herbs and spices, is an irritant and potential allergen.

Benefits Cilantro is a good source of vitamin C. One tablespoon of dried cilantro leaves provides 17 percent of the adult RDA.

Possible Adverse Effects   Handling the coriander plant may cause contact dermatitis (itching, burning, or stinging, plus reddened or blistered skin).

Information for Women Who Are Pregnant or Nursing   * * *

Plant/Drug Interactions   * * *

HOW TO USE THIS PLANT

In Cooking   Store fresh cilantro leaves in plastic wrap or a plastic food bag to keep them from drying out. Check the cilantro daily, discarding any wilted or damaged leaves.

Do not tear cilantro leaves until you are actually ready to use them. When you tear a vegetable rich in vitamin C, its cells release an enzyme called ascorbic acid oxidase which destroys vitamin C and reduces the nutritional value of the food.

Chlorophyll, the green coloring in cilantro leaves, is sensitive to acids. When cilantro is heated, its chlorophyll reacts with natural acids in the leaves or in the cooking water, forming a brown compound called pheophytin. The pheophytin in turn reacts with the yellow carotene pigments in the leaves, turning the cooked cilantro bronze. To prevent this color change, prevent the chlorophyll from reacting with the acids by cooking the cilantro for as short a time as possible. (Commercial herb packagers preserve the color of cilantro and other green herbs by drying the leaves at a very low heat.)

In the Garden   When picking cilantro from your own garden, take the leaves while they are young, before the plant flowers. Leaves from a flowering cilantro plant are bitter.

Cinnamon

ABOUT THIS PLANT

Botanical name(s): Cinnamomum verum (a.k.a. *Cinnamomum zeylanicum*)
Common name(s): Sweetwood, true cinnamon
Native to: Sri Lanka, Sumatra, Borneo
Parts used as food/drink: Bark
GRAS list: Yes
Medicinal properties: Carminative
Other uses: Flavoring for toothpaste, perfume

ABOUT THIS PLANT AS FOOD OR DRINK

Cinnamon is the dried inner bark of a tropical evergreen laurel tree, *Cinnamomum zeylanicum*, called "true cinnamon" to distinguish it from CASSIA (*Cinnamomum cassia*), a spice that looks and tastes like cinnamon.

True cinnamon bark is peeled off the tree, then left to dry and ferment for 24 hours, after which its outer layer is scraped off, leaving the inner, light-colored bark, which curls into quills as it dries. Removing the outer bark makes the cinnamon less biting and mellows its aroma.

In the United States, much of the spice sold as cinnamon is actually a blend of cinnamon and cassia. The marriage of these two spices complements each. Cassia adds a bitter note to cinnamon's warm, sweet flavor, deepens cinnamon's aroma, and lends a dark, reddish-brown tinge to true cinnamon's natural tan color.

Cinnamon sticks made of true cinnamon look like quills (a single tube). Cinnamon sticks made from cassia are rolled from both sides toward the center. They look like scrolls.

Nutritional Profile   One teaspoon (2 g) ground cinnamon has 6 calories. It provides 0.09 g protein, 0.07 g fat, 1.84 g carbohydrates, 1.2 g dietary fiber, 6 IU vitamin A, 0.7 mg vitamin C, 28 mg calcium, and 0.9 mg iron.

HOW THIS PLANT AFFECTS YOUR BODY

Important Phytochemicals   Both the oil of true cinnamon (also known as oil of cinnamon, Ceylon) and oil of cassia (also known as oil of cinnamon) get their flavor and aroma from cinnamaldehyde, a yellow, oily liquid with a strong cinnamon scent. (The value of oil of cassia is determined by its cinnamaldehyde content which can run higher than 80 percent, while oil of cinnamon, Ceylon, is only 50–65 percent cinnamaldehyde.) Oil of true cinnamon also contains eugenol, the flavoring and aroma agents in oil of CLOVES, and several other aromatic oils, including phellandrene. Cinnamaldehyde, eugenol, and phellandrene are irritants and potential allergens.

Benefits   Cinnamon is a antiflatulent (an agent that helps break up intestinal gas). In 1990, the German Commission E approved the use tea prepared from cinnamon bark and other cinnamon preparations as an appetite stimulant and to relieve bloating, intestinal gas and mild intestinal spasms.

Possible Adverse Effects   Some people find cinnamon irritating to the stomach.

People sensitive to cinnamon may develop contact dermatitis (itching, burning, even blistered skin) after handling cinnamon or using perfume or soap scented with cinnamon. Or they may develop cheilitis (irritated, peeling lips) after eating a dish or chewing gum flavored with cinnamon or using mouthwash or toothpaste scented or flavored with cinnamon.

Large doses of cinnamon bark may cause rapid heartbeat and respiration, increased sweating and intestinal contractions, sedation and central nervous system depression.

Information for Women Who Are Pregnant or Nursing   Because cinnamon may trigger intestinal contractions, Commission E has cautioned against its use by pregnant women.

Plant/Drug Interactions   * * *

HOW TO USE THIS PLANT

Around the House   To freshen your kitchen, boil 1 teaspoon of ground cinnamon or one cinnamon stick in 3 cups of water in an open saucepan on top of the stove. To scent your bureau drawers, use cinnamon sticks as natural sachets. Do not use the sticks if you are sensitive to cinnamon. Also see cloves.

As a Home Remedy   The suggested daily dosage is 4 g cinnamon bark steeped in hot water as a tea.

Cloves

ABOUT THIS PLANT

Botanical name(s): Syzygium aromaticum
Common name(s): * * *
Native to: Indonesia
Parts used as food/drink: Flower bud
GRAS list: Yes
Medicinal properties: Topical anesthetic
Other uses: Pharmaceutical and cosmetic flavor and scent; insect attractant

ABOUT THIS PLANT AS FOOD OR DRINK

Cloves are the dried flower buds of a tropical evergreen tree that belongs to the myrtle family. The buds are picked just before they open into pinkish green blossoms, then dried until they turn dark brown.

A pound of cloves equals at least 5,000 to 7,000 dried buds. The spice is available whole or ground to be used as an ingredient in several popular spice mixtures such as pumpkin pie spice and CURRY POWDER.

Oil of cloves is a popular perfume used in a wide variety of cosmetics including toothpastes, soaps, and body lotions.

Nutritional Profile   One tablespoon (7 g) ground cloves has 21 calories. It provides 0.4 g protein, 1.3 g fat, 4.0 g carbohydrates, 2.3 g dietary fiber, 35 IU vitamin A, 5.3 mg vitamin C, 43 mg calcium, 0.6 mg iron, and 73 mg sodium.

One teaspoon (2 g) ground cloves has 7 calories. It provides 0.1 g protein, 0.4 g fat, 1.29 g carbohydrates, 0.7 g dietary fiber, 11 IU vitamin A, 1.7 mg vitamin C, 14 mg calcium, 0.2 mg iron, and 5 mg sodium.

HOW THIS PLANT AFFECTS YOUR BODY

Important Phytochemicals   Cloves get their sweet, spicy flavor and aroma from oil of cloves. The primary (82–87 percent) ingredient in oil of cloves is eugenol. The oil also contains caryophyllene, an oily liquid that smells like a mixture of cloves and turpentine; almond-scented furfural; vanillin; and fruity scented, peppery methyl amyl ketone.

Eugenol is a topical anesthetic used in dental fillings and cement; a rubefacient (an agent that irritates the skin and causes small blood vessels underneath to dilate so that more blood flows to the surface of the skin, making it warmer); and an antiflatulent (an agent that breaks up intestinal gas). It is also an irritant and an allergic sensitizer.

Benefits   In 1985, the German Commission E approved the use of diluted (1–5 percent) oil of cloves from powdered or ground cloves as a wash or gargle to relieve inflammation of mouth and throat.

Possible Adverse Effects   Some people find cloves irritating to the stomach; the spice is often excluded from a bland diet.

People sensitive to cloves may develop contact dermatitis (itching, burning, even blistered skin) after handling the spice or cheilitis (irritated, peeling lips) after eating a dish or chewing gum flavored with cloves or using mouthwash or toothpaste scented or flavored with cloves.

Information for Women Who Are Pregnant or Nursing   * * *

Plant/Drug Interactions   * * *

HOW TO USE THIS PLANT

In Cooking   When using whole cloves, be sure to remove them before you serve the dish. The simplest way is to put the cloves into a tea ball or stud them into an onion or carrot and then lift out the tea ball/onion/carrot before serving the food.

Ground cloves, which do not have the spicy clove heads, is a milder spice, less irritating than whole cloves.

Around the House   To make a nonchemical, perfumed air freshener for your closets, stick whole fresh cloves into the peel of a large firm orange until the entire orange is completely covered. Then roll the clove-studded orange in ground CINNAMON. Wrap the cinnamon-dusted orange in tissue paper, and put it on your kitchen shelf until the orange dehydrates and shrinks. When the orange is completely dried, unwrap it, dust off any loose cinnamon powder and hang the orange "pomander ball" in your closet. The scent will be lovely. Note: Eugenol attracts insects, so be sure your orange is well-protected while drying.

Cocoa

ABOUT THIS CONDIMENT

Botanical name(s): *Theobroma cacao*
Common name(s): Cocoa
Native to: Central America
Parts used as food/drink: Ripe seeds
GRAS list: No
Medicinal properties: Mild diuretic
Other uses: * * *

ABOUT THIS CONDIMENT AS FOOD OR DRINK

Cocoa is a powder made of ground roasted seeds (beans) of the cocoa tree, *Theobroma cacao*.

Like other seeds, cocoa beans are a good source of proteins, carbohydrates (starch), dietary fiber, B vitamins, and minerals. And cocoa powder is a high-fiber food; one-half ounce cocoa has as much dietary fiber as one-third cup baked beans and twice as much as one-half cup cooked broccoli.

Cocoa's proteins are considered incomplete because they lack sufficient amounts of the essential amino acids lysine and isoleucine; adding milk adds these amino acids and "completes" the proteins. Cocoa butter, the fat in cocoa beans, has no cholesterol, but it is the second most highly saturated vegetable fat, second only to coconut oil.

Nutritional Profile   One cup (86 g) unsweetened dry cocoa powder has 197 calories. It provides 16.8 g protein, 11.8 g total fat, 6.9 g saturated fat, 46.7 g carbohydrates, 28.6 g dietary fiber, 110 mg calcium, 11.9 mg iron, and 18.1 mg sodium.

One tablespoon (5.4 g) unsweetened dry cocoa powder has 12 calories. It provides 1 g protein, 0.7 g total fat, 0.4 g saturated fat, 3 g carbohydrates, 1.8 g dietary fiber, 6.9 mg calcium, 0.7 mg iron, and 1.1 mg sodium.

HOW THIS CONDIMENT AFFECTS YOUR BODY

Important Phytochemicals   Cocoa beans contain three stimulants: caffeine (also found in coffee), theophylline (also found in tea), and theobromine. Theobromine has the weakest effects on the central nervous system, but it is also a muscle stimulant. The stimulants are mild diuretics.

Cocoa and chocolate also contain oxalic acid which binds with calcium to form calcium oxalate, an insoluble salt. That is the basis for the notion that chocolate milk is not nutritious. In fact, there is more calcium in the milk than can bind with cocoa or chocolate syrup, so chocolate-flavored milk is still a good source of calcium.

Benefits * * *

Possible Adverse Effects According to *The Merck Manual*, chocolate is one of the 12 foods most likely to trigger classic food allergy symptoms: hives, swelling of the lips and eyes, and upset stomach. The others are berries, corn, fish, legumes (green peas, lima beans, peanuts, soybeans), milk, nuts, peaches, pork, shellfish, and wheat.

Cocoa/chocolate is sometimes linked to migraine headaches in sensitive people. People who develop headaches after eating cocoa and chocolate may be reacting to the naturally occurring mood elevator phenylethylamine (PEA). The PEA-induced headache is unusual in that it is a delayed reaction that usually occurs 12 or more hours after the chocolate is eaten.

People who frequently suffer from heartburn may find the caffeine and fat in cocoa/chocolate irritating. Caffeine and fat loosen the round muscle (sphincter) that holds the esophagus shut, allowing the acid contents of the stomach to flow backwards producing intense discomfort.

Information for Women Who Are Pregnant or Nursing * * *

Condiment/Drug Interactions Monoamine oxidase (MAO) inhibitors are drugs used as antidepressants or antihypertensives. They inhibit the activity of enzymes that break down nitrogen compounds, including PEA, so they can be eliminated from the body. As a result, the amines build in your bloodstream, constricting blood vessels and raising blood pressure. If you eat a food rich in PEA while you are taking an MAO inhibitor, the result may be a hypertensive crisis (sustained elevated blood pressure).

HOW TO USE THIS CONDIMENT

In Cooking To substitute cocoa powder for chocolate, use 3 tablespoons plain cocoa powder plus 1 tablespoon butter, margarine, or corn oil in place of 1 ounce baking chocolate.

Cakes made with cocoa (or chocolate) must be leavened with baking soda, rather than baking powder. Cocoa/chocolate is highly acidic; it can upset the delicate balance of acid (cream of tartar) and base (alkali = sodium bicarbonate = baking soda) in baking powder. But cocoa is not acidic enough to balance plain sodium bicarbonate, so you must add an acid, usually sour cream or buttermilk or yogurt, to a chocolate cake. Without the sour milk, the batter would be so basic that the chocolate would look red, not brown, and it would taste very bitter.

Coffee

ABOUT THIS PLANT

Botanical name(s): *Coffea arabica*
Common name(s): * * *
Native to: Africa
Parts used as food/drink: Seed
GRAS list: No
Medicinal properties: Stimulant
Other uses: * * *

ABOUT THIS PLANT AS FOOD OR DRINK

Coffee beans are the roasted seeds from the fruit of the evergreen *Coffea* tree native to tropical Africa but now cultivated in many tropical countries including Brazil, Costa Rica, and the West Indies.

Roasted coffee beans are about 11 percent protein, 8 percent sugars, up to 15 percent flavoring oils, and up to 2 percent caffeine, with B vitamins (riboflavin and niacin), vitamin C, iron, potassium, and sodium. But brewed coffee retains only negligible amounts of niacin, potassium, sodium, and iron.

Nutritional Profile   One cup (8 oz) brewed coffee has up to 5 calories. It provides less than 1 g protein, fat, and dietary fiber, 1 g carbohydrates, 5 mg calcium, 0.1 mg iron, and 5 mg sodium. (The mineral content of coffee may vary depending on the water in which it is brewed.)

One cup (8 oz) instant coffee has up to 5 calories. It provides less than 1 g protein and fat, 1 g carbohydrates, no dietary fiber, 7 mg calcium, 0.1 mg iron, and 7 mg sodium. (As with brewed coffee, mineral content may vary.)

HOW THIS PLANT AFFECTS YOUR BODY

Important Phytochemicals   Like COCOA, GUARANA, MATE, and TEA, coffee contains caffeine, a central nervous system stimulant that dilates some blood vessels and constricts others, quickens heartbeat, elevates mood, and acts as a mild diuretic. These effects vary widely from person to person. In addition, people who drink coffee every day may develop a tolerance to caffeine, experiencing less stimulation than those who drink coffee only once in a while.

How much caffeine you get from one cup of coffee depends to a great extent on how the coffee was processed and brewed. For example, solu-

ble coffees ("freeze-dried," "instant"), made by dehydrating concentrated brewed coffee, are often lower in caffeine than regular ground coffees because caffeine, which dissolves in water, is lost when the coffee is dehydrated. Decaffeinated coffee (coffee from which the caffeine has been extracted, either with water or with an organic solvent) may have up to 97 percent less caffeine than regular coffee. Note: Removing the caffeine does not change the coffee's flavor.

CAFFEINE CONTENT (5-oz cup of coffee)	
Drip-brewed coffee	110–150 mg
Percolated coffee	64–124 mg
Instant coffee	40–108 mg
Decaffeinated coffee	2–5 mg

Source: Briggs, George M., and Calloway, Doris Howes, *Nutrition and Physical Fitness*, 9th edition (Holt, Rinehart and Winston, 1984)

Benefits   Consuming caffeine may increase alertness and concentration, intensify muscle responses, speed up heartbeat, and elevate mood. It also appears to strengthen analgesia (pain relief), which is why it is often added to over-the-counter painkillers.

Caffeine dilates systemic blood vessels and constricts cerebral blood vessels. This may explain coffee's ability to relieve headaches caused by engorged blood vessels. It may also explain the result of studies showing that regular (not decaffeinated) coffee appears to increase pain-free exercise time in patients with angina.

Caffeine dilates the coronary arteries and increases the coronary blood flow, but it also speeds up heartbeat; medical opinion is divided as to whether patients with heart conditions should drink coffee.

Caffeine is a mild diuretic sometimes included in over-the-counter remedies for premenstrual tension or menstrual discomfort.

Possible Adverse Effects   Both regular and decaffeinated coffees increase the secretion of stomach acid leading to heartburn.

Caffeine is a drug for which people develop a tolerance; the more often you use it, the more likely you are to experience withdrawal symptoms (headache, lassitude, irritability) if you stop using it. Obviously the symptoms of coffee-withdrawal can be relieved immediately by drinking a cup of coffee, but you can lessen withdrawal discomfort by gradually cutting down intake. It may take up to seven hours to metabolize and excrete the caffeine from one cup of coffee.

Caffeinated beverages contain flavoring oils that can upset your stomach, but MATÉ is probably less irritating than coffee or TEA because it contains significantly less flavoring oil.

Information for Women Who Are Pregnant or Nursing   Very small amounts of caffeine (0.6–1.5 percent) from coffee drunk by a nursing mother can show up in her breast milk.

Plant/Drug Interactions   Coffee may intensify the stimulant effects of caffeine-containing over-the-counter cold remedies, diuretics, pain relievers, stimulants, and weight control products. On the other hand, coffee may counteract the drowsiness caused by sedative drugs, a potential benefit for people taking certain antihistamines.

Monoamine oxidase (MAO) inhibitors are drugs used as antidepressants or antihypertensives. They inhibit the natural activity or enzymes that break down "pressor amines," substances that constrict blood vessels and raise blood pressure. If you consume a food, drug, or herb that contains pressor amines while you are taking an MAO inhibitor, the added amine cannot be efficiently eliminated from your body. The result may be potentially fatal sustained high blood pressure. Caffeine is a weak pressor amine.

Coffee may reduce the effectiveness of the antigout drug allopurinol which is designed to inhibit xanthines, such as caffeine.

By increasing stomach acidity, coffee may reduce the absorption of some oral antibiotics such as ampicillin, erythromycin, griseofulvin, penicillin, and the tetracyclines.

Caffeine binds with iron to form insoluble compounds your body cannot absorb. Ideally, iron supplements and coffee should be taken at least two hours apart.

HOW TO USE THIS PLANT

In Cooking   Avoid bulk coffees or coffee beans stored in open bins. When coffee is exposed to air, the volatile molecules that give it its distinctive flavor and richness escape, leaving the coffee tasteless or bitter.

Keep unopened vacuum-packed cans of ground coffee or coffee beans in a cool, dark cabinet where they will stay fresh for six months to a year. They will lose some flavor in storage, though, because it's impossible to can coffee without trapping some flavor-destroying air inside the can.

Once the coffee container is open, beans or ground coffee should be sealed as tightly as possible and stored in the refrigerator. Tightly wrapped, refrigerated ground coffee will hold its freshness and flavor for about a week; whole beans for about three weeks. For longer storage, freeze the coffee or beans in an air- and moisture-proof container. (You can brew coffee directly from frozen ground coffee and you can grind frozen beans without thawing them.)

When making coffee with tap water, let the water run for a while to add oxygen and eliminate any metal contaminants it may have picked up traveling through the pipes to your tap. Soft water makes "cleaner" tasting coffee than mineral-rich hard water.

Always brew coffee in a scrupulously clean pot. Each time you make coffee, it leaves oils on the inside of the pot. If not removed, they will turn rancid and the next pot of coffee you brew will taste bitter.

In making coffee, your aim is to extract flavorful solids (including coffee oils, sucrose, and other sugars) from the ground beans without pulling bitter, astringent tannins along with them. The longer you brew the coffee, the more solids you will extract, and the more bitter the coffee will taste. To make coffee that's strong but not bitter, increase the amount of coffee not the brewing time.

Cola Nut

ABOUT THIS PLANT

Botanical name(s): Cola nitida
Common name(s): Kola nut, Bissynut, guru nut
Native to: West Africa
Parts used as food/drink: Seed
GRAS list: No
Medicinal properties: Stimulant
Other uses: * * *

ABOUT THIS PLANT AS FOOD OR DRINK

The cola nut is the dried seed of one an evergreen tree native to West Africa. It is most famous for being one of the ingredients in the original secret formula for Coca-Cola. Today, the cola nut is used in prepared diet supplements as an energizer (see below, "Important phytochemicals").

Nutritional Profile   * * *

HOW THIS PLANT AFFECTS YOUR BODY

Important Phytochemicals   The cola nut contains up to 3 percent caffeine and 1 percent theobromine (the stimulant in the COCOA bean), plus sugars and gum. In Africa and the West Indies, the nut is chewed as a stimulant. It is also a mild diuretic.

Benefits   In 1991, the German Commission E approved the use of cola nut preparations to relieve mental and physical fatigue.

Possible Adverse Effects   Like COFFEE, TEA, and COCOA, the cola nut may cause nervousness, insomnia, and sleep disorders. Because caffeine and theobromine may irritate the lining of the intestinal tract, Commission E cautions against its use by people with gastric or duodenal ulcers.

Information for Women Who Are Pregnant or Nursing   * * *

Plant/Drug Interactions   Cola nut products may intensify the adverse effects of caffeine and other stimulants in over-the-counter cold medications that contain caffeine.

HOW TO USE THIS PLANT   * * *

Coltsfoot

ABOUT THIS PLANT

Botanical name(s): Tussilago farfara
Common name(s): Coughwort
Native to: Northern Europe, Asia
Parts used as food/drink: Leaves
GRAS list: No
Medicinal properties: Anti-inflammatory
Other uses: * * *

ABOUT THIS PLANT AS FOOD OR DRINK

Coltsfoot is a perennial herb with yellow flowers that look like DANDELIONs and aromatic leaves shaped a bit like hearts, or like colts' feet, hence the plant's name. Coltsfoot is not used as food, but may be used to brew an herbal tea.

Nutritional Profile * * *

HOW THIS PLANT AFFECTS YOUR BODY

Important Phytochemicals Coltsfoot leaves and flowers are rich in mucilage that coats and soothes mucous membranes, plus resins and astringent tannins. The plant's Latin name, *tussilago*, means "cough dispeller." Ancient Greeks and Romans inhaled the vapor from coltsfoot leaves simmering in hot water or inhaled smoke from burning leaves to break up bronchial congestion; the herb has a long history as a folk remedy for colds, coughs, and asthma.

However, like COMFREY, the coltsfoot plant contains known liver toxins/carcinogens called pyrrolizidines. Studies with laboratory rats that date back to the 1970s show that in nearly two-thirds of the animals fed concentrations of dried coltsfoot flower, more than 4 percent develop liver cancer.

Benefits In 1990, the German Commission E approved the use of preparations of fresh or dried coltsfoot leaves to relieve respiratory infection, cough and hoarseness, or mild inflammation of the mouth and throat. In its approval, Commission E limits the daily dose to an amount containing no more than 10 mcg pyrrolizidines and notes that the herb should not be used for longer than four to six weeks a year.

In the United States, the Food and Drug Administration classifies coltsfoot as an herb of undefined safety. The herb is banned in Canada.

Possible Adverse Effects   See above.

Information for Women Who Are Pregnant or Nursing   German Commission E advises against the use of coltsfoot by women who are pregnant or nursing.

Plant/Drug Interactions   * * *

HOW TO USE THIS PLANT   * * *

Coriander

ABOUT THIS PLANT

Botanical name(s): Coriandrum sativum
Common name(s): Coriander seed
Native to: Mediterranean region, eastern Europe
Parts used as food/drink: Fruit
GRAS list: Yes
Medicinal properties: Appetite stimulant, antiflatulent
Other uses: Flavoring agent in cigarettes

ABOUT THIS PLANT AS FOOD OR DRINK

The coriander plant is impressively hardy. It grows easily from seed in virtually any good garden soil, at temperatures as low as 10 degrees F, and provides two popular seasonings. Its flat green leaves are known as CILANTRO; its small white or purple-tinged flowers yield seeds (actually dried fruit) known as coriander. The seeds, which are more intensely flavored than the leaves, taste like a blend of LEMON and SAGE with a scent that turns warm and spicy as the seeds mature.

Most coriander seeds come from either Morocco or Romania. The Moroccan seeds are larger, but the deeper, spicier Romanian seeds are preferred by distillers and food manufacturers, who use them to flavor gin, various liqueurs, and sausages (frankfurters). Coriander is also used in chewing gum.

Nutritional Profile   One tablespoon (5 g) coriander seed has 15 calories. It provides 0.6 g protein, 0.9 g fat, 2.8 g carbohydrates, 2.1 g dietary fiber, 1.1 mg vitamin C, 35 mg calcium, and 0.8 mg iron.

One teaspoon (1.8 g) coriander seed has 5 calories. It provides 0.2 g protein, 0.3 g fat, 1 g carbohydrates, 0.8 g dietary fiber, 0.4 mg vitamin C, 13 mg calcium, and 0.3 g iron.

HOW THIS PLANT AFFECTS YOUR BODY

Important Phytochemicals   Coriander seeds get their fragrance from linalool, which smells like French LAVENDER. The oily substance, also found in CARDAMOM and other herbs, is an irritant and a potential allergic sensitizer.

Benefits   Coriander is a weak antiflatulent, an agent that breaks up intestinal gas. In 1986, the German Commission E approved the use of coriander preparations as an appetite stimulant and to relieve intestinal gas.

Possible Adverse Effects   Contact with coriander plant or seed may cause contact dermatitis (itching, burning, stinging, reddened, or blistered skin) or allergic cheilitis (dry, peeling, blistered lips).

Information for Women Who Are Pregnant or Nursing   * * *

Plant/Drug Interactions   * * *

HOW TO USE THIS PLANT

In Cooking   To make your own coriander-flavored vodka, steep one tablespoon coriander seed in a bottle of vodka for 24 to 48 hours. Then strain the vodka to remove the seeds, and use as you like.

In the Garden   To harvest coriander seed, allow the plant to flower, then gather the blossoms when the seeds are so dry they crack open when squeezed. To retrieve the seeds, hang the coriander upside down over cheesecloth and collect the seeds that fall. Or wrap the plants in cheesecloth and hit them against a hard surface to separate the seeds. Rub the seeds in a strainer small enough to catch the seeds but allow the debris (chaff) and bits of dirt and dust to fall through.

As a Home Remedy   To make a mildly antiflatulent tea, add 2 teaspoons dried coriander seeds to 1 cup boiling water and let steep for three to four minutes. Then strain and serve the tea.

Industrial Uses   Coriander is added to tobacco to give cigarette tobacco a characteristic "American" fragrance and flavor.

Cornflower

ABOUT THIS PLANT

Botanical name(s): Centuarea cyanus
Common name(s): Bachelor's button, cyani flower
Native to: Mediterranean region, Europe
Parts used as food/drink: Flower
GRAS list: No
Medicinal properties: * * *
Other uses: Blue ink

ABOUT THIS PLANT AS FOOD OR DRINK

The cornflower is a garden flower native to the Mediterranean. Widely regarded as a weed, with a tough stem sometimes said to blunt garden tools, the plant produces the brilliantly colored flowers that have given their name to the color known as "cornflower blue." Cornflower is often included as a coloring agent in herbal teas.

Nutritional Profile * * *

HOW THIS PLANT AFFECTS YOUR BODY

Important Phytochemicals Cornflowers have been used in folk medicine to lower fever, alleviate menstrual disorders, as a laxative and diuretic (a drug that increases urination), and as an expectorant (a substance that breaks up mucus and makes it easier to cough up phlegm). Although the herb is considered safe, none of these claims has ever been medically substantiated.

Benefits * * *

Possible Adverse Effects * * *

Information for Women Who Are Pregnant or Nursing * * *

Plant/Drug Interactions * * *

HOW TO USE THIS PLANT

Around the House Because cornflowers hold their bright blue color when dried, they are often used in arrangements of dried flowers, including wreaths.

Costmary

ABOUT THIS PLANT

Botanical name(s): Chrysanthemum balsamita
Common name(s): Alecost, Bible leaf
Native to: Asia
Parts used as food/drink: Leaves
GRAS list: No
Medicinal properties: * * *
Other uses: Moth repellent

ABOUT THIS PLANT AS FOOD OR DRINK

Costmary, a member of the chrysanthemum family related to CHAMOMILE, is a large plant with light green, mint-scented leaves and sparse, small flowers that look like daisies.

The leaves, generally available only from your own garden, may be used in soups, stews, and sauces or to brew a minty tea.

Nutritional Profile * * *

HOW THIS PLANT AFFECTS YOUR BODY

Important Phytochemicals Like other members of the chrysanthemum family, costmary produces natural insecticides called pyrethrins which are extremely strong allergens. Costmary's pollen, which contains pyrethrins, is highly allergenic.

Benefits * * *

Possible Adverse Effects People sensitive to asters, ragweed, and chamomile, are likely to be allergic to costmary. If they touch any part of the costmary plant or inhale its pollen, they may experience severe allergic reactions ranging from contact dermatitis to sneezing, wheezing, numbness of the lips and tongue, ringing in the ears, headache, restlessness, loss of muscular coordination, convulsions, or death due to paralysis of the respiratory muscles.

Information for Women Who Are Pregnant or Nursing * * *

Plant/Drug Interactions * * *

HOW TO USE THIS PLANT

In Cooking   People who are not allergic to the costmary plant or any of its botanical relatives may use its leaves to brew a minty tea or to lend a minty accent to other teas. Heating costmary leaves makes them bitter; do not steep the leaves longer than three or four minutes.

Around the House   Pyrethrins are natural insect repellents and insecticides. If you are not sensitive to the costmary plant or any of its botanical relatives, scattering dried costmary leaves on the floor of your closet may help protect the clothes from moths.

Couch Grass

ABOUT THIS PLANT

Botanical name(s): Agropyron repens
Common name(s): Dog grass, witch grass
Native to: Europe
Parts used as food/drink: Rhizomes
GRAS list: No
Medicinal properties: * * *
Other uses: Animal feed

ABOUT THIS PLANT AS FOOD OR DRINK

Couch grass, whose Latin name means "creeping field wheat," is a plant that really does look like rye or wheat. Unlike these foods grains, however, couch grass's most nutritious parts are its multiple rhizomes, high-carbohydrate underground stems generally used as cattle feed. In times of famine, they have been roasted, ground, and used as a substitute for coffee or dried, ground, and used as a substitute for flour.

Nutritional Profile * * *

HOW THIS PLANT AFFECTS YOUR BODY

Important Phytochemicals   Couch grass contains essential oils and naturally forming substances called saponins.

Benefits   In 1990, the German Commission E approved the use of couch grass preparations, along with copious amounts of liquids, to relieve urinary inflammation and prevent the formation of deposits that can lead to kidney stones. Note: In approving the use of couch grass, Commission E cautioned against its use for people with edema (swelling) due to heart disease or kidney disease.

Possible Adverse Effects   * * *

Information for Women Who Are Pregnant or Nursing   * * *

Plant/Drug Interactions   * * *

HOW TO USE THIS PLANT   * * *

Cream of Tartar

ABOUT THIS CONDIMENT

Chemical name(s): *Potassium bitartrate*
Common name(s): * * *
Native to: * * *
Parts used as food/drink: * * *
GRAS list: No
Medicinal properties: Laxative, diuretic
Other uses: Mordant (color fixative in dyeing)

ABOUT THIS CONDIMENT AS FOOD OR DRINK

Cream of tartar is composed of the white crystals that form naturally in the sediments ("lees") created when grapes are fermented to make wine.

The best known use for cream of tartar is as an acid ingredient in baking powder, but it is also used to intensify the flavor of beverages and candy and as a stabilizing agent to preserve food colors and flavors.

Nutritional Profile One teaspoon cream of tartar has 8 calories. It provides 495 mg potassium, 0.2 mg calcium, 0.1 mg iron, and 2 mg sodium.

HOW THIS CONDIMENT AFFECTS YOUR BODY

Important Phytochemicals Tartrates, which attract and hold water in the digestive tract, are sometimes used in over-the-counter laxatives; sodium bitartrate is used as a strong laxative in veterinary medicine. But in its review of over-the-counter products, the U.S. Food and Drug Administration's Advisory Review Panel on OTC (over-the-counter) Antidiarrheal, Emetic, and Antiemetic Drug Products rated tartrates as "conditionally approved active ingredients" because neither their safety nor their effectiveness as laxatives has been scientifically unproven.

Benefits: * * *

Possible Adverse Effects Tartrates are used in over-the-counter antacid products, a purpose for which the FDA Advisory Review Panel on OTC (over-the-counter) Drugs calls them safe and effective. However, in its evaluation, the review panel cautioned against high doses of tartrates because they might be damaging to the kidneys.

Information for Women Who Are Pregnant or Nursing * * *

Condiment/Drug Interactions   * * *

HOW TO USE THIS CONDIMENT

In Cooking   When you mix flour with water and beat the batter, the long protein molecules in the flour relax and unfold. Internal bonds (bonds between atoms on the same molecule) are broken and new bonds form between atoms on different molecules, creating a network of elastic protein known as gluten.

Baking powders contain two ingredients that stabilize the protein network, a fast-acting leavening agent and a slow-acting leavening agent. These products are called *double-acting* baking powders, because their ingredients work at different times and temperatures.

When you add a baking powder made of baking soda and cream of tartrate to batter, its fast-acting cream of tartar releases carbon dioxide immediately. (You can see the carbon dioxide as bubbles in the batter.) The slow-acting sodium bicarbonate releases carbon dioxide later, when the batter is heated in the oven, stabilizing the batter's protein network into its final ("risen") form.

To make your own tartrate baking powder, combine $1/4$ teaspoon baking soda with $1/2$ teaspoon cream of tartar. This equals the leavening power of 1 teaspoon double acting baking powder. Note: Because tartrate baking powders release their carbon dioxide as soon as they are added to the batter, they should be used only in batters that will go straight into a heated oven. Never use a tartrate baking powder in a dough you plan to refrigerate.

Add a pinch of cream of tartar to an egg white before beating. The acidic cream of tartar will stabilize the foam by making the egg white less basic (alkaline) and preventing the egg proteins (albumen) from bonding tightly to each other (coagulating), a phenomenon often described as "overbeating." Copper ions flaking off the sides of a copper mixing bowl do the same thing. That is why it is standard culinary practice to beat egg whites in a copper bowl.

When making candy or a sugar syrup, add a pinch of cream of tartar to the sugar to slow down crystallization (clumping of sugar molecules). This gives you more time to either cool the candy into a clear syrup or beat it longer and make even more crystals.

To protect the potency of cream of tartar, store it tightly closed in a cool place. Even under the best conditions, baking powders become less potent with time. To test the powder, add 1 teaspoonful to a cup of water. If it bubbles, the powder is still working.

Cumin

ABOUT THIS PLANT

Botanical name(s): Cuminum cyminum
Common name(s): Comino
Native to: Mediterranean region
Parts used as food/drink: Seeds
GRAS list: Yes
Medicinal properties: Carminative
Other uses: * * *

ABOUT THIS PLANT AS FOOD OR DRINK

Cumin is a member of the carrot family, a relative of PARSLEY. The plant produces seeds that look and smell like CARAWAY seeds but are slightly longer, lighter in color, and have a deeper, stronger flavor.

Cumin is best known as an ingredient in CURRY POWDER and CHILI POWDER. It is also the flavoring agent, along with caraway, in Dutch cheeses and the German liqueur known as kummel. (*Kummel* is the German word for caraway.)

Nutritional Profile One tablespoon (6 g) cumin seed has 22 calories. It provides 1.1 g protein, 1.3 g fat, 2.7 g carbohydrates, 0.6 g dietary fiber, 76 IU vitamin A, 0.5 mg vitamin C, 56 mg calcium, 4 mg iron, and 10 mg sodium.

One teaspoon (2 g) cumin seed has 8 calories. It provides 0.4 g protein, 0.5 g fat, 0.9 g carbohydrates, 0.2 g dietary fiber, 27 IU vitamin A, 0.2 mg vitamin C, 20 mg calcium, 1.4 mg iron, and 4 mg sodium.

HOW THIS PLANT AFFECTS YOUR BODY

Important Phytochemicals Cumin seeds contain oil of cumin, which is 30–40 percent cuminaldehyde, an oily liquid with a strong, persistent odor and stinging taste. Oil of cumin also contains turpentine-scented pinene and lemon-scented dipentene.

Benefits * * *

Possible Adverse Effects * * *

Information for Women Who Are Pregnant or Nursing * * *

Plant/Drug Interactions * * *

HOW TO USE THIS PLANT

In Cooking Like capsaicin, the flavoring agent in peppers, cuminaldehyde dissolves in alcohol or milk fat, but not in water. That's why ice water will not cool the burning sensation you experience when you eat a hot curry or chili. Beer, the traditional accompaniment, will soothe the burn. So will whole milk, but that is rarely served with chili although it may be used in an American-made creamy curry sauce. (East Indians use coconut milk).

You can substitute ground caraway seeds for ground cumin. The flavor, though milder, is remarkably similar.

If you shop in Indian grocery stores, you may come across black cumin (*Nigeria sativa*), an unrelated plant also known as nutmeg flower or Roman coriander. Black cumin, which is easier to grow than regular cumin, produces pods with small, dark seeds that smell like FENNEL and taste something like peppery NUTMEG. The flavor is distinctive, so try a little before you season a whole dish.

Curry Powder

ABOUT THIS PLANT

Botanical name(s): * * *
Common name(s): * * *
Native to: India
Parts used as food/drink: * * *
GRAS list: No
Medicinal properties: Diaphoretic, irritant
Other uses: * * *

ABOUT THIS PLANT AS FOOD OR DRINK

Curry powder is a blend of as many as 16 to 20 different spices such as CIN-NAMON, CLOVES, CUMIN, FENUGREEK, GINGER, PEPPER (red and black), and TURMERIC, the one that gives the powder its characteristic golden hue.

For information on any of the spices in curry powder, see the individual listings.

Nutritional Profile One tablespoon (6.3 g) of a representative curry powder made with coriander seed (36 percent), turmeric (28 percent), cumin (10 percent), fenugreek (10 percent), white pepper (5 percent), all-spice (4 percent), yellow mustard seed (3 percent), red pepper (2 percent) and ginger (2 percent) has 20 calories. It provides 0.3 g protein, 0.3 g fat, 3.7 g carbohydrates, 62 IU vitamin A, 0.7 mg vitamin C, 30 mg calcium, and 1.86 mg iron.

HOW THIS PLANT AFFECTS YOUR BODY

Important Phytochemicals Coriander, the main ingredient in most curry powders, is an antiflatulent, a substance that helps expel intestinal gas.

Turmeric is a choleretic, a substance that stimulates the liver to increase its production of bile, the yellow, brown, or green fluid that helps emulsify fats in your duodenum and increases peristalsis, the rhythmic contractions that move food through your gastrointestinal tract. Choleretics are ordinarily beneficial for healthy people but may pose some problems for people with gallbladder or liver diseases.

Black pepper and red pepper are diaphoretics, substances that increase perspiration. Pepper, ALLSPICE, MUSTARD, and GINGER are all irritating to the skin and mucous membranes.

Benefits   Because it promotes perspiration, which cools your body as the moisture evaporates on your skin, curry powder is a popular seasoning in warm climates.

Like other "hot" spices, curry powder may be useful when you have hay fever or a head or chest cold. The pepper in the mixture irritates the mucous membranes lining your nose and throat, causing them to exude a watery secretion. This makes it easier for you to cough up sticky mucus or clear your nose when you blow it.

Possible Adverse Effects   The oils in the spices in curry powder may irritate the lining of your stomach and bladder, causing gastric discomfort or frequent painful urination that mimics a urinary infection.

Information for Women Who Are Pregnant or Nursing   * * *

Plant/Drug Interactions   * * *

HOW TO USE THIS PLANT

In Cooking   For an unusual flavor, sprinkle a pinch of curry powder over an apple before you bake it, or add a pinch to a dish of applesauce, then warm the sauce.

In Indian grocery stores, you may come across a dried herb called curry leaves that looks like small bay leaves. Fresh curry leaves are available in India; in the U.S., the only ones generally available are dried curry leaves which, unfortunately, are much less aromatic and less flavorful than fresh ones.

Cyclamates

ABOUT THIS CONDIMENT

Chemical name(s): Calcium cyclamate, sodium cyclamate
Common name(s): Sucaryl calcium, Sucaryl sodium
Native to: * * *
GRAS list: No
Parts used as food/drink: * * *
Medicinal properties: Nonnutritive sweetener
Other uses: * * *

ABOUT THIS CONDIMENT AS FOOD OR DRINK

Cyclamates, the second substitute sweetener to be identified (after SAC-CHARIN), were isolated at the University of Illinois in 1937.

Cyclamates are 30 to 60 times sweeter than sugar. Most people can detect a sweet taste in a solution containing 1 part cyclamate in 10,000 parts water. It takes 1 part sugar to 140 parts water to produce a solution with the same level of sweetness.

Nutritional Profile Cyclamates have no nutritive value.

HOW THIS CONDIMENT AFFECTS YOUR BODY

Important Chemicals Like saccharin, cyclamates were linked to cancer in laboratory animals. Although there has never been any evidence of ill effects in human beings, the sweeteners have been banned from use in the United States since 1969. But they are available for use as a tabletop sweetener in Canada, and the U.S. Food and Drug Administration is currently reconsidering its ban.

Benefits The cyclamates' chief benefit is their ability to sweeten without calories. They are useful in a diet designed to control weight and for people with diabetes who must control their sugar intake.

Possible Adverse Effects * * *

Information for Women Who Are Pregnant or Nursing * * *

Condiment/Drug Interactions * * *

HOW TO USE THIS CONDIMENT

In Cooking Cyclamates are used as a tabletop sweetener. They can be added to coffee, tea, and other hot/cold drinks or sprinkled on cereals and fruits.

Dandelion

ABOUT THIS PLANT

Botanical name(s): *Taraxacum officinale*
Common name(s): Lion's tooth
Native to: Europe
Parts used as food/drink: Leaf, root
GRAS list: No
Medicinal properties: Diuretic, laxative, appetite stimulant
Other uses: Fabric dye

ABOUT THIS PLANT AS FOOD OR DRINK

The dandelion, a member of the daisy family, has pleasantly bitter, edible leaves that are highly nutritious. Dandelion leaves are rich in beta-carotene, the deep yellow carotenoid pigment your body converts to vitamin A, plus folate (the B vitamin that reduces the risk of birth defects and heart disease), plus vitamin C, iron, and the complex carbohydrates levulin and inulin. Both dandelion leaves and dandelion root contain the soluble dietary fiber pectin.

Fresh raw dandelion leaves may be added to salads or they may be cooked and served as a vegetable. Ground, roasted dandelion roots and rhizomes (underground stems) can be used like ground, roasted CHICORY to deepen the bitter flavor of coffee without adding caffeine. Dandelion flowers are used to flavor and color dandelion wine.

Nutritional Profile   One cup raw dandelion leaves has 25 calories, 2 g protein, less than 1 g fat, 5 g carbohydrates, 2 g dietary fiber, 7,700 IU vitamin A (150–192 percent of the RDA), 15 mcg of the B vitamin folate, 19 mg vitamin C (30 percent of the RDA), and 2 mg iron (20 percent of the RDA).

One cup boiled dandelion leaves has 35 calories, 2 g protein, less than 1 g fat, 7 g carbohydrates, 3 g dietary fiber, 12,285 IU vitamin A, 13 mcg of the B vitamin folate, 19 mg vitamin C, and 2 mg iron.

HOW THIS PLANT AFFECTS YOUR BODY

Important Phytochemicals   Dandelion leaves get their bitter flavor from taraxacin; the roots and rhizomes contain bitter taraxasterol. Both leaves and roots are used in folk medicine as a diuretic; in fact, the French name for dandelions is *pis en lit* ("pee in the bed"). According to the American Pharmaceutical Association Practical Guide to Natural Medicine, that's an accurate description. The liquid produced by steeping dandelion leaves or roots in hot water is mildly diuretic and mildly laxative.

Benefits   Like many other greens such as BORAGE, collard greens, mustard greens, and turnip greens, dandelion leaves are rich in calcium. Three and one-half ounces chopped fresh leaves provides 10 percent of the current calcium RDA for an adult. Dandelion leaves are also a good source of nonheme iron, the form of iron found in plants. (The form of iron found in meat, fish, poultry, milk, and eggs is called heme iron.) Three and a half ounces of fresh dandelion leaves provides 17 percent of adult RDA. You can increase the amount of iron you absorb from dandelion leaves by eating the vegetable with meat. The meat increases the secretion of stomach acids, and iron is absorbed more easily in an acid environment. The vitamin C in dandelion leaves also makes iron more available by changing nonheme iron from ferric iron to ferrous iron, a form of iron your body absorbs more easily.

In 1984 and 1990, the German Commission E approved the use of steeped dandelion liquid (1 tablespoon cut herb per cup hot water) as a diuretic, appetite stimulant, and for the relief of stomach upset. In 1992, the commission approved the use of fresh or dried dandelion leaves as an appetite stimulant and to relieve flatulence, but cautioned against the use of dandelion by people with gallbladder disease or gallstones.

Possible Adverse Effects   The dandelion and its pollen are allergenic. Some sensitive individuals may end up with itchy, burning, red, or blistered skin after handling dandelions, or begin to sneeze and/or cough when exposed to the dandelion flower.

By stimulating the flow of stomach acids, taraxacin and taraxasterol may cause upset stomach in sensitive individuals.

Information for Women Who Are Pregnant or Nursing   * * *

Plant/Drug Interactions   * * *

HOW TO USE THIS PLANT

In Cooking   Dandelions are so easy to find that it can be tempting to pick them off the lawn and toss them in the salad. Resist the urge: Plants growing wild may have been sprayed with pesticides or contaminated with animal matter. Better to shop your local farmers' market for dandelion greens from cultivated plants.

To reduce the natural bitterness of dandelion leaves, store them in the refrigerator or pick them only after the weather turns cold. Chilling dandelion roots also makes them less bitter.

Wash dandelion leaves before refrigerating but do not cut or tear them until you are ready to use them. When you cut the leaves, you tear the cells, which then release an enzyme called ascorbic acid oxidase which destroys vitamin C and reduces the dandelion's nutritional value.

Chlorophyll, the green coloring in dandelion leaves, is sensitive to acids. When the leaves are heated, their chlorophyll reacts with natural acids in the leaves or in the cooking water, forming a brown compound called pheophytin. The pheophytin in turn reacts with the yellow carotene pigments in the leaves, turning the cooked dandelion leaves bronze. To prevent this color change, cook dandelion leaves very quickly or add them to a dish at the very last minute. (Commercial herb packagers preserve the color of green herbs by drying the leaves at a very low heat.)

Around the House   Dandelion flowers yield a golden yellow dye for wool and cotton. Dandelion roots produce a purple dye. To make these coloring agents, steep 1 quart crushed flowers or cut-up roots overnight in a pot with just enough water to cover. The next day, boil the flowers or roots in the same water for 15 minutes to two hours, adding more liquid as needed, until the water has reached the desired color. Let the mixture cool, then strain it through a colander or sieve into a second large pot to remove all the plant material. Wearing rubber gloves to protect your hands, immerse one clean, wet, unlined cotton or woolen T-shirt, blouse, sweater, or other small garment in the bath, swishing it around so the dye comes in contact with every surface of the garment. Then immerse the garment in the dye and boil it for 30 minutes or less, until the color looks right. Turn off the heat, let the dye bath cool, remove the garment, and hold it under cold running water until the water runs clear.

Caution: Do not use these dyes if you are sensitive to dandelions. Always try any dye on an inconspicuous part of the garment first to see if you like the color. Boiling will shrink some cotton or woolen fabrics.

Dill

ABOUT THIS PLANT

Botanical name(s): Anethum graveolens
Common name(s): Dillweed, dillseed
Native to: Asia
GRAS list: Yes
Parts used as food/drink: Leaves, fruit ("seeds")
Medicinal properties: Antispasmodic, antibacterial (dill seed)
Other uses: * * *

ABOUT THIS PLANT AS FOOD OR DRINK

Dill, a member of the PARSLEY family, has feathery leaves and umbrella-like clusters of small, yellow flowers. The plant produces two different herbs: dill seed (dried fruit) and dill weed (the top eight inches of the leaves).

Nutritional Profile   One-half ounce (14 g) fresh dill weed has 6 calories, 0.5 g protein, 0.2 g fat, 21 mcg folate, and 30 mg calcium.

One teaspoon (1 g) dried dill weed has 3 calories. It provides 0.2 g protein, a trace of fat, 0.6 g carbohydrates, 18 mg calcium, and 0.5 mg iron.

One teaspoon (2.1 g) dill seed has 6 calories. It provides 0.3 g protein, 0.3 g fat, 1.2 g carbohydrates, 32 mg calcium, 0.3 mg iron, and 1 IU vitamin A.

HOW THIS PLANT AFFECTS YOUR BODY

Important Phytochemicals   Both dill seeds and dill weed get their slightly bitter flavor and their pungent aroma from carvone, an oily compound also found in CARAWAY, plus lemon-scented limonene and phellandrene.

Carvone is an antiflatulent, an agent that breaks up intestinal gas. Limonene and phellandrene are irritants and photosensitizers, compounds that make skin more sensitive to sunlight and increase the risk of serious sunburn, especially in light-skinned people.

Benefits   In 1990, the German Commission E approved the use of dill seed preparations, including teas made by steeping dill seed in hot water, to relieve upset stomach.

Possible Adverse Effects   Handling the dill plant may cause allergic reactions, including contact dermatitis (itchy, burning, reddened skin) and sunburn in sensitive people.

Information for Women Who Are Pregnant or Nursing   * * *

Plant/Drug Interactions   * * *

HOW TO USE THIS PLANT

In Cooking   Dill is most commonly used to produce the characteristic aroma and flavor of dill pickles and to add piquancy to fish and vegetable dishes, including baked or boiled potatoes, and cucumber and potato salads.

The longer dill leaves are cooked, the less flavor they have. To preserve the herb's pungency, add dill at the last minute, just before you serve the food.

Chlorophyll, the green coloring in dill leaves, is sensitive to acids. When dill is heated, its chlorophyll reacts with natural acids in the leaves or in the cooking water, forming a brown compound called pheophytin. The pheophytin in turn reacts with the yellow carotene pigments in the leaves, turning the cooked dill bronze. To prevent this color change, prevent the chlorophyll from reacting with the acids by cooking the dill for as short a time as possible. (Commercial herb packagers preserve the color of green herbs by drying the leaves at a very low heat.)

Dill seeds taste like caraway seeds, only milder. In a pinch, you can use dill seeds instead of caraway seeds in rye bread or boiled cabbage.

In the Garden   Carvone is a natural insecticide that increases the effectiveness of the highly toxic chemical insecticide parathion, now used only in agriculture. Studies show that only 8 percent of fruit flies exposed to parathion alone die, but 99 percent die when exposed to the same amount of parathion plus carvone. No evidence exists right now to suggest that dill growing in your garden or scattered around the house has any such effect.

Echinacea

ABOUT THIS PLANT

Botanical name(s): Echinacea pallida, Echinacea purpurea
Common name(s): Coneflower, purple coneflower
Native to: Western Canada, southern and southwest United States
Parts used as food/drink: Leaves
GRAS list: No
Medicinal properties: Immune system enhancer
Other uses: * * *

ABOUT THIS PLANT AS FOOD OR DRINK

Echinacea is a member of the daisy family, a perennial plant native to the United States. It produces relatively narrow leaves on a stem that grows as high as 3 feet and is topped with a large, purple flower. The leaves may be used as an herbal tea.

Nutritional Profile   * * *

HOW THIS PLANT AFFECTS YOUR BODY

Important Phytochemicals   The potentially active ingredient in echinacea is echinacin (also known as echinacein), a complex carbohydrate that appears to enhance immune function and quicken wound healing.

In 1997, echinacea was the best-selling herbal supplement in health food stores in the United States, and the fourth best-selling herbal supplement in food, drug and mass market retail stores, behind GINKGO BILOBA, GINSENG, and GARLIC.

Benefits   In studies with animals and human beings, echinacea given by mouth or through injection appears to strengthen the immune system by increasing body temperature and boosting the effectiveness of natural defense mechanisms such as white blood cells (including those called natural killer cells), macrophages, and spleen cells. Note: Most tests of echinacea in Germany have been done with injectible products not available in the United States.

In 1992, the German Commission E approved the use of preparations of dried echinacea roots and rhizomes (underground stems) to relieve the symptoms and shorten the course of respiratory infection. In 1992, the commission approved the use of echinacea preparations as an external dressing to speed wound healing. In both instances, the commission cautioned against using echinacea for longer than 8 weeks at a time and warned against its use for people with progressive systemic diseases such as AIDS, multiple sclerosis, tuberculosis, and other illnesses of the immune system.

Note: The Commission E approval does not apply to preparations of the green parts of *Echinacea pallida* or to the leaves and roots of the *Echinacea angustifolia* (another variety of echinacea). There is no scientific evidence to suggest that these parts or plants have any therapeutic value.

Possible Adverse Effects   Taking echinacea by injection (as in the German trials) may trigger allergic reactions, especially in people sensitive to daisies or related plants such as CHAMOMILE. It may also adversely affect metabolic function in people with diabetes.

In 1999, researchers at Loma Linda University School of Medicine in California incubated hamster eggs for one hour in concentrations of echinacea containing 1/1000th to 1/100th the amount of echinacea customarily found in over-the-counter products. When they added human sperm to the dish, they found that the echinacea damaged the sperms' outer membrane, reducing its ability to penetrate and fertilize the eggs. Sperm not exposed to echinacea penetrated up to 88 percent of the eggs; sperm exposed to echinacea, only 13 percent.

Information for Women Who Are Pregnant or Nursing   Commission E cautions against echinacea injections for pregnant women.

Plant/Drug Interactions   * * *

HOW TO USE THIS PLANT

Around the House   Echinacein is an insecticide, reputed to be particularly effective against houseflies.

Elder

ABOUT THIS PLANT

Botanical name(s): Sambucus nigra
Common name(s): European elder, pipe tree
Native to: Europe
Parts used as food/drink: Fruit (berry)
GRAS list: Yes
Medicinal properties: Diaphoretic (flower)
Other uses: * * *

ABOUT THIS PLANT AS FOOD OR DRINK

The elder, which may grow as high as 30 feet, has paired leaves, clusters of small white flowers, and berries that turn dark purple-blue-black as they ripen. Elderberries are used to make jam and elderberry wine, two traditional European treats.

Nutritional Profile   One-half cup (72 g) raw elderberries has 53 calories. It provides 0.5 g protein, 0.4 g fat, 13.3 g carbohydrates, 5 g dietary fiber, 26 mg vitamin C, 435 IU vitamin A, 27.5 mg calcium, 1.7 mg iron, and 4.4 mg sodium.

HOW THIS PLANT AFFECTS YOUR BODY

Important Phytochemicals   Like BLACK PEPPER and RED PEPPER, the berries and flowers of the European elder contain diaphoretics, substances that increase perspiration.

Caution: Raw elderberries contain small amounts of a poisonous alkaloid (plant chemical) that not only makes the berries smell and taste unpleasant but may also cause nausea and vomiting. The poisonous compound is inactivated when the berries are heated; cooking makes elderberries safe.

Caution: The leaves and stems of the European elder and the leaves, bark, and roots of the American elder (*Sambucus canadensis*, also known as sweet elder) contain cyanide; they are poisonous. To avoid accidental poisoning, do not pick your own elder flowers or berries; use only those sold in by a reputable health food store or mail-order supplier.

Benefits   In 1986, the German Commission E approved the use of tea brewed from dried flowers and flower extracts from the European elder to alleviate symptoms of the common cold.

Possible Adverse Effects   See above.

Information for Women Who Are Pregnant or Nursing   * * *

Plant/Drug Interactions   * * *

HOW TO USE THIS PLANT

In Cooking   Elderberries appear in late summer when the flowers die. To harvest and prepare fresh berries, chill or freeze an entire elder branch, then shake the berries off into a large bowl and rinse to remove dust and insects.

Elderberries may be cooked alone or used to add a spicy tartness to other fruit dishes such as apple pie, or to make a tasty jam. Dried elderberries can be steeped in boiling water (remember: the berries must be cooked) for a strongly fruity tea.

Ephedra

ABOUT THIS PLANT

Botanical name(s): Ephedra sinica
Common name(s): Ma huang
Native to: China, India
Parts used as food/drink: * * *
GRAS list: No
Medicinal properties: Bronchodilator, central nervous system stimulant
Other uses: * * *

ABOUT THIS PLANT AS FOOD OR DRINK

Ephedra plants are evergreen bushes native to China and India. The shrubs, which smell like pine, have small yellowish flowers and fruit. Ephedra is never used in food but may be found in some herbal teas or supplements.

Nutritional Profile * * *

HOW THIS PLANT AFFECTS YOUR BODY

Important Phytochemicals The pharmacologically active ingredients in ephedra are the central nervous system stimulants ephedrine and pseudoephedrine. Note: The only ephedra species used as food is an American variety, *Ephedra nevadensis,* also known as Mormon tea or desert tea. Mormon tea does not contain either ephedrine or pseudoephedrine, but it is very high in astringent tannins that may be irritating to the stomach.

Benefits Pseudoephedrine is widely used as a decongestant (a drug that shrinks swollen tissues) in over-the-counter cold and allergy medication. In 1991, the German Commission E approved the use of ephedra preparations to relieve mild bronchial spasms. In approving the use of ephedra products, the commission cautioned against their use by people with anxiety disorders, high blood pressure, reduced blood circulation in the brain, prostate disorders including prostate cancer, and thyroid disorders.

Possible Adverse Effects The adverse effects of ephedrine and pseudoephedrine may include insomnia, restlessness, irritability; nausea and vomiting; urinary difficulties; chemical dependence and psychosis; seizures; abnormal heartbeat, and heart attack culminating in death.

In the past several years, there have been more more than 800 reports of illness and at least 17 deaths among people taking supplements containing ephedra. As a result, several states have restricted its sale. In 1997, the U.S. Food and Drug Administration proposed mandatory warning labels for supplements containing ephedrine and moved to lower the amount of ephedrine permitted per dose to 8 mg. However, data from a number of studies released in 1999 showed that ephedrine did not begin to produce adverse effects in doses lower than 20 mg. As a result, the General Accounting Office (GAO) concluded that while the FDA was correct in trying to regulate the use of ephedra and ephedrine, the permissible dose should be set higher than 8 mg. New proposals are expected from the FDA.

Information for Women Who Are Pregnant or Nursing   * * *

Plant/Drug Interactions   If you are taking any medication, particularly medication for depression, heart disease or high blood pressure, consult your doctor before using any ephedra product.

Taking ephedra along with a monoamine oxidase (MAO) inhibitor antidepressant may intensify the side effects of the ephedra. Ephedra taken with certain heart medications or the anesthetic halothane may cause irregular heartbeat. Using an ephedra product along with the antihypertensive drug guanethidine may cause high blood pressure.

HOW TO USE THIS PLANT   * * *

Eucalyptus

ABOUT THIS PLANT

Botanical name(s): *Eucalyptus globulis*
Common name(s): Blue gum, fever tree, gum tree
Native to: Australia
Parts used as food/drink: Dried leaves
GRAS list: No
Medicinal properties: Expectorant, mild antispasmodic
Other uses: Pharmaceutical flavoring, roach repellent, perfumery

ABOUT THIS PLANT AS FOOD OR DRINK

Eucalyptus, a member of the myrtle family, is an evergreen with blue-green leaves. It is one of the world's tallest trees, sometimes growing as high as 250 feet with a large root network that soaks up water so efficiently that eucalyptus trees can actually drain swampy land, thus destroying the marsh that harbors mosquitoes and reducing the incidence of malaria—and accounting for the eucalyptus nickname "fever tree."

Dried eucalyptus leaves are often available as tea bags in health food stores.

Caution: Pure eucalyptus oil, sold in some health food, perfume or cosmetics stores, is poisonous. It is meant only for external use in perfumery or steam vaporizer products.

Nutritional Profile * * *

HOW THIS PLANT AFFECTS YOUR BODY

Important Phytochemicals   Eucalyptus leaves get their flavor and aroma from eucalyptus oil (also known as eucalyptol), cineole, or cajepuyol. Eucalyptol, a spicy, camphor-scented oil also found in BASIL, BAY LEAVES, CARDAMOM, and CLOVES, is an expectorant (a substance that liquefies mucus) and a secretory (a substance than causes mucous membranes to secrete liquid). Both effects make it easier to cough up and expel mucus.

Benefits   In 1986 and 1990, German Commission E approved the use of infusions of chopped, dried eucalyptus leaves and eucalyptus oil to relieve congestion caused by upper respiratory infections. In both cases, it cautioned against the use of these products for people with liver disease or inflammation of the gastrointestinal tract or bile duct. In addition, it warned that eucalyptus preparations—which give off potentially irritating vapors—should never be applied to the face, especially of young people and babies.

Possible Adverse Effects Nausea, vomiting, and diarrhea (rare).

Information for Women Who Are Pregnant or Nursing * * *

Plant/Drug Interactions Eucalyptus products may interact indirectly with medications because eucalyptus oil increases the production of liver enzymes used to metabolize and eliminate medical drugs. As a result, using eucalyptus products may weaken the activity of drugs metabolized and excreted through the liver. If you are taking any medication, check with your doctor before using eucalyptus products.

HOW TO USE THIS PLANT

Around the House During the 1980s, several reports suggested that eucalyptol might repel cockroaches, but the results have still not been documented. You may run your own experiments by scattering tea bags containing eucalyptus leaves under the sink or in the back of kitchen cabinets, out of reach of children and pets.

Evening Primrose

ABOUT THIS PLANT

Botanical name(s): Oenothera biennis
Common name(s): Evening star, night willow
Native to: North America
Parts used as food/drink: * * *
GRAS list: No
Medicinal properties: * * *
Other uses: * * *

ABOUT THIS PLANT AS FOOD OR DRINK

The evening primrose, which grows across Canada as well as in the southern and northwestern regions of the United States, is a tall herb with bright yellow flowers and a hairy stem that may reach six feet.

Native Americans once used the plant as food. The oil pressed from its seeds is used as a food ingredient in some parts of the world and as a dietary supplement in many Western countries.

Nutritional Profile   * * *

HOW THIS PLANT AFFECTS YOUR BODY

Important Phytochemicals   Evening primrose seed oil is rich in gamma-linolenic acid (GLA) and cis-linoleic acid, two fatty acids the body uses to make hormones.

During the 1980s, many claims were made for evening primrose's ability to ameliorate medical conditions such as premenstrual syndrome (PMS), prevent heart disease, reduce cholesterol levels, lower blood pressure, and alleviate itching associated with some inflammatory skin disorders. However, the results of clinical trials are controversial, and there is no definitive proof that the oil actually works.

In 1997, evening primose oil was the eighth best-selling herbal supplement in food, drug, and mass market retail stores in the United States, behind GINKGO BILOBA, GINSENG, GARLIC, ECHINACEA, ST. JOHN'S WORT, SAW PALMETTO, and grapeseed extract.

Benefits   * * *

Possible Adverse Effects   Evening primrose oil may increase the risk of seizures.

Information for Women Who Are Pregnant or Nursing * * *

Plant/Drug Interactions   The herb should not be used by people taking anti-seizure medication or medication for schizophrenia.

HOW TO USE THIS PLANT   * * *

Fennel

ABOUT THIS PLANT

Botanical name(s): *Foeniculum vulgare*
Common name(s): Florence fennel, garden fennel, sweet fennel
Native to: Europe, Asia
Parts used as food/drink: Leaves, dried ripe fruit ("seeds")
GRAS list: Yes
Medicinal properties: Carminative, expectorant
Other uses: Anticough ingredient, pharmaceutical/cosmetic fragrance

ABOUT THIS PLANT AS FOOD OR DRINK

Fennel is a tall plant related to CARAWAY. It has small green or yellow-brown fruit ("seeds") that look like tiny watermelons but taste like LICORICE or ANISE.

Sweet fennel oil, the flavoring in fennel, is used to flavor liqueurs, candy, pickles, condiments, sausages such as pepperoni and cappicola, and products such as mouthwash.

Nutritional Profile   One teaspoon (2 g) fennel seed has 7 calories. It provides 0.3 g protein, 0.3 g fat, 1.1 g carbohydrates, 0.8 g dietary fiber, 3 IU vitamin A, 0.4 mg vitamin C, 24 mg calcium, 0.4 mg iron, and 2 mg sodium.

One tablespoon (6 g) fennel seed has 20 calories. It provides 0.9 g protein, 0.9 g fat, 3 g carbohydrates, 2.3 g dietary fiber, 1.2 mg vitamin C, 8 IU vitamin A, 69 mg calcium, 1.1 mg iron, and 5 mg sodium.

One cup sliced raw fennel bulb has 27 calories, 1.1 g protein, 0.2 g fat, 6.3 g carbohydrates, 2.7 g dietary fiber, 117 IU vitamin A, 10.4 mg vitamin C, 42.6 mg calcium, 0.7 mg iron, and 52 mg sodium.

HOW THIS PLANT AFFECTS YOUR BODY

Important Phytochemicals   Oil of fennel is mostly (50–60 percent) anethole, plus anisaldehyde and anisic acid, licorice-flavored and -scented compounds also found in anise. Other aroma compounds in fennel oil are camphor-scented fenchone, turpentine-scented pinene, and lemon-scented limonene and dipentene.

Anethole and fenchone are irritants. Recent studies suggest that they stimulate the secretion of fluids from the mucous membrane lining of the nose and throat.

Limonene is a photosensitizer, a substance that makes your skin more sensitive to sunlight and increases the risk of sunburn, particularly in fair-skinned people.

Benefits   In 1991, the German Commission E approved the use of fennel seed teas and syrups to relieve gastrointestinal spasms and help expel intestinal gas. In addition, it approved the use of fennel seeds and fennel oil syrups and honey to relieve congestion associated with upper respiratory infections, but cautioned against the use of fennel for more than a few weeks without the approval of a physician.

Possible Adverse Effects   Handling the fennel plant may (rarely) cause contact dermatitis (itching, burning, stinging, reddened, or blistered skin), allergic rhinitis (sneezing, runny nose, itchy eyes), or photosensitivity.

Information for Women Who Are Pregnant or Nursing   * * *

Plant/Drug Interactions   * * *

HOW TO USE THIS PLANT

In Cooking   In baking, you can substitute fennel seeds for anise seed. Grilling fish over a fire built of fennel twigs scents the meat with a delicate licorice flavor and aroma. Use only unsprayed plants.

As a Home Remedy   To brew a fennel tea from fennel seed, crush 5 to 7 g seeds and steep in boiling water for approximately five minutes, then strain and serve.

Fenugreek

ABOUT THIS PLANT

Botanical name(s): Trigonella foenum-graecum
Common name(s): Greek hay seed, trigonella
Native to: Southern Europe
Parts used as food/drink: Seeds
GRAS list: Yes
Medicinal properties: Appetite stimulant, mild antiseptic, blood flow stimulant
Other uses: Fabric dye

ABOUT THIS PLANT AS FOOD OR DRINK

Fenugreek is a member of the pea family, producing pods with up to 20 aromatic seeds apiece. Ground fenugreek seeds are used in CURRY POWDERs or to flavor imitation MAPLE SYRUP. Whole fenugreek seeds are added to CHUTNEYs. Vegetarians, particularly in the Middle East, often boil whole fenugreek seeds to serve as a high-protein main dish. Fenugreek tea bags are available at health food stores.

Note: Like raw beans, raw fenugreek seeds contain antinutrient compounds that inactivate trypsin and chymotrypsin, enzymes you need to digest proteins. Cooking inactivates the antinutrients and makes the seeds safe to eat.

Nutritional Profile   3.5 ounces (100 g) fenugreek seeds has 323 calories. It provides 23 g protein, 6.4 g fat, 58.3 g carbohydrates, 24.6 g dietary fiber, 60 IU vitamin A, 3 mg vitamin C, 175.6 mg calcium, 33.5 mg iron, and 67.2 mg sodium.

One tablespoon (11 g) fenugreek seeds has 36 calories. It provides 2.6 g protein, 0.7 g fat, 6.5 g carbohydrates, 2.7 g dietary fiber, 7 IU vitamin A, 0.3 mg vitamin C, 19 mg calcium, 3.7 mg iron, and 7 mg sodium.

One teaspoon (4 g) fenugreek seeds has 12 calories. It provides 0.9 g protein, 0.2 g fat, 2.2 g carbohydrates, 0.9 g dietary fiber, no vitamin A, 0.1 mg vitamin C, 6 mg calcium, 1.2 mg iron, and 2 mg sodium.

HOW THIS PLANT AFFECTS YOUR BODY

Important Phytochemicals   Fenugreek seeds are high (40 percent) in mucilage, a soothing emollient sometimes used as an emulsifier in drugs and food.

Fenugreek seeds contain diosgenin, a plant steroid found primarily in Central and South American yams. Diosgenin, which can be converted to pregnenolone (a steroid formed during the synthesis of hormones), is used as a source of progestins for oral contraceptives.

Benefits   Bitter compounds in fenugreek appear to stimulate the production of stomach acid; they may also act as mild antiseptics and improve blood flow. In 1990, the German Commission E approved the use of fenugreek as an appetite stimulant and as an ingredient in external products such as liniments, ointments, oils, and gels that can be applied to local inflammations or added to the bathwater.

Like legumes (beans and peas), nuts, and other seeds, fenugreek seeds are a high-protein food. While the small amounts of fenugreek used as a spice add only negligible amounts of protein to your diet, 3.5 ounces (100 g) uncooked fenugreek seeds provide 23 g protein, precisely the same amount you get from a 3 to 3.5–ounce serving of meat, fish, or poultry.

Fenugreek seeds contain trigonelline, a nitrogen compound found in many legumes. When trigonelline is heated or comes in contact with acids such as tomatoes or wine, it yields nicotinic acid (niacin), the B vitamin that prevents pellagra. 3.5 ounces fenugreek seeds provides 1.6 mg niacin (12 percent of the RDA for a woman, 9 percent of the RDA for a man).

Possible Adverse Effects   Repeated use of fenugreek as a skin dressing may be irritating.

Information for Women Who Are Pregnant or Nursing   Early reports (1969) suggested that extract of fenugreek might stimulate uterine contractions. These have not shown up in later reports. Today, some experts say to avoid fenugreek while nursing; the American Academy of Pediatrics considers it safe.

Plant/Drug Interactions   * * *

HOW TO USE THIS PLANT   * * *

Filé (Sassafras)

ABOUT THIS CONDIMENT

Botanical name(s): *Sassafras albidum*
Common name(s): Gumbo filé
Native to: United States
Parts used as food/drink: Leaves
GRAS list: No
Medicinal properties: * * *
Other uses: * * *

ABOUT THIS CONDIMENT AS FOOD OR DRINK

Filé, which is used to season Creole and Cajun dishes, is composed of dried sassafras leaves, the flavoring once used in root beer and the original chicle gum patented by Thomas Adams in 1871.

Nutritional Profile * * *

HOW THIS CONDIMENT AFFECTS YOUR BODY

Important Phytochemicals The most important flavoring agent in sassafras leaves is safrole, also found in miniscule quantities in BASIL, PEPPER (BLACK), and NUTMEG. Sassafras root bark also contains anethole, also found in ANISE and FENNEL, plus eugenol, the chief flavoring in oil of cloves; and ginger-flavored asarone.

Safrole is an irritant, a known carcinogen that causes liver tumors in laboratory rats and mice. In large doses it is an hallucinogenic. Only safrole-free sassafras leaves and sassafras extract are approved for use in food in the United States.

Benefits * * *

Possible Adverse Effects Handling sassafras leaves may cause contact dermatitis, (itching, burning, stinging, reddened, or blistered skin).

Information for Women Who Are Pregnant or Nursing * * *

Condiment/Drug Interactions * * *

HOW TO USE THIS PLANT

In Cooking   Sassafras leaves are high in mucilage, a culinary thickener.

To approximate (but not quite match) filé's flavor, combine equal parts ground ANISEED, CLOVES, and GINGER. To avoid overseasoning, add the mixture carefully, a pinch at a time, tasting as you go.

Flaxseed

ABOUT THIS PLANT

Botanical name(s): Linum usitatissimum
Common name(s): Linseed, lint bells
Native to: Europe
Parts used as food/drink: Seeds
GRAS list: No
Medicinal properties: Laxative, emollient, demulcent
Other uses: Seeds: animal feed; Oil: varnishes, paints, artificial rubber, waterproofing products, flooring (linoleum), etc.; Fibers: fabric (linen)

ABOUT THIS PLANT AS FOOD OR DRINK

The tall, slender flax plant produces two foods: seeds and oil. The seeds may be added to salads or casseroles or milled into a meal that can be added to bread dough. The oil pressed from the seeds is often used in salad dressings. All three products—seeds, meal, oil—are generally available in health food stores.

Nutritional Profile   One cup (155 g) flaxseeds has 762 calories. It provides 30.2 g protein, 52.7 g fat (4.9 g saturated fatty acids, 34.7 g polyunsaturated fatty acids, 10.6 g monounsaturated fatty acids), 51.1 g carbohydrates, 43.2 g dietary fiber, 2.0 g vitamin C, 308.5 mg calcium, 9.6 mg iron, and 52.7 mg sodium.

One tablespoon flaxseeds has 59 calories. It provides 2.3 g protein, 4.1 g fat (0.4 g saturated fatty acids, 2.7 g polyunsaturated fatty acids, 0.8 g monounsaturated fatty acids), 4.1 g carbohydrates, 3.3 g dietary fiber, 0.2 mg vitamin C, 23.9 mg calcium, 0.7 mg iron, and 4.1 mg sodium.

One tablespoon flaxseed oil has 126 calories. It provides 14 g fat (1.3 g saturated fatty acids, 10.2 g polyunsaturated fatty acids 2.5 g monounsaturated fatty acids). Its polyunsaturated acids consist of 8 g omega-3 fatty acids and 1.6 g omega-6 fatty acids.

HOW THIS PLANT AFFECTS YOUR BODY

Important Phytochemicals   Flaxseeds are high in dietary fiber and unsaturated fatty acids, including the essential fatty acid linoleic acid. They are also rich in vitamin E, the natural antioxidant first identified as a substance vital for reproduction in rats. (Vitamin E is the collective name for a group of compounds known as *tocopherols*, from the Greek words *tokos* which means "offspring" and *pherein* which means "to bear").

Flaxseeds are an excellent source of lignans, a form of phytoestrogens (estrogen-like compounds in plants) most commonly found in grains. Ounce for ounce, flaxseed has 75 to 800 times more lignans than any other plant food. Bacteria in your gut digests plant lignans and produces "human lignans" called enterodiol (END) and enterolactone (ENL). END and ENL are weakly estrogenic compounds that link up with estrogen receptors in hormone-sensitive tissue such as the breast. Every lignan molecule that joins to an estrogen receptor prevents an estrogen molecule from attaching to the site, which may reduce the risk of estrogen-related cancers. Because human lignans are eliminated in urine, it impossible to estimate the amount of lignans your body makes by measuring the amount of lignans excreted. Generally, women on high-grain diets excrete higher amounts of lignans. In Finland (1982) and Australia (1997), studies of breast cancer patients and controls (women of the same age who do not have breast cancer) suggest that women excreting higher amounts of lignans have a lower risk of breast cancer. The question, though, is whether the lignans lower the risk of breast cancer or are simply a "marker" for some other risk-lowering factor such as individual metabolism.

Benefits Flaxseeds' dietary fiber builds stool bulk and stimulates contractions that move waste more quickly through the intestinal tract. Its outer coating of mucilage is an emollient (a substance that soothes irritated skin) and a demulcent (a substance that soothes irritated mucous membranes). In 1984, the German Commission E approved the use of whole or crushed (not ground) flaxseed to relieve chronic constipation, irritable colon, diverticulitis, gastritis, and enteritis. The commission also approved the use of ground flaxseed products as emollients and demulcents.

All vegetable oils are low in saturated fat and high in monounsaturated and polyunsaturated fatty acids, including omega-3 fatty acids, the polyunsaturates already credited with lowering your risk of heart disease. Your body converts alpha-linolenic acid, the most important omega-3, to hormone-like substances called eicosapentaenoic acid (EPA) and docosahexaenoic acid (DHA) which reduce inflammation, perhaps by inhibiting an enzyme named COX-2 which is linked to inflammatory diseases such as rheumatoid arthritis and skin cancer. According to the Arthritis Foundation, omega-3 fatty acids relieve joint inflammation in people with rheumatoid arthritis. Research at Purdue University suggests that they also prevent the natural breakdown of bone tissue and increase production of a bone-protecting growth factor that steps up new bone formation, at least in laboratory rats whose ovaries have been removed, cutting off their natural supply of bone-protecting estrogen (a condition analogous to menopause in women).

Possible Adverse Effects   * * *

Information for Women Who Are Pregnant or Nursing   * * *

Plant/Drug Interactions   While approving the use of flaxseed as a laxative, Commission E noted that mucilage may interfere with the absorption of other drugs. If you are taking other medication, check with your doctor before using a flaxseed product.

HOW TO USE THIS PLANT

In Cooking   To add a nutty flavor to yeast breads, mill whole flaxseeds in a clean coffee grinder and add the meal to your dough as a fat substitute, 3 parts flax meal for 1 part fat ($1^1/2$ cup milled flaxseed = $^1/2$ cup butter, margarine, shortening or oil).

Whole flaxseeds can be stored at room temperature for up to a year. Milled flaxseeds must be refrigerated or frozen in an airtight container; refrigerated flaxseed should be used within 30 days.

Garam Masala

ABOUT THIS CONDIMENT

Botanical name(s): ✳ ✳ ✳
Common name(s): Hot mixture
Native to: India
Parts used as food/drink: ✳ ✳ ✳
GRAS list: No
Medicinal properties: Diaphoretic, irritant
Other uses: ✳ ✳ ✳

ABOUT THIS CONDIMENT AS FOOD OR DRINK

Garam masala is a CUMIN-based mixture of ground spices that may include BLACK PEPPER, CHILI PEPPER, CARDAMOM, CINNAMON, CLOVES, and CORIANDER.

Nutritional Profile   See individual entries for these ingredients.

HOW THIS CONDIMENT AFFECTS YOUR BODY

Important Phytochemicals   Cumin is a potential irritant. So are peppers. Coriander helps expel intestinal gas. Peppers are diaphoretics, substances that increase perspiration. See individual entries for details.

Benefits   Hot spices such as those in garam masala promote perspiration which cools your body as the moisture evaporates on your skin. In addition, they irritate the mucous membranes lining your nose and throat, causing them to "weep" a watery secretion that makes it easier to cough up sticky mucus or clear your nose when you have a cold or hay fever.

Possible Adverse Effects   The oils in the spices that make up garam masala may irritate the lining of your stomach and bladder, causing gastric discomfort or frequent painful urination that mimics a urinary infection.

Information for Women Who Are Pregnant or Nursing   ✳ ✳ ✳

Condiment/Drug Interactions   ✳ ✳ ✳

HOW TO USE THIS CONDIMENT   ✳ ✳ ✳

Garlic

ABOUT THIS PLANT

Botanical name(s): *Allium sativum*

Common name(s): Allium, the "stinking rose"

Native to: Central Asia, southern Europe

Parts used as food/drink: Bulb

GRAS list: Yes

Medicinal properties: Antibacterial, antifungal, antihypertensive, anti–blood clotting agent, antiflatulent, cholesterol lowering agent

Other uses: * * *

ABOUT THIS PLANT AS FOOD OR DRINK

The garlic plant, with its long, flat, green leaves and white-to-pink flowers, is related to the ONION. The mildest member of the family is elephant garlic (*Allium scorodoprasum*), a cross between garlic and onions that can grow as large as a grapefruit.

Garlic is available fresh and as dried garlic chips (large pieces of dried garlic); minced garlic (small pieces of dried garlic); garlic powder (ground dried garlic plus an anticaking agent such as tricalcium phosphate, which keeps the garlic powder from absorbing moisture); and garlic salt (a mixture of ground garlic and SALT).

Nutritional Profile One clove (3 g) raw garlic has 4 calories. It provides 0.2 g protein, a trace of fat, 1 g carbohydrates, no dietary fiber, 0.9 mg vitamin C, 5 mg calcium, a trace of iron, and no sodium.

One tablespoon (8 g) garlic powder has 28 calories. It provides 1.4 g protein, 0.1 g fat, 6.1 g carbohydrates, 0.8 g dietary fiber, 1.5 mg vitamin C, 7 mg calcium, 0.2 mg iron, and 2 mg sodium.

One teaspoon (3 g) garlic powder has 9 calories. It provides 0.5 g protein, a trace of fat, 2 g carbohydrates, 0.3 g dietary fiber, 0.5 mg vitamin C, 2 mg calcium, 0.1 mg iron, and 1 mg sodium.

HOW THIS PLANT AFFECTS YOUR BODY

Important Phytochemicals Garlic's flavor comes from its pale yellow oil which contains the sulfur compound alliin. When you crush or slice a garlic clove, you tear its cell walls, releasing allinase, an enzyme that converts alliin to allicin.

Alliin and allicin are antibiotics, as shown in several laboratory studies in which garlic juice has slowed the growth of microorganisms (bacteria, yeasts, fungi) growing in test tubes.

Garlic also contains ajoene, a compound that may be as effective as aspirin in keeping blood platelets from clumping. Animal studies conducted during the 1980s in which garlic oil added to animal feeds reduced levels of low-density lipoproteins (LDLs), the "bad" fat and protein particles that carry cholesterol into your arteries, and raised levels of high density lipoproteins (HDLs), the "good" particles that carry cholesterol out of the body. Human studies in which subjects consume 10 cloves of garlic a day for one month have shown similar results as well as increases in the activity of anti-clotting substances in blood.

Other sulfur compounds in garlic include S-allycysteine (SAC), dially disulfide (DAD), and diallyl trisulfide (DATS) appear to slow the growth of cancer cells. Ordinarily, heating, dehydrating, or deodorizing garlic inactivates or removes the biologically active compounds in garlic oil. However, Penn State University researchers have found that chopping or crushing garlic and allowing it to stand for at least 10 minutes before cooking preserves its anticancer activity. And DATS—which is found in processed garlic oil as well as in raw garlic—stopped human lung, skin, and colon cancer cells from growing in a test tube.

Oil of garlic is an antiflatulent (an agent that helps break up and expel intestinal gas) and a rubefacient (a substance that irritates skin and dilates the tiny blood vessels right under the surface, increasing the flow of blood and making the skin feel warmer).

In 1997, garlic was the second best-selling herbal supplement in health food stores in the United States, behind ECHINACEA, and the third best-selling herbal supplement in food, drug, and mass market retail stores.

Benefits   Garlic is a low-calorie, low-fat, no-cholesterol, low-sodium food with lots of vitamins and minerals. For example, an ounce of raw garlic provides 0.07 mg thiamine (twice the amount in 3.5 oz egg white), 0.4 mg iron (2 percent of the RDA for an adult woman), and 4 mg vitamin C (7 percent of the RDA for a healthy adult), but we rarely eat enough garlic to get useful amounts of these nutrients. Note: While garlic is a naturally low in sodium, one teaspoon (6 g) garlic salt has 1,850 mg sodium.

In 1988, the German Commission E approved the use of fresh garlic (4 g per day) as an adjunct to a dietary regimen designed to lower blood cholesterol and prevent age-related changes in blood vessels. However, a 1999 review of eight long-term studies commissioned by the U.S. Agency for Healthcare Research and Quality showed no sustained effect on cholesterol levels.

Possible Adverse Effects   The most common side effect of eating garlic is bad breath caused by the sulfur compound diallyl disulfide, which is excreted in perspiration and in air exhaled from the lungs. Heating garlic destroys its diallyl disulfide, which is why cooked garlic is so much less smelly than raw garlic.

High doses of garlic oil may cause nausea, diarrhea, and vomiting. In rare cases, eating garlic may cause gastric upset due to changes in the bacteria living naturally in your gut; some people are allergic to garlic.

Information for Women Who Are Pregnant or Nursing   The smelly compounds in garlic may be excreted in breast milk.

Plant/Drug Interactions   In a paper delivered to the 1999 annual meeting of the American Society of Anesthesiologists, garlic was identified as one of several herbs including GINGER, GINKGO BILOBA and GINSENG, that may interfere with normal blood clotting. While this has benefits (see above), it may be a problem for people using blood-thinning drugs such as warfarin (Coumadin).

HOW TO USE THIS PLANT

In Cooking   To peel fresh garlic easily, drop the cloves in boiling water for 30 seconds, then drain, cool, and peel. Alternatively, you can put a head of fresh, raw garlic on a flat surface, flat side down, and hit it with the flat side of a knife. The cloves will separate, and the skin should come off easily.

To get the most flavor from fresh garlic, slice through the clove, releasing the odorous strongly flavored oil inside. Mash the cloves, chop them, or wring out the oil with a garlic press.

Store dehydrated garlic products in tightly closed containers to protect them from air and moisture which can cause the powder to clump together or turn the oil in dried garlic rancid.

In cooking, $1/4$ teaspoon garlic powder equals two small, fresh garlic cloves.

Gentian

ABOUT THIS PLANT

Botanical name(s): *Gentiana lutea*
Common name(s): Yellow gentian, bitter root
Native to: Central and southern Europe
Parts used as food/drink: Rhizomes, roots
GRAS list: No
Medicinal properties: Appetite stimulant, antiflatulent
Other uses: * * *

ABOUT THIS PLANT AS FOOD OR DRINK

Gentian is an ornamental plant native to Europe. It is grown commercially for its root and rhizomes (underground stems) which produce a bitter extract used in digestive tonics and in BITTERS.

You may find powdered gentian tea bags at your health food store. Occasionally—more often in Europe than in the United States—gentian is also sold as a dried root you can chop or crush to make your own tea powder.

Note: The gentian plant is not related to gentian violet, a synthetic dye once widely used as an antiseptic.

Nutritional Profile   * * *

HOW THIS PLANT AFFECTS YOUR BODY

Important Phytochemicals   The bitter flavor of gentian roots and rhizomes comes from amarogentin and gentipicroside, plus gentisic acid, an analgesic and antirheumatic compound related to salicylic acid—which is, in turn, a chemical cousin of acetylsalicylic acid (aspirin). The rhizomes also contain yellow pigments (gentisin, isogentisin, and gentioside), astringent tannins, soluble dietary fiber (pectin), and sugars such as sucrose.

Benefits   Like the mustard oils in MUSTARD, the bitter flavor chemicals in gentian stimulate the flow of saliva and digestive juices, triggering the gastric contractions we call hunger pangs. In 1985 and 1990, the German Commission E approved the use of infusions of dried, unfermented gentian roots and rhizomes as an appetite stimulant and to relieve intestinal gas.

Possible Adverse Effects   People sensitive to gentian may develop headaches after consuming the herb. In addition, gentian may irritate the lining of the intestinal tract; in approving the use of gentian products, Commission E cautioned against their use by people who have gastric or stomach ulcers.

Information for Women Who Are Pregnant or Nursing In 1979, one German herbal guide warned against the use of gentian by pregnant women; this warning is not substantiated in later reports.

Plant/Drug Interactions * * *

HOW TO USE THIS PLANT

In Cooking To make a tea with dried gentian root, bring 1 teaspoon chopped gentian root to a boil in 1 cup water, then simmer the liquid for about 15 minutes. Turn off the heat and let the root soak for another 5 minutes. Strain the cooled liquid and sweeten to taste with sugar or honey or add a mint leaf.

Geranium

ABOUT THIS PLANT

Botanical name(s): *Pelargonium graveolens*
Common name(s): Scented geraniums
Native to: South Africa
Parts used as food/drink: Leaves
GRAS list: Yes
Medicinal properties Insect repellent
Other uses: Perfumery, gardening

ABOUT THIS PLANT AS FOOD OR DRINK

Scented geraniums are popular for their small colorful flowers and a variety of aromas including some that resemble apple, CINNAMON, coconut, lemon, MINT, and ROSE. The fresh, edible leaves from scented geraniums can be used to make salads smell wonderful or to flavor desserts, baked goods, jellies, and jams.

Nutritional Profile * * *

HOW THIS PLANT AFFECTS YOUR BODY

Important Phytochemicals The aroma compounds in scented geraniums are irritants and potential allergens.

Benefits * * *

Possible Adverse Effects Prolonged handling of scented geraniums may cause contact dermatitis (itching, burning, stinging, reddened, or blistered skin) in sensitive people.

Information for Women Who Are Pregnant or Nursing * * *

Plant/Drug Interactions * * *

HOW TO USE THIS PLANT

In Cooking Rinse fresh scented geranium leaves thoroughly to remove dirt and debris. When they are dry, tear the leaves to release their oils.

To bake a scented cake, line the pan with the geranium leaves, then pour in the batter and bake as usual. To prepare a tea from geranium leaves, steep the fresh leaves in boiling water and flavor with fresh mint or lemon.

Around the House Dried scented geranium leaves are used to make sachets to scent your drawers and closets (they are also reputed to repel insects) and potpourris to scent your rooms.

In the Garden Like other citronella plants, geraniums may repel garden pests with a risk of poison.

Industrial Uses Scented geraniums are grown commercially for their fragrant oils, such as rose-scented geraniol, which is used in perfumery, and lemon-scented citronella, once widely employed as an insect repellent.

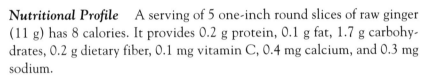

Ginger

ABOUT THIS PLANT

Botanical name(s): Zingiber officinale
Common name(s): Ginger root
Native to: Southern Asia
Parts used as food/drink: Rhizomes
GRAS list: Yes
Medicinal properties: Antiemetic
Other uses: Preservative

ABOUT THIS PLANT AS FOOD OR DRINK

Ginger is a distant relative of the banana. Its name comes from the Sanskrit word *singabera*, meaning "shaped like a horn." The spice is used in baked goods, chewing gum, and soft drinks, especially colas and ginger ale.

Nutritional Profile   A serving of 5 one-inch round slices of raw ginger (11 g) has 8 calories. It provides 0.2 g protein, 0.1 g fat, 1.7 g carbohydrates, 0.2 g dietary fiber, 0.1 mg vitamin C, 0.4 mg calcium, and 0.3 mg sodium.

One tablespoon (5 g) ground ginger has 19 calories. It provides 0.5 g protein, 0.3 g fat, 3.8 g carbohydrates, 0.7 g dietary fiber, 8 IU vitamin A, 0.4 mg vitamin C, 6 mg calcium, 0.6 mg iron, and 2 mg sodium.

One teaspoon (2 g) ground ginger has 6 calories. It provides 0.2 g protein, 0.1 g fat, 1.3 g carbohydrates, 0.2 g dietary fiber, 3 IU vitamin A, 0.1 mg vitamin C, 2 mg calcium, 0.2 mg iron, and 1 mg sodium.

HOW THIS PLANT AFFECTS YOUR BODY

Important Phytochemicals   Ginger's flavor and aroma come from its pungent yellow oil which contains spicy, sweet zingerone; mint-flavored, peppery-scented borneol; camphor-scented eucalyptol; and lemon-scented citral, the dominant flavoring agent in light yellow Indian ginger.

Zingerone, borneol, eucalyptol, and citral are irritants. Like the piperine in BLACK PEPPER and the capsaicin in RED PEPPER, zingerone irritates skin, dilating small blood vessels just under the surface so that more blood flows into the area and the skin feels warmer. Zingerone also irritates the mucous membrane lining of the nose and throat, causing them to "weep" watery secretions which can make it easier to blow your nose or cough up mucus when you have a cold.

Ginger not only adds flavor to food, it may also act as an antioxidant, slowing the rate at which fats combine with oxygen and turn rancid. In 1986 researchers at the University of California at Davis added extract of freshly ground ginger root to salted pork patties, then cooked and refrigerated or froze the patties. The fats in the gingered pork patties turned rancid at a slower rate than the fats in patties that had been prepared without ginger. The more ginger there was in the patty, the slower the rate of the rancidity reaction.

In 1997, ginger was the 18th best-selling herbal supplement in health food stores in the United States.

Benefits   In 1982, researchers at Brigham Young University in Provo, Utah, ran a controlled study with 26 student volunteers which strongly suggests that ginger helps prevent motion sickness. The volunteers were given either two capsules of the antinausea drug Dramamine or two capsules of powdered ginger or two look-alike capsules (placebos) and then spun in a motorized chair for six minutes. If the volunteers got sick or asked the researchers to stop, the test was ended. None of the students who had been given either Dramamine or the placebo capsules were able to remain in the chair for the whole six minutes. Half the students who got the ginger capsules did make it through to the end; those who asked to stop the test lasted longer than any of the students given Dramamine or the placebo.

In 1988 and 1990, the German Commission E approved the use of chopped ginger, ginger teas brewed from dry extract, and other ginger preparations to relieve upset stomach and prevent motion sickness. In its approval, the commission cautioned against the use of ginger by people with gallstones unless prescribed by a physician.

Possible Adverse Effects   In a paper delivered to the 1999 annual meeting of the American Society of Anesthesiologists, ginger was identified as one of several herbs including GARLIC, GINKGO BILOBA, and GINSENG, that may interfere with normal blood clotting. In addition, some people find gingered food irritating to the stomach.

Information for Women Who Are Pregnant or Nursing   Based on two studies published in the 1980s showing that a compound isolated from ginger caused changes in body cells, some herbal medicine experts caution against the use of ginger by pregnant women. However, in a 1991 paper published in the *European Journal of Obstetrics*, 70 percent of the women in the study felt better after taking ginger rather than a placebo. In approving the use of ginger to prevent nausea and motion sickness, Commission E noted the concerns regarding ginger during pregnancy, but said that a review of published reports did not justify the caution.

Plant/Drug Interactions   Ginger should not be used if you are taking anti-inflammatory drugs or anticoagulants ("blood thinners").

HOW TO USE THIS PLANT

In Cooking Ginger is available fresh or preserved, ground to a powder or in large pieces known as "hands."

One-half teaspoon ground ginger equals 1–2 teaspoons chopped fresh ginger. Rinsed preserved ginger can be substituted in equal amounts for fresh ginger.

Choose fresh ginger with smooth skin. If the skin is wrinkled, the root may be dried out. Like garlic, ginger turns milder when cooked. If burned, it becomes bitter.

To make "pink ginger," the garnish commonly served in Japanese restaurants, buy very young ginger roots, peel or scrape away the skin, slice the ginger very thin, dip it in lemon juice and season with salt. The lemon juice will turn the peeled, sliced ginger root pink.

In the Garden Ginger rhizomes can be potted, so you can grow your own ginger plants in your kitchen. When the roots are ready, simply reach in, pull them out and slice or grate to use in cooking.

Ginkgo Biloba

ABOUT THIS PLANT

Botanical name(s): *Ginkgo biloba*
Common name(s): Maidenhair tree, kew tree, Ya-chio
Native to: China
Parts used as food/drink: Nut
GRAS list: No
Medicinal properties: Blood flow enhancer
Other uses: * * *

ABOUT THIS PLANT AS FOOD OR DRINK

If the ginkgo were an animal rather than a plant, you could call it a surviving dinosaur. It is the only living member of a family of the Ginkgoaceae, a family of trees that once dominated the forests of the Northern Hemisphere. The Chinese think ginkgo leaves look like duck's feet (Ya-chio), so that's what they call the tree.

The ginkgo fruit, which has a remarkably unpleasant smell, is wrapped around the ginkgo nut, which is actually the ginkgo seed. Americans do not consider the ginkgo a food plant; the Japanese, however, roast the oval, cream-colored, half-inch-long ginkgo nuts and serve them as a delicacy called *silvernuts* at weddings and other celebrations.

Note: Raw ginkgo fruit contains toxic substances, including ginkgolic acid, which are inactivated by heat. The ginkgo nut is edible only when cooked.

Nutritional Profile   One ounce (28 g) dried ginkgo nuts has 99 calories. It provides 3 g protein, 0.6 g fat, 0.3 g dietary fiber, 311 IU vitamin A, 8.4 mg vitamin C, 5.7 mg calcium, 0.5 mg iron, and 3.7 mg sodium.

HOW THIS PLANT AFFECTS YOUR BODY

Important Phytochemicals   The fruit, leaf, and bark of the ginkgo tree contain flavonoids including quercitin (also found in red wine) and a family of bioactive compounds called ginkgolides that improve blood flow and relieve symptoms associated with blocked blood vessels in the brain, arms, and legs.

In 1997, ginkgo biloba was the third best-selling herbal supplement in health food stores in the United States, behind ECHINACEA and GARLIC, and the best-selling herbal supplement in food, drug, and mass market retail stores.

Benefits   In Asian medicine, ginkgo nuts and ginkgo leaves are used to treat asthma and vascular disorders. In 1994, German Commission E approved the use of products containing extract of ginkgo leaf to treat memory loss, inability to concentrate, dizziness, headache, and ringing in the ears associated with organic brain disease (dementia). The herb is also approved as a treatment for leg pain or dizziness and ringing in the ears cause by blocked blood vessels.

In the United States, a 1997 study reported in the *Journal of the American Medical Association* found some mild improvement in memory and mental performance among dementia patients given ginkgo biloba. At the National Institutes of Health Center for Complementary and Alternative Medicine, a five-year study is in progress to see whether the herb can reduce the risk of dementia or improve memory in healthy people.

Possible Adverse Effects   Handling or consuming ginkgo biloba may cause headache, upset stomach, or allergic skin reactions. Ginko biloba may slow blood clotting.

Information for Women Who Are Pregnant or Nursing   In 1999, researchers at Loma Linda University School of Medicine (California) incubated hamster eggs for one hour in concentrations of ginkgo biloba containing $1/1,000$ to $1/100$ the amount of ginkgo biloba customarily found in over-the-counter products. When they added human sperm to the dish, they found that the herb damaged the sperms' outer membrane, reducing its ability to penetrate and fertilize the eggs. There is little information as to whether a nursing infant will experience coagulation problems if his/her mother takes ginko biloba.

Plant/Drug Interactions   Ginko biloba should not be used if you are taking anticoagulants ("blood thinners"). It may also interact with monoamine oxidase (MAO) inhibitors (a group of antidepressant drugs).

HOW TO USE THIS PLANT   * * *

Ginseng

ABOUT THIS PLANT

Botanical name(s): *Panax ginseng* (Asian ginseng), *Eleuthero senticosus* (Siberian ginseng), *Panax quinquefolius* (American ginseng)

Common name(s): Asian ginseng: Chinese ginseng, Japanese ginseng, Korean ginseng; Siberian ginseng: Eleuthera, pepperbush; American Ginseng: Western ginseng

Native to: Eastern Asia, northern Europe, eastern North America

Parts used as food/drink: * * *

GRAS list: No

Medicinal properties: Energy booster

Other uses: * * *

ABOUT THIS PLANT AS FOOD OR DRINK

In health food parlance, the term *ginseng* usually refers either to Asian ginseng or to Siberian ginseng. The first is a slow-growing perennial herb whose botanical name, *Panax*, comes from the Greek word for healing (as in *panacea*). The second is a shrub found in Russian and Asian forests. A third ginseng plant, American ginseng (*Panax quinquefolius*) is less well known.

The licorice-flavored ginseng root may be used on its own as an herbal tea or in small amounts as a flavoring agent in honeys or other herbal teas.

Nutritional Profile   One-half ounce (14 g) dried Asian ginseng has 39 calories, 1.6 g protein, 0.3 g fat, 1 g dietary fiber, a trace of vitamin A, 41 mg calcium, a trace of iron.

HOW THIS PLANT AFFECTS YOUR BODY

Important Phytochemicals   The active ingredients in the Asian ginseng root and American ginseng are steroid-like plant compounds called ginsenosides. The active ingredients in the Siberian ginseng root are lignans, members of a group of naturally occurring steroid compounds in plants called phytoestrogens (*phyto* means "plant") that can produce effects similar to those of the female sex hormone estrogen.

In 1997, ginseng as a class was the second best-selling herbal supplement in food, drug, and mass market stores in the United States, right behind GINKGO BILOBA. On its own, Asian ginseng was tied with ALOE as the sixth best-selling herbal supplement in health food stores.

Benefits   In 1991, the German Commission E approved the use of teas and preparations made from dried Asian or Siberian ginseng root as a tonic to relieve fatigue, improve concentration, and speed convalescence.

Possible Adverse Effects   In approving the use of ginseng, German Commission E cautioned against the use of Siberian ginseng for people with high blood pressure.

In a paper delivered to the 1999 annual meeting of the American Society of Anesthesiologists, ginseng was identified as one of several herbs including GARLIC, GINGER, and GINKGO BILOBA, that may interfere with normal blood clotting. In addition, there have been some reports of drowsiness after taking ginseng. People sensitive to one ginseng variety are likely to be sensitive to the others.

Information for women who are pregnant or nursing   All forms of ginseng should be avoided during pregnancy or lactation.

Plant/Drug Interactions   Ginseng may interact with monoamine oxidose (MAO) inhibitors (a group of antidepressants), anticoogulants ("blood thinners"), the heart medication digitalis, and all drugs processed in the body by the enzyme CYP 3A-4 (check with your doctor or pharmacist).

HOW TO USE THIS PLANT   * * *

Grenadine

ABOUT THIS CONDIMENT

Botanical name(s): * * *
Common name(s): * * *
Native to: Caribbean region
Parts used as food/drink: * * *
GRAS list: No
Medicinal properties: * * *
Other uses: * * *

ABOUT THIS PLANT AS FOOD OR DRINK

Grenadine is a sweet red syrup originally made from pomegranates grown on the island of Grenada in the Caribbean. Today, red currants and other fruits are used to make this low- or no-alcohol liquid that adds color and sweetness to mixed drinks such as the rum-based mai-tai or the tequila-based tequila sunrise, also made with orange juice. The grenadine, which is heavier than tequila or orange juice, sinks to the bottom of the glass, creating what some people thinks looks like a rising red sun, hence the name.

Nutritional Profile * * *

HOW THIS CONDIMENT AFFECTS YOUR BODY

Important Phytochemicals The only meaningful nutrient in grenadine is sugar. Grenadine contains so little alcohol and so little grenadine is used as flavoring that any alcohol-related effects are due to the primary ingredient (i.e. rum or tequila) in a grenadine-flavored drink.

Benefits * * *

Possible Adverse Effects Grenadine may be on the restricted list for people on a low-sugar or low-carbohydrate diet.

Information for Women Who Are Pregnant or Nursing * * *

Plant/Drug Interactions * * *

HOW TO USE THIS CONDIMENT * * *

Guarana

ABOUT THIS PLANT

Botanical name(s): *Paullinia cupana*
Common name(s): Brazilian cocoa, zoom
Native to: South America
Parts used as food/drink: Seeds
GRAS list: No
Medicinal properties: Stimulant, diuretic
Other uses: * * *

ABOUT THIS PLANT AS FOOD OR DRINK

Guarana is a chocolate-scented paste made of crushed seeds from the *Paullina cupana* plant. The paste is powdered and used as the base for a number of beverages including a soft drink that is as popular in Brazil as colas are in the United States. One guarana soft drink (Bawls) has been introduced in the United States, but Americans are more likely to use guarana as a stimulating herbal tea than as a soft drink (see below).

Nutritional Profile * * *

HOW THIS PLANT AFFECTS YOUR BODY

Important Phytochemicals Guarana contains four important stimulants. The first is caffeine; guarana has about as much caffeine per ounce as do roasted coffee beans. The second is theine, the stimulant in dried tea leaves. The third is theobromine, the muscle stimulant in cocoa beans. The fourth is guaranine, found only in guarana.

Guarana is also high in tannins, bitter astringents that coagulate proteins on the surface of your skin or the mucous membrane lining of your mouth, causing the tissues to pucker so that when you eat or drink a food or beverage high in tannins, you experience a "cool" or "fresh" sensation. In folk medicine, high-tannin plants are commonly used as a remedy for diarrhea.

Brazilians use guarana primarily to boost energy, suppress appetite, alleviate the pain of headache and arthritis, and to increase urination. These are all caffeine-related effects. Guarana is also used to treat chronic diarrhea, a tannin-related effect.

Guarana is an approved food ingredient.

Benefits Caffeine increases alertness and concentration, intensifies muscle responses, speeds up heartbeat and elevates mood. It is often combined with analgesics in over-the-counter painkillers. In addition, caffeine dilates systemic blood vessels and constricts cerebral blood vessels, which may explain guarana's ability to relieve headaches caused by engorged blood vessels. Caffeine dilates the coronary arteries and increases the coronary blood flow, but it also speeds up heartbeat; medical opinion is divided as to whether heart patients should drink beverages containing caffeine or caffeine-like stimulants.

Caffeine's mild diuretic effect may account for its usefulness in over-the-counter remedies for premenstrual tension or menstrual discomfort.

Possible Adverse Effects   Excess consumption of guarana may cause insomnia and/or jittery or nervous behavior.

Information for Women Who Are Pregnant or Nursing   * * *

Plant/Drug Interactions   * * *

HOW TO USE THIS PLANT   * * *

Hawthorn

ABOUT THIS PLANT

Botanical name(s): *Crataegus monogyna*
Common name(s): English hawthorn, maybush, whitethorn
Native to: Europe
Parts used as food/drink: Leaves and flowers
GRAS list: No
Medicinal properties: Cardiac stimulant
Other uses: Hardwood products

ABOUT THIS PLANT AS FOOD OR DRINK

The hawthorn is a member of the rose family, a stout-branched tree native to Europe but now growing wild throughout North America. Its leaves and flowers are used in herbal teas.

Nutritional Profile   * * *

HOW THIS PLANT AFFECTS YOUR BODY

Important Phytochemicals   Hawthorn leaves and flowers are rich in flavonoids such as hyperoside, rutin, vitexin, and vitexinrhamnose. Flavonoids are naturally occurring antioxidants that prevent molecular fragments circulating in your body from joining to form potentially damaging molecules. Hawthorn also contains substances called catechins which appear to dilate blood vessels, including the vessels leading from the heart, and to enhance the pumping action of the heart.

Benefits   In 1994, the German Commission E validated hawthorn's long folk history as a heart "tonic" that benefits the circulatory system: The commission approved the use of preparations containing extract of dried flowering hawthorn twig tips as a treatment for heart failure. (It did not approve use of the hawthorn berry because there is no scientific proof of the berry's effectiveness.)

  Caution: Despite its history as a folk remedy, hawthorn extract is potent medicine that should be used only with medical supervision.

Possible Adverse Effects   * * *

Information for Women Who Are Pregnant or Nursing   * * *

Plant/Drug Interactions   If you are currently taking heart medication, inform your doctor before using any hawthorn product.

HOW TO USE THIS PLANT   * * *

Hibiscus

ABOUT THIS PLANT

Botanical name(s): *Hibiscus sabdariffa, Hibiscus rosa-sinensis*

Common name(s): Jamaica sorrel, Jamaica tea, red tea, roselle, Sudanese tea; China rose, Chinese hibiscus

Native to: Africa, India

Parts used as food/drink: Calyx, flowers

GRAS list: No

Medicinal properties: * * *

Other uses: Fiber

ABOUT THIS PLANT AS FOOD OR DRINK

The hibiscus is a tall tropical plant with brilliant red flowers whose petals, collected before they mature, are used to give a tart crisp flavor to jams, jellies, and beverages including herbal teas.

Nutritional Profile One ounce (28 g) hibiscus leaves has 12 calories. It provides 0.9 g protein, a trace of fat, 2.6 g carbohydrates. 0.5 g dietary fiber, 1,181 IU, 15 mg vitamin C, 60.8 mg calcium, and 1.4 mg iron.

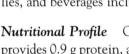

HOW THIS PLANT AFFECTS YOUR BODY

Important Phytochemicals The flavor of hibiscus leaves comes from plant acids including citric acid (also found in citrus fruits), malic acid (also found in apples), oxalic acid (also found in spinach), and tartaric acid (also found in grapes).

Hibiscus rosa-sinensis petals are astringent. The calyxes (petals enclosing the fruit) of *Hibiscus sabdariffa* have been used in folk medicine as an appetite stimulant, a laxative, a diuretic, and to relieve the symptoms of the common cold, but there is no scientific evidence to back up these claims.

Benefits * * *

Possible Adverse Effects * * *

Information for Women Who Are Pregnant or Nursing * * *

Plant/Drug Interactions   In one 1994 study reported in the *Journal of Antimicrobial Chemotherapy*, taking hibiscus tea along with the antimalaria drug chloroquine made the medicine significantly less effective.

HOW TO USE THIS PLANT

Industrial Uses   *Hibiscus sabdariffa* is cultivated for the fiber derived from its stems.

Hops

ABOUT THIS PLANT

Botanical name(s): Humulus lupulus
Common name(s): Common hops
Native to: Europe, North America
Parts used as food/drink: Fruits
GRAS list: No
Medicinal properties: Calming agent, sleep promoter
Other uses: Aromatic stuffing for pillows; brewing

ABOUT THIS PLANT AS FOOD OR DRINK

The hop plant, a botanical cousin of marijuana, is a climbing vine that produces tiny flowers and cone-shaped fruit (the hops) which are covered with yellow hairs called lupulin, which contain the bitter resins and oils that give beer its characteristic flavors and aroma.

Nutritional Profile

HOW THIS PLANT AFFECTS YOUR BODY

Important Phytochemicals   The most important flavoring agents in hops are lupulone and humulone, bitter compounds with antibacterial activity. In laboratory studies, these compounds appear to be active against *Staphylococcus aureus*; during brewing, they may reduce bacteria active in the beer. Hops also contain an essential oil (oil of hops) of irritant compounds including myrcene, lavender-scented linalool, rose-scented geraniol and lemon-scented citral. And, like other fruits, they contain proteins, nitrogen compounds, sugars (fructose and glucose), and pectins. Small amounts of these nutrients are found in beer.

Benefits   Hops have a long-standing reputation as a sedative. Until 1916, they were listed in the U.S. Pharmacopoeia, and the U.S. Food and Drug Administration includes them on the list of herbs generally recognized as safe (GRAS). But not until 1983 was there any proof that eating (or drinking) hops caused to make you sleepy. That year, researchers identified a sedative compound—dimethyl carbinol (also known as 2-methyl-3-butene-2-ol)—in hops. In 1984 and again in 1990, German Commission E, approved the use of hops alone or in combination with other sedative drugs to relieve anxiety, restlessness, and sleep disorders.

Possible Adverse Effects   The pollen of hops is a respiratory allergen. It may also cause contact dermatitis (itching, burning, stinging, reddened, or blistered skin) in sensitive individuals who handle the plant. These reactions are most common among people working with hops. Some reports suggest that as many as one in every 30 workers harvesting hops suffers some skin irritation.

Information for Women Who Are Pregnant or Nursing   * * *

Plant/Drug Interactions   * * *

HOW TO USE THIS PLANT

Around the House   Throw pillows stuffed with dried hops smell good. Like hops themselves, they also enjoy a reputation in folk medicine as sleep aids, but there is no study to show that inhaling the scent of hops will put you to sleep although it may make you sneeze if you are sensitive to the hop plant.

Horehound

ABOUT THIS PLANT

Botanical name(s): Marrubium vulgare
Common name(s): Common horehound, white horehound
Native to: Europe, Asia
Parts used as food/drink: Leaves, stems, flowers
GRAS list: Yes
Medicinal properties: Choleretic, expectorant
Other uses: Candy

ABOUT THIS PLANT AS FOOD OR DRINK

Horehound is native to Europe and Asia but now grows wild in the United States, Canada, and Mexico. The apple-scented, bittersweet plant, a member of the mint family, is used to flavor candy and over-the-counter cold and cough remedies.

Horehound is available in tea bags and as a syrup.

Nutritional Profile   * * *

HOW THIS PLANT AFFECTS YOUR BODY

Important Phytochemicals   The flavoring agent in horehound is marrubiin, a bitter compound in the leaves and stems. Marrubiin is an expectorant, a substance that increases the secretion of watery liquids from the mucous membranes lining the throat and bronchial tubes, making it easier to cough up phlegm and mucus. Horehound leaves and stems are also high in mucilage, a demulcent that soothes irritated mucous membranes. As a result, horehound has long been used as a folk remedy for sore throat and as a cough medicine, but absent clinical studies, the U.S. Food and Drug Administration's Advisory Review Panel on Over-the-Counter Cold, Cough, Allergy, Bronchodilator and Anti-Asthmatic Products calls it "safe/not proven effective."

Marrubiin is also a choleretic, a substance that stimulates the liver to increase its production of bile, the yellow, brown, or green fluid that helps emulsify fats in your duodenum and increases peristalsis, the rhythmic contractions that move food through your gastrointestinal tract. Cholerretics are ordinarily beneficial for healthy people but may pose some problems for people with gallbladder or liver diseases.

Benefits   Like other bitter plants, horehound has often been used as an appetite stimulant. In 1990, the German Commission E approved the use of horehound preparations for this purpose and to relieve upset stomach, bloating, or intestinal gas.

Possible Adverse Effects   In very high doses, horehound is a strong laxative and may cause irregular heartbeat.

Information for Women Who Are Pregnant or Nursing   * * *

Plant/Drug Interactions   * * *

HOW TO USE THIS PLANT

In Cooking   To brew horehound tea, cover leaves and/or stems with water and simmer for 25 minutes, then strain the thickened liquid, and sweeten it with honey or sugar to taste. You can drink this as a warm tea or use it cool as a gargle.

Horseradish

ABOUT THIS PLANT

Botanical name(s): Armoracia rusticana
Common name(s): * * *
Native to: Europe
Parts used as food/drink: Roots
GRAS list: Yes
Medicinal properties: Antimicrobial, rubefacient
Other uses: * * *

ABOUT THIS PLANT AS FOOD OR DRINK

Horseradish is a cruciferous vegetable, a member of the cabbage family that includes broccoli, brussels sprouts, and cauliflower.

Horseradish is available fresh or as a prepared condiment. Wasabi, the pungent green Japanese horseradish, is available in Asian grocery stores as a powder or prepared paste.

Note: The "horseradish tree," *Moringa oleifera*, is an unrelated plant native to India and the Mediterranean. It has thick roots and pods sometimes used in curries and other dishes as a substitute for the more strongly flavored true horseradish.

Nutritional Profile   One ounce (29 g) raw horseradish has 29 calories. It provides 0.9 g protein, a trace of fat, 5.6 g carbohydrates, 40 mg calcium, 0.4 mg iron, and 23 mg vitamin C.

One teaspoon (5 g) prepared horseradish has 2 calories. It provides a trace of protein and fat, 0.6 g carbohydrates, 0.2 g dietary fiber, 1.2 mg vitamin C, 3 mg calcium, a trace of iron, and 1.6 mg sodium.

One tablespoon (15 g) prepared horseradish has 8 calories. It provides 0.2 g protein, 0.1 g fat, 1.7 g carbohydrates, 0.5 g dietary fiber, 3.7 mg vitamin C, 8 mg calcium, 0.1 mg iron, and 47 mg sodium.

HOW THIS PLANT AFFECTS YOUR BODY

Important Phytochemicals   Like other cruciferous vegetables, horseradish root is flavored with mustard oils, sulfur compounds such as allyl isothiocyanate. The sharp odor of horseradish comes from another sulfur compound, sinigrin, which releases acrid constituents when you slice into the radish and tear its cell walls. This reaction is similar to what happens when you slice an onion, releasing sulfur compounds that make your eyes water.

It is now believed that the sulfur compounds in cruciferous vegetables may reduce the risk of some kinds of cancer, perhaps by preventing the formation of carcinogens in your body, blocking cancer-causing substances from reaching or reacting with sensitive body tissues, or by inhibiting the transformation of healthy cells to malignant ones. In studies with laboratory animals, one sulfur compound, sulforaphane, increased body production of phase-2 enzymes, naturally occurring substances that inactivate and help eliminate carcinogens. At Johns Hopkins University in Baltimore, 69 percent of the rats injected with a compound known to cause mammary cancer developed tumors versus only 26 percent of the rats given the carcinogenic compound plus sulforaphane.

Benefits   Fresh horseradish is a good source of vitamin C. One ounce fresh grated horseradish supplies 38 percent of the vitamin C a healthy adult needs each day.

Like MUSTARD, horseradish is a rubefacient. When applied as a poultice, it irritates the skin and causes the small blood vessels just under the surface to dilate, increasing the flow of blood and making the skin feel warm. In 1988, the German Commission E approved the use of preparations of fresh or dried horseradish root as an external dressing to relieve congestion of the common cold and for minor muscle aches and as an oral medication for congestion and urinary infections.

Possible Adverse Effects   Horseradish may irritate the lining of the gastrointestinal tract; concentrated horseradish poultices may burn the skin.

There are at least two early (1988) reports of adverse reactions to wasabi in which diners became pale and confused, began to sweat profusely and collapsed after eating a large serving of the condiment. While there were no long-term effects, both reports suggested that this response may be serious in patients with weakened blood vessels in the heart or brain.

Information for Women Who Are Pregnant or Nursing   * * *

Plant/Drug Interactions   Like other cruciferous vegetables, horseradish contains sulfur compounds known as goitrogens (goitrin, thiocyanate, isothiocyanate). Goitrogens inhibit the thyroid gland's production of thyroid hormones. As a result, the gland enlarges in an attempt to make more hormones. (The swollen thyroid gland is commonly called a goiter.) Goitrogens are not a problem for healthy people who eat moderate amounts of cruciferous vegetables, but they may be hazardous for people who have a thyroid disorder or who are taking thyroid medication.

Cruciferous vegetables, including horseradish, may affect the accuracy of the guaiac slide test for hidden blood in the stool. The active ingredient in this test is alpha-guaiaconic acid, a compound that turns blue in the presence of blood. It also turns blue when it comes in contact with peroxidase, a compound found naturally in crucifers. The result may be a false positive, indicating cancer when there is none present. To prevent this, your doctor may advise you to avoid eating cruciferous vegetables (and some other foods) for three days prior to the test.

HOW TO USE THIS PLANT

In Cooking   For the strongest flavor, use freshly grated horseradish. The sulfur-containing mustard oil in prepared horseradish turns bitter when exposed to air. For the best flavor, use the horseradish within a few weeks after you open the jar.

To reconstitute dried wasabi powder, combine each teaspoon of powder with $1/4$ teaspoon water. For the best flavor, use immediately.

Horsetail

ABOUT THIS PLANT

Botanical name(s): Equisitum arvense
Common name(s): Field horsetail
Native to: North America
Parts used as food/drink: Shoots, green stems
GRAS list: Yes
Medicinal properties: Diuretic
Other uses: Scouring pad

ABOUT THIS PLANT AS FOOD OR DRINK

Horsetail is a tall, rush-like plant related to the ferns. It does not produce flowers. Its sterile, hollow, jointed green stems are used to brew an astringent herbal tea.

Nutritional Profile   * * *

HOW THIS PLANT AFFECTS YOUR BODY

Important Phytochemicals   Horsetail contains silicic acid, plus the astringent bitter flavonoids isoquercitrin, galuteolin, and equisetrin; saponins (naturally foaming substances); and a very small amount of nicotine.

Silicic acid is an irritant. Flavonoids and saponins are mild diuretics.

Benefits   In 1986, the German Commission E approved the use of horsetail preparations as a diuretic to relieve bacterial and inflammatory urinary disease and as a compress to speed wound healing.

In its approval, the commission recommended taking copious amounts of fluids along with the horsetail and cautioned against the use of horsetail for patients with heart and kidney failure.

Possible Adverse Effects   * * *

Information for Women Who Are Pregnant or Nursing   * * *

Plant/Drug Interactions   * * *

HOW TO USE THIS PLANT

In Cooking   Horsetail is available as an herbal tea.

As a Home Remedy For use as an herbal tea, steep the stems in hot water, then strain the liquid. The suggested dosage is 6 g horsetail stems per day.

For external use as a compress, steep 10 g horsetail stems in 1 liter water.

Around the House Perhaps the most interesting thing about horsetail is that its stems contain large amounts of abrasive silica and silicic acids plus saponins (naturally foaming substances). As a result horsetail has traditionally been used to polish metals.

Hyssop

ABOUT THIS PLANT
Botanical name(s): Hyssopus officinalis
Common name(s): Garden hyssop
Native to: Eurasia
Parts used as food/drink: Leaves
GRAS list: Yes
Medicinal properties: Demulcent
Other uses: Perfumery

ABOUT THIS PLANT AS FOOD OR DRINK
Hyssop, a member of the mint family, has small purple flowers and narrow leaves with a spicy mint flavor. Small quantities of fresh hyssop leaves may be used in salads or as a garnish for fruit soups, salads, and desserts. Dried hyssop flowers are sometimes used to decorate soups or to brew an herbal tea.

Dried hyssop leaves may be available as a tea in your health food store; fresh leaves are available only from your own garden. Oil of hyssop is sometimes used to flavor the French liqueurs Chartreuse and benedictine.

Nutritional Profile * * *

HOW THIS PLANT AFFECTS YOUR BODY
Important Phytochemicals Hyssop's flavor and aroma come from oil of hyssop, a clear or greenish-yellow liquid whose primary (50 percent) ingredient is turpentine-scented pinene.

Pinene is an expectorant, an agent that may increase the secretions of the mucous membranes lining the bronchial tubes, liquefying mucus so that you can cough it up more easily. However, hyssop's value in relieving coughs and colds is not documented.

Like other essential oils, pure oil of hyssop is toxic, causing severe muscle spasms in laboratory animals and human beings.

Benefits * * *

Possible Adverse Effects * * *

Information for Women Who Are Pregnant or Nursing * * *

Plant/Drug Interactions * * *

HOW TO USE THIS PLANT

Around the House   To make a greenish dye for natural wool fabrics, chop 1 pint hyssop leaves for each ounce of fabric. Soak the leaves overnight in water. Then discard the soaking water, add fresh water to cover, and simmer the leaves up to an hour, until the water turns the color you want. Strain the liquid and add enough fresh water to make 4 gallons of dye for 1 pound of cloth. Add the garment to be dyed and let it sit until the color is right, then rinse it in cold water until the water runs clear. In theory, you should be able to use this dye on all natural fabrics, but it is much easier to get good results with wool than with silk and cotton. In any case, it's always a good idea to try the dye on a small inside spot on a garment to see how the material reacts before you put the entire garment into the dye bath.

In the Garden   Pinene, the chief constituent of oil of hyssop, is used in making insecticides. Some gardeners believe that its odor, a mixture of camphor and turpentine, is a natural insect repellent. You may try your own experiment by planting hyssop and seeing if it reduces the normal insect population.

Irish Moss

ABOUT THIS PLANT

Botanical name(s): *Chondrus crispus*
Common name(s): Carrageen
Native to: Pacific and Indian Oceans, North Atlantic
Parts used as food/drink: Whole plants or their extracted gums
GRAS list: No
Medicinal properties: Iodine source
Other uses: Laxative, stabilizers

ABOUT THIS PLANT AS FOOD OR DRINK

Irish moss is a seaweed most commonly used as a thickener.

Nutritional Profile   3.5 ounces (100 g) raw Irish moss has 49 calories. It provides 1.5 g protein, 0.2 g fat, 12.3 g carbohydrates, 118 IU vitamin A, 30 mg vitamin C, 72 mg calcium, 9 mg iron, and 67 mg sodium.

HOW THIS PLANT AFFECTS YOUR BODY

Important Phytochemicals   One useful group of compounds in seaweed are alginates, a form of soluble dietary fiber (gums) used as thickeners and gelling agents. Carrageen, the alginate from Irish moss, was used as a substitute for AGAR during World War II.

Benefits   * * *

Possible Adverse Effects   Because seaweed is high in sodium, it is often restricted on a controlled sodium diet. Remember, powdered seaweed is not a low-sodium substitute for table salt.

All seaweed is high in iodine. The exact amount varies from species to species, but it is not uncommon for dried seaweed to have concentrations as high as 0.4–0.6 percent, 116 to 174 mg iodine per ounce, nearly 800 times the RDA (150 mcg). The thyroid gland uses iodine to make thyroid hormones. If you don't get enough iodine, the gland will swell in an attempt to produce more hormone; the swelling is called a goiter. Paradoxically, people who consume too much iodine, defined by the German Commission E as more than 150 mcg per day, may also suffer from goiter because an oversupply of inorganic iodine (the form found in food) keeps the thyroid gland from making organic iodine (the form used to make thyroid hormones). Iodine-overdose goiter is most likely to occur at an iodine consumption exceeding 2,000 mcg (2 mg) a day as in Japan. There seaweed is an important part of the diet, and iodine intake may be as high as 50,000 to 80,000 mcg (50–80 mg) per day.

Some people experience serious allergic reactions to large amounts of iodine, generally defined as more than 150 mcg per day.

Information for Women Who Are Pregnant or Nursing * * *

Plant/Drug Interactions * * *

HOW TO USE THIS PLANT

In Cooking To reduce or eliminate seaweed's "weedy" iodine flavor, soak the seaweed in cool water for at least 2 hours before using.

Jasmine

ABOUT THIS PLANT

Botanical name(s): *Jasminum* species
Common name(s): Catalonian jasmine, common jasmine, royal jasmine
Native to: China, India
Parts used as food/drink: Dried flowers
GRAS list: Yes
Medicinal properties: * * *
Other uses: Perfumery

ABOUT THIS PLANT AS FOOD OR DRINK

Jasmine is an evergreen shrub native to Asia. It has dark green leaves and large, white, showy flowers best known for their strong fragrance. The dried flowers of *Jasminum sambac*, often available in tea bags, are dried and used to brew Chinese jasmine teas.

Note: The *Jasminum* species are not related to *Gelseminium semipervirens*, a flowering plant commonly known as Carolina jasmine or Carolina jessamine.

Nutritional Profile * * *

HOW THIS PLANT AFFECTS YOUR BODY

Important Phytochemicals Jasmine's flavor and aroma come from jasmone, the most important constituent of oil of jasmine, a potential allergen.

In Asia, jasmine is valued for its purported ability to relieve stress, alleviate tension, and enhance libido; there is no scientific documentation for any of these claims. The U.S. Food and Drug Administration considers jasmine a safe flavoring; pure oil of jasmine sold for perfume is potentially toxic and only for external use.

Benefits * * *

Possible Adverse Effects People sensitive to oil of jasmine may experience allergic reactions when they handle the plant or use it in perfumes or for aromatherapy.

Information for Women Who Are Pregnant or Nursing * * *

Plant/Drug Interactions * * *

HOW TO USE THIS PLANT * * *

Juniper

ABOUT THIS PLANT

Botanical name(s): *Juniperis communis*
Common name(s): Common juniper
Native to: Europe, North America
Parts used as food/drink: Berries
GRAS list: No
Medicinal properties: Diuretic
Other uses: Perfumery, cosmetics, soaps, detergents

ABOUT THIS PLANT AS FOOD OR DRINK

Juniper is an evergreen shrub with blue-black/purplish berries that contain juniper oil (also known as juniperberry oil), the spicy clear to pale green liquid that gives gin its distinctive flavor. It is used as a flavoring agent in cola drinks, root beer, ice cream, candy, chewing gum and sauerkraut and a fragrance in perfumes, soaps, detergents, and cosmetic lotions. The riper the berries, the higher the oil content.

Nutritional Profile   One-quarter ounce (9 g) dried juniper berries has 24 calories. It provides 1.3 g protein, 0.4 g fat, 0.8 g dietary fiber, 144 IU vitamin A, 60 mg calcium, 1 mg iron, and a trace of sodium.

HOW THIS PLANT AFFECTS YOUR BODY

Important Phytochemicals   Juniper oil contains 4-terpineol, an irritant and mild diuretic.

The flavor and aroma compounds in juniper oil include bitter thujone, astringent tannins, sugars, turpentine-scented pinene, pleasant-scented myrcene, and lemon-scented limonene. Juniper berries also contain resins and waxes.

Benefits   In 1984, the German Commission E approved the use of preparations of whole, crushed, or powdered fresh or dried ripe juniper berries to relieve symptoms of an upset stomach.

Possible Adverse Effects   4-Terpineol may irritate the kidneys; if taken for prolonged periods of time, it may cause kidney damage. However, the amount of juniper oil in alcoholic beverages is so low (less than 1 percent) that it is unlikely to cause problems for healthy people. But juniper extract used as medication may be hazardous for people with kidney disease.

Information for Women Who Are Pregnant or Nursing In experiments with laboratory animals, juniper preparations caused contractions of smooth muscle such as the muscle lining the uterus. In approving juniper preparations, Commission E advised against their use by pregnant women.

Plant/Drug Interactions * * *

HOW TO USE THIS PLANT

In Cooking Adding juniper berries to a marinade, to beans, or to soups gives the dish a gin-like flavor.

As a flavoring, 1 teaspoon of juniper berries is equivalent to $1/2$ cup gin.

Kava

ABOUT THIS PLANT

Botanical name(s): *Piper methysticum*
Common name(s): Kava kava, kew, tonga
Native to: South Pacific region
Parts used as food/drink: Rhizomes (underground roots)
GRAS list: * * *
Medicinal properties: Antianxiety, antistress
Other uses: * * *

ABOUT THIS PLANT AS FOOD OR DRINK

Kava is a flowering shrub native to the South Pacific region, related to PEP-PER. Its thick rhizomes (underground roots) are used to make a relaxing herbal beverage called kava or added to other herbal teas.

Nutritional Profile * * *

HOW THIS PLANT AFFECTS YOUR BODY

Important Phytochemicals The active constituents in kava are compounds called kavalactones which are central nervous system depressants (substances that slow down breathing, heartbeat and other involuntary body functions). The best known kavalactone in kava is kawain.

The kava root is a potential allergen.

Benefits In 1990, the German Commission E approved the use of preparations of dried kava kava roots to relieve anxiety, stress, and restlessness. In approving the herb, the commission cautioned that it should not be used for longer than three months without medical advice and supervision, a warning repeated in 1997 by the U.S. Food and Drug Administration. The commission also advised against the use of kava by people suffering from depression.

Possible Adverse Effects Using large amounts of kava or using kava for extended periods of time may cause enlarged pupils, disturbances in eye/motor coordination, temporary yellow discoloration of skin, hair, and nails, scaly rashes, muscle weakness, and drowsiness.

In a paper delivered to the 1999 annual meeting of the American Society of Anesthesiologists, kava was identified as an herb that may prolong the effects of general anesthesia in surgery. The report recommended that people cease using kava kava two weeks prior to surgery.

Information for Women Who Are Pregnant or Nursing   In approving the use of kava, Commission E cautioned against its use during pregnancy and lactation.

Plant/Drug Interactions   Kava may intensify the sedative effects of alcoholic beverages, muscle relaxants, sleeping pills (barbiturates), and mood-altering psychiatric medications such as antianxiety medications.

HOW TO USE THIS PLANT   * * *

Kelp

ABOUT THIS PLANT

Botanical name(s): *Laminaria hyperborea*
Common name(s): Brown algae, kombu tangleweed
Native to: Pacific and Indian Oceans, North Atlantic Ocean
Parts used as food/drink: Whole plants or their extracted gums
GRAS list: Yes
Medicinal properties: Iodine source
Other uses: Laxatives, stabilizers

ABOUT THIS PLANT AS FOOD OR DRINK

Kelp, a seaweed, is a nutritious vegetable most commonly used in Japanese cooking.

Nutritional Profile   3.5 ounces (100 g) raw kelp has 43 calories. It provides 1.68 g protein, 0.6 g fat, 9.6 g carbohydrates, 116 IU vitamin A, 3 mg vitamin C, 168 mg calcium, 2.9 mg iron, and 230 mg sodium.

HOW THIS PLANT AFFECTS YOUR BODY

Important Phytochemicals   Alginates are a useful group of compounds present in seaweed. They are a form of soluble dietary fiber (gums) used as thickeners and gelling agents. Powdered kelp is used as a thickener. It is also used as a "natural" alternative to table SALT. In fact, all salt, whether from mineral deposits in the earth, seawater ("sea salt"), or seaweed, has precisely the same chemical structure, a combination of sodium and chloride. The only advantage to sea salt or powdered kelp is its naturally occurring iodine.

Benefits   Most seaweeds are rich in calcium and iron. 3.5 ounces raw kelp provides 21 percent of the RDA for calcium, and 19 percent of the RDA for iron. The iron in seaweed is nonheme iron, a form of iron more difficult for your body to absorb than heme iron, the form of iron present in meat, fish, poultry, milk, and eggs. Eating seaweed with meat increases the amount of iron you absorb from the seaweed because meat triggers the secretion of stomach acids, and iron is absorbed more easily in an acid environment. You can also increase your absorption of nonheme iron by eating the seaweed with a food rich in vitamin C. Vitamic C changes the iron in seaweed from ferric iron to ferrous iron, a more easily absorbed form of iron.

Possible Adverse Effects   Because seaweed is high in sodium, it is often restricted on a controlled-sodium diet. Remember: Powdered seaweed is not a low-sodium substitute for table salt.

All seaweed is high in iodine. The exact amount varies from species to species, but it is not uncommon for dried seaweed to have concentrations as high as 0.4–0.6 percent, 116 to 174 mg iodine per ounce, nearly 800 times the RDA (150 mcg). The thyroid gland uses iodine to make thyroid hormones. If you don't get enough iodine, the gland will swell in an attempt to produce more hormone; the swelling is called a goiter. Paradoxically, people who consume too much iodine, defined by the German Commission E as more than 150 mcg per day, may also suffer from goiter because an oversupply of inorganic iodine (the form found in food) keeps the thyroid gland from making organic iodine (the form used to make thyroid hormones). Iodine-overdose goiter is most likely to occur when iodine consumption exceeds 2,000 mcg (2 mg) per day, as is common in Japan. There seaweed is an important part of the diet, and iodine intake may be as high as 50,000 to 80,000 mcg (50–80) per day.

Some people experience serious allergic reactions to large amounts of iodine, generally defined as more than 150 mcg a day.

Information for Women Who Are Pregnant or Nursing   * * *

Plant/Drug Interactions   * * *

HOW TO USE THIS PLANT

In Cooking   To reduce or eliminate seaweed's "weedy" iodine flavor, soak the seaweed in cool water for at least 2 hours before using.

Ketchup

ABOUT THIS CONDIMENT

Botanical name(s): * * *
Common name(s): catsup, tomato catsup
Native to: Malaysia
Parts used as food/drink: * * *
GRAS list: No
Medicinal properties: Antioxidant, anticarcinogen
Other uses: * * *

ABOUT THIS CONDIMENT AS FOOD OR DRINK

Some food historians believe that ketchup originated in Malaysia and was given a name that comes from the word for "taste." Others say the name *ketchup* come from the Chinese words for "pickled fish sauce." Modern ketchups are usually sweet tomato sauce flavored with onions, pepper, sugar, and vinegar plus assorted spices such as ALLSPICE, CINNAMON, MUSTARD, GARLIC, CLOVES, and NUTMEG.

Nutritional Profile One-quarter cup (61 g) tomato ketchup has 64 calories. It provides 1 g protein, less than 1 g fat, 17 g carbohydrates, 1 g dietary fiber, 62 IU vitamin A, 9 mg vitamin C, 12 mg calcium, 0.4 mg iron, and 726 mg sodium.

One tablespoon (15 g) tomato ketchup has 15.6 calories, 0.2 protein, a trace of fat, 4.1 g carbohydrates, 0.2 g dietary fiber, 152 IU vitamin A, 2.3 mg vitamin C, 2.9 mg calcium, 0.1 mg iron, and 178 mg sodium.

One packet (6 g) tomato ketchup has 6.2 calories, 0.1 mg protein, a trace of fat, 1.6 g carbohydrates, 0.1 g dietary fiber, 50.9 IU vitamin A, 0.9 mg vitamin C, 1.1 mg calcium, and 71.2 mg sodium.

One tablespoon (15 g) low sodium ketchup has 15.6 calories, 0.2 g protein, a trace of fat, 4.1 g carbohydrates 0.2 g dietary fiber, 152 IU vitamin A, 2.3 mg vitamin C, and 3 mg sodium.

HOW THIS CONDIMENT AFFECTS YOUR BODY

Important Phytochemicals Tomatoes and tomato sauces are good sources of vitamin C and a reasonable source of vitamin A. One tablespoon regular ketchup provides 4 percent of the RDA for vitamin C, 4 percent of the RDA for vitamin A for a man, and 5 percent of the RDA for a woman.

(This is an average; not all ketchups provide the same amount of nutrients, so check the label to be sure.)

Cooked tomatoes, including tomato sauces such as ketchup, are an excellent source of lycopene, a red carotenoid pigment that appears to reduce the risk of prostate cancer and cancer of the lung. Note: Because lycopene dissolves in fat, adding a bit of oil or cheese to a cooked tomato product increases the amount of lycopene you absorb.

LYCOPENE CONTENT OF TOMATO PRODUCTS (mg/ounce)	
Tomato ketchup	5 mg/ounce
Tomato sauce	5
Fresh tomato	3
Canned tomatoes	3
Tomato juice	3
Source: Tomato Research Council	

Tomato sauces are also high in antioxidants, naturally occurring compounds that prevent molecular fragments in your body from joining to form potential carcinogens.

Benefits   * * *

Possible Adverse Effects   Regular ketchup is a high-sugar food with moderately high amounts of sodium. One tablespoon regular catsup has up to 3 g (3,000 mg) sugar and 156 mg sodium.

Information for Women Who Are Pregnant or Nursing   * * *

Condiment/Drug Interactions   * * *

HOW TO USE THIS CONDIMENT

In Cooking   Ketchup's antioxidant activity is useful in preventing "warmed-over" flavor, a fat/oxygen reaction in refrigerated cooked meats. When meat is heated, it loses water and shrinks. Its pigments combine with oxygen; they are denatured (broken into fragments) by the heat, so that they turn brown, the natural color of well-done meat. At the same time, the fats in the meat are oxidized, a reaction that produces a characteristic "warmed-over" flavor when the cooked meat is refrigerated and then reheated. Cooking and storing meat under a blanket of antioxidants such as tomato ketchup reduces fat oxidation and lessens the intensity of "warmed-over" flavor.

Lavender

ABOUT THIS PLANT

Botanical name(s): Lavandula officinalis
Common name(s): Garden lavender, true lavender
Native to: Mediterranean region
Parts used as food/drink: Leaves, flowers
GRAS list: Yes
Medicinal properties: Sedative, antiflatulent
Other uses: Moth repellent, fragrance

ABOUT THIS PLANT AS FOOD OR DRINK

Lavender, a perennial plant with narrow, grayish-green leaves and long spikes with purple flowers, is grown primarily for its oil, which is widely used as a flavoring agent in beverages and baked goods and a fragrance in perfumes and cosmetics.

Fresh lavender leaves and flowers may be used in salads or fruit dishes or cooked sauces, candies, and baked goods such as cakes and cookies. Dried leaves and flowers are used to make jams and jellies.

Nutritional Profile   * * *

HOW THIS PLANT AFFECTS YOUR BODY

Important Phytochemicals   Lavender's flavor and aroma come from oil of lavender which contains bitter-tasting, vanilla-scented coumarins; astringent tannins; bergamot-scented linalyl acetate; lavender-scented linalool; turpentine-scented pinene; lemon-scented limonene; and rose-scented geraniol.

Linalool, limonene, geraniol, and pinene are irritants. Limonene is also a photosensitizer, a substance that makes your skin more sensitive to sunlight, increasing the risk of sunburn, particularly for fair-skinned people.

Benefits   In 1984 and 1990, German Commission E approved the use of preparations of lavender flowers gathered and dried before they have fully opened to relieve restlessness, insomnia, and "nervous stomach."

Possible Adverse Effects   Handling the lavender plant or using lavender-scented perfumes and cosmetics may cause contact dermatitis (itching, burning, stinging, reddened, or blistered skin) in sensitive individuals or increase the risk of sunburn.

Information for Women Who Are Pregnant or Nursing * * *

Plant/Drug Interactions * * *

HOW TO USE THIS PLANT

Around the House   Lavender is reputed to repel moths. If you are not sensitive to lavender, you may run your own experiment by tossing dried lavender flowers in your drawers or closets to protect your clothes.

To dry lavender flowers for sachets, pick the flowers just as they open and hang them upside down in an airy room. When the flowers are crinkly and brittle, they are ready for use.

Lemon

ABOUT THIS PLANT

Botanical name(s): Citrus limon
Common name(s): * * *
Native to: Northern India
Parts used as food/drink: Juice, rind
GRAS list: * * *
Medicinal properties: Antiscorbutic (juice)
Other uses: Pharmaceutical flavoring

ABOUT THIS PLANT AS FOOD OR DRINK

Lemons are citrus fruits, members of the family that includes grapefruit, limes, and oranges. The lemon provides two distinct flavoring agents: lemon juice and lemon peel. Lemon peel, the yellow outer rind without the bitter inner white membrane, has a high concentration of lemon oil, so it is more strongly flavored than lemon juice.

Nutritional Profile   One teaspoon (2 g) fresh raw lemon peel has no calories. It provides a trace of protein and fat, 0.3 g carbohydrates, 3 mg calcium, a trace of iron, and 2.6 mg vitamin C.

One ounce (30 g) fresh lemon juice has 7 calories. It provides 0.19 protein, a trace of fat, 2.4 g carbohydrates, 5.7 IU vitamin A, 13 mg vitamin C, 2 mg calcium, a trace of iron, and no sodium.

HOW THIS PLANT AFFECTS YOUR BODY

Important Phytochemicals   The flavor and aroma of lemons comes from lemon oil (also known as cedro oil), a pale yellow or pale green liquid that is about 90 percent limonene. Lemon oil also contains lemon-scented citral and citronellal, turpentine-scented phellandrene and pinene, plus the bitter astringent flavonoid hesperidin.

Citral, citronellal, limonene, phellandrene, and pinene are all irritating to skin and mucous membranes. Hesperidin is a natural antioxidant, a compound that prevents molecular fragments circulating in your body from joining to form potentially damaging molecules.

Benefits   Lemon juice is an excellent source of vitamin C, which protects against scurvy, the disease caused by a deficiency of vitamin C. One ounce of lemon juice provides 21 percent of the RDA for a healthy adult.

Possible Adverse Effects   Oil of lemon can cause contact dermatitis (itching, burning, stinging, reddened, or blistered skin) including cheilitis (chapped, peeling, or bleeding lips) in sensitive people who handle lemons or eat foods made with lemons, lemon juice, or lemon peel.

Information for Women Who Are Pregnant or Nursing   * * *

Plant/Drug Interactions   * * *

HOW TO USE THIS PLANT

In Cooking   One teaspoon grated lemon peel (also known as lemon zest) has flavor equal to 2 tablespoons fresh lemon juice. When grating the peel, use only the lemon-colored part; the white membrane underneath is bitter.

To make lemon-flavored sugar, grate enough lemon peel to make 1 tablespoon zest. Stir the zest into 1 cup granulated sugar and store the sugar, tightly covered, in a cool, dry place. Use as needed. Note: Don't store the lemon-sugar in the refrigerator; the moist air causes it to cake.

One teaspoon freshly grated lemon peel (zest) has flavor equal to 2 teaspoons candied lemon peel.

As a Cosmetic   Lemon juice is a traditional conditioning rinse for blond hair. Old-fashioned, alkaline, soap-based shampoos left a sticky residue on the hair. The acid in lemon juice easily dissolved this residue, leaving hair shinier and more manageable. Modern detergent shampoos are less likely to leave a residue, but lemon juice is still useful for adding a blond shine.

To make the lemon juice rinse, combine the juice of half a lemon with $1/2$ cup warm water. Apply after rinsing shampoo from the hair, then rinse again with warm water to remove all lemon juice.

Lemon Balm

ABOUT THIS PLANT

Botanical name(s): *Melissa officinalis*
Common name(s): Common balm, lemon balm, melissa, sweet balm
Parts used as food/drink: Leaves
GRAS list: Yes
Medicinal properties: Sedative, antiflatulent
Other uses: Perfume, cosmetics, insect repellent

ABOUT THIS PLANT AS FOOD OR DRINK

Lemon balm is a lemon-scented member of the mint family. (It is unrelated to the lemon fruit, but its fresh leaves may be used to add a citric tang to salads.)

Nutritional Profile   * * *

HOW THIS PLANT AFFECTS YOUR BODY

Important Phytochemicals   Lemon balm's flavor and aroma come from an essential oil that contains lemon-scented citral and citronellal; rose-scented geraniol, the primary constituent of oil of roses; and lavender-scented linalool. Lemon balm's oil also contains astringent tannins and bitter flavonoids.

Citral, citronellal, geraniol, and linalool are irritants and potential allergens and allergic sensitizers (compounds that make you sensitive to other compounds).

Benefits   In 1984 and 1990, the German Commission E validated the long-standing folk belief in lemon balm's ability to relieve stress by approving the use of fresh or dried lemon balm leaves to as a mild sedative or carminative (an agent that relieves intestinal gas).

Possible Adverse Effects   Handling the lemon balm plant and leaves may cause contact dermatitis (itching, stinging, burning, reddened, or blistered skin) or sensitize you to other allergens.

Information for Women Who Are Pregnant or Nursing   * * *

Plant/Drug Interactions   * * *

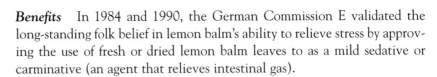

HOW TO USE THIS PLANT

Cooking with This Plant   Fresh lemon balm leaves lose their flavor quickly. To protect both flavor and aroma, dry the leaves and keep them in a cool, dark cabinet in an airtight container.

To get the most lemon flavor from lemon balm leaves, crush the leaves just before you use them. This will release their flavoring oil. Use the leaves in iced tea, carbonated sodas, or fruit punches. To add a lemon tang to wine, add one or two balm leaves to a bottle and leave them there for several hours, until you are ready to serve the wine. The alcohol in the wine draws out the flavor and aroma of the leaves. Note: In Great Britain, wine in which balm leaves have been steeped is sometimes used as a mouthwash.

In the Garden   Plants that contain citronella oil repel mosquitoes and other insects. Their active ingredient appears to be methyl heptanone, a constituent of citronella oil that is non-poisonous to people, pets, or wild animals that wander through to forage. In addition, lemon balm—whose botanical name, *Melissa,* is Greek for "bee"—is sometimes used by beekeepers to attract bees to hives.

As a Home Remedy   Steep lemon balm leaves in hot water for 5–10 minutes; unlike some other fresh herbs, lemon balm leaves do not turn bitter with long steeping. The suggested dose is 1.5–4.5 g fresh or dried leaves per cup, as needed during the day.

Lemongrass

ABOUT THIS PLANT

Botanical name(s): *Cymbopogon nardus* (Ceylon lemongrass), *Cymbopogon citratus* (West Indian lemongrass)

Common name(s): * * *

Native to: Southeast Asia

Parts used as food/drink: Leaves

GRAS list: No

Medicinal properties: * * *

Other uses: Perfume, insect repellent

ABOUT THIS PLANT AS FOOD OR DRINK

Lemongrass, a tall perennial that grows best in the cooler tropical climates, has gray-green, grasslike leaves used to add a lemony flavor and aroma to Asian cooking.

Lemongrass may be used fresh or dried. The fresh leaves are sometimes available in Asian grocery stores; packaged dried leaves may be easier to find on herb and spice shelves in supermarkets.

Nutritional Profile   One-quarter ounce (7 g) dried lemongrass has 28 calories. It provides 0.5 g protein, 0.5 g fat, 27 mg calcium, 3.9 mg iron, and 4.5 mg sodium.

HOW THIS PLANT AFFECTS YOUR BODY

Important Phytochemicals   The flavor and aroma of lemongrass comes from lemongrass oil, which contains lemon-scented citral and citronella, the primary flavoring and aroma compounds in oil of LEMON and other lemon-scented herbs.

Citral and citronella are irritants, potential allergens, and photosensitizers, compounds that make skin more sensitive to sunlight, increasing the risk of serious sunburn, especially for light-skinned people.

Lemongrass is widely used in folk medicine as a mild astringent or a tonic for an upset stomach but there is no scientific documentation for these claims.

Benefits   * * *

Possible Adverse Effects   Handling lemongrass may cause contact dermatitis (itching, burning, stinging, reddened, or blistered skin), as well as severe sunburn.

Information for Women Who Are Pregnant or Nursing   * * *

Plant/Drug Interactions   * * *

HOW TO USE THIS PLANT

In Cooking   When cooking with fresh lemongrass, bend or nick the leaf to release its flavor and aroma.

As a seasoning, 1 stalk fresh lemongrass is equivalent to about 1 teaspoon powdered lemongrass.

In the Garden   Plants containing citronella oil repel mosquitoes and other insects. The active component in citronella appears to be methyl heptanone, an ingredient in many commercial insect repellents. Lemongrass is not toxic to human beings, pets, or wild animals.

Lemon Verbena

ABOUT THIS PLANT

Botanical name(s): Aloysia triphylla
Common name(s): * * *
Native to: Latin America
Parts used as food/drink: Leaves
GRAS list: No
Medicinal properties: * * *
Other uses: Insect repellent, perfumes

ABOUT THIS PLANT AS FOOD OR DRINK

Lemon verbena is a woody shrub with narrow, shiny, pale green leaves that, although unrelated to the LEMON, taste like lemon and smell like a combination of lemons and limes. What makes lemon verbena especially useful is that neither drying nor cooking diminishes their flavor and aroma.

Nutritional Profile * * *

HOW THIS PLANT AFFECTS YOUR BODY

Important Phytochemicals The oil that gives lemon verbena leaves their flavor and aroma is approximately 35 percent lemony-scented citral; borneol, which smells like PEPPER and tastes like mint; lemon-scented citronellal and limonene; camphor-scented eucalyptol; and rose-scented geraniol.

Borneol, citronellal, limonene, and geraniol are irritants and potential allergens.

Benefits * * *

Possible Adverse Effects Handling the lemon verbena plant or eating foods flavored with lemon verbena leaves may cause contact dermatitis (itching, burning, stinging, reddened, or blistered skin) or cheilitis (chapped or bleeding lips) in sensitive people.

Information for Women Who Are Pregnant or Nursing * * *

Plant/Drug Interactions * * *

HOW TO USE THIS PLANT

Around the House Plants that contain citronella oil repel mosquitoes and other insects but are nontoxic to people and pets. The active ingredi-

ent appears to be methyl heptanone, a constituent of citronella oil, an ingredient in many commercial insect repellents. Fresh or dried lemon verbena leaves can be used to scent your closets and drawers and perhaps keep insects away (see below).

In the Garden   Verbena leaves may repel insects around plants.

Licorice

ABOUT THIS PLANT

Botanical name(s): *Glycyrrhiza glabra*
Common name(s): Licorice root, sweet licorice, sweet wood
Native to: Middle East, southern Europe, Asia
Parts used as food/drink: Roots, stems
GRAS list: Yes
Medicinal properties: Demulcent
Other uses: Pharmaceutical flavoring, flavoring for tobacco

ABOUT THIS PLANT AS FOOD OR DRINK

The botanical name for licorice come from the Greek words *glykys* ("sweet"), and *rhiza* ("root"). Licorice grows wild in Europe and Asia, but it has been cultivated in other countries for its sweet-tasting roots and rhizomes (underground stems). The root itself is 50 times sweeter than plain sugar; the extract from the root is a bit less sweet.

Licorice extract is used as a flavoring in candy, cough drops, and medicines. However, in the United States, licorice candy is most likely to be flavored with ANISE (an herb unrelated to licorice) or synthetic licorice flavoring.

Nutritional Profile One-half ounce (14 g) dried licorice root has 38 calories. It provides 1.5 g protein, 1.2 g dietary fiber, 8.8 mg vitamin C, 123 mg calcium, 12.3 mg iron, and 114.5 mg sodium.

HOW THIS PLANT AFFECTS YOUR BODY

Important Phytochemicals As much as 14 percent of the weight of the licorice root is the intensely sweet compound glycyrrhizic acid (also known as glycyrrhizin). Licorice also contains sugars, soothing resins, vanilla-scented coumarins, phytosterols (alcohol compounds found in plants), and antioxidant flavonoids. In laboratory studies, various animals appear to use flavonoids in much the same way as they use vitamin C: to strengthen capillaries, the small blood vessels just under the skin. In human beings, antioxidant flavonoids are valued for their ability to prevent molecular fragments from joining with each other to form potentially cancer-causing compounds.

Benefits Teas made by boiling fresh or dried licorice root in water are a long-standing folk remedy for sore throat and upset stomach. In controlled clinical studies, glycyrrhizic acid and its derivatives appear to hasten the healing of gastrointestinal ulcers.

In 1985, 1990, and 1991, the German Commission E approved the use of licorice teas and other preparations of powdered unpeeled dried licorice root to soothe a sore throat due to the common cold or an upper respiratory infection, and approved the use of licorice preparations to soothe gastric/duodenal ulcers. In its approval, the commission cautioned against the medical use of licorice for longer than 4 to 6 weeks except as directed by a physician.

Possible Adverse Effects   Consuming large amounts of true licorice for prolonged periods of time may cause sodium and fluid retention and loss of potassium. In human beings, doses of 280 mg licorice per kilogram of body weight (an amount equal to approximately 0.5 oz for a 150-pound person) every day for four weeks is reported to cause fluid retention leading to edema (swollen tissues), higher blood pressure, loss of potassium and calcium, gastrointestinal discomfort including diarrhea, constipation, ulceration, and (rarely) blood disorders. These symptoms are reversible when licorice use ceases.

In approving licorice, German Commission E advised against its use by people with liver disease, kidney disease, and low potassium levels. Note: Synthetic licorice flavoring does not cause the adverse effects associated with natural licorice.

Information for Women Who Are Pregnant or Nursing   Because licorice may increase fluid retention, Commission E cautions against pregnant women consuming natural licorice-flavored foods or using licorice as a medication.

Plant/Drug Interactions   Licorice may lessen the effectiveness of diuretic drugs used to treat high blood pressure and heart disease and increase the amount of potassium lost through urination. The loss of potassium increases sensitivity to the heart medication digitalis.

HOW TO USE THIS PLANT

As a Home Remedy   The suggested daily dose for relief of sore throat or upset stomach is 5 to 15 g powdered or finely cut fresh or dried root steeped as a tea.

Industrial Uses   In the United States, licorice extract is used to flavor the tobacco used in cigarettes, cigars, pipe tobacco, and chewing tobacco.

Lovage

ABOUT THIS PLANT

Botanical name(s): *Levisticum officinale*
Common name(s): Love parsley, sea parsley
Native to: Europe, Mediterranean region
Parts used as food/drink: Leaves, stems
GRAS list: Yes
Medicinal properties: Antiflatulent, diuretic
Other uses: * * *

ABOUT THIS PLANT AS FOOD OR DRINK

Lovage, a member of the carrot family, is a tall herb with large dark green leaves that taste and smell like CELERY. Its botanical name, *Levisticum*, comes from the Latin word for Liguria, the part of Italy where the plant originally grew wild. In some parts of Europe, lovage is known as *maggi*, the name of a popular flavoring in which it is an ingredient.

Lovage leaves may be used fresh in salads. Its stems may be blanched and served as a vegetable or candied as a sweet. Both stems and leaves are used to flavor various spirits-based liqueurs, as well as BITTERS.

Nutritional Profile * * *

HOW THIS PLANT AFFECTS YOUR BODY

Important Phytochemicals Lovage contains vanilla-scented coumarins as well as oil of lovage, whose ingredients include phthalides, flavoring and aroma compounds also found in CELERY. Phthalides are allergens and photosensitizers (compounds that make skin more sensitive to sunlight).

Benefits Like celery, lovage has often been used in folk medicine as a diuretic, a compound that increases urination. In 1990, the German Commission E approved the use of preparations of dried lovage roots and rhizomes (underground stems) to relieve minor inflammation of the urinary tract. In its approval, the commission cautioned against the use of lovage for people with kidney disease or impaired kidney function.

Possible Adverse Effects Prolonged handling of lovage plants may cause an increased sensitivity to sunlight, a common problem with members of the carrot family. In approving lovage, Commission E cautioned against exposure to the sun and/or ultraviolet light while using the herb as a medication.

Information for Women Who Are Pregnant or Nursing Oil of lovage contains antispasmodics, compounds that relax smooth muscle tissue such as the muscle lining the uterus. In folk medicine, lovage has sometimes been used as an emmenagogue, a substance that induces a menstrual period. Although there is no scientific evidence to document this effect, some herbalists caution pregnant women not to use lovage or lovage products.

Plant/Drug Interactions * * *

HOW TO USE THIS PLANT

In Cooking Lovage leaves and stems are useful in soups and stews because their strong flavor persists even after long cooking.

Chlorophyll, the green coloring in lovage leaves, is sensitive to acids. When lovage is heated, its chlorophyll reacts with natural acids in the leaves or in the cooking water, forming a brown compound called pheophytin. The pheophytin in turn reacts with the yellow carotene pigments in the leaves, turning the cooked lovage bronze. To prevent this color change, you must keep the chlorophyll from reacting with the acids by cooking the lovage for as short a time as possible. (Commercial herb packagers preserve the color of green herbs by drying the leaves at a very low heat.)

Mace

ABOUT THIS PLANT

Botanical name(s): Myristica fragrans
Common name(s): * * *
Native to: Indonesia
Parts used as food/drink: Seed covering
GRAS list: Yes
Medicinal properties: Hallucinogen
Other uses: Flavoring for tobacco

ABOUT THIS PLANT AS FOOD OR DRINK

Mace is one of two spices from the NUTMEG tree, an evergreen native to Indonesia and now grown in the West Indies. Nutmeg is the seed kernel inside the tree's fruit; mace is made from the aril, a lacy covering on the shell of the seed. When the nutmeg fruit is harvested, the outer husk is broken open and the aril is removed. Broken pieces of the aril ("blades") are dried to bring out their strong aroma. Then they are ground and packaged as mace. The color of the spice tells you where the spice was grown. Indonesian mace is orange; West Indian mace is yellowish brown.

Note: Both the oil extracted from the leaves of the nutmeg tree and the oil from the seed kernel and the aril are called oil of nutmeg, but the oil from the leaves is also known as oil of mace, while the oil from the kernel and the aril are also known as oil of myristica.

Nutritional Profile   One teaspoon (2 g) ground mace has 8 calories. It provides 0.1 g protein, 0.6 g fat, 0.2 g saturated fat, 0.9 g carbohydrates, 0.3 g dietary fiber, 14 IU vitamin A, 0.4 mg vitamin C, 4 mg calcium, 0.2 mg iron, and 1 mg sodium.

One tablespoon (5 g) ground mace has 25 calories. It provides 0.4 g protein, 1.7 g fat, 0.5 saturated fat, 42 IU vitamin A, 1.1 mg vitamin C, 13 mg calcium, 0.7 mg iron, and 4 mg sodium.

HOW THIS PLANT AFFECTS YOUR BODY

Important Phytochemicals   Mace's flavor and aroma come from oil of nutmeg, which contains peppery-scented, mint-flavored borneol; spicy eugenol, the compound that gives CLOVES their unique smell and taste; rose-scented geraniol; and lavender-scented linalool.

Mace and nutmeg appear to relieve intestinal spasms and have been used in folk medicine to treat gastrointestinal problems such as diarrhea, intestinal gas, and gastric spasms. But there is no scientific evidence to show that they are actually effective.

Borneol, geraniol, and linalool are irritants and potential allergens. Oil of nutmeg also contains small amounts of myristicin, an hallucinogen. High doses of myristicin, defined as one to three whole nutmeg or 5 grams ($^1/_6$ oz) powdered nutmeg or mace—may trigger psychological disturbances including euphoria, detachment from reality or the sensation of floating; vomiting; flushed skin; and visual and auditory hallucinations within one to six hours. Very large doses may be fatal; the small amounts of mace commonly used in food are considered safe.

Oil from nutmeg or mace grown in Indonesia contains very small amounts of safrole, the principal flavoring in FILÉ/(sassafras). Safrole is a carcinogen. The U.S. Food and Drug Administration does not permit the use of safrole in food sold in the United States, so the sassafras sold legally in this country must be safrole-free. Again, the small amounts of mace commonly used in food are considered safe.

Benefits * * *

Possible Adverse Effects See above.

Information for Women Who Are Pregnant or Nursing Large amounts of mace (the nutmeg seed plus the aril) may trigger uterine contractions.

Plant/Drug Interactions * * *

HOW TO USE THIS PLANT

In Cooking Although the flavor of mace is stronger than the flavor of nutmeg, the spices substitute for each other. One part ground mace is equivalent to 1 part ground nutmeg.

Mallow

ABOUT THIS PLANT

Botanical name(s): Malva sylvestris
Common name(s): Cheeseplant, common mallow
Native to: Mediterranean region, Asia
Parts used as food/drink: Leaves, shoots, seed pods, flowers
GRAS list: No
Medicinal properties: Demulcent
Other uses: * * *

ABOUT THIS PLANT AS FOOD OR DRINK

Mallow, whose botanical name comes from the Greek word for "soft," is native to Asia and the Mediterranean region; it now grows wild in North America. The plant produces small round leaves that may be boiled and served as a vegetable or brewed into a delicately flavored tea. Its shoots, its green seed capsules (known as "cheeses"), and its pink flowers may be chopped and added to salads.

Nutritional Profile   One ounce (29 g) dwarf mallow leaves provides 36 mg vitamin C.

HOW THIS PLANT AFFECTS YOUR BODY

Important Phytochemicals   Mallow leaves and flowers are high in mucilage; the flowers contain astringent tannins. Mucilage is a demulcent, a substance that soothes irritated mucous membranes such as those lining the mouth and throat.

Tannins coagulate proteins on the surface of skin or mucous membranes, causing the tissues to pucker so that when you eat or drink a food or beverage high in tannins, you experience a "cool" or "fresh" sensation.

Benefits   Teas prepared from mallow's high-mucilage leaves and flowers have long been used in folk medicine to soothe a sore throat. In 1989, the German Commission E approved the use of preparations of dried mallow flowers to relieve irritation of the mouth and throat as well as dry cough.

Mallow leaves are also a good source of vitamin C. One ounce of a dwarf mallow provides 56 percent of the RDA for vitamin C.

Possible Adverse Effects   * * *

Information for Women Who Are Pregnant or Nursing   * * *

Plant/Drug Interactions   * * *

HOW TO USE THIS PLANT

In Cooking   Do not tear or cut mallow leaves until you are ready to use them. When you cut into a food rich in vitamin C, its cells release an enzyme called ascorbic acid oxidase, which destroys vitamin C.

Chlorophyll, the green coloring in mallow leaves, is sensitive to acids. When you heat mallow, its chlorophyll reacts with natural acids in the leaves or in the cooking water, forming a brown compound called pheophytin. The pheophytin in turn reacts with the yellow carotene pigments in the leaves, turning the cooked mallow bronze. To prevent this color change, you must keep the chlorophyll from reacting with the acids by cooking the mallow for as short a time as possible. (Commercial herb packagers preserve the color of green herbs by drying the leaves at a very low heat.)

Maple Syrup

ABOUT THIS CONDIMENT

Botanical name(s): * * *
Common name(s): * * *
Native to: Northeast United States, Canada
Parts used as food/drink: * * *
GRAS list: No
Medicinal properties: * * *
Other uses: * * *

ABOUT THIS CONDIMENT AS FOOD OR DRINK

Maple syrup and maple sugar are made from the sap of the sugar maple. The sap is watery when drawn from the tree, so it is boiled in large vats to evaporate the water and concentrate a thick sweet syrup. Further boiling, which removes more water, creates crystals of maple sugar.

It takes up to 40 gallons of sap to make one gallon of syrup, a fact that may explain why pure maple syrup is so expensive.

Nutritional Profile   One tablespoon (20 g) maple syrup has 52 calories. It provides 13.4 g carbohydrates, 13.4 mg calcium, 0.2 mg iron, and 1.8 mg sodium.

One tablespoon (20 g) pancake syrup made with cane sugar and 15 percent maple syrup has 56 calories. It provides 15 g carbohydrates, 2.6 mg calcium, 0.2 mg iron, and 20.8 mg sodium.

One tablespoon (20 g) pancake syrup with 2 percent maple syrup has 53 calories. It provide 13.9 g carbohydrates, 1 mg calcium, and 12.2 mg sodium.

HOW THIS CONDIMENT AFFECTS YOUR BODY

Important Phytochemicals   The significant nutrient in maple syrup and maple sugar is its carbohydrates, which provide a concentrated source of energy (calories) with a higher mineral (calcium, iron) content than refined SUGAR.

Benefits   Sugars are the most efficient source of glucose, the fuel on which the body runs.

Possible Adverse Effects   All sugars stick to your teeth, providing food for the bacteria that cause cavities.

Some people develop higher levels of triglycerides (fatty acids) in their blood when they eat a diet high in sugar. People with diabetes cannot use sugar efficiently because they lack sufficient amounts of insulin, the enzyme that enables the body to metabolize (digest) sucrose and distribute it to body cells. As a result, the glucose continues to circulate in the blood until it is excreted through the kidneys. This is why one way to diagnose diabetes is to measure the level of sugar in urine.

Information for Women Who Are Pregnant or Nursing   * * *

Condiment/Drug Interactions   * * *

HOW TO USE THIS CONDIMENT

In Cooking   You can make your own maple syrup from maple sugar simply by adding water and slowly warming the mixture.

Marigold

ABOUT THIS PLANT

Botanical name(s): *Calendula officinalis*
Common name(s): Garden marigold, pot marigold, calendula
Native to: Southern Europe
Parts used as food/drink: Flowers, leaves
GRAS list: Yes
Medicinal properties: Anti-inflammatory, healing agent
Other uses: Coloring agent, natural pest repellent

ABOUT THIS PLANT AS FOOD OR DRINK

Marigolds are ornamental plants with large, showy, orange, yellow, or creamy white edible flowers. Fresh young marigold leaves can be used as greens in salads or as a mild flavoring that adds a touch of color to soups and stews. Powdered dried yellow or orange marigold flowers are sometimes used in fish or rice dishes as an inexpensive substitute for SAFFRON, the world's most expensive spice.

Nutritional Profile One ounce (28 g) fresh marigold leaves has 0.2 g protein, 7.4 g fat, 40–88 mg vitamin C, and 856 mg calcium.

HOW THIS PLANT AFFECTS YOUR BODY

Important Phytochemicals The faintly bitter flavor of marigold leaves and flowers comes from tannins, astringent compounds that coagulate proteins on the mucous membrane lining of your mouth, making the tissues pucker and creating a slight tingling effect.

Yellow and orange marigold flowers are colored with a combination of plant pigments including red lycopene, the carotenoid now linked to a lower risk of prostate cancer and cancer of the lung; red rubixanthine and red-blue violaxanthine; and small amounts of deep yellow beta-carotene, the carotenoid your body converts to vitamin A.

Benefits Plants containing astringent tannins are often used to relieve inflammation and speed wound healing. In 1986, the German Commission E approved the use of preparations of dried marigold flowers as an external wound dressing and as a rinse and/or gargle to soothe inflammations of the mouth and throat.

Marigolds are nutritious. A diet rich in carotenoid pigments appears to reduce the risk of some forms of cancer. It also protects your eyes as your body converts beta-carotene to 11-cis retinol, the most important constituent of rhodopsin, a protein in the rods in your retina (the cells that enable you to see in dim light).

Possible Adverse Effects   Marigolds are related to asters, CHAMOMILE, chrysanthemums, and ragweed. People sensitive to any of these plants may also be sensitive to marigolds and may develop respiratory symptoms (asthma, runny nose, hay fever) when exposed to marigolds, or contact dermatitis (itching, burning, stinging, reddened, or blistered skin) when they touch the plant, or cheilitis (peeling, bleeding lips) if they eat the flowers.

Information for Women Who Are Pregnant or Nursing   Although marigolds have been used safely for centuries and there are no scientific studies showing any ill effects of marigolds for women who are pregnant or nursing, some warnings have appeared in lay publications cautioning against the plant's use during pregnancy or lactation.

Plant/Drug Interactions   * * *

HOW TO USE THIS PLANT

In Cooking   Only marigolds cultivated for food use are considered safe to eat. Marigolds sold as cut flowers for decoration, may have been sprayed with toxic chemicals, and should not be used as food.

To prepare marigolds from your garden, snip off the flowers while they are still in bloom. Pull off petals and leaves and rinse them thoroughly to remove dust and insects.

To prepare marigold petals as a substitute for saffron, dry the flowers in a cool, dark place. When the flowers are dried, pull off the petals and pulverize the centers. Store the powder in a tightly sealed glass jar to protect it from air and moisture.

Around the House   In folk art, marigolds are sometimes used as an orange dye for wool. To prepare a dye from marigolds, tear up 1 pint of marigold flowers for each ounce of wool you want to dye. Put the flowers in a large pot, and add enough water to cover. Boil the flowers for 30 minutes; then strain out the flowers and add enough fresh water to make 1 quart of dye solution for each ounce of wool to be dyed. Wet the wool yarn, fabric, or unlined garment in warm water; squeeze out excess water; add the yarn, fabric, or garment to the dye bath; and let simmer (do not boil) for about 30 minutes. Now turn off the heat, let the solution cool, remove the yarn or garment and rinse it in cool water until the water runs clear. In theory, this natural marigold dye works on any undyed, 100 percent wool yarn or fabric, but it is always possible the color may not be to your liking or it may be uneven if the yarn, fabric or garment is stained or faded. It is always a good idea to try any dye on a small inconspicuous spot to see how it looks before you dye the entire garment.

In the Garden   Like BASIL, GARLIC, PEPPERMINT and some other strongly scented garden plants, marigold plants appear to be natural insect repellents that do not pose a hazard to people or pets.

Marjoram

ABOUT THIS PLANT

Botanical name(s): *Majorana hortensis, Marjoram onites*

Common name(s): Sweet marjoram (*M. hortensis*), Pot marjoram (*M. onites*)

Native to: Asia, Mediterranean region

Parts used as food/drink: Leaves

GRAS list: Yes

Medicinal properties: * * *

Other uses: Perfumery

ABOUT THIS PLANT AS FOOD OR DRINK

Sweet marjoram is a member of the mint family, so closely related to OREGANO that botanists sometimes use the same scientific names—*Origanum majorana* and/or *Majorana hortensis*—to describe both plants. The U.S. Department of Agriculture distinguishes between the two by using the name *Majorana hortensis* for the sweet-scented marjoram and the name *Origanum vulgare* for the more acrid oregano.

Sweet marjoram has small green leaves that taste like very mild oregano; pot marjoram (*Origanum onites*) is a related plant with slightly larger leaves. The fresh leaves can be used in salads. Whole or crumbled dried leaves are used to flavor vegetables, meats (including sausages such as liverwurst and bologna), poultry stuffing, and tomato sauces. Pot marjoram, which tastes a bit more like THYME, is sometimes substituted for sweet marjoram.

Nutritional Profile One teaspoon (1 g) dried sweet marjoram leaves has 2 calories. It provides 0.1 g protein, a trace of fat, 0.4 g carbohydrates, 0.2 g dietary fiber, 48 IU vitamin A, 0.3 mg vitamin C, 12 mg calcium, 0.5 mg iron, and no sodium.

One tablespoon (2 g) dried sweet marjoram leaves has 5 calories. It provides 0.2 g protein, 0.1 g fat, 1 g carbohydrates, 0.7 g dietary fiber, 137 IU vitamin A, 0.9 mg vitamin C, 34 mg calcium, 1.4 mg iron, and 1 mg sodium.

HOW THIS PLANT AFFECTS YOUR BODY

Important Phytochemicals Marjoram contains small amounts of arbutin and hydroxyquinone.

Arbutin is a diuretic and urinary antiseptic. According to the German Commission E, marjoram and marjoram oil—perhaps because of their arbutin—appear to have some antibacterial activity, but there is no scientific evidence to support any claim of medical benefits.

Hydroxyquinone, a known animal carcinogen, is better known as a depigmenting compound included in creams used to lighten the skin and/or get rid of brownish "age spots." Although there are no reports of adverse effects linked to skin ointments containing marjoram extract, Commission E cautions that until the effects of hydroxyquinone and the herb itself are clearly documented the products should not be used for infants and small children.

Benefits   * * *

Possible Adverse Effects   Marjoram oil may be irritating to skin or eyes.

Information for Women Who Are Pregnant or Nursing   See above.

Plant/Drug Interactions   * * *

HOW TO USE THIS PLANT

In Cooking   You can substitute marjoram for oregano (and vice versa), but not in equal quantities: When using oregano in place of marjoram, use a little less oregano; when using marjoram instead of oregano, use a little more marjoram or add a pinch of thyme. One and one-half teaspoons marjoram leaves equals the flavor of 1 teaspoon oregano leaves. One-half teaspoon oregano leaves equals the flavor of 1 teaspoon marjoram leaves.

When substituting herbs, always use the same form of the herb—fresh leaves, dried whole leaves, or ground dried leaves.

Marshmallow

ABOUT THIS PLANT

Botanical name(s): *Althaea officinalis*
Common name(s): Althea
Native to: Europe, Asia
Parts used as food/drink: Roots, leaves
GRAS list: No
Medicinal properties: Demulcent
Other uses: Candy making (antiquated)

ABOUT THIS PLANT AS FOOD OR DRINK

Marshmallow is a tall plant with oval leaves and purple or pink-white flowers that bloom from July through October. It is native to Asia and Europe, but now grows wild on the edges of North American marshes.

Marshmallow leaves yield a clear liquid or juice that is rich in mucilage. This was once whipped with eggs and sugar to create a foam that hardened into the original marshmallow candy. Modern-day marshmallows are made from a protein solution such as gelatin which is whipped with sugar syrup and allowed to harden.

Marshmallow roots and young green tops may be used as vegetables. Dried marshmallow root, which may be labeled *althea* (from the Greek "to heal") is occasionally available at health food stores.

Nutritional Profile   * * *

HOW THIS PLANT AFFECTS YOUR BODY

Important Phytochemicals   The mucilage in marshmallow leaf and root is a natural demulcent, a compound that soothes irritated skin and mucous membranes.

Benefits   In 1989, the German Commission E approved the use of preparations of marshmallow leaf and root to relieve a sore throat and dry cough and the use of preparations of the root to relieve mild inflammation of the lining of the stomach. Note: Marshmallow preparations sometimes contain added sugar. As a result, Commission E advises that they should be used only as a gargle by people with diabetes. The caution applies to the added sugar, not the herb or root.

Possible Adverse Effects   * * *

Information for Women Who Are Pregnant or Nursing   * * *

Plant/Drug Interactions   If you consume natural marshmallow along with medication, the marshmallow's mucilage may slow your absorption of the medicine. If you are currently taking medication, check with your doctor before including marshmallow in your diet.

HOW TO USE THIS PLANT

In Cooking   Chlorophyll, the green coloring in marshmallow leaves, is sensitive to acids. When you heat the leaves, their chlorophyll reacts with natural acids in the leaves or in the cooking water, forming a brown compound called pheophytin. The pheophytin in turn reacts with the yellow carotene pigments in the leaves, turning them bronze. To prevent this color change, prevent the chlorophyll from reacting with the acids by adding the leaves at the last minute. (Commercial herb packagers preserve the color of green herbs by drying the leaves at a very low heat.)

As a Home Remedy   Peel the marshmallow root, and boil it with sugar or honey and orange or lemon juice to make a soothing tea or gargle for a sore throat or dry cough.

Maté

ABOUT THIS PLANT

Botanical name(s): *Ilex paraguariensis*
Common name(s): Paraguay tea, St. Bartholomew's tea, yerba maté
Native to: South America
Parts used as food/drink: Leaves
GRAS list: Yes
Medicinal properties: Central nervous system stimulant
Other uses: * * *

ABOUT THIS PLANT AS FOOD OR DRINK

The maté tree, which is native to Argentina, Brazil, and Paraguay, is a member of the holly family that has red berries like its northern cousin. But maté leaves are oval rather than spiky, lighter green in color, and less shiny.

Once maté leaves are harvested, they are dried for 24 to 36 hours, then crumbled into a coarse powder, which is aged in sacks for a year or more. The result is a powder used to brew maté tea, a bitter, aromatic beverage that is extremely popular in South America. In the United States, maté is most commonly found in health food stores where it is sometimes promoted as a natural coffee substitute.

Nutritional Profile   * * *

HOW THIS PLANT AFFECTS YOUR BODY

Important Phytochemicals   Maté's flavor comes from astringent tannins; citric acid, one of the compounds that makes LEMONS sour; malic acid, a flavoring agent that gives immature apples their astringency; and small amounts of vanillin, the principal flavoring agent in VANILLA.

Maté contains caffeine and theophylline, the central nervous system stimulants found in COFFEE, GUARANA, and TEA, plus theobromine, the muscle stimulant in COCOA.

Benefits   Caffeine is a stimulant. It makes you more alert, improves concentration and muscle response, speeds up the heartbeat, and lifts the mood. Caffeine is a mild diuretic that increases urination. It constricts the blood vessels in your brain (that is why caffeinated beverages sometimes relieve headaches caused by engorged blood vessels). On the other hand, caffeine also dilates blood vessels in the rest of the body, increasing the

THE CAFFEINE CONTENT OF VARIOUS STIMULATING BEVERAGES (5-ounce cup)	
Cocoa	2–20 mg caffeine
Drip-brewed coffee	110–150 mg
Percolated coffee	64–124 mg
Decaffeinated coffee	2–5 mg
Maté	21–42 mg
Tea	20–110 mg

Sources: *The American Dietetic Association Handbook of Clinical Dietetics*. New Haven: Yale University Press, 1981; Whitney, Eleanor Noss, Cataldo, Corinne Balog, Rolfes, Sharon Rady, *Understanding Clinical Nutrition*, 4th edition. Minneapolis/St. Paul: West Publishing Company, 1994.

flow of blood to the heart. Studies suggest that it may increase pain-free exercise time in people with angina, but its tendency to make the heart beat faster leaves doctors divided as to whether people with heart disease should use caffeinated beverages such as maté. In 1988, the German Commission E approved the use of maté to relieve mental and physical fatigue.

Information for Women Who Are Pregnant or Nursing   * * *

Plant/Drug Interactions   Caffeine reduces the effectiveness of the antigout drug allopurinol; the antibiotics ampicillin, erythromycin, griseofulvin, penicillin, and tetracyclines; antacids including cimetidine (Tagamet); and iron supplements.

Drinking a caffeine beverage while you are taking any drugs that contain caffeine, such as the antiasthma drug theophylline or nonprescription products such as cold remedies, diuretics, pain relievers, and weight-control products, may intensify caffeine-associated side effects such as jittery behavior, nervousness, insomnia, and sleep disorders.

HOW TO USE THIS PLANT

In Cooking   South Americans sometimes use maté to add a bitter note to baked goods, much as North Americans use coffee to intensify the flavor of chocolate in mocha desserts or Mexicans use bitter chocolate in a molé sauce for chicken. If you have access to a store that carries South American foods or if your local health food store stocks maté, you may wish to experiment, using maté in place of coffee in various recipes.

Mayonnaise

ABOUT THIS CONDIMENT

Chemical name(s): ✳ ✳ ✳
Common name(s): ✳ ✳ ✳
Parts used as food/drink: ✳ ✳ ✳
GRAS list: No
Medicinal properties: ✳ ✳ ✳
Other uses: Cosmetic

ABOUT THIS PLANT AS FOOD OR DRINK

Mayonnaise, a simple food with a sophisticated chemistry, is made of oil and water. Water is a polar molecule (a molecule with a positive electrical charge at one end and a negative electrical charge at the other), while oil is a nonpolar molecule whose electrical charge is evenly distributed. (This is why water and oil do not mix.)

The ingredient food chemists use to keep water and oil from separating in a mixture such as mayonnaise is called an emulsifier. The emulsifier in old-fashioned, homemade mayonnaise is lecithin, found naturally in egg yolks. The virtue of the lecithin molecule is that it is polar at one end, so it can hook onto water, and nonpolar at the other, so it can hook onto oil. As a result, adding egg yolk to oil and water produces a smooth, nonseparating sauce.

Commercial mayonnaise and mayonnaise-type dressings often use flour rather than egg yolk to hold their oil and water together. Flour does not work with electrical charges; it simply traps the oil and water molecules in a starch network. So long as you do not beat the dressing and break the network, the liquids stay together.

The U.S. Food and Drug Administration's "standard of identity" (representative recipe) for a typical commercial mayonnaise is:

Vegetable oil (not less than 65 percent of the total weight of the mayonnaise)

Vinegar or lemon or lime juice (not less than 2.5 percent of the weight of the mayonnaise)

Egg (whole eggs or frozen, liquid or dried yolks)

Salt

Sweetener (sugar, dextrose, honey, corn syrup, etc.)

MSG

Calcium disodium EDTA or disodium EDTA (compounds that attract and hold metal atoms that would otherwise darken the dressing or allow it to become rancid)

Nutritional Profile   One tablespoon (14 g) mayonnaise made with soybean oil has 99 calories. It provides less than 1 g protein and carbohydrates, 11 g fat, 1.6 g sat fat, 3.1 g monounsaturated fat, 5.7 g polyunsaturated fat, 8 mg cholesterol, 1 mcg folate, 2 mg calcium, .1 mg iron, and 78 mg sodium.

One tablespoon (15 g) low-calorie mayonnaise made with soybean oil has 35 calories. It provides a trace of protein, 3 g fat, 0.5 g saturated fat, 0.7 g monounsaturated fat, 1.6 g polyunsaturated fat, 3.6 mg cholesterol, 2.4 g carbohydrates, and 74 mg sodium.

One tablespoon (15 g) mayonnaise-type salad dressing has 57 calories, 0.1 g protein, 4.9 g fat, 0.7 g saturated fat, 1.3 mg monounsaturated fat, 2.6 g polyunsaturated fat, 3.8 mg cholesterol, 32 IU vitamin A, 2 mg calcium, and 104 mg sodium, a trace of protein, 5 g fat, 4 mg cholesterol, 4 g carbohydrates, 2 mg calcium, a trace of iron, 30 IU vitamin A.

HOW THIS PLANT AFFECTS YOUR BODY

Benefits   * * *

Possible Adverse Effects   Commercial mayonnaise and mayonnaise-type dressings that contain egg yolks may be high in fat and cholesterol.

Information for Women Who Are Pregnant or Nursing   * * *

Plant/Drug Interactions   * * *

HOW TO USE THIS CONDIMENT

In Cooking   Contrary to popular belief, mayonnaise does not necessarily speed food spoilage. In 1982 researchers at the Food Research Institute of the University of Wisconsin confirmed that commercially prepared mayonnaise actually protects the food because it contains vinegar or lemon juice, acids that retard the growth of the *Salmonella* and *Staphylococcus* organisms, the commonest causes of food poisoning. This should never be interpreted to mean that any food, including food mixed with mayonnaise, does not need to be refrigerated. Keeping foods properly cold (or properly hot) is the best way to slow bacterial growth and prevent food poisoning. *Caution:* Freezing salads made with mayonnaise may be hazardous. Freezing slows bacterial growth but does not kill bacteria, which begin to multiply quickly again while the food is defrosting.

When you peel or slice a fruit or vegetable, you tear cell walls, releasing polyphenoloxidase, an enzyme that converts phenols in the fruit or vegetable to brownish compounds that darken its flesh. You can slow this reaction by coating the fruit or vegetable with an acid. That's why we dip sliced apples or potatoes in lemon juice, or mix guacamole (avocados), Waldorf salad (apples and walnuts) or potato salad with acidic, commercially prepared mayonnaise. The mayonnaise has two virtues. Not only is it an acid, it is also a protective coating that keeps out oxygen, which also turns the fruit and vegetables dark.

As A Cosmetic   Mayonnaise is an old-fashioned hair conditioner probably first used when the dressing was a home-made blend of olive oil and oil-rich eggs. Modern commercial full-calorie mayonnaise is still oil-rich and will still make your hair shine, although it's certainly harder to rinse out than regular conditioners.

To use, scoop $1/2$ cup mayonnaise out of a jar with a clean spoon. Put the jar back in the refrigerator and rub the mayonnaise on your hair. Then wrap your head in aluminum foil or plastic wrap. Wait for about half an hour, then wash your hair, rinsing thoroughly to remove excess oils.

Meat Tenderizer

ABOUT THIS CONDIMENT

Chemical name(s): Papain
Common name(s): Ać-cent
Native to: * * *
Parts used as food/drink: * * *
GRAS list: Yes (papain)
Medicinal properties: * * *
Other uses: * * *

ABOUT THIS CONDIMENT AS FOOD OR DRINK

The active ingredient in commercial meat tenderizers is papain, also known as vegetable pepsin. Papain is a proteolytic (proteo = protein; lyse = disintegrate) enzyme from fresh papayas. Other proteolytic enzymes are bromelain, from fresh pineapple, and ficin, from fresh figs.

Proteolytic enzymes tenderize meat by breaking long protein molecules in the meat into smaller pieces. Papain is highly effective; as little as one-quarter ounce (7 g) papain will tenderize as much as 8.8 pounds of meat.

In addition to papain, a representative commercial meat tenderizer contains SALT, the sweetener dextrose, the flavor enhancer MSG (MONOSODIUM GLUTAMATE), the anticaking agent tricalcium phosphate, and a partially hydrogenated vegetable oil such as cottonseed oil or soybean oil.

Nutritional Profile   One teaspoon regular meat tenderizer contains 1,750 mg sodium. One teaspoon low-sodium meat tenderizer has 1 mg sodium.

HOW THIS CONDIMENT AFFECTS YOUR BODY

Important Phytochemicals   The active compound in meat tenderizer is papain (see above).

Because papain degrades protein, it is widely believed to inactivate the protein venom injected by many stinging insects, particularly mosquitoes, and a paste made of papain meat tenderizer and water is a time-honored folk remedy. However, the German Commission E has not approved papain for this use, citing insufficient scientific proof. *Caution:* If you are allergic to any insect venom, do not rely on any home remedy. If stung, seek medical advice IMMEDIATELY.

Benefits   * * *

Possible Adverse Effects   Papain is a potential allergen that may cause contact dermatitis (itching, stinging, burning, reddened, or blistered skin).

Meat tenderizers high in sodium are usually prohibited on a controlled-sodium diet.

Papain may cause increased bleeding in people with existing blood-clotting disorders.

Information for Women Who Are Pregnant or Nursing   * * *

Condiment/Drug Interactions   Monoamine oxidase (MAO) inhibitors are drugs used as antidepressants or antihypertensives. They inhibit the activity of enzymes that break down nitrogen compounds (amines) so these compounds can be efficiently eliminated from the body. As a result, the amines build in your bloodstream, constricting blood vessels and raising blood pressure.

When meat is treated with a papain tenderizer, one by-product is tyramine, an amine that constricts blood vessels and raises blood pressure. Ordinarily, tyramine is eliminated from the body by the enzyme monoamine oxidase (MAO), but MAO inhibitors prevent this enzyme from degrading and eliminating tyramine. If you eat tenderized meat while you are taking an MAO inhibitor, the result may be a hypertensive crisis (sustained high blood pressure). Note: Aged meat is also high in tyramine.

HOW TO USE THIS CONDIMENT

In Cooking   Proteolytic enzymes are inactivated by heat. Canned or dried papaya, pineapple, or figs will not tenderize meat.

Milk Thistle

ABOUT THIS PLANT

Botanical name(s): Silybum marianum
Common name(s): Marian thistle, Mary thistle
Native to: Mediterranean region
Parts used as food/drink: Leaves
GRAS list: No
Medicinal properties: Antidote, liver protector
Other uses: * * *

ABOUT THIS PLANT AS FOOD OR DRINK

Milk thistle is a Mediterranean native, a tall plant with purple-red flowers and large, prickly leaves with white veins (the "milk" in milk thistle). The plant is cultivated primarily as an ornamental plant, but its leaves, minus their spikes, may be used fresh as a salad green or cooked as a green vegetable. Milk thistle tea bags may be available at health food stores.

Nutritional Profile * * *

HOW THIS PLANT AFFECTS YOUR BODY

Important Phytochemicals The active compound in milk thistle fruit (also known as milk thistle "seeds"), is silymarin, a collective name for three other compounds: silybin, silidianin, and silicristin. The three are often characterized as a new class of chemical, a combination of plant alcohols with flavonoids, naturally-occurring antioxidants that prevent molecular fragments circulating in your body from joining to form potentially damaging molecules.

In experimental studies, silymarin appears to protect the liver by preventing poisons such as phalloidin and aminitin (the toxins in "death cap" mushrooms), carbon tetrachloride, and FV3, a liver virus found in cold-blooded animals, from penetrating liver cells. In addition, silymarin stimulates the regeneration of liver cells.

Benefits Validating the studies described above, in 1986, the German Commission E approved the use of milk thistle preparations containing at least 70 percent silymarin to relieve upset stomach and as supportive therapy for chronic liver disease.

Like other deep green vegetables, milk thistle leaves contain carotenoid pigments, including beta-carotene, a deep yellow coloring agent the body converts to a form of vitamin A. According to the American Cancer Society, a diet rich in these foods may lower the risk of some forms of cancer. Vitamin A also protects your vision: The body, converts the vitamin A from milk thistle to 11-cis retinol, the most important constituent of rhodopsin, a protein in the rods in your retina (the cells that enable you to see in dim light).

Possible Adverse Effects   Silymarin is a mild laxative.

Information for Women Who Are Pregnant or Nursing   * * *

Plant/Drug Interactions   * * *

HOW TO USE THIS PLANT

In Cooking   Chlorophyll, the green coloring in milk thistle leaves, is sensitive to acids. When milk thistle is heated, its chlorophyll reacts with natural acids in the leaves or in the cooking water, forming a brown compound called pheophytin. The pheophytin in turn reacts with the yellow carotene pigments in the leaves, turning the cooked leaves bronze. To prevent this color change, keep the chlorophyll from reacting with the acids by cooking the milk thistle for as short a time as possible. (Commercial herb packagers preserve the color of green herbs by drying the leaves at a very low heat.)

Mojo

ABOUT THIS CONDIMENT

Botanical name(s): * * *
Common name(s): * * *
Native to: Cuba
Parts used as food/drink: * * *
GRAS list: No
Medicinal properties: * * *
Other uses: * * *

ABOUT THIS CONDIMENT AS FOOD OR DRINK

Mojo (pronounced "mo-ho") is a citrus-based Cuban condiment used as a marinade and dressing. A representative commercial mojo may include grapefruit and/or orange and/or LEMON juice, plus VINEGAR, SALT, GARLIC, ONION, BITTER ORANGE, and assorted spices such as OREGANO and CUMIN. Some mojos also include a thickener (xanthan gum) or a preservative (sodium benzoate is common).

Nutritional Profile Two tablespoons (30 ml) of a representative commercial mojo has 10 calories. It provides 2.5 mg carbohydrates, 100 mg calcium, 2 mg iron, and 270 mg sodium.

HOW THIS CONDIMENT AFFECTS YOUR BODY

Benefits * * *

Possible Adverse Effects Citrus fruits are potential allergens that may cause contact dermatitis (itching, burning, stinging, reddened, or blistered skin) or cheilitis (peeling, bleeding lips).

Information for Women Who Are Pregnant or Nursing * * *

Condiment/Drug Interactions Taking aspirin or other nonsteroidal anti-inflammatory drugs such as naproxen or ibuprofen with acidic foods such as grapefruit juice makes the drugs' more irritating to your stomach.

Drinking grapefruit juice with a wide variety of drugs ranging from antihistamines to blood pressure medication appears to reduce the amount of the drug your body metabolizes and eliminates. The "grapefruit effect" was first identified among people taking the antihypertensive drugs felodipine (Plendil) and nifedipine (Adalat, Procardia). It is not yet known

exactly what the active substance in the juice is. One possibility, however, is bergamottin, a naturally occurring compound in grapefruit juice known to inactivate cytochrome P450 3A4, a digestive enzyme needed to convert many drugs to water-soluble substances that are flushed out of the body. Without an effective supply of cytochrome P450 3A4, the amount of a drug circulating in your body may rise to dangerous levels. Reported side effects include low blood pressure, increased heart rate, headache, flushing, and lightheadedness. Among the drugs with which grapefruit juice is known to interact are the antihistamine terfenadine (Seldane, Hismanal); the anticoagulant warfarin (Coumadin); the benzodiazepines (Valium, Halcion, Restoril); the calcium channel blockers felodipine (Plendil), nifedipine (Adalat, Procardia), and verapimil (Calan, Isoptin, Veralan); the immunosuppressive drugs cyclosporine (Sandimmune), used primarily for organ transplants; and the anti-asthma drug theophylline. However, the amount of grapefruit juice in mojo is so small that there is very little probability of this effect being linked to use of the condiment.

HOW TO USE THIS CONDIMENT

In Cooking   You can make your own mojo at home starting with grapefruit juice, grapefruit-orange juice, or grapefruit-orange-lemon juice. Depending on your own preference, add all or some of the following to taste: sherry vinegar, wine vinegar, or white distilled vinegar; olive oil; garlic; cumin; salt; pepper.

MSG (*Monosodium Glutamate*)

ABOUT THIS CONDIMENT

Chemical name(s): Monosodium glutamate
Common name(s): MSG
Native to: * * *
Parts used as food/drink: * * *
GRAS list: No
Medicinal properties: * * *
Other uses: * * *

ABOUT THIS CONDIMENT AS FOOD OR DRINK

Monosodium glutamate, more commonly known as MSG, is one of a number of compounds derived from glutamic acid, a nonessential amino acid found in meat, fish, cow's milk, cereals, and grains. MSG occurs naturally in SEAWEED; it can be made from the proteins in wheat, corn, or soybeans. Today, more than 90 percent of all MSG is made by bacterial fermentation of carbohydrates such as the sugar from sugar beets.

Contrary to popular belief, MSG does not enhance flavors in food—it adds its own. The Japanese have named this flavor *umami* (pronounced "u-mom-ee"). Umami is neither sweet, nor bitter, nor sour, nor salty; diners asked to describe it usually say it is "rich."

Nutritional Profile   One teaspoon (5 g) MSG contains 492 mg sodium. One serving ($^1/_8$ teaspoon) of a commercial brand name MSG may contain 75 mg sodium.

HOW THIS CONDIMENT AFFECTS YOUR BODY

Important Phytochemicals   Monosodium glutamate is a neurotransmitter, a chemical that enables cells to transmit electrical messages. In the brain, MSG acts as an "excitory neurotransmitter," one that intensifies cell activity. In excessive amounts, MSG may be so stimulating that it causes neurons to expire. MSG is banned from baby foods in the United States.

Benefits   MSG, which does not affect the flavor of sweet foods, has no benefit other than to make protein foods taste better.

Possible Adverse Effects Although many scientific studies have failed to confirm a link between MSG and Kwok's disease, also known as "Chinese restaurant syndrome," many people report a tightening of facial muscles, nausea, headache, dizziness, and heavy perspiration after eating foods made with MSG. These symptoms occur in one of several hundred people within 20 minutes after eating the dish, but they may also occur in anyone who gets a high enough dose of MSG on an empty stomach. People who are especially sensitive to glutamic acid, corn, wheat, or sugar beets (from which MSG may be made) may develop symptoms after eating only minute amounts of MSG.

Because the chemical structure of monosodium glutamate is similar to that of aspartic acid, people who are sensitive to MSG may also be sensitive to the sugar substitute aspartame. In sensitive individuals, the consumption of either MSG or aspartame may cause hives and swelling of tissue in the throat. According to a 1986 study conducted at Washington University in St. Louis, Missouri, these symptoms may show up immediately after eating or they may not appear for several hours.

MSG is high in sodium, so it is usually restricted on a controlled-sodium diet.

Information for Women Who Are Pregnant or Nursing * * *

Condiment/Drug Interactions MSG intensifies the effects of diuretic drugs, increasing urination and the consequent loss of fluids, potassium, and water-soluble nutrients such as vitamin C and the B vitamins.

HOW TO USE THIS CONDIMENT

In Cooking Because MSG dissolves in water but not in fat, it is better to add it to a liquid such as a sauce or a soup rather than sprinkling it directly on solid food.

Mustard

ABOUT THIS PLANT

Botanical name(s): *Brassica nigra* (black mustard), *Brassica juncea* (brown mustard)

Common name(s): * * *

Native to: Europe

Parts used as food/drink: Flowers, leaves, seeds

GRAS list: Yes

Medicinal properties: Counterirritant, appetite stimulant, emetic

Other uses: * * *

ABOUT THIS PLANT AS FOOD OR DRINK

Mustard is a thoroughly economical plant. Its greens may be boiled and served as a vegetable; its flowers and seed pods may be used in salads; and its seeds may be ground to make the condiment we call *mustard*, the second most popular spice in the United States (PEPPER is number one).

Nutritional Profile   One teaspoon (3 g) mustard seed has 15 calories. It provides 0.8 g protein, 1 g fat, 0.4 g polyunsaturated fat, 0.7 g monounsaturated fat, 1.1 g carbohydrates, 2 IU vitamin A, 17 mg calcium, 0.33 mg iron, and 0.2 mg sodium.

One teaspoon or packet (5 g) prepared yellow mustard has 4 calories. It provides less than 1 g protein, fat and carbohydrates, 4 mg calcium, 0.1 mg iron, and 63 mg sodium.

One-half cup (70 g) cooked, drained mustard greens has 11 calories. It provides 0.6 g protein, 0.2 g fat, 1.5 g carbohydrates, 2,122 IU vitamin A, 18 mg vitamin C, 52 mg calcium, 0.5 mg iron, and 0 mg sodium.

HOW THIS PLANT AFFECTS YOUR BODY

Important Phytochemicals   Mustard gets its flavor from mustard oils that contain sinigrin, a bitter-tasting compound. When mustard seeds are cracked or ground, their cell walls are torn, releasing enzymes that convert sinigrin to allyl isothiocyanate, the chemical that gives mustard its characteristic bitter taste.

Mustard oils are counterirritants. When applied to the skin, they cause small blood vessels just under the skin's surface to dilate so that more blood

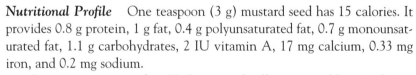

flows to the site. The increased blood flow produces a sensation of warmth, which is why mustard plasters were once used for people with upper respiratory infections. However, in strong concentrations or if left on too long, mustard plasters may burn the skin; modern heating pads that turn off automatically when a lever is released are safer and more efficient.

In concentrated form, mustard powder is an emetic, a substance that causes vomiting. A solution of mustard powder in warm water was once a well-known home remedy for suspected poisoning, but as information about toxins has expanded, home remedies have been replaced with specific antidotes. *Caution:* Never induce vomiting in someone who has swallowed a toxic substance except as directed by a physician.

Benefits   Like other "hot" herbs and spices, mustard irritates the lining of your stomach, triggering the flow of gastric juices and stimulating the contractions called hunger pangs. As a result, mustard has long been used as an appetite stimulant.

Like other dark green leafy vegetables, mustard greens are a good source of deep yellow carotenoid pigments such as beta-carotene that are converted to vitamin A in your body. According to the American Cancer Society, a diet rich in carotenoids appears to reduce the risk of some forms of cancer. Vitamin A also protects your eyes. In your body, the vitamin A from mustard greens is converted to 11-cis retinol, the most important constituent of rhodopsin, a protein in the rods in your retina (the cells that enable you to see in dim light). One-half cup cooked mustard greens provides 53 percent of the vitamin A required each day by a healthy adult woman and 42 percent of the vitamin A required by a healthy adult man.

Possible Adverse Effects   Because it stimulates the production of stomach acid, mustard—like black pepper, CHILI POWDER, CLOVES, NUTMEG, alcohol, COCOA, COFFEE, MATE, and TEA—is generally restricted or prohibited on a bland diet.

Information for Women Who Are Pregnant or Nursing   * * *

Plant/Drug Interactions   * * *

HOW TO USE THIS PLANT

In Cooking   Ground mustard, the powder sold as dry mustard, is also known as mustard flour. To fully develop the sharp, stinging flavor of the mustard oils in the seeds, you must add tepid water, the liquid that most effectively initiates the enzymatic activity that gives mustard its characteristic taste. Acids such as vinegar or wine preserve the flavor of the mustard/water paste. Therefore, the simplest prepared mustard is mustard flour plus a little water, an acid (wine or vinegar), and a coloring agent such as turmeric to make the mustard more yellow. Some prepared mustards also contain sugar, artificial flavors, and perhaps some wheat flour to make the mustard smoother.

To collect your own mustard seeds, harvest the mustard plant when the weather cools, after the pods have browned, but before they have split open. Slice the plant at the bottom, then hang the cut plants over cheesecloth or newspaper to dry. When they are dry, wrap them in a cheesecloth bag and bang the bag against a counter to dislodge the seeds. Finally, sift the seeds through a colander or strainer to get rid of the extraneous debris. *Caution:* Always handle the mustard seeds carefully; if you break the seeds and so release the mustard oils, they may irritate or even blister your skin.

One teaspoon dry mustard equals the flavor of 1 tablespoon prepared mustard.

As a substitute for the very hot mustard customarily served in Chinese restaurants, mix dry mustard with just enough tepid water to make a paste. For the best flavor, wait 10 minutes, then use immediately.

You can use mustard powder to hold an oil and water salad dressing together. Ordinarily, water and oil do not mix. Water is a polar molecule with a positive electrical charge at one end a negative electrical charge at the other. Oil is a nonpolar molecule with its electrical charge evenly distributed all over the molecule. Thus, the two cannot attract each other. But if mustard flour is added, it will absorb both the water and oil molecules, holding them in place and allowing the two to "mix." Mustard flour can hold up to 1.5 times its weight in salad oil and twice its weight in water.

Chlorophyll, the green coloring in mustard greens, is sensitive to acids. When mustard greens are heated, their chlorophyll reacts with natural acids in the leaves or in the cooking water, forming a brown compound called pheophytin. The pheophytin in turn reacts with the yellow carotene pigments in the greens, turning the cooked greens bronze. To prevent this color change, you must keep the chlorophyll from reacting with the acids by cooking the mustard greens for as short a time as possible. (Commercial herb packagers preserve the color of green herbs by drying the leaves at a very low heat.)

Nasturtium

ABOUT THIS PLANT

Botanical name(s): *Tropaeolum majus*
Common name(s): Indian cress
Native to: South America
Parts used as food/drink Leaves, flowers, stems
GRAS list: No
Medicinal properties: Antiscorbutic
Other uses: Natural insect repellent

ABOUT THIS PLANT AS FOOD OR DRINK

Nasturtium is a Peruvian vine with colorful flowers and light green leaves whose peppery flavor is similar to that of WATERCRESS (*Nasturtium officinale*), a botanical cousin. Nasturtium stems, leaves, and flowers can be used fresh in salads, or the leaves may be cooked and served as a green vegetables.

Nutritional Profile   One ounce (28 g) fresh nasturtium leaves and stalks has 14–100 calories. It provides 0.5–3.8 g protein, 0.3–2.5 g dietary fiber, 2.6–19 IU vitamin A, 57–132.8 mg vitamin C, 60–440 mg calcium, and 0.4–2.7 mg iron.

HOW THIS PLANT AFFECTS YOUR BODY

Important Phytochemicals   The flavor of nasturtium leaves comes from spicy mustard oils, similar to those found in MUSTARD, ONIONS, and the cruciferous vegetables (BROCCOLI, brussels sprouts, cabbage, cauliflower, and RADISHES.

Benefits   Nasturtium leaves are high in fiber and are an excellent source of vitamin C, the nutrient that prevents scurvy.

Possible Adverse Effects   * * *

Information for Women Who Are Pregnant or Nursing   * * *

Plant/Drug Interactions   * * *

HOW TO USE THIS PLANT

In Cooking   Chlorophyll, the green coloring in nasturtium leaves, is sensitive to acids. When the leaves are heated, their chlorophyll reacts with natural acids in the leaves or in the cooking water, forming a brown compound called pheo-phytin. The pheophytin in turn reacts with the yellow carotene pigments in the leaves, turn-ing the cooked leaves bronze. To prevent this color change, keep the chlorophyll from reacting with the acids by cooking the nasturtium leaves for as short a time as possible. (Commercial herb packagers preserve the color of green herbs by drying the leaves at a very low heat.)

In the Garden   Like MARIGOLDS, onions, GARLIC, and radishes, nasturtiums have a strong aroma that repels many garden pests. In your garden, nasturtium plants act as a natural insect repellent.

Nettle

ABOUT THIS PLANT

Botanical name(s): Urtica dioica
Common name(s): Common nettle, stinging nettle
Native to: Europe/Asia
Parts used as food/drink: Young tops
GRAS list: No
Medicinal properties: Diuretic, counterirritant
Other uses: Fabric dye

ABOUT THIS PLANT AS FOOD OR DRINK

The nettle, also known as the stinging nettle, is a tall, straight plant with hairy, oval, dark green leaves that can be boiled and served along with young nettle shoots as a green vegetable. Nettle may also be used to brew a flavored beer and as an herbal tea.

Nutritional Profile   One ounce (28 g) dried young nettle provides 8.5 g protein, 0.9 g fat, 2.9 g dietary fiber, 5.6 IU vitamin A, 831 mg calcium, 9 mg iron, 39 mg sodium, and 5.6 IU vitamin A.

HOW THIS PLANT AFFECTS YOUR BODY

Important Phytochemicals   Nettle contains histamine and other compounds that trigger an allergic reaction. It also contains irritants such as carbonic acid, formic acid, and silicic acid (also found in HORSETAIL), plus astringent tannins. Appropriately, the nettle's botanical name (*Urtica*) comes from the Latin "to burn."

Benefits   The U.S. Food and Drug Administration classifies nettle as an herb of undefined safety, but in 1987, the German Commission E approved the use of preparations such as teas made from fresh or dried nettle leaves (and aboveground parts) to relieve urinary inflammation. In its approval, Commission E cautioned against the use of nettle products for patients with edema (swelling) due to heart disease or kidney disease and advised those using nettle to drink copious amounts of fluids.

   Like other dark green leafy vegetables, fresh nettle shoots and leaves contain deep yellow carotenoid pigments such as beta-carotene that are converted to vitamin A in your body. According to the American Cancer Society, a diet rich in carotenoids appears to reduce the risk of some forms

of cancer. Vitamin A also protects your eyes. In your body, the vitamin A from mustard greens is converted to 11-cis retinol, the most important constituent of rhodopsin, a protein in the rods of the retina (the cells that enable you to see in dim light).

Possible Adverse Effects   When you touch or handle the nettle plant, it releases the histamine and other irritants stored in tiny sacs inside the leaves. Because these irritants are potent vasodilators (substances that make blood vessels expand), handling nettle plants may cause hives and/or severe contact dermatitis (itching, burning, stinging, reddened, or blistered skin) and hives. (Hives are sometimes known as *urticaria* and *nettle rash*.)

Information for Women Who Are Pregnant or Nursing   Some herbal sources describe nettle as an emmenagogue, a substance that causes uterine contractions that induce a menstrual period, but this is not mentioned in Commission E's report.

Plant/Drug Interactions   * * *

HOW TO USE THIS PLANT

In Cooking   Always wear protective gloves and long sleeves to cover your arms when handling the nettle plant, either in the kitchen or in the garden.

When cooking nettle, use only the young leaves and shoots at the very top of the plant. Boil the nettle in water for at least 15 minutes to destroy the irritating compounds that make nettle sting. Caution: Unless it is boiled, nettle—including nettle teas—may cause gastric upset, urinary irritation, and cheilitis (irritated, even blistered, lips and mouth).

Chlorophyll, the green coloring in nettle, is sensitive to acids. When nettle is heated, its chlorophyll reacts with natural acids in the leaves or in the cooking water, forming a brown compound called pheophytin. The pheophytin in turn reacts with the yellow carotene pigments in the shoots, turning the cooked shoots bronze. To prevent this color change, keep the chlorophyll from reacting with the acids by cooking the nettle for as short a time as possible. (Commercial herb packagers preserve the color of green herbs by drying the leaves at a very low heat.)

Industrial Uses   Commercially, nettle is used as a source of chlorophyll for green dyes, as livestock feed, and as the source of a fiber similar to hemp or flax.

Nutmeg

ABOUT THIS PLANT

Botanical name(s): Myristica fragrans
Common name(s): Myristica
Native to: Indonesia
Parts used as food/drink: Seed kernel
GRAS list: Yes
Medicinal properties: * * *
Other uses: Flavoring for tobacco and toothpaste

ABOUT THIS PLANT AS FOOD OR DRINK

Nutmeg is one of two spices (the other is MACE) that come from the nutmeg tree, an evergreen member of the myrtle family native to Indonesia but now grown in the West Indies. Nutmeg is the seed kernel inside the tree's fruit; mace is made from the aril, a lacy covering on the shell of the seed. Dried whole nutmegs are yellow-brown; ground nutmeg is tan.

Note: Both the oil extracted from the leaves of the nutmeg tree and the oil from the seed kernel and the aril are called oil of nutmeg, but the oil from the leaves is also known as oil of mace, while the oil from the kernel and the aril are also known as oil of myristica.

Nutritional Profile   One teaspoon (2.2 g) ground nutmeg has 12 calories. It provides 0.1 g protein, 0.8 g fat, 1 g carbohydrates, 4 mg calcium, a trace of iron, and 2 IU vitamin A.

One tablespoon (7 g) ground nutmeg has 37 calories. It provides 0.4 g protein, 2.5 g fat, 3.5 g carbohydrates, 1.5 g dietary fiber, 7 IU vitamin A, 0.2 mg vitamin C, 13 mg calcium, 0.2 mg iron, and 1 mg sodium.

HOW THIS PLANT AFFECTS YOUR BODY

Important Phytochemicals   Nutmeg's flavor and aroma come from oil of nutmeg, which contains peppery-scented, mint-flavored borneol; spicy eugenol, the compound that makes CLOVES smell and taste like cloves; rose-scented geraniol; and lavender-scented linalool.

Nutmeg and mace appear to relieve intestinal spasms. They have been used in folk medicine to treat gastrointestinal problems such as diarrhea, intestinal gas, and gastric spasms, but there is no scientific evidence to show that they are actually effective.

Borneol, geraniol, and linalool are irritants and potential allergens. Oil of nutmeg also contains small amounts of myristicin, an hallucinogen. High doses of myristicin, defined as one to three whole nutmeg or 5 grams ($^1/_6$ oz) powdered nutmeg or mace—may trigger psychological disturbance including euphoria, detachment from reality, or the sensation of floating; vomiting; flushed skin; and visual and auditory hallucinations within one to six hours. Very large doses may be fatal. The small amount of mace commonly used in food is considered safe.

Oil from nutmeg and mace grown in Indonesia contains very small amounts of safrole, the flavoring agent in FILÉ (sassafras). Safrole is a carcinogen. The U.S. Food and Drug Administration does not permit the use of safrole in food sold in the United States; the sassafras sold legally in this country must be safrole-free. The small amount of mace commonly used in food is considered safe.

Benefits   * * *

Possible Adverse Effects   Like black PEPPER, CHILI POWDER, cloves, and MUSTARD seeds, nutmeg is a gastric irritant that increases the secretion of stomach acids. It is usually prohibited on a bland diet. Also, see above.

Information for Women Who Are Pregnant or Nursing   Large amounts of nutmeg (the seed plus the aril) may cause contractions of the uterine muscles.

Plant/Drug Interactions   * * *

HOW TO USE THIS PLANT

In Cooking   One whole nutmeg, grated, equals 2 to 3 teaspoons of ground nutmeg.

Nutmeg has a more delicate flavor than mace, but in a pinch one may be substituted for the other so long as you use the same form of the spice, that is, 1 part ground nutmeg for 1 part ground mace.

Industrial Uses   Nutmeg is used to flavor tobacco used in American cigarettes and other tobacco products.

Olives

ABOUT THIS PLANT

Botanical name(s): Olea europaea
Common name(s): * * *
Native to: Mediterranean region
Parts used as food/drink: Fruit, oil
GRAS list: No
Medicinal properties: Laxative, emollient
Other uses: Cosmetic products

ABOUT THIS PLANT AS FOOD OR DRINK

Olives are the fruit of a tree native to Mediterranean countries, the geographic area that is home to 93 percent of all the olive trees in the world.

Green olives are olives picked before they ripen. Black olives are olives picked ripe and dipped in an iron solution to stabilize their color. After harvesting, all green olives and most black olives are soaked in a mild solution of sodium hydroxide and then washed thoroughly in water to remove oleuropein, a naturally bitter carbohydrate. Green olives are often allowed to ferment before being packed in a brine solution. Black olives are not fermented, which accounts for their milder flavor. The exceptions: Greek olives and Italian olives, salt-cured black olives that have not been soaked to remove the oleuropein and are sold covered with olive oil that preserves the olives by protecting them from oxygen.

Pressed ripe olives yield olive oil, a pale yellow to pale green vegetable oil with a distinctive delicate flavor and aroma. The color is not a guide to quality but an indication of when the olives were pressed; the earlier in the season, the greener the oil. Olive oil is used as a condiment and in packing fish products such as sardines or tuna.

The primary (83.5 percent) fatty acid in olive oil is oleic acid. Olive oils are graded according to the pressing from which they come and their acidity measured by the amount of "free" oleic acid released when the olive is pressed.

Extra virgin olive oil has no more than 1 percent free oleic acid—one gram acid per 100 grams oil. (Virgin olive oil is oil from the very first pressing of the olives.)

Superfine virgin olive oil has not more than 1.5 percent; fine virgin olive oil, no more than 3.3 percent.

Pure olive oil is a blend of virgin olive oil and refined olive oil, oil from a second pressing of the fruit.

Pomace oil is oil obtained by treating olive residue (pomace) from previous pressings with solvents that extract any remaining oil.

Nutritional Profile   A serving of 5 green olives (19 g) has 23 calories. It provides less than 1 gram protein, 2 g fat, 0.3 g saturated fat, 0.2 g polyunsaturated fat, 1.9 g monounsaturated fat, less than 1 gram carbohydrates and dietary fiber, 6 IU vitamin A, 12 mg calcium, 0.3 mg iron, and 468 mg sodium.

A serving of 5 pitted black olives (22 g) has 22 calories. It provides less than one gram protein, 1 g carbohydrates, 1 g dietary fiber, 2 g fat, 0.3 g saturated fat, 0.2 g polyunsaturated fatty acids, 1.8 g monounsaturated fatty acids, 9 IU vitamin A, 20 mg calcium, 0.7 mg iron, and 146 mg sodium. (Note: A 22 g serving of Greek olives has 74 calories. It provides 0.5 g protein, 7.9 g fat, 1.9 g carbohydrates, and 723 mg sodium.)

One tablespoon (14 g) olive oil has 124 calories. It provides 14 g fat, 1.9 g saturated fatty acids, 1.2 g polyunsaturated fatty acids, and 10.3 g monounsaturated fatty acids, and 0.7 g vitamin E.

One tablespoon extra virgin olive oil (14 g) has 126 calories. It provides 14 g fat, 2 g saturated fatty acids, 1.3 g polyunsaturated fatty acids, 10.8 g monounsaturated fatty acids, and 0.7 g vitamin E.

HOW THIS PLANT AFFECTS YOUR BODY

Important Phytochemicals   VEGETABLE OILS such as olive oil are composed primarily of unsaturated fatty acids, molecules that can accommodate extra hydrogen atoms. Monounsaturated fatty acids can accommodate two extra hydrogen atoms; polyunsaturated fatty acids can accommodate four or more extra hydrogen atoms. Most of the fatty acids in olive oil are monounsaturated.

Like other vegetable oils, olive oil is a source of vitamin E, the collective name for a group of antioxidant heart-protective compounds known as tocopherols.

Benefits   People with high cholesterol levels are considered to be at risk for heart disease. The unsaturated fatty acids in vegetable oils appear to lower overall cholesterol levels. Polyunsaturated fatty acids reduce all forms of cholesterol, including high-density lipoproteins (HDLs), the "good" protein and fat particles that carry cholesterol out of the body, but monounsaturated fatty acids protect the HDLs while reducing the levels of low-density lipoproteins (LDLs), the "bad" fat and protein particles that carry cholesterol into arteries. Olive oil is more than 95 percent monounsaturated fatty acids.

In a roundabout way, olive oil may also reduce the risk of some kinds of cancer. Lycopene, a red carotenoid pigment found in tomatoes, appears to reduce the risk of lung cancer and cancer of the prostate, and in one large European study, men who ate a diet high in lycopene were at lower risk of heart attack. Cooked tomatoes, including tomato sauces, provide more lycopene than do fresh tomatoes. Because lycopene dissolves in fat, adding a bit of olive oil to a cooked tomato product increases the amount of lycopene you absorb.

Possible Adverse Effects   * * *

Information for Women Who Are Pregnant or Nursing   * * *

Plant/Drug Interactions   * * *

HOW TO USE THIS PLANT

In Cooking   Small olives taste less "woody" than large ones; pitted olives are the best buy if you want to slice the olives into a salad; otherwise, olives with pits are less expensive.

To make olives less salty, bathe them in olive oil before you use them.

Olive oil is best when used within a year of pressing and packaging; it should not be held longer than two years. Molecules of unsaturated fatty acids may pick up oxygen atoms which oxidize the oil (turn it rancid). To protect olive oil, store it in a tightly closed container in a cool, dark cabinet.

Commercial Uses   Olive oil is used as an emollient in drugs, in cosmetics such as soaps, and in commercial lubricants.

Onions

ABOUT THIS PLANT

Botanical name(s): *Allium cepa*
Common name(s): * * *
Native to: Mediterranean region
Parts used as food/drink: Bulb, leaves
GRAS list: No
Medicinal properties: Appetite stimulant, anticholesterol agent, antihypertensive
Other uses: Insect repellent

ABOUT THIS PLANT AS FOOD OR DRINK

Onions are related to CHIVES and GARLIC, members of a family of pungent vegetables native to countries around the Mediterranean. The most nutritious onions are the immature ones, which are called scallions if they are picked before the bulbs have fully developed and green or spring onions if picked when the bulbs are large.

Nutritional Profile   One-quarter cup (40 g) chopped fresh onion has 15 calories. It provides 0.5 g protein, a trace of fat, 3.5 g carbohydrates, 0.8 g dietary fiber, 2.5 mg vitamin C, 8 mg calcium, 0.1 mg iron, and 65 mg sodium.

One-quarter cup (25 g) chopped green onion bulb and leaves has 8 calories. It provides 0.5 g protein, a trace of fat, 1 g carbohydrates, 0.5 g dietary fiber, 9.5 IU vitamin A, 4.5 mg vitamin C, 18 mg calcium, 0.4 mg iron, and 4 mg sodium.

HOW THIS PLANT AFFECTS YOUR BODY

Important Phytochemicals   Yellow onions, white onions, and the white bulbs of green onions/scallions get their color from creamy pale yellow anthoxanthins. Red onions are red due to red anthocyanins. Neither anthocyanin nor anthoxanthins provide the vitamin A found in the deep yellow carotenoids masked by chlorophyll in the green tops of green onions.

All onions get their flavor and aroma from sulfur compounds such as aliin and MUSTARD oils. These compounds are activated by allinase, an enzyme released when the onion is peeled or sliced. Onions also contain flavonoids, bitter antioxidants sometimes used to stimulate the appetite.

Benefits   The green tops of scallions are a good source of beta-carotene, the vitamin A precursor in deep yellow fruits and vegetables. According to the American Cancer Society, a diet rich in these foods may lower the risk of some forms of cancer. Vitamin A also protects your eyes. In your body, the vitamin A from scallion tops is converted to 11-cis retinol, the most important constituent of rhodopsin, a protein in the rods in your retina (the cells that enable you to see in dim light).

The sulfur compounds in onions appear to reduce the risk of some cancers, perhaps by preventing the formation of carcinogens in your body or by blocking carcinogens from reaching or reacting with sensitive body tissues or by inhibiting the transformation of healthy cells to malignant ones.

In a number of laboratory studies over the past three decades, first in India and then in this country, the oils in onions appear to decrease blood levels of low-density lipoproteins (LDLs), the protein and fat molecules that carry cholesterol into the bloodstream, while increasing the levels of high-density lipoproteins (HDLs), the protein and fat molecules that carry cholesterol out of the body. As early as 1986, the German Commission E approved the use of sliced fresh or dried onions or onion juice to prevent the formation of blood clots that could lead to a heart attack. The amount cited in the Commission E report was 50 g (slightly less than 2 oz) fresh vegetables or 20 grams (slightly less than 1 oz) dried onions a day.

Possible Adverse Effects   The most common adverse effect associated with eating onions (including scallions) is bad breath caused by the sulfur compounds in the onions. When onions are heated, these compounds break down and become less smelly; cooked onions are significantly less pungent than raw onions.

Some people find onions irritating to the stomach.

Information for Women Who Are Pregnant or Nursing   The smelly compounds in onions may be present in a nursing mother's milk.

Plant/Drug Interactions   * * *

HOW TO USE THIS PLANT

In Cooking   Store onions in a cool cabinet or a cool room such as a root cellar where the temperature is 60 degrees F or lower and there is plenty of circulating air to keep the onions dry and prevent them from sprouting. Properly stored, onions should stay fresh for three to four weeks; at 55 degrees F, they may retain all their vitamin C for as long as six months.

Cut the roots from green onions/scallions, trim damaged tops, and refrigerate the vegetables in a tightly closed plastic bag, checking daily to remove wilted tops.

When you cut into an onion, you tear cell walls, releasing propanethial-S-oxide. The sulfur compound, identified in 1985 at the University of St. Louis in Missouri, floats into the air, changing into sulfuric acid when it comes in contact with water, which it why it stings if it gets into your eyes. To prevent this, slice fresh onions under running water to dilute the propanethial-S-oxide before it rises, or chill the onion for an hour before slicing to slow the movement of sulfur molecules so they do not rise from the cutting board.

To peel the outer skin from an onion, immerse the vegetable briefly in boiling water, then lift with a slotted spoon and drop it into cold water. The skin will loosen and come off easily.

Heat converts an onion's sulfurous flavor and aroma compounds into sugars, which is why cooked onions taste sweet. When onions are browned, the sugars and amino acids on their surface caramelize to a deep rich brown and the flavor intensifies. This browning of sugars and amino acids is called the *Maillard reaction* after the French chemist who first identified it.

Onions may also change color when you cook them. Onions get their creamy color from anthoxanthins, pale yellow pigments that turn brown if they combine with metal ions. That's why onions discolor if you cook them in an aluminum or iron pot or slice them with a carbon steel knife. Red onions contain anthocyanin pigments that turn redder in acid (lemon juice, vinegar) and blue in a basic (alkaline) solution.

Use chopped fresh scallion tops as a substitute for chives.

Chlorophyll, the green coloring in scallion tops, is sensitive to acids. When scallions are heated, their chlorophyll reacts with natural acids in the leaves or in the cooking water, forming a brown compound called pheophytin. The pheophytin in turn reacts with the yellow carotene pigments in the leaves, turning the cooked leaves bronze. To prevent this color change, you must keep the chlorophyll from reacting with the acids by cooking the scallion tops for as short a time as possible. (Commercial herb packagers preserve the color of green herbs by drying the leaves at a very low heat.)

In the Garden   In the garden, onions act as natural insect repellents. Some other similarly odiferous herbs are BASIL, MARIGOLD, NASTURTIUM, PEPPERMINT, ROSEMARY, and SAGE.

Onion Seasonings

ABOUT THIS CONDIMENT

Botanical name(s): * * *
Common name(s): * * *
Native to: * * *
Parts used as food/drink: * * *
GRAS list: Yes
Medicinal properties: Appetite stimulant, anticholesterol
Other uses: * * *

ABOUT THIS CONDIMENT AS FOOD OR DRINK

Onions are dried and processed to make onion flakes (large pieces of dried onion); minced onion (small pieces of dried onion); onion powder (ground dehydrated onion); and onion salt (onion powder plus shredded scallions and salt). Note: Onion powder and onion salt usually contain an anticaking agent such as tricalcium phosphate (also known as calcium phosphate, tribasic; or tricalciumorthophosphate) to prevent them from absorbing moisture and clumping.

Nutritional Profile   One-quarter ounce (14 g) dehydrated onion flakes has 25 calories. It provides 0.6 g protein, 0.1 g fat, 6 g carbohydrates, 14 IU vitamin A, 2.5 mg vitamin C, 12 mg calcium, 0.2 mg iron, and 0 mg sodium.
   One teaspoon (2.1 g) onion powder has 7 calories. It provides 0.2 g protein, a trace of fat, 1.7 g carbohydrates, 8 mg calcium, and 0.3 mg vitamin C.
   One teaspoon (5 g) onion salt has 1,620 mg sodium.

HOW THIS CONDIMENT AFFECTS YOUR BODY

Important Phytochemicals   All onions get their flavor and aroma from sulfur compounds such as aliin and MUSTARD oils. These compounds are activated by allinase, an enzyme released when the onion is peeled or sliced. The onion's sulfur compounds appear to reduce the risk of some cancers, perhaps by preventing the formation of carcinogens in your body or by blocking carcinogens from reaching or reacting with sensitive body tissues or by inhibiting the transformation of healthy cells to malignant ones. But heating or drying reduces the intensity of these compounds, so dried onions are unlikely to have the same powers as fresh onions.

Onions also contain flavonoids, bitter antioxidants sometimes used to stimulate the appetite. In laboratory studies, various animals appear to use flavonoids as they do vitamin C to strengthen capillaries, the small blood vessels just under the skin. In human beings, antioxidant flavonoids are valued for their ability to prevent molecular fragments from linking up with each other to form potentially cancer-causing compounds.

Benefits   In a number of laboratory studies over the past three decades, first in India and then in this country, the oils in onions appear to decrease blood levels of low-density lipoproteins (LDLs), the protein and fat molecules that carry cholesterol into the bloodstream, while increasing the levels of high-density lipoproteins (HDLs), the protein and fat molecules that carry cholesterol out of the body. As early as 1986, the German Commission E approved the use of dried onions to protect the heart. The recommended daily dose is 20 g (slightly less than an ounce) of dried onion.

The green tops of scallions are a good source of beta-carotene, the vitamin A precursor in deep yellow fruits and vegetables. According to the American Cancer Society, a diet rich in these foods may lower the risk of some forms of cancer. Vitamin A also protects your eyes. In your body, the vitamin A from scallion tops is converted to 11-cis retinol, the most important constituent of rhodopsin, a protein in the rods in your retina (the cells that enable you to see in dim light).

Possible Adverse Effects   The most common side effect of eating onions (including dried onions) is bad breath caused by the sulfur compounds in the onions. Because heat degrades these compounds, cooked and/or dried onions are less smelly than raw ones.

Some people find onions and onion seasoning irritating to the stomach.

Information for Women Who Are Pregnant or Nursing   The smelly compounds in onions may be present in a nursing mother's milk.

Plant/Drug Interactions   * * *

HOW TO USE THIS PLANT

In Cooking   Because drying removes about 95 percent of the moisture in the onion, it takes nearly 8 pounds of fresh onions to make 1 pound of dried onions. If you plan to add dehydrated onion products to an acid solution (such as a stew flavored with wine) or to a dish that

FLAVOR EQUIVALENTS	
$^1/_2$ cup onion flakes	= 2 tablespoons chopped raw onion
1 tablespoon minced dried onion	= $^1/_4$ cup minced fresh onion
1 tablespoon onion powder + 1 tablespoon water	= one medium onion

does not have enough water to rehydrate the onions, soak the onion products in water first to bring out the flavor, then add them to the pot.

The yellow onions and the white bulbs of green onions used in onion seasonings are colored with creamy pale yellow anthoxanthins. Heating the onions or drying them darkens the pigments which is why onion seasonings look browner than fresh onions.

Orange Peel (Sweet)

ABOUT THIS PLANT

Botanical name(s): *Citrus sinensis*
Common name(s): Orange zest
Native to: Northern India, China
Parts used as food/drink: Rind
GRAS list: Yes
Medicinal properties: Appetite stimulant
Other uses: Pharmaceutical flavoring, perfume

ABOUT THIS PLANT AS FOOD OR DRINK

Sweet orange peel, also known as orange zest, is the grated fresh rind (outer skin) of the familiar fruit from a tree native to northern India and China, but now cultivated in Spain, the West Indies, Florida, and California.

Nutritional Profile One teaspoon fresh orange peel has 2 calories. It provides a trace of protein, a trace of fat, 0.5 g carbohydrates, 0.2 g dietary fiber, 8.4 IU vitamin A, 2.7 mg vitamin C, 3.2 mg calcium.

One ounce (28 g) candied sweet orange peel has 90 calories. It provides a trace of protein and fat and 23 g carbohydrates.

HOW THIS PLANT AFFECTS YOUR BODY

Important Phytochemicals An orange's flavor and aroma come from orange oil, which contains lemon-scented citral and limonene, lavender-scented linalool, and terpineol, an antiseptic in pine oil. Because the oil is concentrated in the rind, the peel is intensely flavorful and aromatic.

The compounds in orange oil are skin irritants and potential allergic sensitizers (compounds that can make you sensitive to other allergens).

Oranges and other citrus fruits also contain bitter flavonoids such as hesperidin, an antioxidant. In laboratory studies, various animals appear to use flavonoids as they do vitamin C to strengthen capillaries, the small blood vessels just under the skin. In human beings, antioxidant flavonoids are valued for their ability to prevent molecular fragments from linking up with each other to form potentially cancer-causing compounds.

Benefits Orange peel is a good source of vitamin C. One ounce of fresh orange peel provides 65 percent of the vitamin C a healthy adult needs each day.

Like other bitter compounds, flavonoids stimulate the release of gastric juices, leading to the contractions we call hunger pangs. As a result, they are often used as appetite stimulants. In 1990, the German Commission E approved the use of teas brewed from sweet orange peel for this purpose.

Possible Adverse Effects Handling orange peel may cause contact dermatitis (itching, burning, stinging, reddened, or blistered skin) in sensitive individuals. Eating a food made with orange peel may cause cheilitis (chapped, blistered, or peeling lips). The oil in the peel may also irritate the intestinal tract.

Information for Women Who Are Pregnant or Nursing   * * *

Plant/Drug Interactions   * * *

HOW TO USE THIS PLANT

In Cooking Sweet orange rind is used to lend dash to marinades, sauces, and baked goods.

Before grating fresh orange peel, scrub the orange to remove any wax. Do not grate past the orange-colored part of the peel—the white tissue underneath is bitter.

One teaspoon grated orange peel equals the flavor of 1 teaspoon dried orange peel, 1 tablespoon fresh orange juice, or 2 teaspoons candied orange peel, washed to remove the sugar.

As a substitute for bitter orange peel, mix 2 parts grated fresh orange peel with 1 part grated lemon peel.

Oregano

ABOUT THIS PLANT

Botanical name(s): Origanum vulgare
Common name(s): Common oregano
Native to: Southern Europe
Parts used as food/drink: Leaves
GRAS list: Yes
Medicinal properties: No
Other uses: Perfumery

ABOUT THIS PLANT AS FOOD OR DRINK

Oregano, popularly known as "the pizza herb," is a member of the mint family, a relative of BASIL and MARJORAM. Its leaves are small, less than an inch long. They are unusual because they dry quickly and hold their flavor well.

Oreganos vary in flavor. Greek oregano (*Origanum heraclites*) and Spanish oregano (*Origanum vivens*) are strongly flavored; Italian oregano (*Origanum onites*) and common oregano (*Origanum vulgare*) are mild. Mexican oregano (*Lippia*), also known as Mexican marjoram or Mexican wild sage, is the strongest of the oreganos, strong enough to be used in CHILI POWDER and dishes flavored with chili peppers.

The oregano sold in the United States is usually a mixture of various species of dried oregano plus marjoram and thyme.

Nutritional Profile   One teaspoon (2 g) ground oregano has 5 calories. It provides 0.2 g protein, 0.2 g fat, 1 g carbohydrates, 0.6 g dietary fiber, 104 IU vitamin A, 0.8 mg vitamin C, 24 mg calcium, 0.7 mg iron, and no sodium.

One tablespoon (5 g) ground oregano has 14 calories. It provides 0.5 g protein, 0.5 g fat, 2.9 g carbohydrates, 1.9 g dietary fiber, 311 IU vitamin A, 2.3 mg vitamin C, 71 mg calcium, 2 mg iron, and 1 mg sodium.

HOW THIS PLANT AFFECTS YOUR BODY

Important Phytochemicals   Oregano's flavor comes from oil of origanum, a yellow-green, pleasantly scented liquid also used to flavor some liqueurs and to perfume toilet soaps. The most important ingredients in oil of origanum are carvacrol (also known as 2-p-cymenol) and thymol, also found in MARJORAM, SAVORY, and THYME.

Carvacrol is an antifungal and anthelmintic (an agent that kills intestinal worms) sometimes used as a disinfectant in the syntheses of organic chemicals, but its most important commercial use is as a perfume.

Benefits   Oregano is a good source of vitamin A. One teaspoon dried oregano provides 3 percent of the RDA for a man and 2 percent of the RDA for a woman.

Possible Adverse Effects   Oregano is a choleretic, an agent that stimulates the liver to increase its production of bile, a yellow, brown or green fluid. Bile helps emulsify fats in the duodenum and increases peristalsis, the rhythmic contractions that move food through the gastrointestinal tract. Choleretics are ordinarily beneficial for healthy people, but may pose some problems for people with gallbladder or liver disease. Some other choleretic herbs are GENTIAN, PEPPERMINT, and ONION.

Information for Women Who Are Pregnant or Nursing   * * *

Plant/Drug Interactions   * * *

HOW TO USE THIS PLANT

In Cooking   You can substitute oregano for marjoram and vice versa, but not in equal quantities. One and one-half teaspoons marjoram leaves equals the flavor of 1 teaspoon oregano leaves. One-half teaspoon oregano leaves equals the flavor of 1 teaspoon marjoram leaves.

When substituting, always use the same form of the herb—fresh leaves for fresh leaves, dried whole leaves for dried whole leaves, and ground leaves for ground leaves.

To extract the most flavor from whole, dried oregano leaves, crumble them before using to release the oils inside.

 *Paprika*

ABOUT THIS PLANT

Botanical name(s): *Capsicum annuum*
Common name(s): * * *
Native to: India
Parts used as food/drink: Dried pods (fruit)
GRAS list: Yes
Medicinal properties: Antiscorbutic
Other uses: Food coloring

ABOUT THIS PLANT AS FOOD OR DRINK

Paprika is the powder made by grinding dried ripe bell peppers, the mildest members of the Capsicum family.

Paprika peppers from Hungary and California are long and conical; those from Spain and Morocco are small and round. Either type of pepper may produce a mild (sweet) paprika or a hot one. The difference lies in which part of the pepper is used. The compounds that make hot peppers hot are carried in the pepper's veins and seeds. Hot paprikas are ground with the veins (no paprikas are ground with the seeds).

Paprika may also be used in salad dressing as an emulsifier (an agent that allows oil and water to mix), and it is sometimes included in spice mixtures, such as CHILI POWDER. The oils and resins extracted from the peppers ground for paprika are used as spices or as food coloring in cheeses and meat products, where they are listed on the label either as "paprika" or as "natural color."

Nutritional Profile   One teaspoon (2 g) paprika has 6 calories. It provides 0.3 g protein, 0.3 g fat, 1.2 g carbohydrates, 0.4 g dietary fiber, 1,273 IU vitamin A, 1.5 mg vitamin C, 4 mg calcium, 0.5 mg iron, and 1 mg sodium.

One tablespoon (7 g) paprika has 20 calories. It provides 1 g protein, 0.9 g fat, 3.9 g carbohydrates, 1.4 g dietary fiber, 4,182 IU vitamin A, 5 mg vitamin C, 12 mg calcium, 1.6 mg iron, and 2 mg sodium.

HOW THIS PLANT AFFECTS YOUR BODY

Important Phytochemicals   All peppers contain capsaicinoids concentrated in the seeds and membranes. Capsaicinoids are irritants that act directly on the pain receptors in your skin and mucous membranes. The strongest capsaicinoids are capsaicin and dihydrocapsaicin. Capsaicin is so potent that a single drop diluted in 1 million drops of water will still warm your tongue. Like dihydrocapsaicin, it delivers a sting all over your mouth. A third capsaicinoid, nordihydrocapsaicin, produces a warmer, mellower sensation in the front of your mouth and palate. A fourth, homodihydrocapsaicin, packs a delayed punch, delivering a stinging, numbing burn to the back of your throat.

Applied to the skin, capsaicin causes the small blood vessels under the skin to dilate, increasing the flow of blood to the area and making the skin feel warm. Once used as a warming poultice, it is no longer considered a safe remedy, as strong concentrations may blister the skin. Capsaicin is also a diaphoretic (an agent that increases perspiration). It stimulates nerve endings in your mouth normally stimulated by a rising body temperature, sending impulses to your brain that trigger facial perspiration.

Benefits   Paprika is a good source of deep yellow carotenoid pigments such as beta-carotene that are converted to vitamin A in your body. A diet rich in carotenoids appears to reduce the risk of some forms of cancer. It also protects your eyes as your body converts beta-carotene to 11-cis retinol, the most important constituent of rhodopsin, a protein in the rods in your retina (the cells that enable you to see in dim light). One tablespoon paprika provides 104 percent of the amount of vitamin A a healthy adult woman needs each day and 84 percent of the daily requirement for a healthy adult man.

Ounce for ounce, fresh sweet red peppers have more than seven times as much vitamin C as fresh oranges (105 mg/oz versus 14 mg/oz). Drying the peppers destroys much of the vitamin C, but 1 tablespoon paprika still provides 8 percent of the RDA for vitamin C.

Possible Adverse Effects   Hot paprikas, like hot red peppers, may irritate the lining of your mouth, throat, stomach, and bladder, causing upset stomach or frequent, painful urination which some people confuse with an aphrodisiac effect.

Information for Women Who Are Pregnant or Nursing   * * *

Plant/Drug Interactions   * * *

HOW TO USE THIS PLANT

In Cooking   Paprika scorches easily. For the best flavor when using it in a stew, add the paprika near the end of the cooking time.

You can use paprika to hold an oil and water salad dressing together. Ordinarily, water and oil do not mix. Water is a polar molecule with a positive electrical charge at one end a negative electrical charge at the other. Oil is a nonpolar molecule with an evenly distributed electrical charge, so the two cannot attract each other. But if paprika is added, it will absorb both water and oil molecules, holding them in place and allowing the two to mix. Paprika may hold several times its own weight in salad oil and twice its weight in water. Each time you use the dressing, you must shake it to make it smooth once again.

Parsley

ABOUT THIS PLANT

Botanical name(s): Petroselinum crispum
Common name(s): Common parsley
Native to: Mediterranean region
Parts used as food/drink: Leaves, stems
GRAS list: Yes
Medicinal properties: Diuretic
Other uses: Fabric dye

ABOUT THIS PLANT AS FOOD OR DRINK

Parsley, a member of the carrot family, comes in two varieties: flat leaf and curly leaf. The curly leaf version is more attractive as a garnish, but flat leaf parsley has a stronger, more intense flavor.

Nutritional Profile One-half cup (30 g) chopped fresh parsley has 11 calories. It provides 1 g protein, a trace of fat, 2 g carbohydrates, 1 g dietary fiber, 1,560 IU vitamin A, 40 mg vitamin C, 41 mg calcium, 1.9 mg iron, and 166 mg sodium.

One tablespoon (1 g) dried parsley has 4 calories. It provides 0.3 g protein, a trace of fat, 0.7 g carbohydrates, 0.4 g dietary fiber, 30 IU vitamin A, 1.6 mg vitamin C, 19 mg calcium, 1.3 mg iron, and 6 mg sodium.

HOW THIS PLANT AFFECTS YOUR BODY

Important Phytochemicals Parsley leaves, both flat and curly, get their flavor and aroma from parsley leaf oil which contains apiole, myristicin, and lavender-scented bergapten. Parsley also contains the yellow pigments, apiin and apigenin, two bitter flavonoids.

In laboratory studies, various animals appear to use flavonoids as they do vitamin C to strengthen capillaries, the small blood vessels just under the skin. In human beings, antioxidant flavonoids are valued for their ability to prevent molecular fragments from joining to form potentially cancer-causing compounds.

Apiole and myristicin are mild diuretics known to stimulate smooth muscle contractions. Bergapten is a photosensitizer.

Benefits   In 1989, the German Commission E validated the long-standing folk use of parsley as a diuretic by approving preparations of fresh or dried parsley leaves and root, along with copious amounts of fluid, to flush out the urinary tract. In approving parsley preparations, the commission warned against their use for people with kidney disease.

Parsley is a good source of deep yellow carotenoid pigments such as beta-carotene that are converted to vitamin A in the body. A diet rich in carotenoids appears to reduce the risk of some forms of cancer. It also protects your eyes as your body converts beta-carotene to 11-cis retinol, the most important constituent of rhodopsin, a protein in the rods in your retina (the cells that enable you to see in dim light). One-half cup chopped parsley provides 31 percent of the RDA for vitamin A for a woman and 31 percent of the RDA for a man.

Parsley is a good source of vitamin C; one-half cup chopped fresh leaves and stems provides 66 percent of the RDA for this nutrient.

Possible Adverse Effects   Bergapten is a furocoumarin, a member of a class of chemicals known to irritate the skin and photosensitize it (make it extremely sensitive to sunlight). Handling parsley plants may cause contact dermatitis (itching, burning, stinging, reddened, or blistered skin) or make your skin more sensitive to sunlight. Both reactions are most likely to occur among food workers who handle large bunches of parsley without wearing protective gloves.

Caution: Commission E has not approved the use of parsley seed or pure parsley oil products. Both the seeds and the oil contain high concentrations of apiol and myristicin. Large doses of apiol cause liver damage; kidney irritation; intestinal bleeding; contractions of the smooth muscle lining the bladder, intestines, and liver; and irregular heartbeat. In laboratory studies with mice, myristicin was found to latch onto the DNA in liver cells. Teas made from parsley seed are less troublesome because they contain less of the essential oil.

Information for Women Who Are Pregnant or Nursing   Because parsley oil may trigger uterine contractions, Commission E cautions pregnant women not to use medical preparations of parsley or parsley oil and suggests they avoid consuming large amounts of fresh parsley.

Plant/Drug Interactions   * * *

HOW TO USE THIS PLANT

In Cooking   Do not tear or cut fresh parsley until you are ready to use it. When you cut into a food rich in vitamin C, its cells release an enzyme called ascorbic acid oxidase that destroys vitamin C and reduces the nutritional value of the food.

Chlorophyll, the green coloring in parsley leaves, is sensitive to acids. When parsley is heated, its chlorophyll reacts with natural acids in the leaves or in the cooking water, forming a brown compound called pheophytin. The pheophytin in turn reacts with the yellow carotene pigments in the leaves, turning the cooked leaves bronze. To prevent this color change, keep the chlorophyll from reacting with the acids by cooking the parsley for as short a time as possible. (Commercial herb packagers preserve the color of green herbs by drying the leaves at a very low heat.)

Adding parsley to the pot decreases the unpleasant odor of vegetables such as onions and cauliflower.

Passionflower

ABOUT THIS PLANT

Botanical name(s): *Passiflora incarnata*
Common name(s): Passion vine
Native to: Southwestern United States
Parts used as food/drink: Flowering tops
GRAS list: No
Medicinal properties: Sedative, analgesic
Other uses: * * *

ABOUT THIS PLANT AS FOOD OR DRINK

The passionflower is a vine, a botanical cousin to the plant that produces the passion fruit. Its flowering tops are used to brew an herbal tea.

Caution: Do not confuse the edible *Passiflora incarnata* with a related variety, *Passiflora caerula*, a toxic plant that contains cyanide.

Nutritional Profile * * *

HOW THIS PLANT AFFECTS YOUR BODY

Important Phytochemicals Passionflower contains a number of bitter compounds including harman and harmaline, the flavonoid vitexin, vanilla-scented coumarin derivatives, and maltol, the sugar compound that lends baking bread its characteristic aroma.

Harman and harmaline are central nervous system stimulants. Vitexin is a natural antioxidant, a compound that prevents molecular fragments circulating in your body from joining to form potentially damaging molecules.

Benefits In 1978, the U.S. Food and Drug Administration Advisory Review Panel on Over-the-Counter Sedative, Tranquilizer, and Sleep Aid Products disapproved the use of passionflower in over-the-counter sleep aids because the panel could not find any evidence that the herb induces drowsiness, which seems logical considering the herb's stimulant content. However, in 1985 and 1990, the German Commission E approved the use of preparations of dried passionflower tops to relieve anxiety-related restlessness. The approval requires that passionflower products contain no more than 0.01 percent harman/harmaline.

Possible Adverse Effects * * *

Information for Women Who Are Pregnant or Nursing   Harman and harmaline may trigger uterine contractions. Although there are no reports of miscarriage linked to use of passionflower, herbal experts often advise pregnant women to avoid the herb. There is no information about passionflower's sedative effect on a nursing infant whose mother uses the herb.

Plant/Drug Interactions   * * *

HOW TO USE THIS PLANT

In Cooking   Passionflower tea bags are available in health food stores.

As a Home Remedy   The suggested daily dose for relief of nervous restlessness is tea brewed from 4–8 g herb.

Pepper, Black

ABOUT THIS PLANT

Botanical name(s): *Piper nigrum*
Common name(s): Pepper
Native to: India, the East Indies
Parts used as food/drink: Fruit (berry)
GRAS list: Yes
Medicinal properties: Counterirritant, diaphoretic
Other uses: Natural insecticide

ABOUT THIS PLANT AS FOOD OR DRINK

Green, black, or white peppercorns are the fruits of a tropical vine, *Piper nigrum*, a species entirely unrelated to the capsicum peppers (bell peppers, cayenne pepper, chili pepper).

Green peppercorns are unripe berries sold as whole, soft seasonings. Black peppercorns are berries picked unripe and allowed to dry in the sun to develop their color and flavor, then marketed as whole peppercorns or a ground spice. White peppercorns, which are also sold whole or as a powder, are berries that are allowed to mature before they are picked. After harvesting, the white peppercorns are soaked in water, stripped of their outer covering and allowed to dry and bleach in the sun.

Visually, white pepper is considered more attractive than black pepper in cream sauces and soups, but the flavor is the same. Green peppercorns have a different flavor, sometimes described as "fresh."

Nutritional Profile One teaspoon (2 g) ground black pepper has 5 calories. It provides 0.2 g protein, a trace of fat, 1.36 g carbohydrates, 0.6 g dietary fiber, 4 IU vitamin A, 0.4 mg vitamin C, 9 mg calcium, and 0.6 mg iron.

One tablespoon (6 g) ground black pepper has 16 calories. It provides 0.7 g protein, 0.2 g fat, 4.2 g carbohydrates, 1.7 g dietary fiber, 12 IU vitamin A, 1.3 mg vitamin C, 28 mg calcium, and 1.9 mg iron.

One teaspoon (2 g) ground white pepper has 7 calories. It provides 0.3 g protein, a trace of fat, 1.7 g carbohydrates, 0.6 g dietary fiber, 0.5 mg vitamin C, 6 mg calcium, 0.3 mg iron, and no sodium.

One tablespoon (7 g) ground white pepper has 21 calories. It provides 0.7 g protein, 0.2 g fat, 4.9 g carbohydrates, 1.9 g dietary fiber, 1.5 mg vitamin C, 19 mg calcium, 1.0 mg iron, and no sodium.

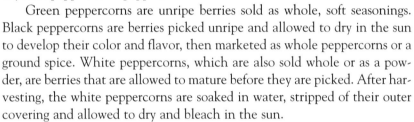

HOW THIS PLANT AFFECTS YOUR BODY

Important Phytochemicals   All peppercorns are flavored with piperine, piperidine, and chavicin. These three compounds are irritants that cause small blood vessels just underneath the skin to expand, increasing the flow of blood to the surface so that your skin feels warmer. Piperine, piperidine, and chavicin are also diaphoretics, substances that increase perspiration.

Black pepper contains small amounts of safrole, a known carcinogen also found in sassafras (see FILÉ). In experimental research, extracts of black pepper have caused tumors in laboratory mice when administered daily for three months. But the doses were more than 80 times as high as the average amount of pepper consumed each day by human beings, and pepper is not considered a human carcinogen.

Benefits   Because pepper irritates mucous membranes, highly spiced foods may be beneficial when you have a stuffy nose due to hay fever or a head cold. The spice irritates tissues inside your nose and throat, causing them to weep a watery secretion that makes it easier for you to cough up mucus or to blow your nose.

Eating pepper also makes you perspire. Because perspiration acts as a natural "air conditioner," cooling your body as the moisture evaporates from your skin, peppery foods are popular in warm climates.

Possible Adverse Effects   Eating peppered foods may upset your stomach and irritate your bladder so that you have to urinate more frequently; you may also find urinating painful. Some people confuse this the urinary irritation with an aphrodisiac effect. Others mistakenly believe that because pepper makes you urinate more frequently, it will cure a hangover. It won't. Your body does eliminate alcohol when you urinate (as well as when you breathe and perspire), but you can only get rid of the alcohol after it has been metabolized (digested) by enzyme action. When you drink more alcohol than your body can metabolize in a given period, the unmetabolized alcohol continues to circulate through your body, causing headache, muscle aches, and upset stomach. As time passes, the excess alcohol is metabolized and eliminated, and your discomfort eases. There is no way to speed up the process because you can't speed up your body's production of the necessary enzymes.

Information for Women Who Are Pregnant or Nursing   * * *

Plant/Drug Interactions   * * *

HOW TO USE THIS PLANT

In Cooking   Whole peppercorns retain their flavor better than ground pepper, which will eventually begin to taste bitter. To retain maximum freshness, store whole peppercorns in the freezer and grind them while still frozen.

A metal pepper grinder provides a clearer flavor than a pepper grinder made of wood because wood absorbs oils from the peppercorns. This also means a wooden grinder is more difficult to keep clean.

Pepper has a natural affinity for dishes made with ALLSPICE, CINNAMON, and CLOVES, deepening the flavor while adding a pleasant bite. Add a pinch of pepper to hot chocolate, eggnog, spiced wine punch, apple pie, baked apples or applesauce, baked pears, or gingerbread. Or try this recipe for peppered hot chocolate: Combine 1 teaspoon plain cocoa powder, 1 teaspoon sugar, a pinch of cinnamon, and a pinch of ground black or white pepper in a coffee cup. Add just enough boiling water or hot milk to make the powder into a smooth paste. Then stir in enough boiling water or hot milk to make 1 cup.

In the Garden Piperine is a natural insecticide considered more toxic to houseflies than pyrethrins, the natural insecticide derived from chrysanthemums. To protect your plants, you may wish to experiment with a pepper spray, a solution of one-half teaspoon ground pepper in 1 quart of warm water.

Pepper, Red

ABOUT THIS PLANT

Botanical name(s): Capsicum
Common name(s): Cayenne pepper
Native to: Mexico, Central America, South America, West Indies
Parts used as food/drink: Dried ripe seeds and pods
GRAS list: Yes
Medicinal properties: Diaphoretic, counterirritant
Other uses: * * *

ABOUT THIS PLANT AS FOOD OR DRINK

Red pepper, also known as cayenne pepper, is made from the seeds and pods of Capsicum peppers, a species completely unrelated to *Piper nigrum*, the plant that produces black, green, and white peppercorns (see PEPPER, BLACK).

The Capsicum peppers, which are native to Mexico, Central America, the West Indies and much of South America, may be long and thin like the cayenne pepper, large and firm like the Anaheim pepper, conical like the jalapeño, or small and round. Tabasco peppers, used to make a popular hot sauce, are a variety of hot peppers known as *Capsicum frutescens*.

Ground sharp red pepper, which is usually labeled *cayenne pepper* or *red pepper*, is made from small, pungent Capsicums. The term *red pepper* may also be used to describe red pepper milder than cayenne. Crushed red pepper, the seasoning popular as a pizza topping, is made from the seeds of the hot Capsicum varieties. CHILI POWDER is a blend of red pepper with other herbs and spices.

Nutritional Profile   One teaspoon (2 g) red or cayenne pepper has 6 calories. It provides 0.2 g protein, 0.3 g fat, 1 g carbohydrates, 0.45 g dietary fiber, 749 IU vitamin A, 1.4 mg vitamin C, 3 mg calcium, 0.1 mg iron, and 1 mg sodium.

One tablespoon (5 g) red or cayenne pepper has 17 calories. It provides 0.6 g protein, 0.9 g fat, 3 g carbohydrates, 1.4 g dietary fiber, 2,205 IU vitamin A, 4.3 mg vitamin C, 8 mg calcium, 0.4 mg iron, and 2 mg sodium.

HOW THIS PLANT AFFECTS YOUR BODY

Important Phytochemicals   The compounds that make hot peppers hot are called capsaicinoids. They are concentrated in the peppers' seeds and membranes, and all are strong irritants that act directly on the pain receptors in the skin and mucous membranes.

The strongest capsaicinoids are capsaicin and dihydrocapsaicin. Capsaicin is so strong that a single drop diluted in 1 million drops of water will warm your tongue. Like dihydrocapsaicin, it delivers a sting all over your mouth. A third capsaicinoid, nordihydrocapsaicin, produces a warmer, mellower sensation in the front of your mouth and palate. A fourth, homodihydrocapsaicin, packs a delayed punch, delivering a stinging, numbing burn to the back of your throat.

Applied to the skin, capsaicinoids dilate small blood vessels just under the surface, increasing the flow of blood to the area and making the skin feel warm. Though once used as a warming poultice, the capsiaicinoids are so irritating that they are no longer considered a safe home remedy.

Capsaicinoids are also diaphoretics (agents that increase perspiration). They work by stimulating endings in your mouth normally stimulated by a rising body temperature, which sends impulses to your brain that trigger facial perspiration.

Benefits   Red pepper is an excellent source of deep yellow carotenoid pigments such as beta-carotene that are converted to vitamin A in your body. A diet rich in carotenoids appears to reduce the risk of some forms of cancer. It also protects your eyes as your body converts beta-carotene to 11-cis retinol, the most important constituent of rhodopsin, a protein in the rods in your retina (the cells that enable you to see in dim light).

Fresh red peppers are also rich in vitamin C. Ounce for ounce, they have more vitamin C than fresh oranges (105 mg/oz versus 50 mg/oz), but drying the fresh peppers to make ground red pepper destroys most of the vitamin C.

VITAMIN A AND VITAMIN C CONTENT OF RED PEPPERS AND RED PEPPER PRODUCTS

Pepper	Serving	Vitamin A (IU)	Vitamin C (mg)
Chili powder	1 tablespoon	2,620	4.8
Chili powder	1 teaspoon	910	1.7
Bell pepper (red, raw, chopped)	1/2 cup	2,850	95
Hot red chili pepper (raw, diced)	1 tablespoon	1,010	23

Source: USDA Nutrient Database: http://www.nal.usda.gov/fnic/cgi-bin/nut_search.pl
Nutritive Value of Foods, USDA Home and Garden Bulletin Number 72 (Washington, D.C., USDA, revised 1989)

Foods spiced with pepper may be beneficial when you have hay fever or a cold. The pepper irritates the mucous membranes lining your nose and mouth, causing them to weep watery secretions. This may make it easier for you to blow your nose. Because peppery foods make you perspire, they are popular in warm climates. The perspiration they inspire acts as a natural air conditioner, cooling the body as the moisture evaporates on the skin. Beverages and food spiced with red pepper also stimulate the flow of saliva and encourage the secretion of gastric fluids that set off the contractions we call hunger pangs, which explains red pepper's reputation as an appetite stimulant.

Possible Adverse Effects   Eating red peppers may upset your stomach, irritate the lining of your stomach (red peppers are among the very few foods prohibited on an ulcer diet), irritate your bladder so that you have to urinate more frequently or even make urination painful. Some people confuse this urinary irritation with an aphrodisiac effect. Others mistakenly believe that because pepper makes you urinate more frequently, it will cure a hangover. That's not true. Your body does eliminate alcohol when you urinate, as well as when you breathe and perspire, but you can only get rid of the alcohol after it has been metabolized (digested) by enzyme action. When you drink more alcohol than your body can metabolize in a given period of time, the unmetabolized alcohol is stored in your body tissues, causing headache, muscle aches and upset stomach. As time passes, the excess alcohol is metabolized and eliminated, and your discomfort goes away. There is no way to speed up this process, because you can't speed up the body's production of the necessary enzyme.

Information for Women Who Are Pregnant or Nursing   * * *

Plant/Drug Interactions   * * *

HOW TO USE THIS PLANT

In Cooking   Never pick or handle fresh hot chili peppers without protective gloves. The capsaicin in the white material surrounding the seeds and veins is a severe skin irritant that can continue to burn your skin hours after you have worked with the peppers. Washing with soapy water won't help: Capsaicin does not dissolve in cold water and dissolves only slightly in hot water. It does dissolve in milk fat, alcohol, or vinegar. Bathing your hands with one of these may ease the pain. As a culinary corollary, keep in mind that beer (alcohol) or milk (milk fat) really are the best beverages to accompany a rousing chili or curry.

Pepper Sauce

ABOUT THIS CONDIMENT

Botanical name(s): * * *
Common name(s): Hot sauce
Native to: * * *
Parts used as food/drink: * * *
GRAS list: No
Medicinal properties: Appetite stimulant, diaphoretic
Other uses: * * *

ABOUT THIS CONDIMENT AS FOOD OR DRINK

Pepper sauce is a traditional condiment made from the seeds and pods of Capsicum (red) peppers plus vinegar and salt. Some hot pepper sauces also include sugar and spices. Perhaps the best-known hot pepper sauce is Tabasco sauce, a brand named for a specific variety of hot red peppers found in southern Louisiana.

Nutritional Profile One teaspoon (5.6 g) of a representative hot pepper sauce has 42 calories. It provides 1 g carbohydrate, 4 IU vitamin A, and 25 mg sodium.

HOW THIS CONDIMENT AFFECTS YOUR BODY

Important Phytochemicals The capsaicinoids that make hot peppers hot are strong irritants that act directly on the pain receptors in your skin and mucous membranes. The strongest capsaicinoids are capsaicin and dihydrocapsaicin. Capsaicin is so strong that a single drop diluted in 1 million drops of water will warm your tongue. Like dihydrocapsaicin, it delivers a sting all over your mouth. A third capsaicinoid, nordihydrocapsaicin, produces a warmer, mellower sensation in the front of your mouth and palate. A fourth, homodihydrocapsaicin, packs a delayed punch, delivering a stinging, numbing burn to the back of your throat.

Benefits Capsaicin is a diaphoretic (an agent that increases perspiration). It stimulates nerve endings in your mouth normally stimulated by a rising body temperature, sending impulses to your brain that trigger facial perspiration. Foods spiced with pepper may be beneficial when you have hay fever or a cold. The pepper irritates the mucous membranes lining your nose and mouth, causing them to weep a watery secretion. This may make it easier for you to blow your nose.

Because peppery foods make you perspire, they are popular in warm climates. The perspiration they inspire acts as a natural air conditioner, cooling your body as the moisture evaporates on your skin. Beverages and food spiced with red pepper also stimulate the flow of saliva and encourage the secretion of gastric fluids that set off the contractions we call hunger pangs, which explains red pepper's reputation as an appetite stimulant.

Possible Adverse Effects   Capsaicin is a strong irritant. Applied to the skin, it causes the small blood vessels under the skin to dilate, increasing the flow of blood to the area and making the skin feel warm. Though once used as a warming poultice, it is so irritating that it is no longer considered a safe remedy.

Pepper sauce may upset your stomach, irritate the lining of your stomach (red peppers are among the very few foods prohibited on an ulcer diet), irritate your bladder so that you have to urinate more frequently, or even make urination painful. Some people confuse this urinary irritation with an aphrodisiac effect. Others mistakenly believe that because pepper sauce makes you urinate more frequently, it will cure a hangover. That's not true. Your body does eliminate alcohol when you urinate, as well as when you breathe and perspire, but you can only get rid of the alcohol after it has been metabolized (digested) by enzyme action. When you drink more alcohol than your body can metabolize in a given period of time, the unmetabolized alcohol is stored in your body tissues, causing headache, muscle aches and upset stomach. As time passes, the excess alcohol is metabolized and eliminated, and your discomfort goes away. There is no way to speed up this process, because you can't speed up your body's production of the necessary enzyme.

Information for Women Who Are Pregnant or Nursing   * * *

Condiment/Drug Interactions   * * *

HOW TO USE THIS CONDIMENT
In Cooking   When adding pepper sauce to food, use discretion. A little goes a long way.

Peppermint

ABOUT THIS PLANT

Botanical name(s): *Mentha piperta*
Common name(s): Black mint, white mint
Native to: Europe
Parts used as food/drink: Leaves
GRAS list: Yes
Medicinal properties: Antispasmodic, antiflatulent, mild topical anesthetic
Other uses: Pharmaceutical flavor and scent, perfume

ABOUT THIS PLANT AS FOOD OR DRINK

Peppermint is a SPEARMINT hybrid with two-inch-long oval leaves. It ranks among the most intensely flavored of the mint herbs, a group that includes not only spearmint but also the fruit-flavored mints such as lemon mint, orange mint, and pineapple mint. Most of the dried "mint" leaves sold in grocery stores are spearmint leaves. The best sources of true, fresh peppermint leaves are plants in your own garden.

Nutritional Profile   Two fresh peppermint leaves (0 g) have no calories. They provide a trace of carbohydrates, 4 IU vitamin A, a trace of iron, and 1 mg sodium.

 Two tablespoons fresh peppermint leaves have 2.2 calories, 0.1 g protein, a trace of fat, 0.5 g carbohydrates, 0.3 g dietary fiber, 136 IU vitamin A, and 1 mg vitamin C.

HOW THIS PLANT AFFECTS YOUR BODY

Important Phytochemicals   Peppermint's flavor and aroma come from oil of peppermint, a colorless to pale yellow liquid whose most important constituent (not less than 50 percent) is peppermint-flavored and scented menthol.

 Menthol, a naturally occurring plant alcohol, is an effective local anesthetic used in topical lotions as well as sprays and lozenges for sore throats. It works by increasing the sensitivity of the receptors in the skin that perceive the sensation of coolness while at the same time reducing the sensitivity of the receptors that perceive pain and itching (a mild form of pain).

 Menthol is also a counterirritant, an agent that causes the small blood vessels under the skin to dilate, increasing the flow of blood to the area and making the skin feel warm. When you apply a skin lotion made with menthol, your skin feels cool for a minute, then warm.

Other compounds in oil of peppermint include pleasantly scented cadinene, lemony limonene, peppermint-scented menthone, and turpentine-scented pinene. Peppermint leaves also contain bitter tannins, astringents that coagulate proteins on the mucous membrane lining of the mouth, making the tissues pucker and creating a slight tingling effect. (Drinking milk relieves the tingling.)

Benefits   Teas brewed from peppermint leaves have a long-standing reputation as a home remedy for colds and coughs, but the U.S. Food and Drug Administration's Advisory Review Panel on OTC (Over-the Counter) Cold, Cough, Allergy, Bronchodilator and Anti-Asthmatic Products rated oil of peppermint and menthol as safe but not proven effective for use in various cold and allergy remedies.

However, in 1985, the German Commission E approved the use of peppermint leaf products to relax the smooth muscle of the digestive tract, relieving intestinal spasms. And in 1993, the commission approved the use of peppermint products to relieve intestinal spasms, alleviate congestion due to upper respiratory infection, and soothe irritated membranes lining the mouth.

Possible Adverse Effects   Menthol is an allergic sensitizer that may cause hives. Like limonene and pinene, it is an irritant that may cause contact dermatitis (itching, stinging, burning, reddened, or blistered skin).

Like coffee oils, fatty foods, and carbonated beverages, menthol may irritate the sphincter (muscle ring) at the base of the esophagus, triggering gastric reflux (acid flowing back from the stomach into the esophagus), causing "heartburn."

Peppermint leaf and peppermint oil are choleretics, agents that stimulate the liver to increase its production of bile, a yellow, brown or green fluid. Bile helps emulsify fats in the duodenum and increases peristalsis, the rhythmic contractions that move food through your gastrointestinal tract. Choleretics are ordinarily beneficial for healthy people but may pose some problems for people with gallbladder or liver disease. Some other choleretic herbs are GENTIAN, ONION, and OREGANO.

In approving the use of peppermint leaf products, Commission E warned against their use by people with gallstones except as directed by a physician. In approving peppermint oil, the commission warned against its use by people with gallbladder disease, liver disease, or bile duct obstruction except as directed by a physician.

In addition, because peppermint oil fumes can be irritating, the commission warned against using the oil on the face or near the nose, particularly by children.

Information for Women Who Are Pregnant or Nursing   * * *

Plant/Drug Interactions   * * *

HOW TO USE THIS PLANT

In Cooking   To preserve the flavor of fresh-picked mint leaves, store them in the refrigerator or freeze them in airtight plastic bags or containers.

To preserve the flavor of dried mint leaves, do not crumble them until you are ready to use them.

Caution: Peppermint tea may be hazardous to very young children, who may experience a choking sensation from the menthol.

As a Home Remedy   The suggested daily dose to relieve congestion or ease intestinal spasms is tea brewed from 3–6 g peppermint leaves.

Industrial Uses   Oil of peppermint is among the most popular of all the perfumed oils derived from herbs and spices. It is used not only in foods but in all kinds of cosmetics including shampoo, body oils, toilet soaps, toothpastes and tooth powders, and face masks.

Pine nuts

ABOUT THIS CONDIMENT

Botanical name(s): *Pinus species*
Common name(s): Pignoli, pinyon
Native to: Europe
Parts used as food/drink: Seeds
GRAS list: No
Medicinal properties: * * *
Other uses: * * *

ABOUT THIS CONDIMENT AS FOOD OR DRINK

Pine nuts are seeds from the cones of various kinds of pine trees. The creamy-white nuts may be thin and tapered or wide and round, or they may look like small kernels of corn; the shape depends on the tree from which they come. All pine nuts are soft and oily, and their flavor varies from sweet to pungent, again depending on the tree. Because they must be gathered by hand, pine nuts are relatively expensive. The two most widely available varieties of pine nuts are pinyon and pignoli. In the United States, pine nuts were once called "Indian nuts."

Like other seeds, pine nuts are high in proteins and rich in soluble dietary fiber (gums and pectins in the nut). They are an excellent source of B vitamins, including folate, which is known to protect the heart and reduce the risk of birth defects. Their oils are composed primarily of unsaturated fatty acids, a good source of vitamin E, but nuts have so much fat that even a small serving is high in saturated fat.

Nutritional Profile   A serving of 10 (1 g) dried pinyon/pine nuts has 6.3 calories. It provides 0.1 g protein, 0.6 g fat, 0.1 g saturated fat, 0.3 g polyunsaturated fat, 0.2 g monounsaturated fat, 0.2 g carbohydrates, 0.1 g dietary fiber, 0.1 mg calcium, and 0.7 mg sodium.

One ounce (28 g) dried pinyon/pine nuts has 178 calories. It provides 3.3 g protein, 17.3 g fat, 2.7 g saturated fat, 7.3 g polyunsaturated fat, 6.5 g monounsaturated fat, 5.5 g carbohydrates, 3 g dietary fiber, 100 IU vitamin A, 1 mg vitamin C, 2.2 mg calcium, 0.9 mg iron, and 20.4 mg sodium.

A serving of 10 (1.8 g) dried pignoli/pine nuts has 10 calories. It provides 0.4 g protein, 0.9 g fat, 0.1 g saturated fat, 0.4 g polyunsaturated fat, 0.3 g monounsaturated fat, 0.3 g carbohydrates, 0.1 g dietary fiber, 0.5 mg calcium, 0.2 mg iron, and a trace of sodium.

One ounce (28 g) dried pignoli/pine nuts has 160 calories. It provides 6.8 g protein, 14.4 g fat, 2.2 g saturated fat, 6.1 g polyunsaturated fat, 5.4 g monounsaturated fat, 4 g carbohydrates, 1.3 g dietary fiber, 8.2 IU vitamin A, 0.5 mg vitamin C, 7.4 mg calcium, 2.6 mg iron, and 1.3 mg sodium.

HOW THIS CONDIMENT AFFECTS YOUR BODY

Important Phytochemicals   The proteins in nuts, including pine nuts, are called *limited* or *incomplete* because they are deficient in the essential amino acid lysine. Combining pine nuts with grains produces complete proteins because grains, which are limited in cystine and methionine (found in the seeds), have sufficient amounts of lysine.

Pignoli have up to four times the protein found in pinyon, a fact of primary importance to vegans, vegetarians who do not eat foods from animals and get their protein entirely from plants.

Benefits   In the spring of 1998, an analysis of data from more than 80,000 women enrolled in the long-running Nurses Health Study at the Harvard School of Public Health/Brigham and Women's Hospital in Boston demonstrated that a diet providing more than 400 mcg folate and 3 mg vitamin B_6 per day from either food or supplements—more than twice the current RDA for each—may reduce a woman's risk of heart attack by almost 50 percent. Although men were not included in the analysis, the results are assumed to apply to them as well. (Fruit, green leafy vegetables, beans, whole grains, meat, fish, poultry, and shellfish are good sources of vitamin B_6.)

Although nuts are high in fat, their high level of monounsaturated fatty acids appears to reduce the amount of cholesterol and low-density lipoproteins (LDLs), fat and protein particles that carry cholesterol into arteries.

Possible Adverse Effects   According to *The Merck Manual*, nuts are one of the 12 foods most likely to trigger classic food allergy symptoms: hives, swelling of the lips and eyes, and upset stomach. (The other foods are chocolate, corn, eggs, fish, legumes [green peas, lima beans, peanuts, soybeans], milk, peaches, pork, shellfish, and wheat.)

Information for Women Who Are Pregnant or Nursing   As many as two of every 1,000 babies born in the United States each year may have cleft palate or a neural tube (spinal cord) defect due to their mother's not having gotten adequate amounts of folate during pregnancy. The current RDA for folate is 180 mcg for a woman and 200 mcg for a man, but the U.S. Food and Drug Administration now recommends 400 mcg for a woman who is or may become pregnant. Taking folate supplements before becoming pregnant and continuing through the first two months of pregnancy reduces the risk of cleft palate in the fetus; taking folate throughout the entire pregnancy reduces the risk of neural tube defects.

Condiment/Drug Interactions   * * *

FOLATE CONTENT OF PINE NUTS (1 ounce serving)			
Pignoli	4.9 mcg	3% RDA/women	2.5% RDA/men
Pinyon	16.4 mcg	9% RDA/women	8% RDA/men

Source: USDA Nutrient Database www.nal.usda.gov/fnic/cgi-bin/nut_search.pl

HOW TO USE THIS CONDIMENT

In Cooking   The unsaturated fats in nuts are very sensitive to oxygen and will eventually turn rancid, which means they react with oxygen to produce compounds called hydroperoxides that will break apart into smelly, foul-tasting components. Rancidity is a natural chemical reaction that can be slowed, but not entirely halted, by storing high-fat foods such as nuts in a tightly closed container in a cool, dry place. Shelled nuts may keep best in the refrigerator or they may be frozen for longer storage.

To make a less expensive substitute for pine nuts, shell pumpkin seeds or seeds from another winter squash and toast them at low heat in an ungreased skillet on top of the stove or on a cookie sheet in the oven. Stir often to keep the seeds from burning. The seeds are done as soon as they are nicely golden. Salt to taste and serve.

Poppy Seed

ABOUT THIS CONDIMENT

Botanical name(s): Papaver somniferum
Common name(s): * * *
Native to: Europe, Asia
Parts used as food/drink: Seeds
GRAS list: Yes
Medicinal properties: * * *
Other uses: Soap, paints, varnishes (poppy seed oil)

ABOUT THIS CONDIMENT AS FOOD OR DRINK

Poppy seeds, found in the pods of the poppy plant, are so small that it takes nearly 10 million to make one pound. The seeds are harvested by slicing open the pods. Unripe pods ooze a thick liquid latex whose constituents include morphine and codeine. But the latex rarely touches the seeds inside the pod, and when ripe pods are harvested, there are no narcotic compounds in either the poppy seeds or the oil pressed from the seeds, a pale yellow liquid with a pleasant odor and flavor. Edible grades of poppy seed oil are widely available in Europe and Asia where they are commonly used in cooking. (In this country, poppy seed oil is more likely to be used in making soap, paints, and varnishes.)

Nutritional Profile One teaspoon (3 g) poppy seed has 15 calories. It provides 0.5 g protein, 1.3 g fat, 0.1 g saturated fat, 0.9 g monounsaturated fat, 0.2 g polyunsaturated fat, 0.7 g carbohydrates, 0.3 g dietary fiber, 0.3 mg vitamin C, 41 mg calcium, 0.3 mg iron, and 1 mg sodium.

One tablespoon (9 g) poppy seed has 47 calories. It provides 1.6 g protein, 3.9 g fat, 0.4 g saturated fat, 2.7 g polyunsaturated fat, 0.6 g monounsaturated fat, 2.1 g carbohydrates, 0.9 g dietary fiber, 0.3 mg vitamin C, 127 mg calcium, 0.8 mg iron, and 2 mg sodium.

HOW THIS CONDIMENT AFFECTS YOUR BODY

Important Phytochemicals Poppy seeds are a good source of protein. One tablespoon of seeds has as much protein as one ounce cooked, drained lima beans. The proteins in poppy seeds are called "limited" or "incomplete" because they are deficient in the essential amino acid lysine, but combining the seeds with grains (flour) as a cake filling or as a topping for bread provides complete proteins because grains, which are limited in cystine and methionine (found in the seeds), have sufficient amounts of lysine.

Benefits   See above.

Possible Adverse Effects   Poppy seeds that have been contaminated with even infinitesimal traces of the poppy pod latex may produce a false positive result on a urine test for drugs, suggesting that you have used morphine or the morphine derivative heroin even though you have not.

Information for Women Who Are Pregnant or Nursing   * * *

Condiment/Drug Interactions   * * *

HOW TO USE THIS CONDIMENT

In Cooking   The simplest way to crush poppy seeds for use as a cake filling is to wrap the seeds in a kitchen towel and hammer them with a wooden mallet or rolling pin. A more elegant way to do the job is to pulverize the seeds with a mortar and pestle or to put them through a special mill designed for grinding seeds.

Pumpkin Seeds

ABOUT THIS PLANT

Botanical name(s): Cucurbita pepo
Common name(s): ＊＊＊
Native to: North America
Parts used as food/drink: Flesh, flowers, seeds
GRAS list: No
Medicinal properties: ＊＊＊
Other uses: Decoration

ABOUT THIS PLANT AS FOOD OR DRINK

The pumpkin is a New World original now grown on every continent except Antartica. A member of the squash family, it provides two condiments: pumpkin flowers used as nutritious green vegetable garnishes and high-protein seeds used as high fiber snacks.

The most nutritious pumpkin meat comes from varieties such as "Dickensons" used in canned pumpkin. Ounce for ounce, plain canned pumpkin has up to 20 times as much vitamin A, 50 percent more folate (a B vitamin that protects the heart), and up to 2.5 times as much calcium as boiled meat from an orange Jack O'Lantern type.

Nutritional Profile   One ounce (28 g) dried pumpkin seeds has 153 calories. It provides 6.9 g protein, 13 g fat, 2.5 g saturated fat, 5.9 g polyunsaturated fatty acids, 4.0 g monounsaturated fatty acids, 5.0 g carbohydrates, 1.1 g dietary fiber, 107 IU vitamin A, 0.5 mg vitamin C, 12.2 mg calcium, 4.2 mg iron, and 5.1 mg sodium.

One cup (134 g) boiled pumpkin flowers has 20 calories. It provides 1.5 g protein, 0.1 g fat, 4.4 g carbohydrates, 1.2 g dietary fiber, 2,323 IU vitamin A, 6.7 mg vitamin C, 49.6 mg calcium, 1.2 mg iron, and 8 mg sodium.

HOW THIS PLANT AFFECTS YOUR BODY

Benefits   Like other seeds, pumpkin seeds are high in protein, but limited or "incomplete" because they are deficient in the essential amino acids methionine and cystine. Combining pumpkin seeds with a grain, such as pasta, which is limited in lysine but contains sufficient amounts of the essential amino acids methionine and cystine, makes the proteins "complete."

Like other dark green leafy vegetables, pumpkin flowers contain deep yellow carotenoid pigments such as beta-carotene that are converted to vitamin A in the body. According to the American Cancer Society, a diet rich in carotenoids appears to reduce the risk of some forms of cancer. Vitamin A also protects your eyes. In your body, the vitamin A from pumpkin flowers is converted to 11-cis retinol, the most important constituent of rhodopsin, a protein in the rods in your retina (the cells that enable you to see in dim light).

Possible Adverse Effects   * * *

Information for Women Who Are Pregnant or Nursing   * * *

Plant/Drug Interactions   * * *

HOW TO USE THIS PLANT

In Cooking   To toast pumpkin seeds, remove the outer cover and warm at low heat in an ungreased skillet on top of the stove or on a cookie sheet in a 350-degree F oven. Stir often to keep the seeds from burning. They are done as soon as they are nicely golden.

Toasted pumpkin seeds (and seeds from other winter squash) may be used as a less expensive substitute for pine nuts.

Radish

ABOUT THIS PLANT

Botanical name(s): *Raphamus sativus*
Common name(s): Red radish
Native to: China, Mediterranean region
Parts used as food/drink: Root
GRAS list: No
Medicinal properties: Irritant, appetite stimulant, intestinal stimulant, antimicrobial
Other uses: * * *

ABOUT THIS PLANT AS FOOD OR DRINK

The common radish, also known as the red radish, is a member of the cabbage family, a root with moderate amounts of dietary fiber (insoluble cellulose and lignin). Radishes are a good source of vitamin C. One serving of 10 red radishes has 1 g dietary fiber and 10 mg vitamin C (16.6 percent of the RDA). Ounce for ounce, radishes have about 50 percent as much vitamin C as fresh oranges. (Red radishes have about 7 mg of vitamin C per ounce; daikon radishes, about 9 mg, a fresh orange, about 14 mg.)

Nutritional Profile   A serving of 10 red radishes has 8 calories. It provides less than 1 g protein, 2 g carbohydrates, 1 g dietary fiber, less than 1 g fat, less than 1 IU vitamin A, 10 mg vitamin C, 9 mg calcium, 0.1 mg iron, and 11 mg sodium.

HOW THIS PLANT AFFECTS YOUR BODY

Important Phytochemicals   Like other cruciferous vegetables, the radish contains mustard oils (isothiocyanates).

Benefits   Mustard oils irritate the mucous membrane lining of the respiratory and intestinal tract. This causes the tissues in the nose and throat to secrete liquid that makes it easier to cough up mucus and it triggers the gastric contractions we call hunger pangs. In 1985 and 1991, the German Commission E approved the use of radish juice for these purposes.

The mustard oils in radishes, broccoli, brussels sprouts, cabbage, cauliflower, and other cruciferous vegetables appear to reduce the risk of some cancers, perhaps by preventing the formation of carcinogens in your body, blocking cancer-causing substances from reaching or reacting with sensitive body tissues, or inhibiting the transformation of healthy cells to malignant ones.

Brussels sprouts, broccoli, cauliflower, and other cruciferous vegetables all contain sulforaphane, a member of a family of compounds known as isothiocyanates. In experiments with laboratory rats, sulforaphane appears to increase the body's production of phase-2 enzymes, naturally occurring substances that inactivate and help eliminate carcinogens. At the Johns Hopkins University in Baltimore, Maryland, 69 percent of the rats injected with a chemical known to cause mammary cancer developed tumors versus only 26 percent of the rats given the carcinogenic chemical plus sulforaphane.

Although the sulforaphane levels of other cruciferous vegetables have yet to be calculated, in 1997 the Johns Hopkins researchers discovered that broccoli seeds and three-day-old broccoli sprouts contain a compound that is converted to sulforaphane when the seed and sprout cells are crushed. Five grams of three-day-old broccoli sprouts contain as much sulforaphane as 150 grams of mature broccoli.

Possible Adverse Effects   Cruciferous vegetables, including radishes, contain goitrin, thiocyanate, and isothio-cyanate. These compounds, known collectively as goitrogens, inhibit the formation of thyroid hormones and cause the thyroid to enlarge in an attempt to produce more. Goitrogens are not hazardous for healthy people who eat moderate amounts of cruciferous vegetables, but they may be troublesome for people who have thyroid problems or are taking thyroid medication.

Information for Women Who Are Pregnant or Nursing   * * *

Plant/Drug Interactions   The active ingredient in the guaiac slide test for hidden blood in feces is alphaguaiaconic acid, a chemical that turns blue in the presence of blood. Alphaguaiaconic acid also turns blue in the presence of peroxidase, a naturally occurring compound in radishes. Eating radishes in the 72 hours before taking the guaiac test may produce a false positive result in people who do not actually have any blood in their stool.

HOW TO USE THIS PLANT

In Cooking   Cut off the green tops and refrigerate fresh radishes in plastic bags or covered containers to prevent them from drying out. Don't slice or grate a radish until you are ready to use it. When you cut into a radish, you tear its cells, releasing moisture which converts otherwise mild sinigrin into an irritant mustard oil that gives radishes their hot taste. Tearing the radish's cells also releases polyphenoloxidase, an enzyme that hastens the oxidation of phenols (alcohols) in the radish, producing brown compounds that darken the radish. Storing peeled, sliced, or grated radishes in ice water slows down the browning reaction (and keeps the radishes crisp), but it also destroys vitamin C, which leaches out into the water.

Raspberry Leaf

ABOUT THIS PLANT

Botanical name(s): Rubus idaeus
Common name(s): Red raspberry, garden raspberry
Parts used as food/drink: Leaves, roots
GRAS list: No
Medicinal properties: Astringent
Other uses: * * *

ABOUT THIS PLANT AS FOOD OR DRINK

The raspberry is a member of the rose family, a shrub with prickly stems, pale green leaves, and white flowers followed by small red, yellow, black, or purple berries.

The raspberry bush's tannin-rich, astringent leaves are a good source of vitamin C and iron. One-quarter ounce dried raspberry leaves provides 43 percent of the RDA for vitamin C and 72 percent of the RDA for iron.

Nutritional Profile   One-eighth ounce (3.5 g) dried raspberry leaves has 10 calories. It provides 0.4 g protein, 0.05 g fat, 0.3 g dietary fiber, 0.7 IU vitamin A, 13 mg vitamin C, 43 mg calcium, 3.6 mg iron, and 0.3 mg sodium.

HOW THIS PLANT AFFECTS YOUR BODY

Important Phytochemicals   The raspberry leaf contains bitter tannins, astringent compounds that coagulate proteins on the surface of the mucous membrane lining of the mouth causing the tissue to pucker and tingle. Tannins have the same effect on the skin and on the membranes lining the intestinal tract, so tannin-rich plants (including TEA leaves) have often been used as poultices to stop bleeding from minor cuts or as teas to relieve minor diarrhea. However, the efficacy of raspberry leaves has not been scientifically evaluated.

Benefits   Foods high in vitamin C cure or prevent scurvy, a disease of vitamin C deficiency that is characterized by bleeding gums and slow healing of wounds.

Possible Adverse Effects   * * *

Information for Women Who Are Pregnant or Nursing   * * *

Plant/Drug Interactions   * * *

HOW TO USE THIS PLANT

In Cooking   To make raspberry leaf tea, steep 1 tablespoon clean, fresh leaves in 2 cups of boiling water. Steep the leaves for 15 minutes, then strain the tea and sweeten it to taste with orange juice, apple juice, honey, or sugar.

Raspberry leaf tea bags are available at many health food stores. When you shop, read the fine print on the label, because raspberry leaves don't taste or smell like raspberries, and many "raspberry" tea mixes are actually ordinary tea with added raspberry flavoring.

As a Home Remedy   Raspberry leaf tea may be used as a refreshing mouthwash or to relieve the pain of a minor sore throat. It has no effect on the organisms causing the infection, but it makes your mouth feel pleasantly tingly.

Red Clover

ABOUT THIS PLANT

Botanical name(s): *Trifolium pratense*
Common name(s): Cow grass, cow clover, sweet clover
Native to: Mediterranean region
Parts used as food/drink: Leaves, flowers
GRAS list: Yes
Medicinal properties: * * *
Other uses: * * *

ABOUT THIS PLANT AS FOOD OR DRINK

Red clover is a member of the legume family, related to beans and peas. The plant is also known as *cow grass* because it once grew wild, serving as a forage crop for livestock (and poultry).

Red clover's flowers and its dark green leaves may be used fresh in salads. The flowers may also be dried and used to brew an aromatic herbal tea. An extract of red clover is sometimes used to flavor jams and jellies. Note: Most clover leaves are grouped in threes. The rare four-leafed plant is widely considered to be a lucky charm.

Nutritional Profile One-eighth ounce (3.5 g) dried red clover blossoms has 3.6 calories. It provides 0.4 g protein, 0.1 g fat, 0.4 g dietary fiber, 71.7 IU vitamin A, 10.5 mg vitamin C, 46.7 mg calcium, a trace of iron, and 0.6 mg sodium.

HOW THIS PLANT AFFECTS YOUR BODY

Important Phytochemicals Red clover contains the phytoestrogens daidzein and genistein, estrogen-like plant compounds also found in soybeans. The aroma of red clover comes from vanilla-scented coumarin.

Benefits Like other dark green leaves, red clover leaves are a source of beta-carotene, the vitamin A precursor in deep yellow fruits and vegetables. According to the American Cancer Society, a diet rich in these foods may lower the risk of some forms of cancer. Vitamin A also protects your eyes. In your body, the vitamin A from clover is converted to 11-cis retinol, the most important constituent of rhodopsin, a protein in the rods in your retina (the cells that enable you to see in dim light).

Clover leaves are a good source of vitamin C. One-eighth ounce dried red clover provides 17 percent of the RDA.

Possible Adverse Effects   As with all flowers, red clover produces a potentially allergenic pollen that may cause respiratory symptoms (itchy eyes, runny nose) in sensitive individuals.

Information for Women Who Are Pregnant or Nursing   Because the effects of phytoestrogens remain to be documented, it may be sensible to avoid herbs containing these estrogen-like compounds while pregnant or nursing.

Plant/Drug Interactions   Theoretically, red clover could interact with hormone medications such as birth control pills or postmenopausal hormone replacement therapy, but there are currently no scientific studies to show whether this is true or what the effects might be.

HOW TO USE THIS PLANT

In Cooking   If you dry clover heads quickly, they will retain their pinkish-red color and their fragrance.

To brew red clover tea, use 3 to 4 teaspoons dried flower tops per 1 cup of boiling water. Tea bags are available at your health food store.

Rose (Flower)

ABOUT THIS PLANT

Botanical name(s): *Rosa gallica*
Common name(s): * * *
Native to: Mediterranean region, Europe
Parts used as food/drink: Flower petals
GRAS list: No
Medicinal properties: Astringent
Other uses: Decoration

ABOUT THIS PLANT AS FOOD OR DRINK

The rose's name comes from *rodon,* the Greek word for "red." Roses are edible flowers, rich in tannins that give them a crisp tang. Fresh rose petals may be tossed in salads, used to decorate cake icing, added to egg dishes such as omelets, dipped in batter and fried, or steeped in vinegar to make a rose-scented condiment. Fresh or dried rose petals may be used to brew a fragrant tea.

Nutritional Profile * * *

HOW THIS PLANT AFFECTS YOUR BODY

Important Phytochemicals   The primary aroma compound in oil of roses is geraniol. Rose leaves and flowers also contain tannins, astringents that coagulate the proteins on the surface of the mucous membrane lining of the mouth, making it pucker. Because tannins have similar effects on the skin and on the membranes lining your gut, plants high in tannins have often been used in folk medicine as poultices to stop bleeding from minor cuts or to brew teas that relieve minor diarrhea.

Benefits   In 1990, the German Commission E approved the use of tea brewed from dried rose petals to relieve mild inflammation of the mouth and throat.

Possible Adverse Effects   Like other flowering plants, roses produce a potentially allergenic pollen that may cause allergic rhinitis (sneezing, runny nose, itchy or watery eyes) in sensitive people.

Geraniol is an irritant that may cause contact dermatitis (itching, burning, stinging, reddened, or blistered skin) in people who handle rose plants.

Information for Women Who Are Pregnant or Nursing   * * *

Plant/Drug Interactions   * * *

HOW TO USE THIS PLANT

In Cooking   To keep roses and rose petals fresh, keep them in water until you are ready to use them.

   Caution: Only roses cultivated for food use are considered safe to eat. Roses sold as cut flowers or for decoration may have been sprayed with toxic chemicals. They are not considered edible.

As a Home Remedy   The suggested daily dose for a tea used to relieve oral discomfort is 1–2 g dried rose petals steeped in 1 cup of hot water.

Rose Hips

ABOUT THIS PLANT

Botanical name(s): *Rosa species*
Common name(s): Hipberries
Native to: Europe
Parts used as food/drink: Seed covering
GRAS list: No
Medicinal properties: Antiscorbutic, diuretic
Other uses: * * *

ABOUT THIS PLANT AS FOOD OR DRINK

Rose hips are the bright red outer covering of the seed of various species of wild rose bushes, including *Rosa canina* ("dog rose"), *Rosa gallica*, *Rosa condita*, and *Rosa rugosa* (the Japanese rose).

Rose hips may be used straight off the bush as a delicate, fruity garnish for fruit dishes and beverages or to brew an herbal tea. Or you can remove the seeds and use the rose hips to make a jelly or syrup. Commercially, rose hips are available in tea bags and as loose tea blends. Extracts of rose hips are used in "natural" vitamin C supplements.

Nutritional Profile   One-eighth ounce (3.5 g) dried rose hips has 12 calories, 0.5 g protein, a trace of fat, 1 g dietary fiber, 250 vitamin A, 25 mg vitamin C, 28.9 mg calcium, and a trace of iron and sodium.

HOW THIS PLANT AFFECTS YOUR BODY

Important Phytochemicals   Fresh rose hips are an excellent source of vitamin C. Ounce for ounce, they have three times as much vitamin C as fresh citrus fruits (156 mg/oz rose hips versus 50 mg/oz citrus fruit).

Rose hips are also rich in hesperidin, a yellow flavonoid (pigment). Flavonoids are antioxidants, compounds that prevent molecular fragments in your body from joining to form potentially damaging molecules.

Benefits   Fresh rose hips are an antiscorbutic, a food that prevents or cures the vitamin C deficiency disease scurvy. Depending on where the rose hips were grown and how they were collected, dried, and stored, dried rose hips may have only 10 percent to 55 percent as much vitamin C as fresh rose hips. Steeping rose hips in boiling water extracts about 40 percent of the vitamin C from fresh rose hips and slightly more than 50 percent of the vitamin C in dried rose hips. One cup of tea brewed from 1 oz fresh rose hips provides 62 mg vitamin C, 104 percent of the RDA for a healthy adult.

Possible Adverse Effects   Although rose pollen is an allergen that may cause allergic rhinitis (sneezing, runny nose, itchy, watery eyes) in sensitive people, and the geraniol in oil of roses may cause contact dermatitis (itching, burning, stinging, reddened, or blistered skin) in people who handle the rose bushes, rose hips themselves do not contain either pollen or oil of roses.

Information for Women Who Are Pregnant or Nursing   * * *

Plant/Drug Interactions   * * *

HOW TO USE THIS PLANT

In Cooking   To brew a fragrant, mildly diuretic rose hip tea, add 2 tablespoons fresh or 1 tablespoon dried rose hips to $1^1/2$ cups fresh water. Bring the water to a boil, turn off the heat and let the rose hips steep for 15 minutes. Then strain the tea and use plain or sweetened to taste with orange juice, apple juice, sugar, or honey.

Caution: When picking fresh rose hips, be sure the rose bushes from which you gather the fruits have neither been sprayed with pesticides nor grown with fertilizer that contains pesticides.

Rosemary

ABOUT THIS PLANT

Botanical name(s): *Rosmarinus officinalis*
Common name(s): Garden rosemary
Native to: Mediterranean region
Parts used as food/drink: Leaves
GRAS list: Yes
Medicinal properties: Antispasmodic, counterirritant
Other uses: Perfume, preservative, insect repellent

ABOUT THIS PLANT AS FOOD OR DRINK

Rosemary is a member of the mint family, an evergreen shrub related to BASIL, MARJORAM, and OREGANO. Rosemary often grows by the ocean; in fact, its botanical name, *Rosmarinus,* is a combination of the Latin words for "dew of the sea" (*ros* = dew; *marinus* = sea).

Rosemary leaves look like tiny pine needles, dark green with silver tips. Those harvested for use as an herb are dried quickly to protect their oil and their color. Rosemary is widely available as whole or ground leaves. Oil of rosemary, extracted from the leaves and flowering tops of the plant, is used to flavor candies, baked goods, and liqueurs and to perfume a variety of cosmetics, including soaps, creams, lotions, deodorants, and hair tonics.

Like basil, PEPPERMINT, SAGE, and TANSY, rosemary plants have a strong, distinctive odor and appear to act as natural insect repellents in the garden.

Nutritional Profile   One teaspoon (1 g) fresh rosemary leaves has 1 calorie. It provides a trace of protein and fat, 0.1 g carbohydrates, 0.1 g dietary fiber, 20 IU vitamin A, 0.2 mg vitamin C, 2 mg calcium, a trace of iron, and no sodium.

One tablespoon (2 g) fresh rosemary leaves has 2 calories. It provides 0.1 g protein, 0.1 g fat, 0.4 g carbohydrates, 0.2 g dietary fiber, 50 IU vitamin A, 0.4 mg vitamin C, 5 mg calcium, 0.1 mg iron, and no sodium.

One teaspoon (1 g) dried rosemary leaves has 4 calories. It provides no protein, 0.2 g fat, 0.8 g carbohydrates, 38 IU vitamin A, 0.7 mg vitamin C, 15 mg calcium, 0.4 mg iron, and 1 mg sodium.

One tablespoon (3 g) dried rosemary leaves has 11 calories. It provides 0.2 g protein, 0.5 g fat, 2.1 g carbohydrates, 1.4 g dietary fiber, 103 IU vitamin A, 2 mg vitamin C, 42 mg calcium, 1 mg iron, and 2 mg sodium.

HOW THIS PLANT AFFECTS YOUR BODY

Important Phytochemicals   Rosemary's bittersweet, slightly piney flavor and aroma comes from oil of rosemary, a colorless or pale yellow liquid that contains astringent tannins; peppery-scented, sharp, mint-flavored borneol; camphor and eucalyptol, which have a penetrating odor and a slightly bitter but cooling taste; and pinene, which smells like turpentine.

Rosemary also contains the antioxidant flavonoids (pigments) apigenin, diosmetin, diosmin, and luteolin. In laboratory studies, animals seem to use flavonoids as they do vitamin C to strengthen capillaries, the small blood vessels just under the skin. In human beings, the flavonoids are valued as antioxidants, compounds that prevent molecular fragments from linking up with each other to form potentially cancer-causing compounds.

Benefits   Borneal, camphor, eucalyptol, and pinene are skin irritants. In 1985, 1986, and 1990, the German Commission E approved the use of preparations of fresh or dried rosemary leaves as counterirritants, agents that irritate the skin, causing small blood vessels underneath to dilate so that more blood flows into the area and the skin feels warm. This temporarily relieves pain and discomfort such as that associated with arthritis or muscle injuries.

Commission E also approved the use of rosemary leaf products to relieve gastrointestinal spasms, an effect observed in experimental situations.

Possible Adverse Effects   Handling fresh rosemary plants or using cosmetics scented with rosemary oil may cause contact dermatitis (itching, burning, stinging, reddened, or blistered skin).

Information for Women Who Are Pregnant or Nursing   * * *

Plant/Drug Interactions   * * *

HOW TO USE THIS PLANT

In Cooking   To dry fresh rosemary, hang the sprigs in a cool, dry place, and dry them quickly. (An extra benefit: a lovely fragrance in the air.) Store the dried rosemary in airtight containers (glass jars are usually most protective), and use as needed. If you prefer, simply freeze whole sprigs of rosemary; use them as needed in cooking, directly from the freezer.

Rosemary is a very pungent herb. As little as $1/2$ teaspoon fresh or dried rosemary leaves will season a dish for four people.

To make rosemary vinegar, immerse a sprig of fresh rosemary in a bottle of vinegar and let it steep for two weeks. Shake every other day to distribute the flavor. Remove the rosemary, and use the vinegar in salad dressings or as a marinade.

Add a sprig of fresh rosemary to a jar of honey or orange marmalade to give the sweet honey a pleasantly bitter undertone.

As a Home Remedy   The suggested daily dose to relieve intestinal spasms is 4–6 g rosemary brewed as a tea. The suggested daily dose as a counterirritant is 50 g rosemary added to warm bath water, once a day.

Saccharin

ABOUT THIS CONDIMENT

Chemical name(s): 1, 2-Benzisothiazol-3(2H)-one; 1,1-dioxide
Common name(s): Sweet'N Low
Parts used as food/drink: * * *
GRAS list: No
Medicinal properties: Noncalorie sweetener
Other uses: Pharmaceutical flavoring

ABOUT THIS CONDIMENT AS FOOD OR DRINK

Saccharin was the first synthetic sweetener, a crystalline by-product of petroleum identified by accident at Johns Hopkins University in 1879.

The compound was originally used as an antiseptic and food preservative. Not until World War II, when sugar was in short supply, did saccharin become popular as a food sweetener. It was used in diet products until 1977, when it was temporarily banned in the United States after being linked to bladder cancer in rats. It has since been cleared by the U.S. Food and Drug Administration, and in the spring of 2000, when the National Institute of Environmental Health Sciences released its ninth National Toxicology Report on Carcinogens, saccharin was dropped from the list. Currently, in the United States, the amount of saccharin in a food product is limited to no more than 12 mg/oz in liquids, 20 mg per each sweetener equivalent to 1 teaspoon sugar, and no more than 30 mg per food serving. The amount of saccharin in a food, sugar substitute, cosmetic, or drug product must be listed on the label.

Saccharin is 200 to 700 percent sweeter than sugar, so sweet that you can taste it even when it is diluted to a concentration of 1 part saccharin in 1 million parts water. The saccharin powder sold as a sweetener is made with soluble saccharin, a form of saccharin treated to make it 150 to 225 times more soluble than ordinary saccharin. It takes 290 ml (9 oz) cold water or 25 ml (0.8 oz) boiling water to dissolve 1 g regular saccharin, but 1 g soluble saccharin dissolves in 1.2 ml (0.04 oz) cold water. The packets of saccharin powder sold in grocery stores may contain dextrose (sugar), soluble saccharin, cream of tartar to keep the powder from darkening, and calcium silicate or silicon dioxide, anticaking agents that keep the powder from absorbing moisture.

Nutritional Profile   A typical 1 g packet of saccharin has 2 to 4 calories. It provides no protein, up to 0.5 g carbohydrates, no fat, and 3.3 mg sodium.

HOW THIS CONDIMENT AFFECTS YOUR BODY

Important Phytochemicals   Technically, saccharin is considered sodium free. However, persons on low-salt diets should check with their doctors before using saccharin.

Most people find saccharin very sweet, but those who find broccoli bitter are likely to find saccharin bitter, too, almost certainly because they are among the two-thirds of the human race that carries a gene that makes them extraordinarily sensitive to bitter flavors including very small concentrations of a compound called phenylthiocarbamide (PTC). In addition to saccharine, those who are sensitive to PTC generally dislike cruciferous vegetables (broccoli, cabbage, etc.), caffeine, the salt substitute potassium chloride, and the food preservatives sodium benzoate and potassium benzoate.

Benefits   Theoretically, saccharin's benefit lies in its ability to reduce the calories in your diet. But most people who save calories by drinking diet sodas or using saccharin instead of sugar in their coffee or tea add calories in other ways. The true value of artificial sweeteners such as saccharin and ASPARTAME is for people who have diabetes or other medical conditions that require them to avoid sugar.

Nonnutritive sweeteners reduce the incidence of dental cavities.

Possible Adverse Effects   * * *

Information for Women Who Are Pregnant or Nursing   * * *

Condiment/Drug Interactions   * * *

HOW TO USE THIS CONDIMENT

In Cooking   A 1-g packet of saccharin powder equals the sweetening power of 2 teaspoons table sugar.

One-quarter teaspoon liquid saccharin solution equals the sweetening power of one packet powdered saccharin or 2 teaspoons granulated table sugar.

Saffron

ABOUT THIS PLANT

Botanical name(s): *Crocus sativus*
Common name(s): * * *
Native to: Western Asia, southern Europe
Parts used as food/drink: Stigma
GRAS list: Yes
Medicinal properties: Choleretic
Other uses: Natural coloring agent

ABOUT THIS PLANT AS FOOD OR DRINK

Saffron comes from a flower belonging to the crocus family. The herb itself is made of the flower's dried red brown stigmas, threadlike parts inside the flower that receive pollen so that the plant may reproduce itself. Each saffron flower has only three stigmas, which must be picked by hand as soon as the flowers open. It takes nearly 60,000 flowers to yield the 225,000 stigmas needed to make one pound of saffron, which is why saffron is the world's most expensive seasoning.

Note: There are a number of other plants whose name includes the word *saffron*. American saffron is safflower, the plant from which we get safflower oil. Indian saffron is a common name for TURMERIC, which may be used as an honest substitute for saffron or, unscrupulously, to stretch saffron powder.

Caution: AUTUMN CROCUS (also known as meadow saffron/*Colchicum autumnale*) is neither a crocus nor a saffron. It is a poisonous plant, the source of colchicine, a drug used to treat gout.

NUTRITIONAL PROFILE

One teaspoon (1 g) saffron has 2 calories. It provides 0.1 g protein, a trace of fat, 0.5 g carbohydrates, no dietary fiber, 0.6 mg vitamin C, 1 mg calcium, 0.1 mg iron, and 1 mg sodium.

HOW THIS PLANT AFFECTS YOUR BODY

Important Phytochemicals Saffron's strong, bitter, medicinal flavor comes from oil of saffron, which contains picrocrocin (saffron bitter). As

the saffron stigmas dry, picrocrocin yields bitter safranal. Oil of saffron also contains turpentine-scented pinene plus eulcalyptol, which smells like camphor and has a spicy flavor.

Saffron's distinctive dark red/golden color comes from carotenoid pigments, chiefly red crocetin and crocin, a reddish-yellow coloring agent so potent that 1 part pure crocin dissolved in 150,000 parts water turns the water distinctively yellow. Saffron also contains lycopene, the anticancer red pigment in tomatoes and watermelon; xanthophyll, the yellow pigment in egg yolks; zeaxanthin, the yellow pigment in yellow corn; and yellow alpha-, beta- and gamma-carotene, the pigments your body converts to vitamin A. However, saffron contains such small amounts of the carotenoids that it is not considered a source of vitamin A.

Crocin is a choleretic, an agent that stimulates the liver to increase its production of bile, a yellow, brown, or green fluid. Bile helps emulsify fats in the duodenum and increases peristalsis, the rhythmic contractions that move food through the gastrointestinal tract. Some other choleretic herbs are GENTIAN, ONION, OREGANO, and turmeric. While choleretics are ordinarily beneficial for healthy people, they may pose problems for people with gallbladder or liver disease. However, as the U.S. Food and Drug Administration notes, so little saffron is used in food that it is unlikely to cause harm.

Benefits   * * *

Possible Adverse Effects   * * *

Information for Women Who Are Pregnant or Nursing   The German Commission E warns against the use of large doses of saffron by pregnant women. The documented safe amount is 1.5 g/day. In quantities higher than 5 g/day, saffron is known to cause uterine bleeding, blood disorders, kidney failure, bloody diarrhea, bleeding from eyes, nose, and mouth, dizziness, numbness, and yellow discoloration of the skin and mucous membranes.

Plant/Drug Interactions   * * *

HOW TO USE THIS PLANT

In Cooking   Saffron stigmas are sold whole (threads) or powdered. Powdered saffron, more concentrated than whole saffron threads, is usually sold in small opaque plastic packets containing about $1/16$ teaspoon. Thread saffron is usually available in small packets containing about $1/4$ g saffron, equal to about $1/2$ teaspoon.

Saffron's color, flavor, and aroma are extremely sensitive to light. Protect your investment in this expensive seasoning by storing it in tightly closed containers in a cool, dark place.

Saffron holds its flavor best in acidic foods.

To bring out the flavor of saffron, stir it into 1 tablespoon hot water before adding it to your dish. For saffron rice, add the saffron to the boiling water before you add the rice. For saffron rolls and biscuits, add $1/4$ teaspoon saffron steeped in 2 tablespoons hot water for each 6 cups of flour.

A little bit of saffron's strong, medicine-like flavor goes a very long way. If you are using saffron mainly for color, use no more than $^1/_4$ teaspoon saffron in 2 tablespoons hot water or white wine to season a dish meant for up to eight people.

ANNATTO or turmeric may be used as less expensive substitutes for saffron. Like saffron itself, they have a very strong acrid flavor. For the best results, use only very small amounts of annatto or turmeric; otherwise, their flavor may easily overwhelm the food.

Sage

ABOUT THIS PLANT

Botanical name(s): *Salvia officinale*
Common name(s): Salvia
Native to: Southern Europe
Parts used as food/drink: Leaves, blossoms
GRAS list: Yes
Medicinal properties: Astringent
Other uses: Insect repellent

ABOUT THIS PLANT AS FOOD OR DRINK

Sage is a woody evergreen shrub with violet blue flowers and wooly, gray-green leaves. A member of the mint family, related to BASIL, MARJORAM, and OREGANO, it is native to Albania, Italy, Turkey, and Yugoslavia.

Fresh, rinsed purple or white sage blossoms may be used to add a mildly spicy flavor to salads, cheese, or fruit dishes. The more intensely flavored leaves are used whole or ground in cooked meat and poultry dishes.

Nutritional Profile   One teaspoon (1 g) ground sage has 2 calories. It provides 0.1 g protein, 0.1 g fat, 0.4 g carbohydrates, 0.3 g dietary fiber, 41 IU vitamin A, 0.2 mg vitamin C, 12 mg calcium, 0.2 mg iron, and no sodium.

One tablespoon (2 g) ground sage has 6 calories. It provides 0.2 g protein, 0.3 g fat, 1.2 g carbohydrates, 0.8 g dietary fiber, 118 IU vitamin A, 0.6 mg vitamin C, 33 mg calcium, 0.6 mg iron, and no sodium.

HOW THIS PLANT AFFECTS YOUR BODY

Important Phytochemicals   Sage's flavor and aroma come from oil of sage. The aroma compounds in the oil include camphor (26 percent), lemon-scented limonene, pleasantly scented ocimene, and turpentine-scented pinene. Sage's flavor comes from bitter-tasting thujone, spicy eucalyptol (which smells like camphor), and astringent tannins.

Camphor, eucalyptol, limonene, linalool, pinene, and thujone are irritants. Astringent tannins coagulate proteins on the surface of the mucous membrane lining of the mouth, making the tissues pucker.

Alpha-thujone, an important constituent of oil of sage, is also a major component of oil of WORMWOOD, the herb used to flavor absinthe, a cordial banned in the United States since the 1920s. Thujone can cause

---

gastric upset, irritability, stupor, convulsions resembling epileptic seizures, and death. Although a plant containing thujone cannot be considered completely harmless, using dried sage leaves as a seasoning is unlikely to be hazardous because most of its thujone evaporates when the herb is dried and when it is heated in cooking.

Benefits   Astringent sage tea, used as a gargle, has long been used as a folk remedy to alleviate the discomfort of a sore mouth or throat. In 1985 and 1990, the German Commission E validated this custom, approving the use of fresh or dried sage leaf preparations for this purpose.

Possible Adverse Effects   Handling the sage plant may cause contact dermatitis (itching, burning, stinging, reddened, or blistered skin). Drinking sage tea may cause cheilitis (peeling, cracked, or bleeding lips) or stomatitis (an inflammation of the mucous membranes lining the mouth) in sensitive people.

Information for Women Who Are Pregnant or Nursing   The German Commission E warns against the use of essential oil of sage or alcohol extracts of sage during pregnancy.

Plant/Drug Interactions   * * *

HOW TO USE THIS PLANT

In Cooking   Sage is available either "rubbed" or ground. Rubbed sage, which has been only minimally ground, is a fluffy, velvety powder. Ground sage is a finely ground powder.

As a Home Remedy   The suggested dose for a sage gargle is 2.5 g leaves steeped in a large glass of warm water.

As a Cosmetic   If you are not sensitive to sage, you can use the herb to make a scented aftershave. Buy two bottles of plain witch hazel. Pour $1/2$ cup liquid out of one of the bottles, and add 1 cup crumbled dried sage leaves. Cap the bottle and shake it thoroughly. Let it stand for a week, shaking vigorously each morning and night. At the end of the week, pour out all the witch hazel in the second bottle, and strain the scented liquid from the first bottle into the second through a coffee filter or a clean linen handkerchief. Discard the wet sage leaves. The witch hazel now has a distinct herbal aroma. If you prefer a stronger scent, repeat the process, adding another $1/4$ cup crumbled dried sage leaves to the liquid. At the end of the second week, strain the liquid back into the empty witch hazel bottle, discard the sage leaves and the empty bottle, and use the liquid as an astringent aftershave.

Sage tea can be used as an after-shampoo rinse to make brunette hair shiny and smooth. To make the rinse, pour 1 cup boiling water over 1 tablespoon rubbed or ground sage. Let the mix steep for 15 minutes. Then strain the liquid through a coffee filter or a clean linen handkerchief; use after shampooing.

St. John's Wort

ABOUT THIS PLANT

Botanical name(s): *Hypericum perforatum*
Common name(s): Klamath weed, goatweed
Native to: Europe
Parts used as food/drink: Leaves
GRAS list: No
Medicinal properties: Antidepressant
Other uses: * * *

ABOUT THIS PLANT AS FOOD OR DRINK

St. John's wort is a tall, perennial herb with oval leaves and yellow flowers. It is native to Europe, but now grows in northern North America as well. It is not used in food, but may be brewed into an herbal tea.

Nutritional Profile * * *

HOW THIS PLANT AFFECTS YOUR BODY

Important Phytochemicals The active component in St. John's wort is hypericin, a mild antidepressant.

In 1997, St. John's wort was the fifth best-selling herbal supplement in the United States, after GINKGO BILOBA, GINSENG, GARLIC, and ECHINACEA.

Benefits In 1984 and 1990, the German Commission E approved the use of preparations of dried St. John's wort flowers, leaves, and stems to relieve depression, anxiety, and "nervous unrest."

Caution: Early studies suggested that hypericin might belong to the class of antidepressants known as monoamine oxidase (MAO) inhibitors, drugs that inhibit the activity of naturally occurring enzymes that break down nitrogen compounds (amines) such as tyramine, a by-product of protein metabolism, so they can be eliminated from the body. As a result, the amines build up in the bloodstream, constricting blood vessels and raising blood pressure. If you eat a food high in tyramine while you are taking an MAO inhibitor, the result may be a hypertensive crisis (sustained high blood pressure). According to Commission E, more recent research shows either no MAO activity or very slight MAO activity with hypericin, but it would be well to check with your doctor regarding dietary restrictions before using St. John's wort.

Possible Adverse Effects   Hypericin is a photosensitizer, a substance that makes skin more sensitive to sunlight. In approving the use of St. John's wort products, Commission E cautioned people using the herb, especially those with fair, easily burned skin, to avoid long exposure to the sun.

In a paper delivered to the 1999 annual meeting of the American Society of Anesthesiologists, St. John's wort was identified as one of several herbs that may prolong the effects of general surgical anesthesia. As a result, the researchers recommended that people stop taking this and all other herbal products two weeks prior to surgery.

In 1999, researchers at Loma Linda University School of Medicine in California incubated hamster eggs for one hour in a solution containing $1/1,000,000$ to $1/100$ the amount of St. John's wort customarily found in over-the-counter products. When the researchers added human sperm to the dish, they found that the herb damaged the sperm's outer membrane, reducing its ability to penetrate and fertilize an egg. Sperm not exposed to St. John's wort penetrated 88 percent of the eggs; sperm exposed to St. John's wort did not penetrate any eggs.

Information for Women Who Are Pregnant or Nursing   See above.

Plant/Drug Interactions   St. John's wort should not be taken along with other antidepressant medications; combining these drugs may intensify their adverse effects. In one 1999 report, a 50-year-old woman began taking 600 mg of St. John's wort per day, 10 days after she stopped taking 40 mg of paroxetine (Paxil) per day, which she had taken for eight months. One night, when she had trouble sleeping, she took 20 mg paroxetine along with the St. John's wort. The next day, she was incoherent, groggy, and slow-moving, with nausea, weakness, and fatigue.

Taking St. John's wort may reduce the effectiveness of the heart medication digitalis, the anti-asthma drug theophylline, the transplant anti-rejection drug cyclosporine, and the birth control pill. In February 2000, the National Institutes of Health announced that taking St. John's wort along with the protease inhibitor indinavir (Crixivan), a medication used to suppress the AIDS virus, may decrease the blood levels of indinavir 49 to 99 percent, allowing the HIV virus to resurface and possibly mutate to a drug-resistant form.

HOW TO USE THIS PLANT   * * *

Salsa

ABOUT THIS CONDIMENT

Botanical name(s): * * *
Common name(s): * * *
Native to: Mexico, Central America
Parts used as food/drink: * * *
GRAS list: No
Medicinal properties: * * *
Other uses: * * *

ABOUT THIS CONDIMENT AS FOOD OR DRINK

Salsa is a spicy, tomato-based condiment customarily made with tomatoes, onions, and bell peppers, and flavored with chili, vinegar, and salt.

Nutritional Profile   The nutritional value of a salsa varies with its ingredients. Fresh salsas are generally higher in vitamin C than commercially made salsas.

HOW THIS CONDIMENT AFFECTS YOUR BODY

Important Phytochemicals   Salsas are high in vitamin C, vitamin A, and lycopene, the red pigment in tomatoes and watermelon that is believed to reduce the risk of certain cancers, among them prostate cancer and lung cancer.

Benefits   As noted above, cooked tomatoes are an excellent source of lycopene. Because lycopene dissolves in fat, serving the salsa with a bit of cheese increases the amount of lycopene you absorb.

LYCOPENE CONTENT OF SELECTED TOMATO PRODUCTS (mg/ounce)	
Tomato ketchup	5 mg/ounce
Tomato sauce	5
Fresh tomato	3
Canned tomatoes	3
Tomato juice	3

Source: Tomato Research Council

Tomatoes and tomato products are also high in antioxidants, naturally occurring compounds that prevent molecular fragments in your body from joining together to form potential carcinogens.

Possible Adverse Effects   * * *

Information for Women Who Are Pregnant or Nursing   * * *

Condiment/Drug Interactions   * * *

HOW TO USE THIS CONDIMENT

In Cooking   Tomatoes' antioxidant activity is useful in preventing "warmed-over" flavor, a fat/oxygen reaction in refrigerated cooked meats. When meat is heated, it loses water and shrinks. The pigments in meat combine with oxygen; they are denatured (broken into fragments) by the heat, so that they turn brown, the natural color of well-done meat. At the same time, the fats in the meat are oxidized, a reaction that produces the characteristic "warmed-over" flavor when the cooked meat is refrigerated and then reheated. Cooking and storing meat under a blanket of antioxidants such as tomato salsa reduces fat oxidation and lessens the intensity of the warmed-over flavor.

Salt

ABOUT THIS CONDIMENT

Chemical name(s): Sodium chloride
Common name(s): Common or table salt, NaCl
Native to: ✳ ✳ ✳
Parts used as food/drink: ✳ ✳ ✳
GRAS list: Yes
Medicinal properties: Essential nutrient
Other uses: Fire extinguisher

ABOUT THIS CONDIMENT AS FOOD OR DRINK

Table salt is a compound made of sodium (60.7 percent), the sixth most common element on earth, and chlorine (39.3 percent), a greenish-yellow, suffocating gas that is found in seawater and in the earth's crust. When combined, these compounds form sodium chloride (NaCl), a white, crystalline substance that occurs in nature as the mineral halite. The only difference between "mined" salt and salt obtained by evaporating seawater is that sea salt is naturally iodized. The introduction of iodized salt in 1924 has virtually eliminated goiter in the United States but worldwide, an estimated 600,000,000 people still suffer chronic iodine deficiency.

Note: Sodium chloride crystals cake when they absorb moisture from the air. To keep salt flowing smoothly, some manufacturers add anticaking ingredients such as calcium or magnesium chloride to their products. At home, adding a few grains of raw rice to the salt shaker serves the same purpose.

Nutritional Profile   One teaspoon (6 g) table salt has no calories. It provides 2,235 mg sodium. A salt made with an anticaking agent provides 1 mg calcium.

One tablespoon (18 g) table salt has no calories. It provides 6,976 mg sodium. A salt made with an anticaking agent provides 4 mg calcium.

HOW THIS CONDIMENT AFFECTS YOUR BODY

Important Phytochemicals   Salt is an essential nutrient that enables your body to maintain its fluid balance (the proper amount of fluid inside and around cells) and to regulate chemicals called electrolytes that enable your nerve cells to produce the electrical charges that move muscles, activate your organs, and send messages from your brain to other parts of your body.

The adequate dietary consumption of sodium for a healthy adult is estimated to be 1,100 to 3,300 mg a day depending on age, sex, and level of physical activity.

Benefits   See above.

Possible Adverse Effects   Some people are sensitive to salt, which means that they experience a rise in blood pressure when they eat a high-salt diet.

Information for Women Who Are Pregnant or Nursing   Salt holds water in body cells. During pregnancy, some women are advised to reduce the amount of salt in the diet so as to reduce edema (swelling of ankles and wrists).

Condiment/Drug Interactions   Excess sodium is excreted in urine; diuretics (drugs that make you urinate more frequently) increase the loss of sodium and chloride.

The antigout medication colchicine reduces the absorption of sodium.

HOW TO USE THIS CONDIMENT

In Cooking   To clean leafy vegetables such as broccoli, brussels sprouts, and cabbage, rinse first in cool running water then put the vegetable upside down into a pan of salted water (1 tsp salt to 1 quart water) and soak for 15–30 minutes to drive out insects hiding inside.

To cook without fat in a pan that does not have a nonstick surface, pour 1 tablespoon salt into the pan, rub the salt into the pan with a paper towel or a dish towel, then pour out the salt. You should now be able to cook pancakes, waffles, potatoes, or meat without having the food stick.

Do not salt meat or meat stews before cooking. By osmotic action, the salty water on the meat's surface will draw moisture out of the meat, making it tough. Add salt only when the meat is nearly done.

To cook pasta faster, use salted water. At sea level, water boils at 212 degrees F (100 degrees C), the temperature at which its molecules have enough energy to escape from the surface as steam. If you add salt, the water molecules will need to pick up more energy so that they can push the salt molecules aside and escape from the surface. In effect, adding salt makes water boil at a higher temperature, so the pasta cooks faster.

Salt is a preservative. Salt- or sugar-curing preserves meat through an osmotic reaction that destroys microorganisms living on the meat and dries the meat so that it is less likely to decay quickly. Osmosis is the physical reaction in which liquids flow across a membrane, such as the wall of a cell, from a less dense to a more dense solution. The salt or sugar used in curing dissolves in the liquid on the surface of the meat to make a solution that is more dense than the liquid inside the cells of the meat. Water flows out of the meat and out of the cells of any microorganisms living on the meat, killing the microorganisms and protecting the meat from bacterial damage. Because salt retards the combination of fats with oxygen (a reaction that causes rancidity), salted butter or margarine stays fresh longer than plain butter or margarine.

As a Cosmetic   A slushy paste of salt and water is a cheap, effective toothpaste; a saltwater solution is a cheap and effective mouthwash.

As a Home Remedy   To relieve a sore throat, gargle with warm saltwater solution. The warm salt gargle appears to loosen and wash away the sticky material in an inflamed throat, momentarily easing discomfort.

Salt Substitutes

ABOUT THIS CONDIMENT

Chemical name(s): Potassium chloride
Common name(s): Sylvite, sylvine
Native to: ✳ ✳ ✳
Parts used as food/drink: ✳ ✳ ✳
GRAS list: Yes
Medicinal properties: Electrolyte replenisher
Other uses: Photography

ABOUT THIS CONDIMENT AS FOOD OR DRINK

There are two types of salt substitutes, those made with potassium chloride and those which are simply highly seasoned combinations of herbs and spices. Salt substitutes made with potassium chloride are meant to be used only by people who must limit the amount of sodium in their diet; herb and spice products may be used by anyone.

Potassium chloride salt substitutes may also contain antioxidants such as potassium bitartrate (CREAM OF TARTAR) and fumaric acid to keep the seasoning from darkening, plus adipic acid to give it a tart flavor. Salt substitutes made from herbs and spices may contain garlic, sugar, onion, paprika, and other flavorings. Some salt substitutes contain very small amounts of salt, so small (less than 5 mg) that the product is legally defined as salt-free.

Nutritional Profile One-half teaspoon potassium chloride salt substitute has no calories. It provides 664 mg potassium.

HOW THIS CONDIMENT AFFECTS YOUR BODY

Important Phytochemicals Potassium chloride is an odorless, salty, white, crystalline powder that occurs in nature as a deposit of the mineral sylvine (also known as sylvite). Potassium chloride also occurs naturally in dairy foods, meat, fish, poultry, cereals, and potatoes.

Potassium is an essential nutrient that helps regulate the body's acid/base (pH) balance; aids in metabolizing carbohydrates in the muscles; and protects against the hypertensive effect of sodium. As a medicine, potassium chloride is given intravenously for the potassium depletion that may accompany kidney, liver, or heart failure. Depending on age and sex, a healthy adult requires 1,875 to 5,625 mg potassium a day.

Benefits   Potassium chloride salt substitutes enable people on a sodium-restricted diet to season their food with a condiment that tastes like salt without salt's drawbacks.

Possible Adverse Effects   Consuming excessive amounts of potassium chloride may cause pallor; numbness and tingling in your hands and feet; muscle weakness; gastrointestinal irritation; violent diarrhea; mental confusion; and irregular heartbeat. Although the amount of potassium chloride we get from salt substitutes is generally considered too small to pose problems for healthy people, the substitutes may be hazardous for people with heart disease, kidney disease, diabetes, hyperkalemia (too much potassium in the blood), or oliguria (insufficient urination). For these reasons, the safest course is to use these products only on the advice of a physician.

People who are sensitive to any ingredient in an herb and spice salt substitute may react to the substitute.

Information for Women Who Are Pregnant or Nursing   Like other consumers, pregnant or nursing women should use potassium chloride salt substitutes only as directed by a physician.

Condiment/Drug Interactions   Potassium chloride salt substitutes may cause hyperkalemia if taken along with certain diuretics.

HOW TO USE THIS CONDIMENT

In Cooking   Salt substitutes made with potassium chloride are substituted in equal amounts for sodium chloride (salt).

Herb and spice salt substitutes are used according to taste.

Savory

ABOUT THIS PLANT

Botanical name(s): Satureja hortensis, Satureja montana

Common name(s): Garden savory, summer savory; winter savory, Spanish savory

Native to: Mediterranean

Parts used as food/drink: Leaves

GRAS list: Yes

Medicinal properties: Antiseptic, astringent

Other uses: Perfumery

ABOUT THIS PLANT AS FOOD OR DRINK

Summer savory, also known as garden savory, is a compact plant with pink or white flowers. It is a member of the mint family, related to BASIL, MARJORAM, and OREGANO.

Winter savory, also known as Spanish savory, is an evergreen plant with stiff, dark green, pointed leaves that tastes like summer savory, but stronger.

The ground savory sold in grocery stores is summer savory. Winter savory is generally available only from your own garden, where it can be harvested at any time. Despite its name, however, it is likely to be less flavorful in winter.

Nutritional Profile   One teaspoon (1 g) ground summer savory has 4 calories. It provides 0.1 g protein, 0.1 g fat, 1 g carbohydrates, 0.6 g dietary fiber, 72 IU vitamin A, 0.7 mg vitamin C, 30 mg calcium, 0.5 mg iron, and no sodium.

One tablespoon (4 g) ground summer savory has 12 calories. It provides 0.3 g protein, 0.3 g fat, 3 g carbohydrates, 2 g dietary fiber, 226 IU vitamin A, 2.2 mg vitamin C, 94 mg calcium, 1.7 mg iron, and 1 mg sodium.

HOW THIS PLANT AFFECTS YOUR BODY

Important Phytochemicals   Summer savory's peppery flavor and the spicy aroma of its small green or bronze leaves come from oil of savory, which contains carvacrol, the chief constituent of oil of thyme; cymene, which is used in lemon- and spice-flavored candy and chewing gum; lemon-scented limonene; and astringent tannins.

The flavor and aroma of winter savory come from an oil whose main ingredient may be either carvacrol, cymene, or lavender-scented linalool, depending on where the plant is grown.

Carvacrol and cymene are antiseptics. Tannins are astringents; they coagulate proteins on the surface of your skin or the mucous membranes lining your mouth, making the tissues pucker. The astringent tea brewed from summer savory has long been used in folk medicine to relieve the sore throat that comes with a cold or to help control mild diarrhea, but there is no scientific evidence to document these claims.

Benefits   * * *

Possible Adverse Effects   * * *

Information for Women Who Are Pregnant or Nursing   * * *

Plant/Drug Interactions   * * *

HOW TO USE THIS PLANT

In Cooking   Summer savory adds a peppery flavor and pungent aroma to meats and vegetables, particularly beans. Winter savory is traditionally used in salamis.

Saw Palmetto

ABOUT THIS PLANT

Botanical name(s): *Serenoa repens* or *Sabal serrulata*
Common name(s): Cabbage palm
Native to: Mediterranean region
Parts used as food/drink: Berry
GRAS list: No
Medicinal properties: Antiandrogen (male hormone)
Other uses: * * *

ABOUT THIS PLANT AS FOOD OR DRINK

Saw palmetto is a shrublike palm that grows in sandy soils around the Mediterranean and in the southeastern part of the United States. It is not used as food, but is available as an herbal tea.

Nutritional Profile * * *

HOW THIS PLANT AFFECTS YOUR BODY

Important Phytochemicals The dried ripe fruit (berry) of the saw palmetto plant contains fatty oil with sugar compounds and steroid-like substances.

In 1997, saw palmetto was the sixth best-selling herbal supplement in the United States in 1997, after GINKGO BILOBA, GINSENG, GARLIC, ECHINACEA, and ST. JOHN'S WORT.

Benefits As-yet-unidentified substances in saw palmetto appear to inhibit the activity of male hormones (androgens), but do not lower hormone levels. Saw palmetto products seem to relieve urinary symptoms such as frequent urination associated with benign prostate enlargement; whether they actually shrink the prostate remains an open question. In 1989, 1990, and 1991 the German Commission E approved the use of these products for benign prostate enlargement under a doctor's supervision.

Possible Adverse Effects Saw palmetto may cause headache or upset stomach; very large doses may cause diarrhea.

In 1999, researchers at Loma Linda University School of Medicine in California incubated hamster eggs for up to seven days in solutions containing $1/1{,}000$ to $1/100$ the amount of saw palmetto customarily found in over-the-counter products. When they added human sperm to the dish, they found that exposure to the herb reduced the sperm's ability to penetrate and fertilize the eggs.

Information for Women Who Are Pregnant or Nursing   Because saw palmetto appears to affect levels of human hormones, it should not be used during pregnancy or while a woman is nursing.

Plant/Drug Interactions   Saw palmetto products may interact with other prostate medications or hormone therapy.

HOW TO USE THIS PLANT   ✻ ✻ ✻

Senna

ABOUT THIS PLANT

Botanical name(s): Cassia senna
Common name(s): * * *
Native to: Africa, India
Parts used as food/drink: Leaves
GRAS list: No
Medicinal properties: Cathartic
Other uses: * * *

ABOUT THIS PLANT AS FOOD OR DRINK

Senna, a plant native to Egypt and southern India, is a cathartic (a strong laxative). Its leaves may be dried and used as a laxative in herbal teas and commercially prepared laxatives. Senna is not a food plant, nor is it related to CASSIA (*Cinnamomun cassia*), the cinnamon-flavored spice.

Nutritional Profile * * *

HOW THIS PLANT AFFECTS YOUR BODY

Important Phytochemicals The active ingredients in senna's dried leaves and fruit (pods) are emodin and aloe-emodin anthraquinones, cathartics (strong laxatives) similar to those found in ALOE.

Benefits In 1993, the German Commission E approved the use of preparations of dried senna leaflets to relieve constipation. However, the commission cautioned against using senna preparations for longer than one to two weeks except on the advice of a physician. Also, it specifically warned against the use of senna by children younger than 12 or people with intestinal obstruction or acute intestinal inflammation, ulcerative colitis, appendicitis, or pain of unknown origin.

Possible Adverse Effects Senna irritates the gastrointestinal tract and may cause violent purging. Even the standardized doses of senna in commercial laxative products may cause adverse effects such as diarrhea, dependence on laxatives, dehydration due to a critical loss of fluids and electrolytes (minerals such as sodium, potassium, and chloride that regulate the body's fluid balance).

Note: Because herbal products such as teas are not as closely regulated as medications, the amount of active ingredient in a product may vary from brand to brand and even among different lots of the same brand, posing a risk of unexpected high doses.

Information for Women Who Are Pregnant or Nursing   Commission E cautions against the use of senna by women who are pregnant or nursing because there is insufficient information about its toxic effects. In addition, gastrointestinal contractions triggered by cathartics, including senna, may set off uterine contractions.

Plant/Drug Interactions   Long-term use of cathartics, including senna, may cause a loss of potassium severe enough to affect drugs used to regulate heart rhythm.

HOW TO USE THIS PLANT   * * *

Sesame Seeds

ABOUT THIS PLANT

Botanical name(s): *Sesamum indicum*
Common name(s): Benne seed
Native to: Africa, India, Afghanistan, Indonesia
Parts used as food/drink: Seeds, oil
GRAS list: Yes
Medicinal properties: Emollient, laxative
Other uses: Medical solvent

ABOUT THIS PLANT AS FOOD OR DRINK

The sesame plant is a tall herb whose single hairy stalk may grow as high as seven feet, although stalks two to four feet high are more common.

Sesame seeds are small flat ovals, less than $1/8$ inch long and $1/20$ inch thick. Whole sesame seeds may be dark (with their hulls), white (hulled), or tan (hulled and roasted). Crushed sesame seeds are known as *tahini*, an oily paste that looks and tastes something like peanut butter. Sesame oil, also known as *benne oil* from an African-language word for sesame, is clear and golden when pressed from unroasted seeds and dark amber when pressed from roasted seeds. Golden sesame oil is used in cooking, in margarines, in cosmetics, and as a pharmaceutical solvent. Dark sesame oil is used mainly in Asian cuisine.

Nutritional Profile One-quarter cup (38 g) dried, hulled sesame seeds has 223 calories. It provides 10 g protein, 21 g fat, 2.9 g saturated fat, 9.1 g polyunsaturated fat, 7.9 g monounsaturated fat, 4 g carbohydrates, 3 g dietary fiber, 3 IU vitamin A, 50 mg calcium, 2.96 mg iron, and 15 mg sodium.

One tablespoon (15 g) tahini (ground sesame seeds) has 91 calories. It provides 3 grams protein, 8 grams fat, 1.2 g saturated fat, 3.7 g polyunsaturated fat, 3.2 g monounsaturated fat, 3 g carbohydrates, 1 g dietary fiber, 1 IU vitamin A, 21 mg calcium, 0.1 mg iron, 1 mg vitamin C, and less than 1 mg sodium.

One tablespoon sesame oil has 14 g fat, 2 g saturated fat, 5.6 g monounsaturated fat, and 5.8 g polyunsaturated fat.

HOW THIS PLANT AFFECTS YOUR BODY

Important Phytochemicals   Like other vegetable oils, sesame oil is low in saturated fatty acids and high in unsaturated fatty acids, the source of vitamin E, the collective name for a group of antioxidant heart-protective compounds known as tocopherols.

Benefits   Polyunsaturated fatty acids reduce blood levels of all types of cholesterol, including high-density lipoproteins (HDLs), the "good" fat and protein particles that carry cholesterol out of the body. Monounsaturated fatty acids protect the HDLs while reducing the levels of low-density lipoproteins (LDLs), which carry cholesterol into arteries. Sesame oil, which is approximately 37–41 percent monounsaturated fatty acids, reduces cholesterol levels while preserving HDLs.

Sesame seeds are a good source of protein. One ounce of sesame seeds has as much protein as 8 ounces of milk, 1 ounce of cheddar cheese or 14 cups of cottage cheese. The proteins in sesame seeds are considered limited (or incomplete) because they are deficient in the essential amino acid lysine. But the seeds contain sufficient amounts of other amino acids, including methionine and tryptophan. Combining sesame seeds with grains or beans, which are limited in methionine and cystine, provides complete proteins.

Possible Adverse Effects   * * *

Information for Women Who Are Pregnant or Nursing   * * *

Plant/Drug Interactions   * * *

HOW TO USE THIS PLANT

In Cooking   To preserve the flavor and freshness of sesame oil and sesame seeds, store them in a cool, dark cabinet. In warm weather, refrigerate the oil and the seeds. Sesame seed oil is exceptionally stable and less likely than other vegetable oils to turn rancid.

Sesame seeds may be used as a substitute for finely chopped almonds.

To make $1/2$ cup tahini, put 2 tablespoons sesame seeds in a blender. Combine $1/2$ teaspoon sesame oil, $1/8$ teaspoon salt, and $1/2$ cup cool water. Stir. Blend with sesame seeds, using enough liquid to make a thick, smooth paste that can be used as a substitute for peanut butter.

Shallots

ABOUT THIS PLANT

Botanical name(s): Allium ascalonicum
Common name(s): * * *
Native to: Western Asia
Parts used as food/drink: Bulbs, tops
GRAS list: No
Medicinal properties: * * *
Other uses: Insect repellent

ABOUT THIS PLANT AS FOOD OR DRINK

Shallots are members of the ONION family that look like dark GARLIC, with clusters of brown-skinned bulbs at the bottom of the plant. Gray-skinned shallots have a sharper, stronger flavor than the brown-skinned ones. Shallots are available fresh or freeze-dried.

Nutritional Profile   One tablespoon (10 g) chopped raw shallots has 7 calories. It provides 0.3 g protein, a trace of fat, 1.7 g carbohydrates, 4 mg calcium, 0.1 mg iron, and 0.8 mg vitamin C.

One tablespoon (0.9 g) freeze-dried shallots has 3 calories. It provides 0.1 g proteins, no fat, 0.7 g carbohydrates, 2 mg calcium, a trace of iron, and 0.4 mg vitamin C.

HOW THIS PLANT AFFECTS YOUR BODY

Important Phytochemicals   Like yellow onions, white onions, and the white bulbs of green onions/scallions, shallots get their color from creamy, pale yellow anthoxanthins. Their flavor and aroma comes from sulfur compounds such as aliin and mustard oils, which are activated by allinase, an enzyme released when the onion is peeled or sliced. Cooking converts the sulfur compounds to sugars, which is why cooked shallots taste sweet, not sharp.

Shallots also contain bitter flavonoids. In laboratory studies, various animals appear to use flavonoids as they do vitamin C to strengthen capillaries, the small blood vessels just under the skin. In human beings, antioxidant flavonoids are valued for their ability to prevent molecular fragments from joining to form potentially cancer-causing compounds.

Benefits   The sulfur compounds in onions appear to reduce the risk of some forms of cancer, perhaps by preventing the formation of carcinogens in your body, blocking carcinogens from reaching or reacting with sensitive body tissues, or by inhibiting the transformation of healthy cells to malignant ones.

In a number of laboratory studies conducted over the past three decades, first in India and then in the United States, the oils in onions appear to decrease blood levels of low-density lipoproteins (LDLs), the protein and fat molecules that carry cholesterol into the bloodstream, while increasing the levels of high-density lipoproteins (HDLs), the protein and fat molecules that carry cholesterol out of the body. As early as 1986, the German Commission E approved the use of dried onions or onion juice to prevent the formation of blood clots leading to a heart attack. The amount cited in the Commission E report was 50 g (slightly less than 2 ounces) fresh vegetables or 20 grams (slightly less than 1 ounce) dried onions per day.

Possible Adverse Effects   The most common side effect of eating onions (including shallots) is bad breath caused by the sulfur compounds in the onions. Cooking breaks down these compounds, so cooked onions are less smelly than raw ones.

Some people find onions and onion seasonings irritating to the stomach.

Information for Women Who Are Pregnant or Nursing   The odorous compounds in onions may be present in breast milk.

Plant/Drug Interactions   * * *

HOW TO USE THIS PLANT

In Cooking   Store shallots and other onions in a cool cabinet or a cool room such as a root cellar where the temperature is 60 degrees F or lower and there is plenty of circulating air to keep the onions dry and prevent them from sprouting. Properly stored, they should stay fresh for three to four weeks; at 55 degrees F, they may retain all their vitamin C for as long as six months.

When you cut into a shallot, you tear cell walls, releasing propanethial-S-oxide. The sulfur compound, identified in 1985 at the University of St. Louis in Missouri, floats into the air, changing into sulfuric acid when it comes in contact with water, which it why it stings if it gets into your eyes. To prevent this, slice fresh shallots under running water to dilute the propanethial-S-oxide before it rises, or chill them for an hour before slicing to slow the movement of sulfur molecules so they do not rise from the cutting board.

To peel shallots easily, immerse them in boiling water, then lift them out with a slotted spoon, and plunge them into cold water. The papery skin should now slip off easily.

Heat converts a shallot's sulfur flavor and aroma compounds into sugars, which is why cooked shallots taste sweet. When you brown a shallot, the sugars and amino acids on its surface caramelize to a deep, rich brown and the flavor intensifies. This browning of sugars and amino acids is called the *Maillard reaction* after the French chemist who first identified it.

Shallots may also change color when you cook them; their anthoxanthin pigments turn brown if they combine with metal ions. That's why shallots discolor if they are cooked in an aluminum or iron pot or sliced with a carbon steel knife.

If you grow your own shallots, you can pull the green tops and use them as a substitute for green onions/scallions or CHIVES. Chlorophyll, the green coloring in the leaves, is sensitive to acids. When you heat the leaves, their chlorophyll reacts with natural acids in the leaves or in the cooking water, forming a brown compound called pheophytin. The pheophytin in turn reacts with the yellow carotene pigments in the leaves, turning them bronze. To prevent this color change, prevent the chlorophyll from reacting with the acids by adding the leaves at the last minute. (Commercial herb packagers preserve the color of green herbs by drying the leaves at a very low heat.)

Three to four medium shallot bulbs equal one medium yellow onion.

In the Garden   Strongly scented herbs such as shallots appear to act as natural insect repellents. Other such plants are BASIL, MARIGOLD, NASTURTIUM, PEPPERMINT, ROSEMARY, SAGE, AND TANSY.

Shepherd's Purse

ABOUT THIS PLANT

Botanical name(s): *Capsella bursis pastoris*
Common name(s): Caseheart, lady's purse, mother's-heart
Native to: Europe
Parts used as food/drink: Leaves, seeds
GRAS list: No
Medicinal properties: Blood vessel constrictor
Other uses: * * *

ABOUT THIS PLANT AS FOOD OR DRINK

Shepherd's purse, a member of the MUSTARD family, is an annual plant native to Europe that now grows in temperate zones around the world. It is named for its seed pods which resemble the leather pouches carried by ancient shepherds.

Young shepherd's purse leaves may be used fresh to add a peppery flavor to salads or they may be added to soup or boiled and served as a pleasantly bitter cooked green vegetable. The plant's spicy seeds may be used as a substitute for mustard seeds.

Nutritional Profile * * *

HOW THIS PLANT AFFECTS YOUR BODY

Important Phytochemicals Shepherd's purse leaves get their flavor and aroma from mustard oils released when the leaves are crushed or broken.

Benefits Shepherd's purse leaves contain astringent compounds that coagulate proteins on the surface of skin or mucous membranes, causing the tissues to pucker. For centuries, the plant was used to control bleeding from an open wound. Later, extracts were used to reduce swollen hemorrhoids. In 1986 and 1990, the German Commission E validated these folk remedies by approving the use of preparations of fresh or dried shepherd's purse leaves and seeds as a topical dressing for nosebleeds, for bleeding from a minor injury, or as a tea to treat mild excess bleeding during a menstrual period.

Like other dark green leaves, shepherd's purse is a source of beta-carotene, the vitamin A precursor in deep yellow fruits and vegetables. According to the American Cancer Society, a diet rich in these foods may lower the risk of some forms of cancer. Vitamin A also protects your eyes. In your body, the vitamin A from the plant is converted to 11-cis retinol, the most important constituent of rhodopsin, a protein in the rods in your retina (the cells that enable you to see in dim light).

Possible Adverse Effects * * *

Information for Women Who Are Pregnant or Nursing Products containing shepherd's purse, including herbal teas, are thought to control heavy menstrual bleeding by causing contractions of the smooth muscle lining of the uterus. The active ingredient in the plant has not been identified, so some herbal experts caution pregnant women not to use this plant.

Plant/Drug Interactions * * *

HOW TO USE THIS PLANT

In Cooking Chlorophyll, the green coloring in shepherd's purse leaves, is sensitive to acids. When the leaves are heated, their chlorophyll reacts with natural acids in the leaves or in the cooking water, forming a brown compound called pheophytin. The pheophytin in turn reacts with the yellow carotene pigments in the leaves, turning the cooked leaves bronze. To prevent this color change, keep the chlorophyll from reacting with the acids by cooking the leaves for as short a time as possible. (Commercial herb packagers preserve the color of green herbs by drying the leaves at a very low heat.)

Sorrel

ABOUT THIS PLANT

Botanical name(s): *Rumex acetosa*
Common name(s): Garden sorrel
Native to: Europe
Parts used as food/drink: Leaves
GRAS list: No
Medicinal properties: Antiscorbutic
Other uses: * * *

ABOUT THIS PLANT AS FOOD OR DRINK

Sorrel is a member of the Rumex family, a group of plants that includes YEL-LOW DOCK (*Rumex crispus*). Sorrel's dark green, arrow-shaped leaves, with a bitter flavor reminiscent of spinach, may be used as a vegetable , as a garnish, to season eggs, meat, or sauces, or as one of the herbs on which fish is steamed.

Nutritional Profile One-half cup (67 g) chopped fresh sorrel leaves has 15 calories. It provides 1.3 g protein, 2.1 g carbohydrates, 2,680 IU vitamin A, 32.2 mg vitamin C, 29 mg calcium, 1.6 mg iron, and 0 mg sodium.

HOW THIS PLANT AFFECTS YOUR BODY

Important Phytochemicals Sorrel's distinctive bitter flavor comes from a combination of sharp-tasting compounds, including oxalic acid, which is also found in spinach; malic acid, the compound that gives immature apples and some mature sour apples their bite; astringent tannic acid; tartaric acid; and vitamin C (ascorbic acid).

Like spinach, sorrel is high in oxalates, which may be hazardous in large quantities. Oxalic acid is a caustic chemical that may irritate your skin and the lining of your stomach. It is also mildly laxative.

Benefits Rumex leaves, including sorrel, are rich in vitamin A and so high in vitamin C that they were once used as an antiscorbutic (a food that prevents or cures scurvy, a disease resulting from vitamin C deficiency). One-half cup chopped fresh Rumex leaves such as sorrel provides 67 percent of RDA for vitamin A for a woman and 54 percent of the RDA for a man, plus 54 percent of the RDA for vitamin C.

Possible Adverse Effects   The pollen present in sorrel is a potential allergen that may trigger allergic rhinitis (sneezing, runny nose, itchy or watery eyes) and bronchial asthma in sensitive people.

Foods such as spinach and sorrel, which are high in calcium and oxalates, may be prohibited on a low-calcium, low-oxalate diet for people who form calcium-oxalate kidney stones. They may also be prohibited for people with arthritis or gout.

Information for Women Who Are Pregnant or Nursing   * * *

Plant/Drug Interactions   * * *

HOW TO USE THIS PLANT

In Cooking   Do not tear or cut fresh sorrel leaves until you are ready to use them. When you cut into a food rich in vitamin C, its cells release an enzyme called ascorbic acid oxidase that destroys vitamin C and reduces the nutritional value of the food.

Like spinach and other highly acidic foods, sorrel reacts with metal ions (tiny particles) that may flake off the surface of pots and pans, forming dark pigments. If you cook sorrel or spinach in an aluminum or iron pot, these pigments discolor the pot and the leaves as well. To avoid this, cook sorrel in a glass pot or a pot with an enameled surface.

To reduce the oxalic acid content of sorrel leaves, plunge the leaves into boiling water, let sit for a minute or two, then drain the water and repeat the process two more times.

Chlorophyll, the green coloring in sorrel leaves, is sensitive to acids. When the leaves are heated, their chlorophyll reacts with natural acids in the leaves or in the cooking water, forming a brown compound called pheophytin. The pheophytin in turn reacts with the yellow carotene pigments in the leaves, turning the cooked leaves bronze. (Commercial herb packagers preserve the color of green herbs by drying the leaves at a very low heat.)

Soy Sauce

ABOUT THIS CONDIMENT

Botanical name(s): * * *
Common name(s): Kikkoman, La Choy, et al.
Native to: * * *
Parts used as food/drink: * * *
GRAS list: No
Medicinal properties: * * *
Other uses: * * *

ABOUT THIS CONDIMENT AS FOOD OR DRINK

Soy sauce is a condiment made by adding SALT to cooked soybeans and then setting the mixture aside to ferment. The result is a liquid containing amino acids, proteins, carbohydrates, and other organic compounds in a solution of sodium chloride (salt).

The smoothest, most flavorful soy sauces are the Asian varieties made from fermented soybeans, roasted wheat, salt, yeast or malt, and sugar. They are sometimes allowed to ferment for as long as a year and a half. *Tamari* is a soy sauce made from plain beans. *Teriyaki* is a soy sauce made from plain beans, then thickened with SUGAR and seasoned with VINEGAR and other spices. *Shoyu* is a soy sauce made from soy beans and wheat. "Light" soy sauces are paler and less intensely flavored but saltier than "dark" soy sauces.

Nutritional Profile   One tablespoon (18 g) tamari has 11 calories, 1.9 g protein, a trace of fat, 1 g carbohydrates, 0.1 g dietary fiber, 3.3 mcg folate, 3.6 mg calcium, 0.4 mg iron, and 1,005 mg sodium.

One tablespoon (16 g) shoyu has 9 calories, 0.8 g protein, a trace of fat, 1.5 g carbohydrates, 0.1 g dietary fiber, 2.5 mcg folate, 2.7 mg calcium, 0.3 mg iron, and 914 mg sodium.

One tablespoon (18 g) low-sodium shoyu has 10 calories, 0.9 g protein, a trace of fat, 1.5 g carbohydrates, 0.1 g dietary fiber, 2.8 mcg folate, 3.1 mg calcium, 0.4 mg iron, and 560 mg sodium.

HOW THIS CONDIMENT AFFECTS YOUR BODY

Important Phytochemicals   During fermentation, up to 70 percent of the vitamins in soybeans are destroyed. Among the nutrients remaining in soy

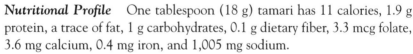

sauce are the essential amino acids arginine (also found in gelatin) and lysine; the nonessential amino acid glutaminic acid (its sodium salt, MONOSODIUM GLUTAMATE [MSG] is used as a flavor enhancer); and choline (a vitamin-like compound in plant and animal cells that enables cells to transmit electrical impulses.

Note: Soy sauces are not a source of isoflavones, the phytoestrogens (estrogen-like plant compounds) in soy foods believed to reduce the risk of hormone-related cancers and heart disease.

Benefits Adding soy sauce to vegetables appears to increase the amount of iron the body can absorb from the vegetables. Nonheme iron, the form of iron found in plant foods, is much less easily absorbed than heme iron, the form of iron found in meat, fish, poultry, and eggs. In 1988 scientists from the United States, China, and Great Britain released the results of a five-year study showing that people in China have no widespread iron deficiencies even though they get their iron primarily from vegetables. The scientists concluded that soy sauce and other fermented condiments used by the Chinese make nonheme iron more available to the body; the mechanism remains unknown.

Possible Adverse Effects Soy sauce, which is high in sodium, is usually prohibited on a sodium-restricted diet.

People who are sensitive or allergic to peanuts or beans may also react to soybeans or other soy foods such as soy milk, soy sauce, tofu, and tempeh. After eating a soy food, they may experience irritated, swollen lips; stomach cramps; chills; or vomiting. (Some people who have an allergic reaction to a soy product may actually be reacting to corn, if the soybeans or soy food was stored, carried, or prepared in a container previously used for corn.)

Cooks often tenderize meat by marinating it in an acidic solution such as wine, vinegar, or soy sauce to break down the muscle fibers in the beef. But acidic marinades also destroy thiamine (vitamin B1) in the meat. A 1986 study from the Hawkesbury Agricultural College in Richmond, Australia, suggests that marinating beef in soy sauce may reduce the thiamine content of the beef by as much as 44 percent.

Information for Women Who Are Pregnant or Nursing * * *

Condiment/Drug Interactions Soy sauce is high in tyramine, a natural by-product formed when proteins are fermented. Tyramine is a pressor amine, a compound that constricts blood vessels and triggers an increase in blood pressure. Monoamine oxidase (MAO) inhibitors—drugs used as antidepressants—interfere with the action of enzymes that break down tyramine. If you eat a food such as soy sauce (which is high in tyramine) while taking an MAO inhibitor, the tyramine cannot be efficiently eliminated from your body. The result may be a hypertensive crisis (sustained elevated blood pressure).

HOW TO USE THIS CONDIMENT
In Cooking Soy sauces may be stored at room temperature or refrigerated.

You may use soy sauce instead of salt on fish, chicken, and beef, as a flavor accent in dipping sauces for dumplings or other prepared foods, or as an ingredient in a marinade.

As a general rule, light soy sauces work well with fish and chicken, when you don't want the color or the flavor of the sauce to overwhelm the dish, while dark soy sauces work best in stews or with beef.

Spearmint

ABOUT THIS PLANT

Botanical name(s): Mentha spicata
Common name(s): Mint
Native to: Mediterranean region
Parts used as food/drink: Leaves; oil
GRAS list: Yes
Medicinal properties: Antiflatulent, choleretic, expectorant
Other uses: Pest repellent

ABOUT THIS PLANT AS FOOD OR DRINK

Spearmint is a member of the mint family with pointed, slightly crinkled, pale green leaves whose flavor and aroma are sweeter and less pungent than those of PEPPERMINT leaves.

Nutritional Profile   Two tablespoons (11 g) fresh spearmint leaves has 5 calories. It provides 0.4 g protein, 0.1 g fat, 1.0 g carbohydrates, 0.8 g dietary fiber, 462 IU vitamin A, 1.5 mg vitamin C, and 22.7 mg calcium, 1.4 mg iron, and 3 mg sodium.

One teaspoon (1 g) dried spearmint leaves has 1 calorie. It provides 0.1 g protein, a trace of fat, 0.3 g carbohydrates, 0.1 g dietary fiber, 55 IU vitamin A, no vitamin C, 7 mg calcium, 0.4 mg iron, and 2 mg sodium.

One tablespoon (2 g) dried spearmint leaves has 5 calories. It provides 0.3 g protein, 0.1 g fat, 0.8 g carbohydrates, 0.5 g dietary fiber, 169 IU vitamin A, no vitamin C, 24 mg calcium, 1.4 mg iron, and 6 mg sodium.

HOW THIS PLANT AFFECTS YOUR BODY

Important Phytochemicals   Spearmint's flavor and aroma come from oil of spearmint, a sometimes colorless, sometimes yellow or yellow-green liquid that is at least 50 percent spearmint-scented l-carvone. (A related compound, d-carvone, is the primary aroma ingredient in oil of CARAWAY.) Oil of spearmint also contains lemon-scented limonene; turpentine-scented pinene; and a small amount of mint-scented menthol.

Carvone, limonene, menthol, and pinene are irritants and allergic sensitizers (compounds that make you sensitive to other chemicals). Carvone and menthol are antiflatulants, agents that help break up and expel intestinal gas.

Benefits   * * *

Possible Adverse Effects Handling the spearmint plant may cause contact dermatitis (itching, burning, stinging, reddened, or blistered skin) or allergic reactions to other plants.

Like coffee, fatty foods, and carbonated beverages, mint oils may irritate the sphincter (muscle ring) at the base of the esophagus, permitting food from the stomach to flow back into the esophagus, creating the painful sensation called heartburn.

Information for Women Who Are Pregnant or Nursing * * *

Plant/Drug Interactions * * *

HOW TO USE THIS PLANT

In Cooking To protect the flavor of fresh spearmint leaves, store them in the refrigerator or freeze them in airtight plastic bags or containers.

To protect the flavor of dried spearmint leaves, do not crumble them until you are ready to use them.

Adding two or three spearmint leaves per pint to your favorite recipe for tomato sauce will give the sauce a surprising, zesty note.

Chlorophyll, the green coloring in spearmint leaves, is sensitive to acids. When the leaves are heated, their chlorophyll reacts with natural acids in the leaves or in the cooking water, forming a brown compound called pheophytin. The pheophytin in turn reacts with the yellow carotene pigments in the leaves, turning the cooked leaves bronze. To prevent this color change, you must keep the chlorophyll from reacting with the acids by cooking the spearmint for as short a time as possible. (Commercial herb packagers preserve the color of green herbs by drying the leaves at a very low heat.)

In the Garden To experiment with spearmint as a natural pest repellent, pour 3 cups boiling water over 1 cup spearmint leaves and let steep for 30 minutes. Then strain the liquid and spray your garden plants.

Spirulina

ABOUT THIS PLANT

Botanical name(s): Spirulina
Common name(s): * * *
Native to: Pacific and Indian Oceans, North Atlantic
Parts used as food/drink: Whole plants or their extracted gums
GRAS list: No
Medicinal properties: Iodine source
Other uses: Laxatives, stabilizers

ABOUT THIS PLANT AS FOOD OR DRINK

Spirulina is a seaweed, a nutritious vegetable most commonly used in Japanese cooking.

Nutritional Profile   3.5 ounces (100 g) raw spirulina has 25 calories. It provides 5.9 g protein, 0.4 g fat, 2.4 g carbohydrates, 56 IU vitamin A, 0.9 mg vitamin C, 12 mg calcium, 2.8 mg iron, and 98 mg sodium.

Three and one-half ounces (100 g) dried spirulina has 290 calories. It provides 57.4 g protein, 7.7 g fat, 23.9 g carbohydrates, 3.6 g dietary fiber, 570 IU vitamin A, 10.1 mg vitamin C, 120 mg calcium, 28.5 mg iron, and 1,048 mg sodium.

HOW THIS PLANT AFFECTS YOUR BODY

Important Phytochemicals   One useful group of compounds in seaweed are alginates, a form of soluble dietary fiber (gums) used as thickeners and gelling agents.

Benefits   Most seaweeds are rich in calcium and nonheme iron, the form of iron found in vegetables. It is more difficult for your body to absorb non-heme iron than heme iron, the iron found in meat, fish, poultry, milk, and eggs. Eating seaweed with meat increases the amount of iron you absorb from the seaweed because meat triggers the secretion of stomach acids, and iron is absorbed more easily in an acid environment. You can also increase your absorption of heme iron by eating the seaweed with a food rich in vitamin C. Vitamin C changes the iron in seaweed from ferric iron to ferrous iron, a more easily absorbed form of iron.

Possible Adverse Effects   Because seaweed is high in sodium, it is often restricted on a controlled sodium diet. Remember, powdered seaweed is not a low sodium substitute for table salt.

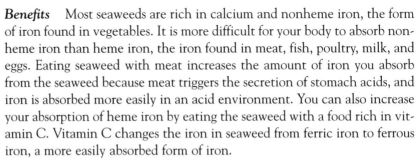

All seaweed is high in iodine. The exact amount varies from species to species, but it is not uncommon for dried seaweed to have concentrations as high as 0.4–0.6 percent or 116 to 174 mg iodine per ounce, nearly 800 times the RDA (150 micrograms). The thyroid gland uses iodine to make thyroid hormones. If you don't get enough iodine, the gland will swell in an attempt to produce more hormone; the swelling is called a goiter. Paradoxically, people who consume too much iodine, defined by the German Commission E as more than 150 mcg per day, may also suffer from goiter because an oversupply of inorganic iodine (the form found in food) keeps the thyroid gland from making organic iodine (the form used to make thyroid hormones). Iodine-overdose goiter is most likely to occur at an iodine consumption exceeding 2,000 mcg (2 mg) per day, as is common in Japan. There seaweed is an important part of the diet, and iodine intake may be as high as 50,000 to 80,000 mcg (50–80 mg) per day.

Some people experience serious allergic reactions to large amounts of iodine, generally defined as more than 150 mcg a day.

Information for Women Who Are Pregnant or Nursing   * * *

Plant/Drug Interactions   * * *

HOW TO USE THIS PLANT
In Cooking   To reduce or eliminate seaweed's "weedy" iodine flavor, soak the seaweed in cool water for at least 2 hours before using.

Star Anise

ABOUT THIS PLANT

Botanical name(s): *Illicium verum*
Common name(s): Chinese anise
Native to: Far East
Parts used as food/drink: Dried fruit
GRAS list: Yes
Medicinal properties: Antiflatulant, expectorant
Other uses: Fragrance

ABOUT THIS PLANT AS FOOD OR DRINK

Star anise is a small evergreen tree that grows wild in southern China. The tree produces fruits that open out into the shape of a star as they ripen, which is how the tree got half its name. The "anise" part comes from the fact that star anise tastes and smells like true ANISE.

Although they come from totally different plants, oil of anise and oil of star anise may substitute for each other. Both are widely used as flavorings in commercial baked goods, cough syrups, cough drops, dentifrices, chewing gum, tobacco, and the LICORICE-flavored liqueurs ouzo and anisette. Anisette is a safe alternative to absinthe, the cordial banned in the United States since the 1920s because it is made from oil of WORMWOOD (*Absinthum*), a poisonous herb that contains thujone, a central nervous system poison related to THC (tetrahydrocannabinol), the active ingredient in marijuana. Thujone may cause gastrointestinal upset, nervousness, stupor, convulsions, and even death.

Caution: Do not confuse Chinese star anise with Japanese star anise (*Illicium lanceolatum*), a poisonous plant used as an agricultural pesticide in the Far East.

Nutritional Profile   * * *

HOW THIS PLANT AFFECTS YOUR BODY

Important Phytochemicals   The flavor of star anise comes from licorice-flavored anethole; spicy methylchavicol, which is related to chavicol, one of the compounds that gives black pepper its bite; and vanilla-flavored anisaldehyde. Oil of star anise also contains estragole, the main constituent of oil of TARRAGON; camphor-scented eucalyptol; lemony-scented limonene; acrid quinic acid; penetrating terpineol; and salty trigonelline (nicotinic acid).

Anethole (also known as anise camphor), limonene, and phellandrene are irritants. They may cause contact dermatitis (itching, burning, stinging, reddened, or blistered skin). In laboratory animals anethole is poisonous when absorbed through the skin.

Eucalyptol and terpineol are expectorants, agents that increase the secretion of liquid from the mucous membranes lining the respiratory tract, thus making it easier to cough up mucus. Oil of anise is an antiflatulent, an agent that helps break up and expel intestinal gas. However, we use such small amounts of star anise to flavor food that we are unlikely to experience these effects.

Benefits   * * *

Possible Adverse Effects   Toothpastes, tooth powders, and mouthwashes flavored with oil of anise have been reported to cause cheilitis (dry, peeling, and bleeding lips), sometimes mistaken for the simple chapping that occurs in cold weather.

Information for Women Who Are Pregnant or Nursing   * * *

Plant/Drug Interactions   * * *

HOW TO USE THIS PLANT

In Cooking   Star anise is the main ingredient in Chinese five spice powder, which also contains FENNEL, CINNAMON/CASSIA, CLOVES, and Szechwan peppercorns.

To brew star anise tea, pour 1 cup boiling water over 1 teaspoon crushed star anise seeds. Let the tea steep for 5 minutes. Then strain into a warmed cup and, if desired, sweeten to taste with honey or sugar.

As a Cosmetic   The Chinese chew whole star anise seeds as a breath sweetener.

Around the House   The scent of anise is attractive to rodents. Dusting star anise seeds on your mousetraps may make them more effective.

Stevia

ABOUT THIS PLANT

Botanical name(s): *Stevia rebaudiana*
Common name(s): Sweet leaf
Native to: South America
Parts used as food/drink: Leaves and twigs
GRAS list: No
Medicinal properties: Digestive aid, mild diuretic
Other uses: * * *

ABOUT THIS PLANT AS FOOD OR DRINK

Stevia is an herb native to South America. For centuries, Peruvians have used its leaves to brew a sweet tea sometimes used as a mild diuretic and digestive aid.

Nutritional Profile   * * *

HOW THIS PLANT AFFECTS YOUR BODY

Important Phytochemicals   The sweetener in stevia is stevioside, a sugar compound said to be 30 to 300 times sweeter than table SUGAR (sucrose).

Benefits   In Japan, dental studies suggest that stevioside may suppress the growth of bacteria that cause cavities.

Possible Adverse Effects   In Japan and the Far East, stevia has been used in products such as soft drinks since 1970, but as late as 1991, the U.S. Food and Drug Administration (FDA) still classified stevia as an herb of unproven safety. In 1995, after passage of the 1994 Dietary Supplement Health and Education Act, the FDA finally agreed to permit stevia to be imported into the United States but requires the herb to be sold as a nutritional supplement, not as a sweetener or a food (tea).

Information for Women Who Are Pregnant or Nursing   In South America, stevia has been used as a contraceptive, but animal studies of its effectiveness are inconclusive. In some animal studies, stevia rendered mice less fertile; in others, there was no evidence either of impaired fertility or birth defects. There have been no studies of stevia's effects on human reproduction.

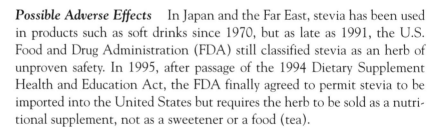

336

Plant/Drug Interactions   * * *

HOW TO USE THIS PLANT

In Cooking   Stevia does not lose its sweetness when heated.

Sucralose

ABOUT THIS CONDIMENT

Chemical name(s): Trichlorogalactosucrose
Common name(s): Splenda
Native to: * * *
Parts used as food/drink: * * *
GRAS list: Yes
Medicinal properties: Noncaloric sweetener
Other uses: * * *

ABOUT THIS CONDIMENT AS FOOD OR DRINK

Sucralose, identified in 1976, is the only calorie-free sweetener made from sugar. In 1998, based on more than 110 studies in human beings and animals over a 20-year period, the U.S. Food and Drug Administration approved the use of sucralose, which is 6 times sweeter than sugar, as a tabletop sweetener and as a sweetener in candy, baked goods, frozen desserts, and nonalcoholic beverages.

Nutritional Profile Sucralose has no calories and no nutritive value. The suggested daily allowance of sucralose is 15 mg per kilogram (2.2 pounds) of body weight.

HOW THIS CONDIMENT AFFECTS YOUR BODY

Important Phytochemicals Your body does not recognize sucralose as a carbohydrate. The compound moves unchanged through your intestinal tract.

Benefits Sucralose's benefit is its ability to sweeten without calories. It is useful in a diet designed to control weight and for people with diabetes who must limit their sugar intake.

Like other nonnutritive sweeteners, sucralose sweetens without increasing the incidence of dental cavities.

Possible Adverse Effects * * *

Information for Women Who Are Pregnant or Nursing * * *

Condiment/Drug Interactions * * *

HOW TO USE THIS CONDIMENT

In Cooking Sucralose does not lose its sweetness when heated. It remains stable when used in cooked or baked dishes.

Sugar

ABOUT THIS CONDIMENT

Chemical name(s): Sucrose
Common name(s): Table sugar, white sugar, refined sugar, granulated sugar
Native to: Tropical areas
Parts used as food/drink: * * *
GRAS list: Yes
Medicinal properties: Demulcent, antiseptic
Other uses: Preservative

ABOUT THIS CONDIMENT AS FOOD OR DRINK

Sugar, also known as table sugar, white sugar, refined sugar, or granulated sugar, is a sweetener made from sugarcane and sugar beets, a crystalline powder that can absorb up to 1 percent of its weight in water from the air. Brown sugar is table sugar with molasses added. Confectioner's sugar is table sugar plus cornstarch.

Table sugar provides no nutrients other than calories (energy) from simple carbohydrates. Brown sugar provides small amounts of B vitamins and minerals (calcium and iron) from the molasses.

Nutritional Profile   One packet (6 g) table sugar has 25 calories. It provides 6 g carbohydrates and a trace of calcium and iron.

One tablespoon (12 g) table sugar has 45 calories. It provides 12 g carbohydrates and a trace of calcium and iron.

One cup (200 g) table sugar has 770 calories. It provides 199 g carbohydrates, 3 mg calcium, and 0.1 mg iron.

One cup (220 g) brown sugar has 820 calories. It provides 212 g carbohydrates, 187 mg calcium, and 4.8 mg iron.

HOW THIS CONDIMENT AFFECTS YOUR BODY

Important Phytochemicals   Carbohydrates are composed of units of sugar. A simple carbohydrate, or a *monosaccharide* (*mono* = one; *saccharide* = sugar), has one unit of sugar. Fructose, the sugar in fruit, is a monosaccharide. So are glucose (blood sugar, the sugar produced when carbohydrates are digested) and galactose, the sugar produced when lactose, the sugar in milk, is digested.

A carbohydrate with two units of sugar is called a double sugar or a disaccharide (*di* = two). Sucrose (table sugar) is a disaccharide composed of one unit of fructose and one unit of glucose. Other disaccharides are lactose (glucose plus galactose) and maltose (two units of glucose). A carbohydrate with more than two units is called a *polysaccharide* (*poly* = many). Raffinose, an indigestible sugar in beans, is a polysaccharide with one unit each of galactose, glucose, and fructose. Starches, which are made of many units of glucose, are also polysaccharides.

Benefits   The body metabolizes all carbohydrates, from simple sugars to complex ones, to either glucose or sugar units that can be converted quickly to glucose. The glucose is then carried into the cells with the help of insulin, an enzyme secreted by the pancreas. Inside the cells, the glucose is burned to produce energy. Carbohydrates also protect the muscles. If there are no carbohydrates available to burn for energy, perhaps as a result of a severe reducing diet, the body will start to burn its own protein tissues (muscles), which is why a carbohydrate-rich diet is sometimes called "protein sparing."

Possible Adverse Effects   People with diabetes cannot metabolize sucrose efficiently because they do not produce sufficient amounts of insulin, the pancreatic enzyme that enables the body to absorb and use sugar. As a result, the unmetabolized sugar continues to circulate in their blood until it is excreted through the kidneys, which is why one way to tell if someone has diabetes is to test the level of sugar in his or her urine. Eating sugared foods does not cause diabetes, an inherited condition, but it may raise blood sugar levels and exacerbate some of the symptoms of diabetes: dehydration, thirst, fatigue.

Caution: Honey, a disaccharide composed of sucrose and fructose, is not a "safe" sweetener for people with diabetes, as it, too, must be metabolized with insulin.

Some people experience higher blood levels of triglycerides, a form of fatty acids, when they eat sugar, but there is no evidence that eating sugar causes heart disease.

A diet high in carbohydrates, including sugar, increases the incidence of dental cavities because the sugar sticks to your teeth, providing food for the bacteria that cause cavities.

Sugar is hydrophilic (*hydro* = water; *philic* = loving). If you drink a highly sweetened liquid when you are dehydrated, the sugar will pull water from your body tissues into your intestinal tract, increasing your dehydration.

Information for Women Who Are Pregnant or Nursing   * * *

Condiment/Drug Interactions   * * *

HOW TO USE THIS CONDIMENT

In Cooking   One cup of white sugar has the sweetening power of 1 cup packed brown sugar or $3/4$ cup confectioner's sugar or 2 cups corn syrup or $1/3$ cup molasses. However, these sweeteners each contain different amounts of moisture; do not substitute them in cooking or baking without adjusting the liquid content of the recipe.

Sweet Cicely

ABOUT THIS PLANT

Botanical name(s): Myrrhis odorata
Common name(s): British myrrh, sweet chervil
Native to: Europe
Parts used as food/drink: Flowers, leaves, seeds
GRAS list: No
Medicinal properties: * * *
Other uses: * * *

ABOUT THIS PLANT AS FOOD OR DRINK

Sweet cicely is a decorative plant with lacy, fernlike leaves and small white flowers. The entire plant—leaves, flowers, stems, seeds, roots— smells like ANISE and tastes sweet, with a mild LICORICE flavor. In French cooking, it is often used along with TARRAGON.

Cicely leaves, flowers, and stems may be used fresh in salads or boiled to make a licorice-flavored liquid used in fruit pies and compotes. The small green or black seeds may also be used in salads and fruit dishes or steeped in vodka to make a licorice-flavored drink. The root was once cooked, mashed, or pureed, and served as a vegetable.

Versatile though it may be, sweet cicely is generally available only from your own garden.

Nutritional Profile * * *

HOW THIS PLANT AFFECTS YOUR BODY

Important Phytochemicals * * *

Benefits * * *

Possible Adverse Effects * * *

Information for Women Who Are Pregnant or Nursing * * *

Plant/Drug Interactions * * *

HOW TO USE THIS PLANT

In Cooking When stewing fruit, substitute 2 to 4 teaspoons chopped fresh cicely leaves for 1 teaspoon sugar. Or, when poaching fruit, boil ¹/4 cup cicely leaves and stem tips in 1 cup water, strain the liquid, and substitute for 1 cup water plus 2 teaspoons sugar.

In baking, sprinkle dried cicely seeds on cookies for a sweet licorice flavor.

Around the House Dried sweet cicely leaves and seeds add a licorice scent to potpourris and sachets.

Sweet Clover

ABOUT THIS PLANT

Botanical name(s): Melilotus officinalis
Common name(s): Melilot, yellow sweet clover
Native to: Europe, Asia
Parts used as food/drink: Leaves
GRAS list: No
Medicinal properties: Anti-inflammatory, anti-edema
Other uses: Livestock feed, tobacco flavoring, cheese flavoring

ABOUT THIS PLANT AS FOOD OR DRINK

Sweet clover, also known as yellow sweet clover, has been cultivated as a food forage plant for livestock and its flowers are a source of honey. It has been used to flavor cheeses and tobacco.

Nutritional Profile * * *

HOW THIS PLANT AFFECTS YOUR BODY

Important Phytochemicals The flavor and aroma of sweet clover come from vanilla-scented coumarin, plus bitter flavonoids and resins.

Benefits In 1986 and 1990, the German Commission E approved the use of fresh or dried leaves and flowering tops of sweet clover to reduce swelling, inflammation, and leg cramps from venous insufficiency as well as hemorrhoids and blood clots. *Caution:* These are potentially serious conditions that should not be treated without the advice and supervision of your physician.

Possible Adverse Effects Large amounts of sweet clover are toxic and may cause headache, nausea, vomiting, and general weakness. The seeds are known to poison farm animals.

Information for Women Who Are Pregnant or Nursing * * *

Plant/Drug Interactions * * *

HOW TO USE THIS PLANT * * *

Sweet Woodruff

ABOUT THIS PLANT

Botanical name(s): Galium odoratum
Common name(s): Waldmeister
Native to: Asia, North Africa
Parts used as food/drink: Leaves
GRAS list: No
Medicinal properties: * * *
Other uses: Wine and spirits flavoring

ABOUT THIS PLANT AS FOOD OR DRINK

Sweet woodruff, also known as waldmeister, is the herb used to flavor German May wine, as well as BITTERS and vermouth.

Nutritional Profile * * *

HOW THIS PLANT AFFECTS YOUR BODY

Sweet woodruff contains bitter tasting, vanilla-scented coumarin. When fed to laboratory animals, extract of sweet woodruff containing large amounts of coumarin damages the liver, shrinks the testicles, and inhibits normal growth. These effects have not been linked to the herb itself.

Benefits * * *

Possible Adverse Effects In human beings, drinking excess amounts of tea brewed from sweet woodruff may cause dizziness and vomiting. As a result, the U.S. Food and Drug Administration has approved the use of coumarin as a flavor only in alcohol beverages. It is no longer allowed in food.

Information for Women Who Are Pregnant or Nursing * * *

Plant/Drug Interactions * * *

HOW TO USE THIS PLANT * * *

Tarragon

ABOUT THIS PLANT

Botanical name(s): *Artemisia dracunculus*
Common name(s): Dragon herb, estragon, French tarragon
Native to: North America, Europe
Parts used as food/drink: Leaves
GRAS list: Yes
Medicinal properties: * * *
Other uses: Perfumery

ABOUT THIS PLANT AS FOOD OR DRINK

Tarragon is a tall weedy plant with slender stems and narrow, dark blue-green leaves. Its name is an anglicized version of the French word *estragon* which is itself derived from the Greek word for "little dragon," a reference to tarragon's snakelike roots.

Tarragon leaves are used as a seasoning; oil of tarragon is used as a food flavoring, particularly in vinegar and pickles, and to scent perfumes.

Nutritional Profile   One teaspoon (2 g) ground tarragon has 5 calories. It provides 0.4 g protein, 0.1 g fat, 0.8 g carbohydrates, 0.1 g dietary fiber, 67 IU vitamin A, 0.8 mg vitamin C, 18 mg calcium, 0.5 mg iron, and 1 mg sodium.

One tablespoon (5 g) ground tarragon has 14 calories. It provides 1.1 g protein, 0.4 g fat, 2.4 g carbohydrates, 0.4 g dietary fiber, 202 IU vitamin A, 2.4 mg vitamin C, 55 mg calcium, 1.6 mg iron, and 4 mg sodium.

HOW THIS PLANT AFFECTS YOUR BODY

Important Phytochemicals   The primary flavoring compound in oil of tarragon is estragole, which tastes and smells like LICORICE. Tarragon also contains the bitter flavonoid rutin, an antioxidant.

Benefits   Like other dark green leaves, tarragon is a source of beta-carotene, the vitamin A precursor in deep yellow fruits and vegetables. According to the American Cancer Society, a diet rich in these foods may lower the risk of some forms of cancer. Vitamin A also protects your eyes. In your body, the vitamin A from tarragon is converted to 11-cis retinol, the most important constituent of rhodopsin, a protein in the rods in your retina (the cells that enable you to see in dim light).

In laboratory studies, various animals appear to use flavonoids as they do vitamin C to strengthen capillaries, the small blood vessels just under the skin. In human beings, antioxidant flavonoids are valued for their ability to prevent molecular fragments from joining to form potentially cancer-causing compounds.

Possible Adverse Effects   Tarragon may cause upset stomach in people sensitive to the herb.

Estragole (but not tarragon) is reported to have produced tumors in laboratory mice; no such effects have been reported in human beings.

Information for Women Who Are Pregnant or Nursing   There are anecdotal tales of tarragon's causing miscarriage. Although there are no scientific studies to prove this effect, pregnant women may wish to avoid this herb.

Plant/Drug Interactions   * * *

HOW TO USE THIS PLANT

In Cooking   Tarragon's flavoring oils evaporate quickly when the herb is dried; fresh tarragon is much more flavorful than dried tarragon.

To preserve the flavor of fresh tarragon leaves, freeze the leaves in an airtight container. Unlike drying, which evaporates the flavoring oils, freezing protects them; frozen tarragon leaves will hold their flavor for as long as three to five months. Use the leaves right out of the freezer—there's no need to defrost them first.

For a flavorful tarragon VINEGAR, add a sprig of clean, freshly cut tarragon to a bottle of distilled white vinegar. Let it steep for three to four days, and then taste the vinegar. If desired, continue steeping until the flavor meets your preference.

Chlorophyll, the green coloring in tarragon leaves, is sensitive to acids. When the leaves are heated, their chlorophyll reacts with natural acids in the leaves or in the cooking water, forming a brown compound called pheophytin. The pheophytin in turn reacts with the yellow carotene pigments in the leaves, turning the cooked leaves bronze. To prevent this color change, keep the chlorophyll from reacting with the acids by cooking tarragon for as short a time as possible. (Commercial herb packagers preserve the color of green herbs by drying the leaves at a very low heat.)

Tea

ABOUT THIS PLANT

Botanical name(s): Camellia sinensis
Common name(s): * * *
Native to: Asia
Parts uses as food/drink: Leaves
GRAS list: No
Medicinal properties: Stimulant, diuretic
Other uses: * * *

ABOUT THIS PLANT AS FOOD OR DRINK

Tea is a beverage brewed from the bright green leaves of a shrub native to Asia. The three major forms of tea—green tea, black tea, and oolong tea—come from the same plant, differing only in their processing.

Green tea is composed of leaves dried right after harvesting so they remain green, with a delicate flavor. Black tea is composed of leaves allowed to ferment after harvesting. During fermentation, the naturally occurring enzyme polyphenoloxidase alters phenols (alcohols) in the leaves, creating tannins, brown pigments that darken the leaves and intensify their flavor. Oolong tea is composed of leaves which have been allowed to ferment for only a short time, turning brownish-green with a flavor somewhere between green tea and the strong black tea.

Note: The terms *souchong*, *orange pekoe*, and *pekoe* describe grades or shapes of black tea leaves. Souchong leaves are round; orange pekoe leaves are thin and wiry; pekoe leaves are shorter and rounder than orange pekoe.

Nutritional Profile One 8-ounce cup brewed green, black, or oolong tea has 2 calories. It provides 1 g carbohydrates, a trace of fat, no calcium, 0.1 mg iron, and 7 mg sodium. The mineral content of tea varies with the mineral content of the water in which it is brewed.

HOW THIS PLANT AFFECTS YOUR BODY

Important Phytochemicals Like COCOA, COFFEE, GUARANA, and MATE, tea contains the central nervous system stimulants theophylline and caffeine and the muscle stimulant theobromine. Coffee has more caffeine; tea has more theophylline; and chocolate has more theobromine.

Theophylline extracted from tea leaves is used as an antiasthma medication that effectively relaxes the smooth muscles in the bronchi, the small passages that carry air into the lungs, but there is no evidence the relatively low con-centrations of theophylline in brewed tea have the same effect.

Tea is high in tannins, astringent compounds that coagulate proteins on the surface of the mucous membrane lining of your mouth, making the tissues pucker.

All tea is high in fluorides. It is not uncommon to find a tea plant with a fluoride con-centration of 100 ppm (parts per million). By comparison, fluoridated water is generally 1 ppm fluoride.

Benefits   The caffeine and theophylline in tea increase alertness and concentration, inten-sify muscle responses, speed up the heartbeat, and elevate mood. However, these effects vary widely from person to person, and if you drink tea every day, you may develop a tolerance for caffeine and theophylline so that they provide less of a lift than if you drink tea only once in a while.

The stimulant effect of a cup of tea depends on its caffeine content and that depends on how the tea is brewed. As a rule, tea brewed from loose leaves almost always has more caffeine than tea made from tea bags or instant tea.

CAFFEINE CONTENT OF BREWED TEAS (mg per 5 oz cup)	
Tea bags (black tea)	
5 min brew	47 mg
1 min brew	29 mg
Loose tea	
Black, 5 min brew	41 mg
Green, 5 min brew	36 mg
Green (Japanese) 5 min brew	21 mg
Drip-brewed coffee	139 mg

Source: *Handbook of Clinical Dietetics*, The American Dietetic Association (Yale University Press, 1981)

Drinking green tea appears to reduce the risk of dental cavities, an effect once attributed to the tea's naturally high fluoride content. But later research suggests it may be due to the oily, flower-scented insoluble compounds such as caryophyllene and indole that give tea its distinctive flavor. To date, nine of the 10 most abundant flowery compounds hexanes in green tea have been shown to inhibit bacterial production of glucans, a sticky material that allows the bacteria to bind to your teeth and cause decay.

In 1991, at the Fourth Chemical Congress of North America, a number of scientific teams announced the identification of compounds in green and black teas that reduce the incidence of tumors of the skin, esophagus, gastrointestinal tract tumors, lung, liver, and pancreas in laboratory animals. Eight years later, in January 1999, Purdue University researchers released a study showing that EGCg, a compound in green tea, inhibits an enzyme required for cancer cell growth, killing cancer cells in laboratory dishes without harming healthy cells. The Purdue findings suggest that drinking four cups of green tea per day may produce a lower overall risk of cancer.

Note: People who drink very hot tea (131–153 degrees F) have a higher risk of esophageal cancer than do people who drink tea at a temperature of 95–117 degrees F. The higher rate of cancer is almost certainly due to the tissues being injured repeatedly by the extremely hot liquid.

Possible Adverse Effects   Like coffee, tea may cause restlessness, nervousness, hyperactivity, insomnia, flushing, and upset stomach after as little as one cup a day. It is possible to develop a tolerance for caffeine, so people who drink tea every day are likely to find it less immediately stimulating than those who drink it only once in a while. It may take up to seven hours to metabolize and excrete the caffeine from one cup of tea.

The tannins in tea may be constipating.

Caffeinated beverages contain flavoring oils that can upset your stomach, but mate is probably less irritating than coffee or tea because it contains significantly less flavoring oil. One pound of mate has about 4.5 mg flavoring oils; one pound of coffee, about 200 mg flavoring oils; one pound of tea, up to 3,600 mg flavoring oils.*

Information for Women Who Are Pregnant or Nursing   * * *

Plant/Drug Interactions   The naturally occurring theophylline and caffeine in brewed tea may intensify the effects of the antiasthma drug theophylline.

Drinking tea may intensify the stimulant effects of caffeine-containing over-the-counter cold remedies, diuretics, pain relievers, stimulants, and weight control products. On the other hand, tea may counteract the drowsiness caused by sedative drugs, a potential benefit for people taking certain antihistamines.

Monoamine oxidase (MAO) inhibitors are drugs used as antidepressants or antihypertensives. They inhibit the natural activity of enzymes that break down pressor amines, substances that constrict blood vessels and raise blood pressure. If you ingest a food, drug, or herb high in tyramine while you are taking an MAO inhibitor, the added tyramine cannot be efficiently eliminated from your body. The result may be potentially fatal sustained high blood pressure. The caffeine in tea is a weak pressor amine.

Tea may reduce the effectiveness of the antigout drug allopurinol, which is designed to inhibit xanthines, such as caffeine.

---

* Coffee seems so much more strongly flavored than tea, so how come tea has a higher amount of flavoring oils? Because an individual tea leaf weighs less than an individual coffee bean. It takes more tea leaves than coffee beans to make a pound. More leaves, more flavoring oils.

By increasing the acidity of stomach fluids, tea may reduce the absorption of some oral antibiotics such as ampicillin, erythromycin, griseofulvin, penicillin, and the tetracyclines.

Caffeine binds with iron to form insoluble compounds your body cannot absorb. Ideally, iron supplements and tea should be taken at least two hours apart.

Tea contains vitamin K, the blood-clotting vitamin produced naturally by bacteria in the intestines. Using foods rich in vitamin K while you are taking an anticoagulant (warfarin [Coumadin, Panwarfin]) may reduce the effectiveness of the anticoagulant.

HOW TO USE THIS PLANT

In Cooking   Store tea in a cool, dark cabinet, in an air- and moisture-proof container, preferably a glass jar.

When brewing tea, always start with an absolutely clean glass, china, or enamel pot and, if possible, soft, mineral-free water. The tannins in tea leaves bond to metals and minerals to create the film sometimes seen floating on top of a cup of tea.

When tea leaves are immersed in water, they release flavoring agents plus bitter tannins, the astringent chemicals that coagulate proteins on the surface of the mucous membranes lining the mouth, making the tissues pucker. The best tea is brewed at water's boiling point (212 degrees F/100 degrees C), a temperature that allows the tea leaves to release flavoring agents quickly without overloading the tea with bitter tannins. If the brewing water is 25 degrees or more below the boiling point, the leaves will release their flavoring agents so slowly that by the time enough flavor molecules have been released into the brew, the ratio of bitter tannins will be so high that the tea tastes bitter. On the other hand, brewing tea in water that is too hot also makes a bitter drink. At temperatures above boiling, the tannins are released so fast that they turn tea bitter in a minute or two.

When tea brewed in hot water is chilled to make iced tea, some pigments precipitate out, making the tea look cloudy. To avoid cloudiness, brew tea for ice tea in lukewarm water.

Thyme

ABOUT THIS PLANT

Botanical name(s): *Thymus vulgaris*
Common name(s): Common thyme, garden thyme
Native to: Southern Europe
Parts used as food/drink: Leaves
GRAS list: Yes
Medicinal properties: Expectorant, bronchial antispasmodic, antibacterial
Other uses: Insect repellent

ABOUT THIS PLANT AS FOOD OR DRINK

Thyme (pronounced "time") is a member of the mint family, a relative of BASIL, MARJORAM, and OREGANO. It has woody stems, clusters of small, lavender-colored flowers, and $1/4$-inch long oval, gray-green leaves.

There are more than 100 varieties of thyme, each slightly different in appearance, each with a slightly different flavor and aroma. For example, thyme from England has broad leaves; French thyme has narrow leaves; winter thyme from Germany stays green all winter. There are also thymes that taste and smell like LEMON, mint, pine, LICORICE, CARAWAY, or NUT-MEG. The whole or ground thyme you get at the grocery store is dried *Thymus vulgaris*.

Nutritional Profile   One teaspoon (1 g) fresh thyme has 1 calorie. It provides a trace or protein and fat, 0.2 g carbohydrates, 0.1 g dietary fiber, 38 IU vitamin A, 1.3 mg vitamin C, 3 mg calcium, 0.1 mg iron, and no sodium.

One teaspoon (1 g) ground thyme has 4 calories. It provides 0.1 g protein, 0.1 g fat, 0.9 g carbohydrates, 0.9 g dietary fiber, 53 IU vitamin A, 0.7 mg vitamin C, 26 mg calcium, 1.7 mg iron, and 1 mg sodium.

One tablespoon (4 g) ground thyme has 12 calories. It provides 0.4 g protein, 0.1 g fat, 2.8 g carbohydrates, 1.6 g dietary fiber, 163 IU vitamin A, 2.1 mg vitamin C, 81 mg calcium, 5.3 mg iron, and 2 mg sodium.

HOW THIS PLANT AFFECTS YOUR BODY

Important Phytochemicals   Oil of thyme, a colorless to reddish-brown liquid, contains thymol, the most important flavoring agent in thyme, plus

sharp-tasting, peppery-scented borneol, carvacrol (which smells like thymol), linalool (which smells like French lavender) and pinene (which smells like turpentine).

Linalool and pinene are irritants. Thymol, an antiseptic that kills mildew and mold, is used in medical laboratories to preserve anatomical specimens and urine samples.

Benefits   Thymol is an expectorant, an agent that causes the mucous membranes lining the respiratory tract to "weep" watery secretions, making it easier for you to cough up mucus. In 1984, 1990, and 1992, the German Commission E approved the use of preparations of dried thyme leaves and flowers to relieve coughs due to upper respiratory infections and whooping cough.

Dried thyme is a source of beta-carotene, the vitamin A precursor in deep yellow fruits and vegetables. According to the American Cancer Society, a diet rich in these foods may lower the risk of some forms of cancer. Vitamin A also protects your eyes. In your body, the vitamin A from thyme is converted to 11-cis retinol, the most important constituent of rhodopsin, a protein in the rods in your retina (the cells that enable you to see in dim light).

Possible Adverse Effects   Handling the thyme plant may cause contact dermatitis (itching, burning, stinging, reddened, or blistered skin). Cosmetics such as bath oils or soaps that are perfumed with oil of thyme may be irritating. Toothpastes flavored with oil of thyme may cause cheilitis (cracked and bleeding lips) and glossitis (irritation of the tongue).

Information for Women Who Are Pregnant or Nursing   * * *

Plant/Drug Interactions   * * *

HOW TO USE THIS PLANT

In Cooking   One sprig fresh thyme equals the flavoring power of $1/2$ teaspoon ground dried thyme. The leaves are sweetest if picked just as the flowers appear.

Thyme leaves hold their flavor better than most herbs when dried. To dry thyme leaves, hang them upside down in an airy room for 10 days. To release the flavor of thyme leaves, crush or crumble them just before using.

Chlorophyll, the green coloring in thyme leaves, is sensitive to acids. When the leaves are heated, their chlorophyll reacts with natural acids in the leaves or in the cooking water, forming a brown compound called pheophytin. The pheophytin in turn reacts with the yellow carotene pigments in the leaves, turning the cooked leaves bronze. To prevent this color change, you must keep the chlorophyll from reacting with the acids by cooking thyme for as short a time as possible. (Commercial herb packagers preserve the color of green herbs by drying the leaves at a very low heat.)

As a Home Remedy   To soothe a sore throat or ease a cough related to a cold, the suggested daily dose is 1–2 g thyme brewed as a tea, several times a day as needed.

Around the House   Scatter dried thyme leaves or flowers in your linen closet. They will scent the closet, sheets, and towels and are reputed to repel insects as well.

In the Garden   Lemon-scented plants such as lemon thyme (*Thymus citriodorus*) seem to repel insects in the garden and may act as safe, natural pest repellents.

Turmeric

ABOUT THIS PLANT

Botanical name(s): Curcuma longa, Curcuma xanthorrhizia (Javanese turmeric)

Common name(s): * * *

Native to: India, China, East Indies

Parts used as food/drink: Rhizomes (underground stems)

GRAS list: Yes

Medicinal properties: Choleretic

Other uses: Fabric dye

ABOUT THIS PLANT AS FOOD OR DRINK

Turmeric is a member of the GINGER family. Its thick rhizomes (underground stems) are ground to make an aromatic yellow powder used as a flavoring and/or coloring agent in a wide variety of foods including butter, cheese, CURRY POWDERs, fruit drinks, liqueurs, margarine, MUSTARDs and pickles.

Nutritional Profile One teaspoon (2 g) ground turmeric has 8 calories. It provides 0.2 g protein, 0.2 g fat, 1.4 g carbohydrates, 0.5 g dietary fiber, no vitamin A, 0.6 g vitamin C, 4 mg calcium, 0.9 mg iron, and 1 mg sodium.

One tablespoon (7 g) turmeric has 24 calories. It provides 0.5 g protein, 0.7 g fat, 4.4 g carbohydrates, 1.4 g dietary fiber, no vitamin A, 1.8 mg vitamin C, 12 mg calcium, 2.8 mg iron, and 3 mg sodium.

HOW THIS PLANT AFFECTS YOUR BODY

Important Phytochemicals Turmeric's mild, slightly bitter, peppery flavor and aroma come from oil of turmeric, which contains peppery-scented, mint-flavored borneol; spicy eucalyptol, which smells like camphor; and zingerone, the spicy sweet flavoring in ginger.

The pigment in turmeric is curcumin, also known as "turmeric yellow." It was once used as a fabric dye, but it has since been replaced by synthetic dyes derived from coal tar.

Benefits Turmeric is a choleretic, an agent that stimulates the liver to increase its production of bile, a yellow, brown, or green fluid. Bile helps to

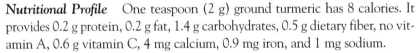

emulsify fats in the duodenum and increases peristalsis, the rhythmic contractions that move food through the gastrointestinal tract. Some other choleretic herbs are GENTIAN, ONION, and OREGANO, and TURMERIC. While choleretics are ordinarily beneficial for healthy people, they may pose problems for people with gallbladder or liver disease. However, according to the U.S. Food and Drug Administration, the very small amounts of turmeric normally used in food are unlikely to cause harm.

In 1985 and 1990, the German Commission E approved the use of preparations of scalded dried turmeric rhizomes to relieve upset stomach. In its approval, the committee cautioned against the use of turmeric for people with gallbladder disease (including gallstones) except as directed by a physician.

Possible Adverse Effects   Long-term use of the turmeric variety known as Javanese turmeric may cause stomach discomfort.

Information for Women Who Are Pregnant or Nursing   * * *

Plant/Drug Interactions   * * *

HOW TO USE THIS PLANT

In Cooking   Curcumin is very sensitive to light. Protect the color of your turmeric by storing the spice in a cool, dark cabinet.

Turmeric is an inexpensive substitute for SAFFRON, the world's most expensive spice and food coloring. Turmeric's flavor is stronger than saffron's, so use it with a light hand.

Valerian

ABOUT THIS PLANT

Botanical name(s): *Valeriana officinalis*
Common name(s): Garden heliotrope, allheal
Native to: North America, Europe, Asia
Parts used as food/drink: Rhizomes (underground stems)
GRAS list: Yes
Medicinal properties: Sedative, antispasmodic
Other uses: * * *

ABOUT THIS PLANT AS FOOD OR DRINK

Valerian is a perennial herb with tiny, sweet-smelling white or pink flowers and long, slender, fringed leaves. Its rhizomes (underground stems) may be used in an herbal tea.

Note: Do not confuse this plant with the poisonous plants American valerian (lady's slipper, *Cypripedium calceolus*) or false valerian (golden ragwort, *Senecio aureus*).

Nutritional Profile * * *

HOW THIS PLANT AFFECTS YOUR BODY

Important Phytochemicals The active compounds in valerian are the valpotriates, substances generally regarded as natural sedatives. Valerian also contains an unpleasantly scented oil.

Benefits The U.S. Food and Drug Administration does not permit valerian in over-the-counter sleep aids. However, in Britain, there are more than 80 such products containing valerian. And, in 1985 and 1990, the German Commission E approved the use of preparations of fresh valerian rhizomes or valerian rhizomes dried at temperatures below 72 degrees F (40 degrees C) to relieve anxiety-related restlessness or insomnia. (The valpotriates are heat sensitive. Valerian must be dried at relatively low temperatures to preserve their chemical potency.)

Possible Adverse Effects Excessive amounts of valerian may cause shakiness, blurred vision, upset stomach, weakened heartbeat, and liver damage.

Information for Women Who Are Pregnant or Nursing Nursing infants whose mothers use valerian should be monitored for sedation.

Plant/Drug Interactions   Although there are no studies showing the interaction between the valpotriates and sedatives/sleep aids, prudence dictates against combining the two.

HOW TO USE THIS PLANT

As a Home Remedy   To alleviate insomnia, the suggested dose is 1–2 teaspoons dried valerian brewed in 1 cup water as a tea.

Vanilla

ABOUT THIS PLANT

Botanical name(s): *Vanilla planifolia*
Common name(s): * * *
Native to: Mexico, East Indies
Parts used as food/drink: Unripe fruits ("beans")
GRAS list: Yes
Medicinal properties: * * *
Other uses: * * *

ABOUT THIS PLANT AS FOOD OR DRINK

The vanilla plant is the only member of the orchid family used as a flavoring. Its unripe fruit, which looks like a pod, is popularly known as a vanilla bean. The most intensely flavored vanilla beans are called Bourbon beans, from a variety native to Mexico but now imported primarily from Madagascar.

A natural vanilla flavoring is labeled *vanilla extract*; it contains only vanilla and alcohol. A representative imitation vanilla flavoring may contain water, propylene glycol (a moisturizing agent), alcohol, artificial and natural flavorings (up to 20 percent pure vanilla extract), SUGAR, caramel color, dextrose, and sodium benzoate (a preservative).

Vanilla is used in baked goods, candies, frozen desserts, and beverages, and as a pharmaceutical flavoring.

Nutritional Profile   One teaspoon (4 g) vanilla extract has 12 calories. It provides 0.5 g carbohydrates, and a trace of calcium and sodium.

One tablespoon (13 g) vanilla extract has 37 calories. It provides 1.6 g carbohydrates, 1 mg calcium, and 1 mg sodium.

HOW THIS PLANT AFFECTS YOUR BODY

Important Phytochemicals   Vanilla's flavor and aroma come from vanillin, a white or yellowish compound whose pleasant taste and scent develop when vanilla beans are allowed to dry and ferment ("cure") after picking. In unripe vanilla beans, vanillin is bound to a sugar molecule. During fermentation, naturally occurring enzymes in the beans separate the vanillin from the sugar molecule. The cured beans are then packaged and sold whole or chopped and covered with a warm alcohol/water solution that extracts flavoring compounds from the bean. When the flavor of

the solution is sufficiently intense, the liquid, called an extract, is poured off, strained, and aged for about a month to smooth out the flavor.

Natural vanillin is an irritant and a choleretic, an agent that stimulates the liver to increase its production of bile, a yellow, brown, or green fluid. Bile helps emulsify fats in the duodenum and increases peristalsis, the rhythmic contractions that move food through the gastrointestinal tract. Some other choleretic herbs are GENTIAN, ONION, OREGANO, and TURMERIC. While cholerics are ordinarily beneficial for healthy people, they may pose problems for people with gallbladder or liver disease.

Synthetic vanilla flavoring is made from eugenol (the primary flavoring ingredient in oil of CLOVES), guaiacol (white or yellow crystals isolated either from a resin in hardwoods or from lignin, a woody fiber in plants). Ethyl vanillin is a strongly flavored synthetic vanillin.

Benefits   * * *

Possible Adverse Effects   Prolonged handling of vanilla beans may cause contact dermatitis (itching, burning, stinging, reddened, or blistered skin) and headaches, symptoms most commonly found among food workers who sort and process vanilla beans.

Information for Women Who Are Pregnant or Nursing   * * *

Plant/Drug Interactions   * * *

HOW TO USE THIS PLANT

In Cooking   As a general rule, the more intensely flavored the vanilla extract or beans, the higher the cost. To preserve the flavor of vanilla beans and natural vanilla extract, protect them from air and light. Keep the beans in an airtight, dark or opaque container in a cool dark cabinet.

One 1-inch vanilla bean, scraped, equals the flavor of 1 teaspoon natural vanilla extract.

To make vanilla-flavored sugar, place one whole vanilla bean in an airtight container with 2 cups table sugar. The bean can be reused until its aroma fades.

To make your own vanilla extract, put one vanilla bean into a 350 ml bottle of vodka or brandy. (If necessary, break the bean into two or three pieces.) Close the bottle tightly, and let it stand for at least three weeks; then use the vodka or brandy as a substitute for commercial vanilla extract. Remember, the longer the bean is left in the bottle the stronger the vanilla flavor will be.

Around the House   Make your own sachet by scenting a cotton ball with vanilla extract to perfume a dresser drawer.

Vegetable Oils

ABOUT THIS CONDIMENT

Botanical name(s): * * *
Common name(s): * * *
Native to: * * *
Parts used as food/drink: * * *
GRAS list: No
Medicinal properties: Cardiovascular protector
Other uses: Cosmetics

ABOUT THIS CONDIMENT AS FOOD OR DRINK

Vegetable oil is a term given to the fatty liquids extracted from a variety of fruits, vegetables, nuts, and seeds.

Margarines have traditionally been made from hydrogenated vegetable oils. Hydrogenation—adding hydrogen atoms—changes the structure of some of the fats in the oils from a form known as "cis fatty acids" to a form known as "trans fatty acids." Adding hydrogenated fatty acids turns the oils to a semisolid material that can be molded into bars or packed in tubs. In 1998, food marketers introduced margarines made without hydrogenated oils.

Margarine may also contain ingredients such as coloring agents (to make the margarine look like butter), emulsifiers, and milk or animal fats (including butter).

Nutritional Profile   One tablespoon (14 g) vegetable oil has 124 calories. It provides 14 g fat.

HOW THIS CONDIMENT AFFECTS YOUR BODY

Important Phytochemicals   Vegetable oils are low in saturated fat and high in monounsaturated and polyunsaturated fatty acids, including the essential fatty acid linoleic acid. Vegetable oils are also rich in omega-3 fatty acids, the polyunsaturates credited with lowering the risk of heart disease. The body converts alpha-linolenic acid, the most important omega-3, to hormone-like substances called eicosapentaenoic acid (EPA) and docosahexaenoic acid (DHA) which reduce inflammation, perhaps by inhibiting an enzyme named COX-2, which has been linked to inflammatory diseases such as rheumatoid arthritis and skin cancer. In addition, the

Arthritis Foundation says omega-3 fatty acids relieve joint inflammation in people with rheumatoid arthritis. Research at Purdue University suggests that they may also prevent the natural breakdown of bone tissue and increase production of a bone-protecting growth factor that steps up new bone formation, at least in laboratory rats whose ovaries have been removed, cutting off their natural supply of bone-protecting estrogen (a condition analogous to menopause in women).

FATTY ACID CONTENT 1 tablespoon vegetable oil			
	Saturated fatty acids (g)	Monounsaturated fatty acids (g)	Polyunsaturated fatty acids (g)
Canola oil	1	8.2	4.1
Corn oil	1.8	3.4	8.2
Olive oil	1.9	10.3	1.2
Peanut oil	2.4	6.5	4.5
Safflower oil	1.3	1.7	10.4
Butter	7.1	3.3	0.4
Source: USDA Nutrient Database www.nal.usda.gov/fnic/cgi-bin/nut_search.pl			

Polyunsaturated fatty acids are excellent sources of vitamin E, the collective name for a group of compounds called tocopherols. The tocopherol with the most vitamin E activity is alpha-tocopherol; the RDA for vitamin E is stated as milligrams of alpha-tocopherol equivalents (mg a-TE), 10 mg a-TE for a man, 8 mg a-TE for a woman.

VITAMIN E CONTENT 1 tablespoon vegetable oil	
	Vitamin E (alpha-TE) (mg)
Canola oil	2.93
Corn oil	2.94
Olive oil	0.7
Peanut oil	1.82
Safflower oil	5.46
Source: USDA Nutrient Database: www.nal.usda.gov/fnic/ cgi-bin/nut_search.pl	

Fats are a concentrated source of energy. Gram for gram, fats contain more than twice as many calories as proteins and carbohydrates: 9 calories per gram versus 4 calories per gram.

Like proteins, which contain some essential amino acids that cannot be manufactured in the human body, fats contain some essential fatty acids that must come from food. One essential fatty acid is linoleic acid, from which our bodies can make another essential fatty acid, arachidonic acid. The best sources of linoleic acid are vegetable oils other than olive oil and coconut oil. The best sources of arachidonic acid are dairy foods, meat, fish, and poultry.

Benefits A diet high in cholesterol and saturated fats increases the amount of cholesterol circulating through your arteries and raises your risk of coronary artery disease (heart attack). To reduce the risk, the U.S. Department of Agriculture/Health and Human Services Dietary Guidelines for Americans recommends limiting the amount of cholesterol in your diet to no more than 300 mg a day. The guidelines also recommend limiting the amount of fat consumed to no more than 30 percent of your total calories, and holding your consumption of saturated fats to no more than 10 percent of your total calories (the calories from saturated fats are counted as part of the total calories from fat). Substituting highly unsaturated vegetable oils for saturated fats from animal foods helps limit cholesterol and saturated fats.

Possible Adverse Effects Trans fatty acids are even more likely to cause atherosclerosis than are saturated fats.

Information for Women Who Are Pregnant or Nursing * * *

Condiment/Drug Interactions * * *

HOW TO USE THIS CONDIMENT

In Cooking To protect the freshness of vegetable oils, store them in tightly closed containers in a cool, dark cabinet. When exposed to air, fatty acids become rancid, which means that they combine with oxygen to form bad-tasting, odorous hydroperoxides that can destroy the vitamin E in the oil. Fats high in unsaturated fatty acids spoil more quickly than fats high in saturated fatty acids. To prevent spoilage (rancidity), many salad and cooking oils contain antioxidant preservatives such as BHT and BHA.

Margarines should be refrigerated and closely wrapped to protect them from absorbing food odors. Most margarines stay fresh for about two weeks in the refrigerator.

When cooking with oils, especially when deep-frying (cooking food in a deep pot filled with oil), watch the temperature carefully. Most fats begin to decompose below 500 degrees F; they may burst into flame without boiling or smoking first. The temperature at which a fat decomposes and burns is called the *smoking point*. Vegetable shortening may burn at 375 degrees F; vegetable oils, at close to 450 degrees F. As a rule, safflower oil, soybean oil, cottonseed oil, and corn oil have higher smoking points than peanut oil and sesame oil.

Vinegar

ABOUT THIS CONDIMENT

Chemical name: Acetic acid
Also known as: * * *
Native to: * * *
Parts used as condiment: * * *
GRAS list: Yes
Medicinal properties: Acidifier
Other uses: Household cleanser, hair rinse

ABOUT THIS CONDIMENT AS FOOD AND FLAVORING

Vinegar is water plus acetic acid, a compound produced naturally when bacteria metabolize alcohols.

White vinegar is made from acetic acid derived from ethyl alcohol, the alcohol used in alcoholic beverages. Cider vinegar, which is amber-colored with a fruity aroma, contains acetic acid made from the bacterial fermentation of apple juice. Malt vinegars are made with acetic acid derived from the fermentation of barley or other cereals. Wine vinegars are made with acetic acid derived from wine, usually red wine. Herb vinegars are made by adding specific herbs to any of the above.

Nutritional Profile   One tablespoon (15 g) cider vinegar has 2 calories. It provides 0.9 mg carbohydrates, 1 mg calcium, 0.1 mg iron, and no sodium.

One cup (140 g) cider vinegar has 34 calories. It provides 14.2 g carbohydrates, 14 mg calcium, 1.4 mg iron, and 2 mg sodium.

HOW THIS CONDIMENT AFFECTS YOUR BODY

Important Phytochemicals   Acetic acid is an acidifier, a compound used to make solutions or tissues more acid. It is a mild urinary irritant.

Benefits   The naturally acid pH of the vagina usually prevents the overgrowth of yeast infections. To increase this protective acidity, distilled white vinegar is often used as an ingredient in vaginal douches, commercial as well as homemade. According to the U.S. Food and Drug Administration's Advisory Review Panel on OTC (Over-the-Counter) Contraceptives and Other Vaginal Drug Products, a dilute solution of vinegar and water (1.5 teaspoons distilled white vinegar in 1 quart of warm water) is a safe acid douche. However, there are no scientifically controlled studies showing that it is actually effective in preventing or curing a yeast infection.

Possible Adverse Effects   Eating foods marinated in vinegar may cause you to urinate more frequently or cause a slight burning sensation while urinating.

Information for Women Who Are Pregnant or Nursing   * * *

Condiment/Drug Interactions   Wine-based or malt vinegars may be high in tyramine, a natural by-product formed when proteins are fermented. Tyramine is a pressor amine, a compound that constricts blood vessels and triggers an increase in blood pressure. Monoamine oxidase (MAO) inhibitors—drugs used as antidepressants—interfere with the action of enzymes that break down tyramine. If you eat a food high in tyramine, such as a wine- or malt-based vinegar, the tyramine cannot be efficiently eliminated from your body. The result may be a hypertensive crisis (sustained elevated blood pressure).

HOW TO USE THIS PLANT

In Cooking   Because acetic acid breaks down protein fibers on the surface of meat, vinegar is a useful tenderizing marinade.

As an acid, vinegar reacts with metal ions from the surface of aluminum, copper, iron, or zinc-lined dishes or pots, producing dark compounds that discolor the pot or the food. To prevent this, dishes made with vinegar should be cooked and stored in an enameled or glass vessel.

Vinegar can be used as a substitute for LEMON juice. If you are out of lemon juice or are allergic to citrus fruit, try a drop or two of vinegar in your sweetened tea. The tart taste matches that of lemons. You can also use a little vinegar in place of lemon juice to give a tart taste to fruit pies (especially apple pies).

Around the House   After washing glass tumblers or dishes, dip them in a solution of warm water plus a tablespoon of white distilled vinegar, then rinse with water to remove soap scum and other residue. The glass will sparkle.

To clean a coffee pot, fill it with water plus a tablespoon of white distilled vinegar, and then run the pot through its cycle to remove coffee oils. Pour out the vinegar/water solution, fill the pot with plain water and repeat the cycle, then dry the pot. (This method will also remove mineral deposits from home humidifiers.)

As a Cosmetic   Before the introduction of residue-free detergent shampoos, rinsing dark hair with a vinegar/water solution was an effective way to remove soap scum. It can still be used to make dark hair shine. (The traditional rinse for blonde hair is lemon juice and water.)

Violets, Sweet

ABOUT THIS PLANT

Botanical name(s): Viola odorata
Common name(s): Garden violet, sweet violet
Native to: Europe
Parts used as food/drink: Flowers
GRAS list: No
Medicinal properties: * * *
Other uses: Perfume, flavoring

ABOUT THIS PLANT AS FOOD OR DRINK

Sweet violets, with their heart-shaped leaves and creeping root stalks, are one of the most fragrant of the more than 600 species of violets.

The purple flowers can be candied or used fresh as a garnish in salads. Violets are also a source of an extract used as a flavoring or in perfumes, but the "violet" scent in many products is actually an extract of orris root.

Nutritional Profile * * *

HOW THIS PLANT AFFECTS YOUR BODY

Important Phytochemicals   The flowers are the only edible part of the violet plant. The leaves contain laxative compounds; the rhizomes (underground stems), roots, and seeds contain purgatives (strong laxatives) and emetics (substances that induce vomiting) that may cause severe gastric upset or well as depression of the respiratory and circulatory system. The larger the dose, the more serious the adverse effects.

Benefits * * *

Possible Adverse Effects   See above.

Information for Women Who Are Pregnant or Nursing * * *

Plant/Drug Interactions * * *

HOW TO USE THIS PLANT

In Cooking   In the kitchen, use only violets grown for food. Violets sold in flower shops may have been sprayed with toxic pesticides.

To make candied violets, choose *Viola odorata*, one of the few violet species whose petals are strong enough to hold their shape when dipped in a sugar syrup.

Wakame

ABOUT THIS PLANT

Botanical name(s): *Undaria*
Common name(s): * * *
Native to: Pacific and Indian Oceans, North Atlantic Ocean
Parts used as food/drink: Whole plants or their extracted gums
GRAS list: No
Medicinal properties: Iodine source
Other uses: Laxatives, stabilizers

ABOUT THIS PLANT AS FOOD OR DRINK

Wakame is a seaweed, a nutritious vegetable most commonly used in Japanese cooking.

Nutritional Profile 3.5 ounces (100 g) raw wakame has 45 calories. It provides 3 g protein, 0.6 g fat, 9 g carbohydrates, 0.5 g dietary fiber, 360 IU vitamin A, 3 mg vitamin C, 150 mg calcium, 2.2 mg iron, and 870 mg sodium.

HOW THIS PLANT AFFECTS YOUR BODY

Important Phytochemicals One useful group of compounds in seaweed are alginates, a form of soluble dietary fiber (gums) used as thickeners and gelling agents.

Benefits Most seaweeds are rich in calcium and nonheme iron, the form of iron found in plants. For example, 3.5 ounces raw wakame provides 15 percent of the RDA for iron. It is more difficult for your body to absorb nonheme iron than heme iron, the iron found in meat, fish, poultry, milk, and eggs. Eating seaweed with meat increases the amount of iron you absorb from the seaweed because meat triggers the secretion of stomach acids, and iron is absorbed more easily in an acid environment. You can also increase your absorption of heme iron by eating the seaweed with a food rich in vitamin C. Vitamin C changes the iron in seaweed from ferric iron to ferrous iron, a more easily absorbed form of iron.

Possible Adverse Effects Because seaweed is high in sodium, it is often restricted on a controlled-sodium diet. Remember, powdered seaweed is not a low sodium substitute for table salt.

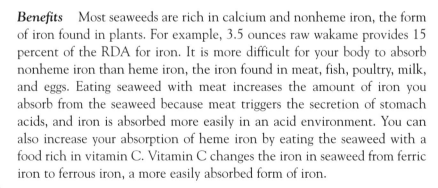

366

All seaweed is high in iodine. The exact amount varies from species to species, but it is not uncommon for dried seaweed to have concentrations as high as 0.4–0.6 percent, 116–174 mg iodine per ounce, nearly 800 times the RDA (150 mcg). The thyroid gland uses iodine to make thyroid hormones. If you don't get enough iodine, the gland will swell in an attempt to produce more hormone; the swelling is called a goiter. Paradoxically, people who consume too much iodine, defined by the German Commission E as more than 150 mcg per day, may also suffer from goiter because an oversupply of inorganic iodine (the form found in food) keeps the thyroid gland from making organic iodine (the form used to make thyroid hormones). Iodine-overdose goiter is most likely to occur at an iodine consumption exceeding 2,000 mcg (2 mg) per day, as is common in Japan. There seaweed is an important part of the diet, and iodine intake may be as high as 50,000 to 80,000 mcg (50 to 80 mg) per day.

Some people experience serious allergic reactions to large amounts of iodine, generally defined as more than 150 mcg per day.

Information for Women Who Are Pregnant or Nursing   * * *

Plant/Drug Interactions   * * *

HOW TO USE THIS PLANT
In Cooking   To reduce or eliminate seaweed's "weedy" iodine flavor, soak the seaweed in cool water for at least 2 hours before using.

Watercress

ABOUT THIS PLANT

Botanical name: *Nasturtium officinale*
Common name: Cress
Also known as: Cress, scurvy grass
Native to: Europe
Parts used as food/drink: Leaves, stems
GRAS list: No
Medicinal properties: Antiscorbutic
Other uses: * * *

ABOUT THIS HERB AS FOOD AND FLAVORING

Watercress is a cruciferous vegetable, a member of the MUSTARD family and a relative of SHEPHERD'S PURSE. A water-loving plant with shiny, dark green leaves, it is native to Europe, but now grows easily in Canada and the United States.

Watercress is used in salads, to flavor soups, as a garnish for roast meats, and as an attractive filling for tea sandwiches or hors d'oeuvres.

Nutritional Profile One-half cup (17 g) chopped fresh watercress has 2 calories. It provides less than 1 g protein, fat, carbohydrates, and dietary fiber, 800 IU vitamin A, 7 mg vitamin C, 20 mg calcium, a trace of iron, and 7 mg sodium.

HOW THIS HERB AFFECTS YOUR BODY

Important Phytochemicals Watercress's dark green, spicy leaves are flavored with peppery mustard oils similar to those found in GARLIC, MUSTARD SEED, ONIONS, and PEPPER (BLACK).

Benefits Like other dark green leaves, watercress is rich in beta-carotene, the vitamin A precursor in deep yellow fruits and vegetables. According to the American Cancer Society, a diet rich in these foods may lower the risk of some forms of cancer. Vitamin A also protects your eyes. In your body, the vitamin A from watercress is converted to 11-cis retinol, the most important constituent of rhodopsin, a protein in the rods in your retina (the cells that enable you to see in dim light). One-half cup chopped fresh watercress provides 16 percent of the RDA for vitamin A for a woman and 20 percent of the RDA for a man.

Watercress, a good source of vitamin C, was once used medically to prevent or cure scurvy, a disease resulting from vitamin C deficiency. One-half cup chopped fresh watercress provides 12 percent of the RDA for vitamin C.

Possible Adverse Effects   All cruciferous vegetables contain naturally occurring goitrogens, sulfur compounds that slow the thyroid gland's production of thyroid hormones, causing the gland to swell in an effort to produce larger amounts of hormones. The swollen gland is known as a *goiter;* the goitrogen in watercress is gluconasturtim. Cruciferous vegetables, including watercress, are not likely to be hazardous for healthy people who eat them in moderation, but they may be troublesome for people who have a thyroid disorder or are using thyroid medication.

HOW TO USE THIS PLANT

In Cooking   Do not tear or cut watercress until you are ready to use it. When you cut into a food rich in vitamin C, its cells release an enzyme called ascorbic acid oxidase which destroys vitamin C and reduces the nutritional value of the food.

Chlorophyll, the green coloring in watercress leaves, is sensitive to acids. When the leaves are heated, their chlorophyll reacts with natural acids in the leaves or in the cooking water, forming a brown compound called pheophytin. The pheophytin in turn reacts with the yellow carotene pigments in the leaves, turning the cooked leaves bronze. To prevent this color change, you must keep the chlorophyll from reacting with the acids by cooking watercress as quickly as possible. (This has the added benefit of preventing the cress from turning stringy.)

Note: Commercial herb packagers preserve the color of green herbs by drying the leaves at a very low heat.

Worcestershire Sauce

ABOUT THIS CONDIMENT

Chemical name: * * *
Also known as: Lea & Perrins, Angostura, et al.
Native to: England
Parts used as condiment: * * *
GRAS list: No
Medicinal properties: * * *
Other uses: * * *

ABOUT THIS CONDIMENT AS FOOD AND FLAVORING

Worcestershire sauce is an anchovy-based condiment, a modern British adaptation of *garum*, the ancient Roman seasoning made of rotted fish.

A typical modern Worcestershire sauce contains water, VINEGAR, sweeteners (molasses, corn sweeteners), anchovies, natural flavorings (perhaps including ASAFETIDA), and spices such as ONIONS, SALT, GARLIC, CLOVES, CHILI PEPPERS, and SHALLOTS.

Nutritional Profile One teaspoon Worcestershire sauce may provide up to 206 mg sodium. One teaspoon low-sodium Worcestershire sauce may provide up to 55 mg sodium.

HOW THIS CONDIMENT AFFECTS YOUR BODY

Important Phytochemicals See onions, salt, garlic, cloves, chili powder, and shallots.

Benefits * * *

Possible Adverse Effects Because Worcestershire sauce contains anchovies, people sensitive to anchovies or other fish may be sensitive to the condiment.

Anchovies are preserved (salted) fish, high in tyramine, a natural by-product of protein fermentation. Tyramine is a pressor amine, a compound that constricts blood vessels and triggers an increase in blood pressure. Monoamine oxidase (MAO) inhibitors—drugs used as antidepressants—interfere with the action of enzymes that break down tyramine. If you eat a food such as vinegar made from wine or a malt base (which is high in tyramine) while taking an MAO inhibitor, the tyramine cannot be efficiently eliminated from your body. The result may be a hypertensive crisis (sustained elevated blood pressure).

Yarrow

ABOUT THIS PLANT

Botanical name(s): Achillea millfolium
Common name(s): Milfoil, soldiers' herb
Native to: Europe
Parts used as food/drink: Flowers
GRAS list: No
Medicinal properties: Appetite stimulant, antispasmodic
Other uses: * * *

ABOUT THIS PLANT AS FOOD OR DRINK

Yarrow is a decorative plant prized for its spicy aroma and small, delicate, white flowers. Yarrow may be used to brew astringent herbal tea.

Nutritional Profile * * *

HOW THIS PLANT AFFECTS YOUR BODY

Important Phytochemicals   Yarrow contains crisp astringent tannins.

Benefits   Astringent beverages such as yarrow or TEA stimulate the flow of saliva and encourage the secretion of gastric fluids that set off the contractions we know as hunger pangs. In 1990, the German Commission E approved the use of preparations of fresh or dried yarrow flowers to stimulate appetite and relieve mild intestinal spasms.

Possible Adverse Effects   Like other flowering plants, yarrow produces a pollen that may cause respiratory symptoms (itchy eyes, runny nose) in sensitive individuals.

Information for Women Who Are Pregnant or Nursing   * * *

Plant/Drug Interactions   * * *

HOW TO USE THIS PLANT

Around the House   Even when dried, yarrow retains a spicy scent that makes it a valued addition to dried flower arrangements and sachets.

As a Home Remedy   As an appetite stimulant, the suggested daily dose is a tea brewed from 3 g yarrow flowers. As a bath to relieve cramps, the suggested dose is 100 g (3.5 oz) yarrow in a warm bath.

Yeast

ABOUT THIS PLANT

Botanical name(s): Saccharomyces cerevisiae
Common name(s): * * *
Native to: * * *
Parts used as food/drink: * * *
GRAS list: Yes
Medicinal properties: * * *
Other uses: * * *

ABOUT THIS PLANT AS FOOD OR DRINK

Yeast is a living organism, a member of the fungus family that includes mushrooms as well as uncounted numbers of yeasts and molds living in the air and soil around us.

Baker's yeast is used to make bread rise by digesting sugars and starches to produce alcohols and carbon dioxide as by-products. When you mix flour and water and beat the batter, the long protein molecules in the flour relax and unfold, breaking internal bonds (bonds between atoms on the same molecule) and forming new external bonds between atoms in adjoining molecules. The resulting network of elastic gluten (protein) stretches (rises) as it fills with the carbon dioxide released when baker's yeast digests sugars in the flour. When the batter or dough is heated, the stretched protein network hardens (bakes) into place. Baker's yeast comes in two forms: compressed yeast cakes and packets of active dry yeast, differentiated by the temperature at which they become active (see below, How to Use This Plant).

Brewer's yeast is a by-product of beer production, composed of yeast cells that are rinsed and dried to be sold as a nutritional supplement. Smoked yeast, a flavoring agent used in prepared foods, including cheese spreads, is made by exposing dried yeast to wood smoke.

Nutritional Profile   One tablespoon (12 g) active dry baker's yeast has 35 calories. It provides 4.5 g protein, 0.6 g fat, 4.6 g carbohydrates, 2.5 g dietary fiber, 2.6 mg calcium, 0.7 mg iron, 2 mg sodium.

One package (7 g) active dry baker's yeast has 20.7 calories. It provides 2.7 g protein, 0.3 g fat, 2.7 g carbohydrates, 1.5 g dietary fiber, 4.5 mg calcium, 1.2 mg iron, and 3.5 mg sodium.

One cake (17 g) baker's compressed yeast has 17.0 calories. It provides 1.4 g protein, 0.3 g fat, 3.1 g carbohydrates, 1.4 g dietary fiber, 3.2 mg calcium, 0.5 mg iron, and 5.1 mg sodium.

HOW THIS PLANT AFFECTS YOUR BODY

Important Phytochemicals   See above.

Benefits   Baker's yeast is a good source of the B vitamin folate, which is now known to reduce the risk of heart disease and birth defects. About 50 percent of the folate in homemade breads comes from yeast. One packet of baker's yeast has 286 mcg (0.286 mg) folate, about 72 percent of the RDA. One tablespoon brewer's yeast has 313 mcg (0.313 mg) folate, about 78 percent of the RDA.

All yeasts are good sources of protein. This makes them particularly useful in bread because the proteins in cereal grains are limited in the essential amino acid lysine, which is plentiful in yeast. Combining yeast with flour "completes" the proteins, a process called *complementarity.*

In 1988, the German Commission E approved the use of brewer's yeast as a nutritional supplement and to treat chronic acne. Yeast approved as a nutritional supplement must be at least 40 percent protein and contain not less than 0.12 mg thiamine, 0.04 mg riboflavin, and 0.25 mg nicotinic acid per gram.

In 1994, the commission approved the use of brewer's yeast to inhibit the activity of organisms that cause acute diarrhea, including certain strains of *Clostridium, Escherichia coli, Proteus, Pseudomonas, Salmonella,* and *Staphylococcus.*

Possible Adverse Effects   Consuming large amounts of yeast (as a supplement, for example) may cause nausea and diarrhea, symptoms reported in people who took as little as 20 grams (about $2/3$ oz) yeast. People sensitive to brewer's yeast may develop migraine headaches if they consume products containing it.

Yeasts are high in nucleic acids, which are converted to uric acid when metabolized by the human body. Uric acid consists of sharp crystals that may cause gout if they collect in your joints or kidney stones if they collect in your urine. Although controlling the amount of uric acid in your diet may not necessarily control gout (which is most effectively treated with allopurinol, a medicine that inhibits the formation of uric acid), limiting foods high in uric acid is still part of many gout regimes.

Information for Women Who Are Pregnant or Nursing   * * *

Plant/Drug Interactions   Using brewer's yeast as a supplement or consuming beef-flavored yeast extracts such as Marmite and Bovril while you are taking an monoamine oxidase (MAO) inhibitor, a class of drugs used as antidepressants, may cause a rise in blood pressure. Both yeasts and the beef-flavored extracts contain tyramine, a natural by-product of protein metabolism. Tyramine, also found in other foods such as aged cheeses and red wines, constricts blood vessels and may trigger an increase in blood pressure. MAO inhibitors interfere with the action of the enzymes that break down tyramine. If you eat a food high in tyramine while taking an MAO inhibitor, the tyramine cannot be efficiently eliminated from your body. The result may be a hypertensive crisis (sustained high blood pressure). Note: The yeast used in baking bread does not pose this problem.

HOW TO USE THIS PLANT

In Cooking   Compressed yeast becomes active at about 50 degrees F, releases carbon dioxide most effectively at 78–82 degrees F, and dies at 120 degrees F. It must be kept in the refrigerator, where it will stay fresh for about two weeks. For longer storage (up to two months), freeze the yeast.

Packets of active dry yeast are easier to store and use. The packets, which are dated, have a life span of about a year. Active dry yeast goes to work at temperatures of about 120 to 130 degrees F.

One packet (1 tablespoon) active dry yeast equals the leavening power of one 3.5-oz or 100-g cake of compressed moist yeast.

Yellow Dock

ABOUT THIS PLANT

Botanical name(s): Rumex crispus
Common name(s): Curly dock
Native to: Europe
Parts used as food/drink: Leaves
GRAS list: No
Medicinal properties: * * *
Other uses: * * *

ABOUT THIS PLANT AS FOOD OR DRINK

Yellow dock is a member of the *Rumex* genus and thus a botanical relative of SORREL (*Rumex acetosa*). Yellow dock's slender, curly leaves have a sharp, bitter flavor similar to that of spinach. They are used as a vegetable and as a "pot herb," an herb used to flavor soups and stews.

Nutritional Profile One-half cup (67 g) chopped fresh yellow dock leaves has 15 calories. It provides 1.3 g protein, 2.1 g carbohydrates, 0.5 g dietary fiber, 2,680 IU vitamin A, 32.2 mg vitamin C, 29 mg calcium, 1.6 mg iron, and no sodium.

HOW THIS PLANT AFFECTS YOUR BODY

Important Phytochemicals Yellow dock leaves get their sharp, piquant flavor from irritant oxalates (calcium oxalate, oxalic acid, and potassium oxalate) and astringent tannins that coagulate the proteins on the surface of the skin, the mucous membrane lining of the mouth and the lining of the gut, making the tissues pucker.

Caution: The root of the yellow dock plant is inedible. It contains strong anthraquinone cathartics such as those found in ALOE and SENNA. Anthraquinones severely irritate the lining of the gut. They are included in some over-the-counter medicines, but the yellow dock root itself is no longer used as a food or medicine.

Benefits Yellow dock leaves are high in vitamin C. One-half cup chopped fresh leaves provides 54 percent of the RDA.

Like other dark green leaves, yellow dock is high in beta-carotene, the vitamin A precursor in deep yellow fruits and vegetables. According to the American Cancer Society, a diet rich in these foods may lower the risk of some forms of cancer. Vitamin A also protects your eyes. In your body, the vitamin A from sorrel is converted to 11-cis retinol, the most important constituent of rhodopsin, a protein in the rods in your retina (the cells that enable you to see in dim light). One-half cup chopped fresh yellow dock leaves provides 67 percent of the RDA for a man, 54 percent of the RDA for a woman.

Possible Adverse Effects   Yellow dock's pollen is an allergen that may trigger allergic rhinitis (hay fever) and bronchial asthma in sensitive people.

Foods such as spinach and yellow dock leaves, which are high in calcium and oxalates, may be prohibited on a low-calcium, low-oxalate diet for people who form calcium-oxalate kidney stones. They may also be prohibited for people with arthritis or gout.

Handling the yellow dock plant may cause contact dermatitis (itching, burning, stinging, reddened, or blistered skin).

Information for Women Who Are Pregnant or Nursing   * * *

Plant/Drug Interactions   * * *

HOW TO USE THIS PLANT

In Cooking   Do not tear or cut yellow dock leaves until you are ready to use them. When you cut into a food rich in vitamin C, its cells release an enzyme called ascorbic acid oxidase. This enzyme destroys vitamin C. Use only unsprayed leaves.

To reduce the oxalic acid content of yellow dock leaves, blanch the leaves three times in boiling water, discarding the water each time, before using as directed in your recipe for a vegetable dish or green sauce.

The tannins in yellow dock react with metals to form dark pigments. If you cook yellow dock or spinach in an aluminum or iron pot, these pigments will discolor the pot and the leaves as well. To keep yellow dock and spinach from darkening, cook them in a glass pot or a pot with an enameled surface.

Chlorophyll, the green coloring in yellow dock leaves, is sensitive to acids. When the leaves are heated, their chlorophyll reacts with natural acids in the leaves or in the cooking water, forming a brown compound called pheophytin. The pheophytin in turn reacts with the yellow carotene pigments in the leaves, turning the cooked leaves bronze. To prevent this color change, you must keep the chlorophyll from reacting with the acids by cooking the leaves for as short a time as possible. (Commercial herb packagers preserve the color of green herbs by drying the leaves at a very low heat.)

Yohimbe

ABOUT THIS PLANT

Botanical name(s): *Pausinystalia yohimbe (Coryanthe johimbe)*
Common name(s): * * *
Native to: West Africa
Parts used as food/drink: * * *
Medicinal properties: Anti-adrenergic, blood vessel dilator
Other uses: * * *

ABOUT THIS PLANT AS FOOD OR DRINK

Yohimbe bark is the dried bark from the trunk or branches of a West African evergreen tree. It has large leaves and clustered white flowers. The herb is not used as food, but in Africa it may be brewed as an herbal tea.

Nutritional Profile   * * *

HOW THIS PLANT AFFECTS YOUR BODY

Important Phytochemicals   The active compound in yohimbe bark is yohimbine, a central nervous system stimulant that is an antiadrenergic (a chemical that blocks impulses between nerve cells) and a blood vessel dilator.

Although yohimbe is reputed to be an aphrodisiac and has been prescribed as a folk remedy for chest pain, high blood pressure and to improve athletic performance, the German Commission E found insufficient proof of its safety (see below) and effectiveness. The U.S. Food and Drug Administration classifies it as both unsafe and ineffective.

Benefits   * * *

Possible Adverse Effects   Yohimbine may cause anxiety, shakiness, nausea and vomiting, insomnia, rapid heartbeat, and elevated blood pressure. It is specifically hazardous to people with liver disease, kidney disease, diabetes, or high (or low) blood pressure. Yohimbe should be taken only under medical supervision.

Yohimbe may interact with herbal products used to treat psychiatric conditions. There are no studies of its interactions with psychotropic drugs.

Information for Women Who Are Pregnant or Nursing   * * *

Plant/Drug Interactions   Yohimbe is a monoamine oxidase (MAO) inhibitor, a substance that inhibits the activity of enzymes that metabolizes tyramine, a compound that constricts blood vessels. As a result, if you eat a tyramine-rich food such as liver, aged cheese, or red wine while you are using yohimbe or any of the MAO inhibitors used as antidepressants, the tyramine will accumulate in your bloodstream, constricting blood vessels. The result may be a hypertensive crisis (sustained elevated blood pressure). Yohimbe should not be combined with MAO inhibitor drugs.

HOW TO USE THIS PLANT   * * *

Zedoary

ABOUT THIS PLANT

Botanical name(s): Curcuma zedoaria
Common name(s): * * *
Native to: India, Asia
Parts used as food/drink: Shoots, rhizomes (underground stems)
GRAS list: No
Medicinal properties: * * *
Other uses: * * *

ABOUT THIS PLANT AS FOOD OR DRINK

Zedoary is a perennial herb native to northern Africa and southern Asia. The flavor of zedoary leaves has been compared to that of LEMONGRASS; in Asia they are said to be used fresh in salads or cooked as a green vegetable. Zedoary's rhizomes (underground stems), which turn yellow when dried, taste and smell something like GINGER. The rhizomes are high in starch; in India, powdered zedoary root is sold as a thickener.

Nutritional Profile   * * *

HOW THIS PLANT AFFECTS YOUR BODY

Important Phytochemicals   Zedoary is rich in complex carbohydrates (starches)—see below.

In Asia, zedoary is used to alleviate intestinal spasms, but the German Commission E notes there are no scientific studies to document its effectiveness.

Benefits   * * *

Possible Adverse Effects   * * *

Information for Women Who Are Pregnant or Nursing   * * *

Plant/Drug Interactions   * * *

HOW TO USE THIS PLANT

In Cooking   All starches, including zedoary, consist of molecules of complex carbohydrates packed into bundles called starch granules. The carbohydrates inside the starch granule are amylose (a long, straight molecule)

and amylopectin (a short, branched molecule). When you heat a starch in liquid, its starch granules absorb the heated water. The amylose and amylopectin molecules inside relax, breaking some of their internal bonds (bonds between atoms on the same molecules) and forming new bonds between atoms on different molecules. The result is a network of carbohydrate molecules that traps and holds water molecules, immobilizing them and thus thickening the liquid.

It takes less energy (heat) to break and re-form bonds between the long, straight amylose molecules than it takes to do the same thing with the short, branched amylopectin molecules. Therefore, starches such as zedoary that have a higher proportion of amylose molecules cook at a lower temperature than starches such as cornstarch and wheat starch, which are higher in amylopectin. As a result, sauces made with starches such as zedoary are much less likely to burn. Zedoary also has less protein than cornstarch and wheat starch, which is why it makes a clear sauce rather than one clouded with protein.

APPENDIX I

Herbs Used Only in Commercial Pharmaceuticals

The following is a list of plants that are unsafe for use either as food or home remedy but which serve as valuable sources of effective medication.

Arnica Flower

ABOUT THIS PLANT

Botanical name(s): Arnica montana
Common name(s): Bane, leopard's bane, mountain tobacco
Native to: Europe
Parts used as food/drink: None
GRAS list: No
Medicinal properties: Analgesic, anti-inflammatory, antiseptic (external use only)
Other uses: * * *

ABOUT THIS PLANT AS FOOD OR DRINK

Arnica is a plant native to Western Europe; it now grows wild in North America. The plant is poisonous. It is never used in food or beverages.

Nutritional Profile * * *

HOW THIS PLANT AFFECTS YOUR BODY

Important Phytochemicals   The arnica flower contains helanalin and dihydrohelanin, two natural antiseptic and anti-inflammatory painkillers that appear to reduce pain and swelling when applied as an external dressing.

    Caution: Arnica is poisonous, and is used only as an ingredient in commercially prepared products for external use only.

Benefits   Until 1960, arnica was listed in the U.S. Pharmacopoeia, but was then removed as a poisonous plant. In 1990, however, the German Commission E approved infusions of arnica, as well as commercial gels, ointments, and creams containing minute amounts of arnica oil or a diluted solution of arnica flowers (usually dried arnica flowers) for use solely as external dressings to relieve arthritic joint pain and muscle pain, or the contusion, swelling, and blood clots following an injury.

Possible Adverse Effects   If swallowed, the arnica flower can cause serious gastroenteritis, intense muscular weakness, elevated blood pressure, irregular heartbeat, and depression of the central nervous system leading to collapse and death. Arnica is also an allergen; handling the plant may cause contact dermatitis (itching, burning, stinging, reddened, or blistered skin).

Information for Women Who Are Pregnant or Nursing * * *

Plant/Drug Interactions * * *

HOW TO USE THIS PLANT * * *

Autumn Crocus

ABOUT THIS PLANT

Botanical name(s): Colchicum autumnale
Common name(s): Meadow saffron
Native to: Europe
Parts used as food/drink: None
GRAS list: No
Medicinal properties: Antigout drug
Other uses: * * *

ABOUT THIS PLANT AS FOOD OR DRINK

Autumn crocus, also known as meadow saffron, is not a crocus nor is it closely related to SAFFRON, the yellow spice used in Eastern and Spanish cuisine. It is a poisonous plant that is never used in food or beverages.

Nutritional Profile * * *

HOW THIS PLANT AFFECTS YOUR BODY

Important Phytochemicals The dried seeds and tubers and the fresh flowers of the autumn crocus, a poisonous plant, are the source of the drug colchicine, which is used to treat gout and familial Mediterranean fever, an inherited condition that causes recurring fever, peritonitis, arthritis, skin lesions, and infection of the heart. In 1986 the German Commission E approved the use of autumn crocus as the source for colchicine.

Benefits * * *

Possible Adverse Effects Consuming any part of the autumn crocus plant may cause numbness in the throat followed by kidney and respiratory failure.

Colchicine, the drug derived from the autumn crocus, may cause diarrhea, nausea, vomiting, and abdominal pain, as well as abnormal bleeding, leukopenia (reduced production of white blood cells), or aplastic anemia, a potentially fatal reduction in the production of red blood cells.

People sensitive to the autumn crocus plant may develop skin rash, hives, and fever if they touch the plant or use colchicine.

Information for Women Who Are Pregnant or Nursing While definitive information regarding pregnant women is not available, female laboratory animals (hamsters, rabbits) given colchicine produced offspring with serious birth defects. Colchicine is rated positive for fetal abnormalities in animals. Because colchicine interferes with the normal production of sperm, leading to birth defects in children conceived while the father is using the drug, some experts rate it positive for human fetal abnormalities as well.

Plant/Drug Interactions   * * *

HOW TO USE THIS PLANT   * * *

Belladonna

ABOUT THIS PLANT

Botanical name(s): Atropa belladonna
Common name(s): Deadly nightshade
Native to: Southern and central Europe, southern Asia, northern Africa
Parts used as food/drink: None
GRAS list: No
Medicinal properties: Antispasmodic
Other uses: * * *

ABOUT THIS PLANT AS FOOD OR DRINK

Belladonna is a poisonous plant, whose ripe berries and other parts may be lethal even in minute amounts. It is never used in food or beverages.

Nutritional Profile * * *

HOW THIS PLANT AFFECTS YOUR BODY

Important Phytochemicals Belladonna, also known as deadly nightshade, contains L-hyoscyamine, atropine, and scopolamine—three important anticholinergics, substances that inhibit the parasympathetic nervous system, which controls automatic body functions such as breathing, heartbeat, dilation and contraction of blood vessels and the pupils of the eyes.

Benefits L-hyoscyamine, atropine, and scopolamine derived from belladonna relieve spasms in smooth muscle such as the muscle lining the intestinal tract, uterus, and bladder and the muscle that controls the opening and closing of the pupil of the eye. They are used medically as antispasmodics and in the drops ophthalmologists use to dilate the pupils so that eyes can be examined. In 1985, the German Commission E approved the use of belladonna as a source of these drugs.

Possible Adverse Effects Dry mouth is a common side effect of normal doses of anticholinergic drugs, as are dry skin and elevated body temperature. Higher doses or overdoses may cause hallucinations and muscle spasms.

Information for Women Who Are Pregnant or Nursing * * *

Plant/Drug Interactions Belladonna increases the anticholinergic effects of tricyclic antidepressants such as amitriptyline (Elavil, Endep),

SOME BRAND NAME DRUGS CONTAINING ATROPINE, HYOSCYAMINE, AND SCOPOLAMINE

Product name	Form	Use	Contains
Arco-Lase Plus (Arco)	tablets	antispasmodic	atropine, hyoscyamine
Atrohist Plus (Medeva)	tablets	decongestant	atropine, hyoscyamine, scopolamine[1]
Donnatal (Robins)	capsules, elixir, tablets	antispasmodic	atropine, hyoscyamine, scopolamine[2]
Levsin (Schwarz)	elixir, tablets	antispasmodic	hyoscyamine
Lomotil (Searle)	liquid, tablets	antidiarrheal	atropine[3]
Motofen (Carnrick)	tablets	antidiarrheal	atropine[4]
Trans-derm scop (Ciba)	patch	motion sickness preventive	scopolamine
Urised (Poly-Medica)	tablets	urinary antiseptic	atropine, hyoscyamine[5]

[1] also contains antihistamine and decongestants
[2] also contains sedative
[3] also contains antidiarrheal
[4] also contains antidiarrheal
[5] also contains antibiotics
Source: *Physicians' Desk Reference*, 51st edition (Montvale, N.J.: Medical Economics, 1997)

the anti-Parkinson drug amantadine (Symadine, Symmetrel), and quinidine, a drug used to control irregular heartbeat (Cardioquin, Duraquin).

HOW TO USE THIS PLANT * * *

Castor Bean

ABOUT THIS PLANT

Botanical name(s): Ricinus communis
Common name(s): * * *
Native to: Africa
Parts used as food/drink: None
GRAS list: No
Medicinal properties: Cathartic
Other uses: Emollient, constituent of chemical coatings, resins, fibers; industrial lubricant; manufacturing fabric dyes and texturizers

ABOUT THIS PLANT AS FOOD OR DRINK

Castor beans are seeds of a perennial tree that may grow to a height of 30 feet in warm climates. Castor beans are poisonous; they are never used in food or beverages.

Nutritional Profile * * *

HOW THIS PLANT AFFECTS YOUR BODY

Important Phytochemicals Every part of the castor bean plant, including the seeds (beans), contains ricin, a potent poison that can burn skin and mucous membranes, increase thirst, cause gastric upset (pain, nausea, and vomiting), kidney failure, blurred vision, convulsions, and death. If chewed, as few as one or two beans may be lethal.

Castor bean oil, also known as ricinus oil, oil of Palma Christi, or tangantangan oil, is considered safe because it is extracted by "cold pressing," a method that allows the beans to release oil without ricin. The active ingredient in castor oil is ricinolein, a laxative that irritates the intestines, triggering contractions that move food through the intestinal tract.

Benefits * * *

Possible Adverse Effects Castor oil is a cathartic, a very strong laxative that may cause excessive loss of fluids and electrolytes (mineral ions that regulate the body's fluid balance and assist in the transmission of impulses between cells). The American Pharmaceutical Association's *Handbook of Nonprescription Drugs,* 11th edition, recommends against the use of castor oil for constipation.

Information for Women Who Are Pregnant or Nursing Like other products that cause intestinal contractions, castor oil is best avoided by pregnant women.

Plant/Drug Interactions * * *

HOW TO USE THIS PLANT * * *

Comfrey

ABOUT THIS PLANT

Botanical name(s): *Symphytum officinale*
Common name(s): Ass ear, blackwort, knitbone
Native to: North America
Parts used as food/drink: None
GRAS list: No
Medicinal properties: Anti-inflammatory
Other uses: * * *

ABOUT THIS PLANT AS FOOD OR DRINK

Comfrey, a member of the borage family, contains liver toxins/carcinogens (see below). It is never used as a food or beverage.

Nutritional Profile * * *

HOW THIS PLANT AFFECTS YOUR BODY

Important Phytochemicals Like COLTSFOOT, comfrey contains pyrrolizidines (PSs), naturally occurring liver toxins/carcinogens. Comfrey contains allantoin, a soothing substance used to treat skin ulcers.

Benefits In 1990, the German Commission E approved the use of comfrey in ointments and other external dressings for bruises and sprains.

Possible Adverse Effects In studies with laboratory rats, comfrey caused cancerous tumors when the animals were fed amounts as low as 0.5 percent to 8 percent of the diet. In approving comfrey leaf and root preparations as an external dressing, Commission E cautioned that the dressing should be applied only to intact skin, must contain no more than 100 mcg PAs per dose, and should not be used for longer than 4–6 weeks a year.

Information for Women Who Are Pregnant or Nursing According to Commission E, comfrey should not be used during pregnancy except with the advice and supervision of a physician.

Plant/Drug Interactions * * *

HOW TO USE THIS PLANT * * *

Foxglove

ABOUT THIS PLANT

Botanical name(s): *Digitalis purpurea*
Common name(s): Witch's bells
Native to: Europe
Parts used as food/flavoring: None
GRAS list: No
Medicinal properties: Cardiac stimulant
Other uses: * * *

ABOUT THIS PLANT AS FOOD OR DRINK

Foxglove is a poisonous plant that is never used in food or beverages.

Nutritional Profile   * * *

HOW THIS PLANT AFFECTS YOUR BODY

Important Phytochemicals   Foxglove is the source of the cardiac stimulant digitalis, also known as digoxin, the first effective drug for heart disease.

Known Benefits   Digitalis makes the heart muscle beat more effectively. It is also a diuretic that helps lower blood pressure by eliminating excess fluids from body tissues.

Possible Adverse Effects   Foxglove is considered safe as used in medicine, but the foxglove plant is poisonous. Chewing even one leaf may cause paralysis or sudden heart failure, and fatalities have been reported in people who drank a tea brewed from foxglove. Symptoms of digitalis poisoning include visual disturbances such as a yellow cast over your field of vision, upset stomach (pain, nausea, diarrhea), severe headache, irregular heartbeat and pulse, tremors, convulsions, and death. Note: Foxglove, which cannot be sold legally outside a pharmacy in Germany, was not reviewed by Commission E.

Information for Women Who Are Pregnant or Nursing   * * *

Plant/Drug Interactions   * * *

HOW TO USE THIS PLANT   * * *

Lily of the Valley

ABOUT THIS PLANT

Botanical name(s): Convallaria majalis
Common name(s): May lily
Native to: Europe
Parts used as food/drink: None
GRAS list: No
Medicinal properties: Cardiac stimulant
Other uses: * * *

ABOUT THIS PLANT AS FOOD OR DRINK

The U.S. Food and Drug Administration classifies lily of the valley as a poisonous plant that may cause gastric upset (nausea, vomiting, diarrhea) or sudden death due to irregular heartbeat. It is never used as food or beverage.

Nutritional Profile * * *

HOW THIS PLANT AFFECTS YOUR BODY

Important Phytochemicals The medically active compounds in lily of the valley are the cardiac stimulants convallatoxin, convallarin, and canvallamarin.

Benefits Convallatoxin, convallarin, and canvallamarin enable the heart muscle to beat more efficiently. In 1987 and 1990, the German Commission E approved the use of the dried flowers of lily of the valley to relieve mild cardiac insufficiency, particularly that due to old age or chronic heart disease. The drug is to be used only with medical supervision.

Possible Adverse Effects Convallatoxin, convallarin, and canvallamarin may cause nausea and vomiting, as well as irregular heartbeat.

Information for Women Who Are Pregnant or Nursing * * *

Plant/Drug Interactions If taken along with cardiac medication, convallatoxin, convallarin, and canvallamarin may make these drugs more effective but may also intensify their adverse effects. The same thing holds true if convallatoxin, convallarin, and canvallamarin are taken along with laxatives or steroid drugs.

HOW TO USE THIS PLANT * * *

APPENDIX II

Hazardous Herbs

The following is a representative, but by no means complete, list of poisonous herbs known to be unsafe for human consumption.

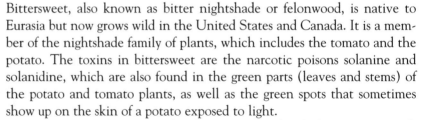

Bittersweet
(*Solanum dulcamara*)

Bittersweet, also known as bitter nightshade or felonwood, is native to Eurasia but now grows wild in the United States and Canada. It is a member of the nightshade family of plants, which includes the tomato and the potato. The toxins in bittersweet are the narcotic poisons solanine and solanidine, which are also found in the green parts (leaves and stems) of the potato and tomato plants, as well as the green spots that sometimes show up on the skin of a potato exposed to light.

Consuming solanine or solanidine may cause headache, upset stomach (pain, vomiting, diarrhea), disturbances of the central nervous system (dizziness, dilated pupils, difficulty in breathing and speaking), coma, and death.

Blue Cohosh
(*Cimicifuga racemosa*)

Blue cohosh, also known as blueberry root, papoose root, and squawroot, is considered hazardous to women of childbearing age. Studies conducted on rats by the U.S. Food and Drug Administration from 1996 to 1998 show that blue cohosh produces significant birth defects such as nerve damage, twisted tail, and eye malformations when fed to pregnant rats.

Note: Blue cohosh should not be confused with BLACK COHOSH, a safe and totally unrelated plant.

Bloodroot
(*Sanguinaria canadensis*)

Bloodroot is a member of the poppy family. It is also known as Indian paint because it yields a red juice that was once used as war paint by Native Americans.

The toxic compounds in bloodroot are protopine (which may cause irregular heartbeat) and sanguinarine (which causes glaucoma in laboratory animals). Consuming bloodroot may cause disturbances in vision, and leave opium-like residues in the urine. In large amounts, bloodroot causes burning pain in the stomach, intense thirst, a feeling of faintness, dizziness, paralysis, and collapse.

In addition, bloodroot is a severe irritant; its juice is so caustic that it can burn and destroy skin and mucous membranes.

Blue Flag
(Iris versicolor)

The active compound in blue flag, also known as liver lily or water flag, is iridin, a potent diuretic and liver toxin. Blue flag is also a cathartic (strong laxative) and an emetic (an agent that causes vomiting). Consuming large amounts of this plant may lead to collapse and/or death.

Caper Spurge
(Euphorbia lathyris)

The caper spurge buds are sometimes mistaken for true capers, the edible buds of the spiny shrub *Capparis spinosa*. Unlike true capers, however, caper spurge buds are severe irritants that contain poisons that may cause gastric upset, dizziness, irregular heartbeat, delirium, collapse, and/or death.

Cherry Laurel
(Prunus laurocerasus)

The leaves of the cherry laurel (*Prunus laurocerasus*) are poisonous. They contain prulaurasin, a compound that releases cyanide in your stomach. These leaves should never be mistaken for true bay leaves (*Lauris nobilis*).

Comfrey
(Symphytum peregrinum)

Comfrey, once cooked and served as a vegetable or added fresh to salads, is no longer considered safe to eat. In laboratory studies, it causes cancer when fed to rats in concentrations as small as 0.5–8 percent of the diet. In addition, comfrey contains the liver toxins known as pyrrolizidines.

Jimsonweed
(Datura stramonium)

Jimsonweed, also known as mad apple, is a member of the nightshade family. Like BELLADONNA, it contains the anticholinergic compounds atropine, hyoscyamine, and hyoscine (scopolamine), but unlike belladonna, it is not used in medicine. The symptoms of jimsonweed poisoning include dimmed vision, dilated pupils (which may occur if you simply handle the plant and then touch your eyes), reddened face and neck, abnormal heartbeat, and delirium.

Lobelia
(Lobelia inflata)

Lobelia, also known as wild tobacco or Indian tobacco because it was once smoked by Native Americans to relieve asthma, is a poisonous plant that contains the respiratory stimulant lobeline. Swallowing the plant or drinking a tea made from its leaves or fruit may cause vomiting, profuse perspiration, paralysis, pain, lowered temperatures, rapid pulse, collapse, coma, and death.

Mandrake
(Mandragora officinarum)

Mandrake, also known as love apple, contains atropine and hyoscyamine, the anticholinergic compounds also found in BELLADONNA and JIMSONWEED, plus mandragorine, a similar compound found only in the mandrake plant. Once thought to increase male fertility, mandrake is now known to be poisonous. Symptoms of mandrake poisoning include profuse perspiration, paralysis of the gastrointestinal tract, quickened heartbeat, dilated pupils, and an extreme sensitivity to light.

May Apple
(Podophyllum peltatum)

May apple, also known as American mandrake, contains poisonous compounds called *podophyllotoxins*. All parts of the plant except its ripe fruit are considered hazardous and may cause nausea, potentially fatal inflammation of the stomach and intestines, and collapse of the circulatory system.

Podophyllotoxins are also strong irritants. Handling the may apple's rhizomes (underground stems) and then touching your eyes or skin may cause inflamed eyes or skin ulcers.

Mistletoe
(Phoradendron serotinum, Phoradendron fiavescens, or Viscum flavescens)

Mistletoe, once considered a symbol of fertility, has poisonous berries. Despite annual warnings, each year poison control centers report cases of children and pets suffering severe gastroenteritis after swallowing the bright red fruits. There has been at least one fatality reported due to acute gastroenteritis and heart failure after drinking a tea brewed of mistletoe berries.

The plant is also an irritant that can cause contact dermatitis (itching, burning, stinging, reddened, or blistered skin).

Mountain Laurel
(Kalmia latifolia)

The leaves and flowers of the mountain laurel (*Kalmia latifolia*) contain andromedotoxin, a narcotic poison so potent that it may poison honey made by bees that alight on the mountain laurel. Consuming mountain laurel leaves or flowers may cause excess salivation and watering of the eyes, vomiting, convulsions, and paralysis leading to death.

Pennyroyal
(Mentha pulegium)

Pennyroyal oil contains pulegone, a potent toxin. As little as one-half teaspoon of the pure oil may cause delirium, muscle spasms, shock, and loss of consciousness. Two tablespoons have proved fatal.

Pennyroyal is also an irritant. Handling the plant may cause contact dermatitis (itching, burning, stinging, reddened, or blistered skin).

Peony
(*Paeonia officinalis*)

The toxic compounds in peony are peonal and peregrinine. Eating peony flowers and seeds may cause serious gastric upset (nausea, cramps, and diarrhea). Consuming the root may cause constriction of the small blood vessels in the kidneys, reducing the body's ability to eliminate fluids.

Poison Hemlock
(*Conium maculatum*)

Poison hemlock, also known as fool's parsley, contains coniine, a colorless liquid that turns dark when exposed to air. If swallowed it may cause muscle weakness, drowsiness, nausea, breathing difficulties, and death. This plant is also an irritant; touching it may cause contact dermatitis (itching, burning, stinging, reddened, or blistered skin).

Rue
(*Ruta graveolens*)

Rue's silvery blue green leaves contain oil of rue, a pale yellow, odorous liquid that is 90 percent methyl nonyl ketone and methyl heptyl ketone, two unpleasantly scented substances occasionally used in dog and cat repellents. Oil of rue also contains the bitter furocoumarins bergapten, psoralen, and xanthotoxin, all of which the plant uses to repel insects and fungi.

Rue is an internal and external irritant. Eating rue may cause flushed skin, irritation of the lungs, vomiting, and collapse in sensitive people. Handling the plant may cause severe contact dermatitis (itching, burning, stinging, reddened, or blistered skin), as well as photosensitivity, severe sensitivity to sunlight. Rue also contains compounds reputed to relax smooth muscles, such as the uterus, and may trigger premature labor.

Scotch Broom
(Cytisus scoparius)

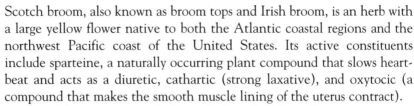

Scotch broom, also known as broom tops and Irish broom, is an herb with a large yellow flower native to both the Atlantic coastal regions and the northwest Pacific coast of the United States. Its active constituents include sparteine, a naturally occurring plant compound that slows heartbeat and acts as a diuretic, cathartic (strong laxative), and oxytocic (a compound that makes the smooth muscle lining of the uterus contract).

Dried broom tops, picked just before the plant flowers, were once widely used in folk medicine as a diuretic, a laxative, an emetic (a drug that induces vomiting), and to slow down rapid heartbeat. But the herb has been replaced by newer drugs, and the U.S. Food and Drug Administration now classifies scotch broom as an unsafe herb.

Overdoses of scotch broom may cause headache and dizziness, rapid heartbeat, upset stomach (nausea and diarrhea), and circulatory collapse. The herb, which contains tyramine, is particularly hazardous to people with high blood pressure or those using monoamine oxidase (MAO) inhibitors, drugs used as antidepressants or antihypertensives. Tyramine raises blood pressure; MAO inhibitors reduce the effectiveness of enzymes that eliminate excess tyramine. If you consume a food high in tyramine while you are taking an MAO inhibitor, the added tyramine cannot be efficiently eliminated from your body. The result may be potentially fatal sustained high blood pressure.

Shave Grass
(Equisetum hyemale)

Shave grass contains two important natural nerve poisons, equisetine and nicotine. Eating shave grass causes loss of appetite, followed eventually by loss of muscular control, breathing difficulties, a weakened pulse rate, convulsions, coma, and death.

Tansy
(Tanacetum vulgare or Chrysanthemum vulgare)

Tansy, also known as bitter buttons, is a member of the chrysanthemum family, a strongly aromatic herb with bright yellow flowers. Once valued for its bitter flavor, tansy is no longer used in cooking because its oil contains thujone, a toxin also found in WORMWOOD. Consuming thujone may cause thirst, restlessness, dizziness, a tingling in your ears, trembling and numbness in the extremities, loss of muscular power, delirium, paralysis, and death.

Tansy also contains arbusculin-A and tanacetin, two irritants that may cause contact dermatitis (itching, burning, stinging, reddened, or blistered skin) if the plant is touched; as many as 61 percent of patients given a patch test for allergy to tansy experienced a reaction.

Tonka Bean
(Dipteryx odorata)

Tonka bean contains large amounts of coumarin, a vanilla-scented compound found in a wide variety of herbs and spices. In laboratory studies, rats and dogs fed tonka beans have suffered liver damage, retarded growth, and testicular atrophy.

Virginia Snakeroot
(Aristolochia serpentaria)

Virginia snakeroot, also known as snakeweed because it was once used to treat snakebite, contains aristolochine, a compound that may cause violent irritation of the gastrointestinal tract and kidneys as well as coma and death from respiratory paralysis. The plant is also a mutagen (an agent that causes changes in cell structure) and a suspected carcinogen.

Wahoo
(Euonymus atropurpureus)

Wahoo, also known as burning bush, contains a resin called euonymin, a cathartic (strong laxative) that irritates the lining of the stomach. Eating wahoo may cause severe gastric upset (vomiting and diarrhea), plus weakness, chills, convulsions, and loss of consciousness.

White Snakeroot
(*Eupatorium rugosum*)

White snakeroot, also known as snakeroot, contains a nerve poison that may trigger an effect known as trembles in cattle and other livestock who forage on any part of the plant. The poison remains in the animals; people who drink milk or eat meat or butter taken from animals who have eaten white snakeroot may also be poisoned.

Wintergreen
(*Gaultheria procumbens*)

Wintergreen, also known as teaberry, is native to North America. Its leaves contain methyl salicylate (wintergreen oil), an oily liquid that smells and tastes like wintergreen. Swallowing even small amounts of wintergreen oil may cause severe poisoning: nausea, vomiting, acidosis, pulmonary edema, pneumonia, convulsions, and death.

Wormwood
(*Artemisia absinthium*)

Oil of wormwood contains as much as 13 percent thujone, a narcotic poison that can damage the nervous system and cause mental deterioration. The oil, which tastes like LICORICE, was once used to flavor absinthe, a liqueur that is now illegal in the United States. Symptoms of wormwood poisoning include thirst, restlessness, dizziness, a tingling in your ears, trembling and numbness in your arms, hands, legs and feet, loss of muscular power, delirium, general paralysis, and death.

Note: The U.S. Food and Drug Administration has approved some thujone-free derivatives of oil of wormwood.

❧ Bibliography ❧

INTERNET DATABASES

American Dietetic Association: http://www.eatright.org
Food Allergy Network: http://www.foodallergy.org
USDA Nutrient Database: http://www.nal.usda.gov/fnic/cgi-bin/nut_search.pl

BOOKS

AMA *Drug Evaluations*. 5th ed. Chicago: American Medical Association, 1983.

American Dietetic Association. *Handbook of Clinical Dietetics*. New Haven: Yale University Press, 1989.

Beers, Mark H., and Robert Berkow, eds. *The Merck Manual*. 17th ed. Rahway, N.J.: Merck Research Laboratories, 1999.

Berkow, Robert, ed. *The Merck Manual*. 15th ed. Rahway, N.J.: Sharp & Dohme Research Laboratory, 1987.

Blumenthal, Mark, et al., eds. *The Complete German Commission E Monographs*. Boston, Mass./Austin Tx.: American Botanial Council and Integrative Medicine Communications, 1998.

Briggs, George M., and Doris Howes Calloway. *Nutrition and Physical Fitness*. New York: Holt, Rinehart and Winston, 1984.

Budavari, Susan, et al., eds. *The Merck Index*, 11th ed. Rahway, N.J.: Merck, 1989.

Duke, James A. *Handbook of Medicinal Herbs*. Boca Raton, Fla.: CRC Press, 1988.

Fauci, Anthony S., et al., eds. *Harrison's Principles of Internal Medicine*. 14th edition. New York: McGraw-Hill, 1998.

Fisher, Joe, and Dennis Fisher. *The Homebrewer's Garden*. Pownal, Vt.: Storey Books, 1998.

Freydberg, Nicholas, and Willis Gortner. *The Food Additive Book*. New York: Bantam Books, 1982.

Gardiner, Anne, and Sue Wilson. *The Inquisitive Cook*. New York: Henry Holt & Co., 1998.

Gilman, Alfred Goodman, Louis S. Goodman, Alfred Gilman. *The Pharmacological Basis of Therapeutics*. 6th ed. New York: Macmillan, 1980.

Gosselin, Robert E., Harold C. Hodge, Roger P. Smith, and Marion N. Gleason, eds. *Clinical Toxicology of Commercial Products*. 4th ed. Baltimore: Williams & Wilkins, 1977.

Grosser, Arthur E. *The Cookbook Decoder*, New York: Warner Books, 1981.

Handbook of Nonprescription Drugs. 8th ed. Washington D.C.: American Pharmaceutical Association, 1986.

Handbook of Nonprescription Drugs. 11th ed. Washington D.C.: American Pharmaceutical Association, 1996.

Jaffrey, Madhur. *World-of-the-East Vegetarian Cooking*. New York: Alfred A. Knopf, 1981.

Krupp, Marcus A., Milton J. Chatton, and Lawrence M. Tierney, eds. *Current Medical Diagnosis and Treatment, 1986*. Los Altos, Calif.: Lange Medical Publications, 1986.

Lewis, Walter H., and Memory P. F. Elvin-Lewis. *Medical Botany*. New York: John Wiley & Sons, 1977.

Logue, A. W. *The Psychology of Eating and Drinking*. 2nd ed. New York: W.H. Freeman and Co., 1991.

Long, James W. *The Essential Guide to Prescription Drugs*. New York: Harper & Row, 1987.

Lust, John. *The Herb Book*. New York: Bantam Books, 1983.

Magic and Medicine of Plants. Pleasantville, N.Y.: Reader's Digest Association, 1986.

McGee, Harold. *On Food and Cooking*. New York: Scribner, 1984.

Merenstein, Gerald B., et al., eds. *Silver, Kempe, Bruyn & Fulginiti's Handbook of Pediatrics*. 16th ed. Norwalk, Conn.: Appleton & Lange, 1991.

National Research Council. *Recommended Dietary Allowances*. 10th ed. Washington D.C.: National Academy Press, 1989.

Onstad, Dianne. *Whole Foods Companion*. White River Junction, Vt.: Chelsea Green, 1996.

Peckenpaugh, Nancy J., and Charlotte M. Poleman. *Nutrition Essentials and Diet Therapy*. 7th ed. Philadelphia: W.B. Saunders, 1995.

Peirce, Andrea. *The American Pharmaceutical Association Practical Guide to Natural Medicine*. New York: Morrow, 1999.

Physicians' Desk Reference. 51st ed. Montvale, N.J.: Medical Economics, 1997.

Poister, John J. *The New American Bartender's Guide*. 2nd ed. New York: New American Library, 1999.

Rinzler, Carol Ann. *The New Complete Book of Food*. 2nd ed. New York: Facts On File, 1999.
———. *Nutrition for Dummies*. 2nd ed. Chicago: IDG, 1999.

Rombauer, Irma S., Marion Rombauer Becker, and Ethan Becker. *New Joy of Cooking*. New York: Scribner, 1997.

Rosengarten, Frederic, Jr. *The Book of Spices*. New York: Jove Publications, 1981.

Rybacki, James J., and James W. Long. *The Essential Guide to Prescription Drugs*. 1998 ed. New York: HarperPerennial, 1997.

Steiner, Richard P. *Folk Medicine*. Washington, D.C.: American Chemical Society, 1986.

Taylor's Guide to Vegetables & Herbs. Boston: Houghton Mifflin, 1987.

Tierney, Lawrence M., Stephen J. McPhee, Maxin A. Papadakis, eds. *Current Medical Diagnosis and Treatment 1998*. Stamford, Conn.: Appleton & Lange, 1998.

Toxicants Occurring Naturally in Foods. 2nd ed. Washington, D.C.: National Academy of Sciences, 1973.

Tyler, Varro E. *Hoosier Home Remedies*. West Lafayette, Ind.: Purdue University Press, 1985.
———. *The New Honest Herbal*. Philadelphia: George F. Stickley Co., 1987.

The Way Things Work. 2 vols. New York: Simon and Schuster, 1967.

Whitney, Eleanor Noss, Corinne Balog Cataldo, and Sharon Rady Rolfes. *Understanding Clinical Nutrition*. 4th ed. Minneapolis/St. Paul: West Publishing Company, 1994.

Windholz, Martha, ed. *The Merck Index*. 10th ed. Rahway, N.J.: Merck & Co., 1987.

Zapsalis, Charles, and R. Anderle Beck. *Food Chemistry and Nutritional Biochemistry*. New York: John Wiley & Sons, 1985.

Zimmerman, David R. *The Essential Guide to Nonprescription Drugs*. New York: Harper & Row, 1983.

PAMPHLETS AND PRESS RELEASES

"Aspartame helps keep weight off," IFIC Foundation Food Insight Media Guide, n.d.

"Cockroaches beware! This house has been treated with catnip," American Chemical Society, August 23, 1999.

Composition of Foods, Spices and Herbs. Agriculture Handbook no. 8-2. Washington, D.C.: Government Printing Office, 1977.

"Diet supplement crackdown criticized," The Associated Press, August 4, 1999.

Does Nature Know Best? Natural Carcinogens in American Food. New York: American Council on Science and Health, October 1985.

Enjoy Your Plants . . . But Protect Your Family. Public Information Bulletin, National Poison Center Network, Children's Hospital of Pittsburgh, n.d.

"Garlic capsules lower cholesterol levels in men," Penn State University, April 16, 1999.

"Garlic may help prevent bowel cancer," Reuters, May 27, 1999.

Gastrointestinal Disease Symposium Issues & Answers. Dallas: Texas Health Sciences Center, n.d.

Gebhardt, Susan E., and Ruth H. Matthews. *Nutritive Value of Foods*. USDA Home and Garden Bulletin no. 72, 1985.

A Glossary of Spices. Englewood Cliffs, N.J.: American Spice Trade Association, 1982.

Health News Tips. New York: Empire Blue Cross and Blue Shield, fall 1985.

"Hold the mayo questions," Cooperative Extension Service, Michigan State University & USDA, July 18, 1979.

The McCormick/Schilling Guide to Gourmet Spices. Baltimore, Md.: McCormick & Company, Inc., n.d.

"Questions and answers about sucralose," IFIC Foundation Food Insight Media Guide, n.d.

"Sweet facts about sugars and health," IFIC Review, August 1995.

"Sweetener fact sheet," Atlanta, Ga.: Calorie Control Council, April 1983.

Watt, Bernice K., and Annabel L. Merrill. *Composition of Foods*. Agriculture Handbook no. 8. Washington, D.C.: Government Printing Office, 1975.

What You Should Know About . . . series (Allspice, Basil, Capcisum Spices, Celery Seed, Cinnamon, Cloves, Coriander, Cumin Seed, Dehydrated Garlic, Dehydrated Onion, Dill, Fennel Seed, Mustard Seed, Nutmeg & Mace, Oregano, Paprika, Pepper, Sage, Sesame Seed, Thyme, Turmeric). Englewood Cliffs, N.J.: American Spice Trade Association, n.d.

PERIODICALS

Ames, Bruce N. "Dietary carcinogens and anticarcinogens," *Science*, September 21, 1983.

"Aspartame not linked to headaches," *Calorie Control Commentary*, spring 1988.

Baker, Beth. "Be smart, beware," *AARP newsletter*, May 1999.

"Beware the bay leaf," *British Medical Journal*, December 20–27, 1980.

Brody, Jane E. "Herbal remedies tied to pregnancy risks," *The New York Times*, March 9, 1999.

———. "Taking a gamble on herbs as medicine," *The New York Times*, February 9, 1999.

Combest, Wendell L. "Black cohosh," *U.S. Pharmacist*, September 1999.

———. "Lavender," *U.S. Pharmacist*, April 1999.

———. "Licorice," *U.S. Pharmacist*, April 1998.

———. "Milk thistle," *U.S. Pharmacist*, September 1998.

————. "Tea tree," *U.S. Pharmacist*, April 1999.

Duke, James. "The joy of ginger," *American Health*, May 1988.

"An expert answers questions on herbal teas," Tufts University Diet & Nutrition Letter, June 1986.

"Folk cure for the seasick," *The New York Times*, April 13, 1982.

"Food and Drug Interactions," *FDA Consumer*, March 1978.

"Food Preservative Made from Rosemary," *The New York Times*, January 24, 1987.

"Garlic: Benefits beyond the basic," *Food Insight*, January/February 1999.

Gianni, Laura, and William B. Dreitlein. "Some popular OTC herbals can interact with anticoagulant therapy," *U.S. Pharmacist*, May 1998.

Gossel, Thomas A. "A review of aspartame: characteristics, safety and uses," *U.S. Pharmacist*, January 1984.

Hamilton, William, and William Kirchain. "Ginseng," *U.S. Pharmacist*, July 1999.

"Healthwise," *U.S. Pharmacist*, May 1984, April 1987.

"Horseradish Horrors," *Newsearch*, vol. 5, October 3, 1988.

"Hot Pepper and Pain," *The New York Times*, June 28, 1983.

"Hot prospects for quelling cluster headaches," *Science News*, July 13, 1991.

"The hot side of chiles," *Science News*, July 16, 1988.

"Hot stuff: A receptor for spicy foods," *Science News*, November 8, 1997.

"How chili peppers deliver their fire," *The New York Times*, October 28, 1997.

"If supping on sushi, watch that wasabi," *Science News*, January 16, 1988.

Jacknowitz, Arthur I. "Artificial sweeteners: how safe are they?" *U.S. Pharmacist*, January 1988.

Jackson, Nancy Beth. "Doctors' warning: beware of herbs' side effects," *The New York Times*, November 18, 1998.

Kiesel, Marcia. "From the Herb Garden," *Food & Wine*, March 1987, July 1987.

Kolata, Gina. "In ancient times, flowers and fennel for family planning," *The New York Times*, March 8, 1994.

Larkin, Tim. "Herbs are often more toxic than magical," *FDA Consumer*, October 1983.

"Low calorie allergy," *Science News*, June 18, 1986.

Moffatt, Anne Simon, and Cathy Sears. "Plant power," *American Health*, April 1987.

"More evidence on the safety of aspartame," Tufts University Diet & Nutrition Letter, February 1988.

Nagourney, Eric. "A warning not to mix surgery and herbs," *The New York Times*, July 6, 1999.

————. "Untapped potential for a common herb," *The New York Times*, October 26, 1999.

Phipps, et al. "Effect of flaxseed ingestion on the menstrual cycle," *Journal of Clinical Endocrinology Metabolism* 77 (1993): 1215–19.

Nemecz, George. "Chamomile," *U.S. Pharmacist*, March 1998.

————. "Saw palmetto," *U.S. Pharmacist*, January 1999.

Nemecz, George, and Troy J. Lee. "Kava Kava," *U.S. Pharmacist*, June 1999.

Nemecz, George, and Wendell L. Combest. "Feverfew," *U.S. Pharmacist*, November 1997.

————. "Ginkgo biloba," *U.S. Pharmacist*, September 1997.

Nice, Frank. "Herbs and Breat-feeding," *U.S. Pharmacist*, September 2000.

O'Neill, Molly. "Cutting the mustard," *The New York Times Magazine*, August 8, 1999.

Oxford Health Plans. "Herbs and prescription drugs don't always mix," *Mind Healthy Body*, Summer 2000.

"Position of the American Dietetic Association: use of nutritive and non-nutritive sweeteners," *The Journal of the American Dietetic Association*, May 1998.

"Questions of Taste," *Food & Wine*, September 1986, October 1987.

Raloff, Janet. "Some herbals may threaten fertility," *Science News*, March 27, 1999.

"Red pepper eases pain of cutaneous nerve disorders," *Medical World News*, January 11, 1988.

Robbins, Wayne. "Find your mojo," *New York Daily News*, October 24, 1999.

"Salt-sensitive genes," *Science News*, November 29, 1986.

Schardt, David. "Garlic: Case unclosed," *Nutrition Action Newsletter*, October 2000.

Schneider, Elizabeth. "The era of the edible blossoms: innovation and rediscovery," *The New York Times*, August 24, 1988.

Siegal, Nina. "A black cloud over blue cohosh," *The New York Times*, October 5, 1999.

"Study finds that mayonnaise can inhibit spoilage of food," *The New York Times*, May 12, 1982.

"The sweet and sour history of saccharin, cyclamate, aspartame," *FDA Consumer*, February 1980.

Thomas, Patricia. "Chinese data base may shed light on diet, heart disease," *Medical World News*, May 23, 1988.

"Toxic reactions to plant products sold in health food stores," *The Medical Letter*, April 6, 1979.

Tropp, Barbara. "All about peppercorns," *Food & Wine*, May 1985.

"Vitamin and nutritional supplements," Mayo Clinic Health Letter, June 1997.

"When hot may be anticarcinogenic," *Science News*, July 16, 1988.

INTERNET ARTICLES

"A focus on fatty acids," The Flax Council, http://www.flaxcouncil.ca/flaxnut9

"Food sources of alpha-linolenic acid (ALA)," The Flax Council, http://www.flaxcouncil.ca/flaxnut9

"General olive FAQs," The Olive Press, http://www.theolivepress.com

Ouellette, Rebecca H. "Medicinal characteristics of garlic," April 10, 1996. http://www.rouellet@moose.uvm.edu

"Warnings in the pipeline," International MS Support Foundation, January 2, 1997. http://aspin.asu.edu/msnews/warnings

Index

Boldface page numbers indicate main headings.